Readings Exclusive
of Brief Examples

Student Authors

Professional Authors

The Contemporary Writer

A PRACTICAL RHETORIC

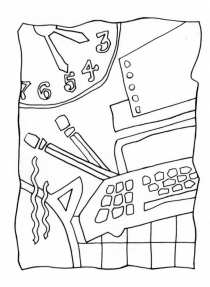

THIRD EDITION

The Contemporary Writer

A PRACTICAL RHETORIC

THIRD EDITION

W. ROSS WINTEROWD
University of Southern California

with

JOHN S. NIXON
Rancho Santiago College

HARCOURT BRACE JOVANOVICH, PUBLISHERS
San Diego   New York   Chicago   Austin   Washington, D.C.
London   Sydney   Tokyo   Toronto

Preface

 The guiding principle of this thoroughgoing revision of *The Contemporary Writer* was the interests and needs of student writers in colleges and universities. I want instructors to find the book effective and students to find it useful and interesting.

Paradoxically, students and their instructors seldom enjoy the rhetorics and handbooks used in composition classes. I have tried to make *The Contemporary Writer* not only useful but also readable and interesting, and to demonstrate that I am not only a textbook writer but a writer in the generic sense. As I said in the preface to the first edition, "I view *The Contemporary Writer* as a real book."

A glance at the table of contents and the index will give some idea of the completeness of the book: all modes of writing are dealt with, and the major concepts in regard to writing and language are covered in detail. Furthermore, the scholarly background that informs the book makes for high reliability of both general concepts and specific information.

The book is contemporary—both in tone and in theory. Again, a survey of the index will demonstrate that important contemporary thought and thinkers are amply represented.

And the book is useful, in that it is carefully designed to be practical for students with the widest range of abilities. All aspects of the book contribute to the goal of helping students learn to write effectively for given purposes and audiences.

No one could have been more fortunate than I in having editors whose judgment was excellent, who understood and valued the craft of writing, and who were admirably patient. This edition began under the aegis of Marlane Agriesti Miriello, who responded almost line by line to the Second Edition and provided me with both an overall sense of what needed to be done and specific reactions to important details. I then worked with Paul Nockleby, perhaps the most tenacious editor in the business. I learned to admire Paul's intelligence and understanding of the field of composition. Finally, Tom Broadbent inherited the project, and my debt to him is incalculable. His sure sense of what instructors want and need and his taste and intelligence make him the sort of editor that authors dream of but encounter rarely.

One of the most odious tasks in preparing a book for publication is obtaining permissions to reprint selections. However, the nitpicking drudgery of this job was, paradoxically, a happy circumstance, for it put me once again in touch with my old friend Eleanor Garner, whose cheerfulness and meticulousness buoyed my spirits and saved me endless frustrations.

Catherine Fauver edited the manuscript, the galleys, and the page proofs. Her careful, intelligent work has, of course, disappeared into the printed book, but her contribution to the quality of the edition was significant.

The work of Cheryl Solheid has not disappeared, for it was she who designed the book. I leave judgment of her taste and skill to the reader, but can report that my wife and I fairly glowed when we saw the cover designed by Ms. Solheid and her colleague, Linda Wild.

I would like to thank the following reviewers, whose reactions and suggestions have been invaluable to me: Carol A. Barnes, Kansas State University; Sondra M. Cooney, Kent State University–Stark Campus; Michael Feehan, University of Texas–Arlington; Standish Henning, University of Wisconsin–Madison; Laura Quinn, University of Wisconsin–River Falls; Tilly Warnock; Suzanne S. Webb, Texas Woman's University; and Barbara D. Winder, Western Connecticut State University.

My thanks also to those who were kind enough to offer other comments and suggestions: Gregory Anderson, Ohio University–Athens; Elmer Baker, York College; R. Michael Barrett, University of Wisconsin–River Falls; Tom Barton, Washington

State University; June Berkley, Ohio University–Athens; Robert Burcaw and Lloyd Burkhart, Moravian College; Enid Cocke, Kansas State University; Kathleen E. Culler, Tulane University; Cynthia Dubielak and John Fallon, Ohio University—Athens; Sherman Han, Brigham Young University–Hawaii; John Hanes, Duquesne University; Richard Hannaford, University of Idaho; Karen R. Keim, Moravian College; Charles Kerlin, St. Joseph's College; Patricia Kolonosky, Kansas State University; William Kuhre, Ohio University–Athens; Albert Labriola, Duquesne University; Debbie Dietrich Leasure, Kansas State University; James Machor, Ohio State University–Lima; Barry M. Maid, University of Arkansas–Little Rock; Cathy McDaniel, Ohio University–Athens; Eugene Nolan, University of Wisconsin–River Falls; Les Perelman, Tulane University; William Prewett, Jr., Tulane University; Brian Railsback, Ohio University–Athens; Paula C. Resch, Loras College; Florence Roberts, University of Idaho; Gary Ross, Texas A&M University; Charles Schuster, University of Washington; Michele Geslin Small, Northland College; Timothy Steury, University of Idaho; Patricia L. Stewart, Kansas State University; Gary Tolliver, Ohio University–Athens; Eric Von Fuhrman, Indiana State University; and Curtis Yehnert, Ohio University–Athens.

My sons, Geoff and Tony; my daughter-in-law, Fran; my grandson, Christopher "Topher" Ross; my mother; and Norma, my wife and best pal—these make my circle just, and make me end where I began.

W. Ross Winterowd

Contents

II

THE USES OF WRITING

3

The Writer's Journal / 60

4

Narration / 77

5

Exposition / 101

6

Argumentation and Persuasion / 133

A Spectrum of Student Writing / 161

III

SPECIAL USES OF WRITING

10

Writing Business Letters / 274

IV ▬▬
STRUCTURE AND STYLE

11
Paragraphs / 312

12
Rewriting Sentences / 355

V

REFERENCE GUIDE

The Contemporary Writer

A PRACTICAL RHETORIC

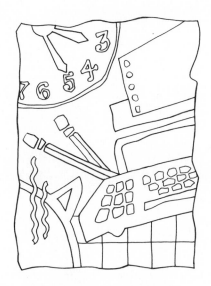

THIRD EDITION

I

THE
WRITING
TRANSACTION

1

From Writer to Reader

The term "writing" is one that we use every day. It can mean (a) what a writer produces (books, essays, letters, reports), or (b) the process of producing it, or (c) handwriting. Thus,

(a) Hemingway's *writing* is always interesting.
(b) Smith is now in the process of *writing* her autobiography.
(c) Uncle Elmer's *writing* is hard to decipher.

THE MEANING OF "WRITING"

We will use the word "text" to mean "that which is written down (or printed) in some way." The book that you are now reading is a textbook, but also a text, and so is the page now before you and the paragraph that you are reading. And when you write, you produce texts. In this book, then, the word "text" means any stretch of written discourse, whether one sentence, one paragraph, one page, or a whole volume. If we discuss handwriting, we will use that term, not "writing."

In this book, the word "writing" will always mean the process, not the product or handwriting.

WHY WRITE?

There are obvious and practical reasons for becoming a good writer. According to Paul A. Strassman, a vice president of Xerox Corporation,

> Since the 1950s our country has become predominantly occupied with the creation, distribution, and administration of information. By 1990, only about fifty percent of the work force will be manufacturing objects and producing food. The rest will occupy most of the time just communicating.[1]

In our "information society," the ability to write effectively can mean success.

However, this immediately practical motive is not the only, or perhaps even the most important, reason for learning to write well. To gain an idea of the *uses* of writing, we can think about some of the *purposes* for writing.

We often use language merely for *self-expression,* to get something off our chest, to let off steam, to release the internal pressure that silence creates. When you stub your toe on a chair at night and curse a blue streak, you are using language self-expressively—not to convey information, not to convince anyone of anything, but merely as a safety valve.

Under self-expression, we can classify any kind of writing that is for the writer him- or herself. Self-expressive writing, as in the following reminiscence of a writer about his past, is reflexive: writer and reader are the same.

> Two odors, aromas, smells. Frying pork chops and burning leaves—one richly oleaginous, the other spicily acrid.
> In the almost dark of a mid-October six o'clock, the entry light and the windows of the red-brick apartment house glow through the chilly haze. The poplars between the sidewalk and the curb are bare, their brittle gold and brown leaves filling the gutter and lying in puddles on the lawn. Parked at the curb is a shining new Hudson Hornet, silver and gray, sleek, streamlined. A radio somewhere in the building,

turned too high (or at least high enough to be heard on the sidewalk), plays "On the Steppes of Central Asia."

The building is two-story, with a front door of oval plate glass set in heavy, much-varnished hardwood, with a brass loop handle and thumb-trigger.

The carpeting in the hall is worn maroon, with large, stylized flowers in green and yellow. The chipped paint on the wainscoting is off-white, an almost ashy gray. The doors to the apartments are the same much-varnished hardwood as the front door, and each has a brass number: 1, 3, 5, 7, 2, 4, 6, 8. "On the Steppes of Central Asia" is now virtually a roar, but then sudden silence: the radio has been snapped off. The smell of pork chops frying is almost palpable.

Before the door of apartment 3 lies the evening paper. The door opens, and a woman in a cotton housedress (white, printed with violets) stoops, picks up the paper, and glances momentarily down the hall. She has the classic, almost masculine face of a Venus de Milo; her hair is drawn into a bun at the back of her neck; her breasts are full, and her hips are broad and capable.

The hall is lighted by three meager frosted-glass, one-bulb fixtures spaced down the ceiling, and in the light, almost as if from candles or lanterns, the aura is golden, mellow, with the maroon of the carpet, the rich smell of the pork chops, the dark wood of the doors, and the many-layered paint on the woodwork. A woman's gentle laugh is barely audible. And then a metallic clang, perhaps a pan that has fallen, and a man's voice: "Damn!"

The radio plays again, now softly, "In a Persian Market."

A woman appears beyond the glass of the front door and, holding a large brown paper sack in one arm, opens the door and enters the hall. Her tan plaid skirt stops just above her knees. The coat, with its fur collar, is chocolate brown. Her brown hair tumbles from beneath a brown tam. Her shoes are spike-heel black patent leather. She glances down the hall and then hurries up the stairs, which creak slightly with her every step. Behind her hovers the aroma of cosmetics, face powder, and perfume.

Throughout the city, brick apartment houses: sooty yellow or deep red. At six o'clock of an October evening, they glow at entryways and windows. They smell of frying meat. Their halls are musty and dimly lighted. From behind the doors come muted sounds of voices.

In the chill haze of an October evening, brick apartment houses. Mystery and romance.

Writing is most often used for *referential* purposes, *to explain:*

- directions for getting from one place to another
- instructions for assembling a new vacuum cleaner
- reasons for making a given choice
- the basis for one's religious belief
- a textbook, such as this one

to demonstrate or prove, through data and reasoning:

- a report in *Consumer's Research*
- a scientific report
- a research or library paper
- a tightly logical argument

and *to explore* ideas:

- a discussion of a subject about which the writer has not yet reached a firm conclusion

In the following example of referential prose, the Canadian writer Farley Mowat *explains* one of the religious beliefs of the Ihalmiut, people who live in the barrens of the arctic north:

> At the peak of the hierarchy of spiritual beings stand those elemental forces of nature which have no concrete form. At their head is Kaila, the god of weather and of the sky. Kaila is the creator and thus the paramount godhead of the People. He is aloof, as the mightiest deity should be, and man is no more than dust under his feet. He demands neither abasement nor worship from those he has created. But Kaila is a just god, for he is all things brought about by the powers of nature, and nature, who is completely impartial, cannot be unjust.
>
> *—People of the Deer*

Persuasive writing is action oriented, intended to make readers do something: buy a product, vote for a candidate, give up smoking. The audience for a persuasive text is usually rather clearly defined. There is a world of difference between writing a clear set of instructions for planting a vegetable garden and persuading one's brother to follow those instructions.

For example, a public service advertisement headlined "We're All Disabled," placed in the January 21, 1986, issue of the *Los Angeles Times* by Mobil Corporation, persuades readers to employ the handicapped, to help provide special facilities, and to donate money to the National Organization on Disability. Here are the last two paragraphs of that advertisement:

> All of us should be partners (and we are, whether we realize it or not). But what can we, as partners, do? As employers we must look beyond the obvious disability and judge each job applicant on the skills or knowledge he or she has to offer. As citizens, we must work to make the community serve everyone, and provide the special facilities

needed by some. And as neighbors, we can make our own tax deductible contribution to the National Organization on Disability, Suite 234, 2100 Pennsylvania Avenue, N.W., Washington, D.C. 20037.

In proclaiming 1983–1992 the Decade of Disabled Persons, President Reagan said it all in a letter to N.O.D.: "There is a long tradition in America of neighbor helping neighbor, and your program shows that spirit is still alive today."

And, of course, many people write to create art: poems, stories, dramas. You need not be a professional musician to enjoy singing or playing an instrument, and you can enjoy "creative" writing without intending to make your living at it.

WHAT THIS BOOK CAN DO FOR YOU: AN OVERVIEW

The Contemporary Writer begins, in the present chapter, with some general concepts that will help you create texts that accomplish what you want them to do; the most important point being what readers expect writers to provide. Through the discussion and exercises in the chapter, *you will learn some of the basic principles of adapting texts to the readers for whom they are intended.*

The second chapter of part I, "The Writing Transaction," is *a guided tour through the writing of one text.* You will see how the writer gathers ideas, organizes them, puts them into sentences and paragraphs, and makes revisions. You will learn that writing involves trial and error and that writers must be ready to make changes all along the way: adding new ideas that pop up, deleting ideas that don't work, substituting one idea for another, and rearranging large and small sections of the text to achieve unity and the proper emphasis.

Part II, "The Uses of Writing," begins with a chapter that talks about *the writer's journal,* explaining why a journal is useful and also why many people gain pleasure from keeping a journal.

The fourth chapter deals with *narration,* or writing that, like history, tells of events in a chronological sequence. The chapter will show you how to bring a narrative to life and make it interesting and believable for your readers. The chapter will also help you learn to use narration as a powerful way to explain ideas and to argue for points of view.

As you read and think about the fifth chapter and do the exercises, you will gain power in the use of writing to *explain* ideas and processes and to *explore* concepts and problems. The chapter concerns *exposition,* which in many ways is the very bread and butter of writing, for expository texts (such as sets of instructions, essays, scientific reports, extended definitions, and business proposals) are necessary to the multiple worlds in which we live: learning, business, science, government.

The sixth chapter will help you use informal logic and evidence to develop effective *arguments* for your opinions. The chapter will also explain how you can *persuade* your readers to take action.

Following the sixth chapter you will find a spectrum of student writing for analysis and discussion.

The third part of the book deals with some special uses of writing. Literature has always been an important part of a liberal education, and most college students are asked to write papers concerning poems, stories, and plays. The seventh chapter will help you write successful *texts about literature.*

Most college and university students need to be skilled takers of *essay examinations.* The eighth chapter will show you how you can be more successful when you write answers in these tests.

The *research paper* (library paper, documented paper) is one of the most common sorts of writing that college students must do. In composing these texts, students learn to assemble and evaluate information and how to provide documentation for the reader. The ninth chapter of this book is a guide to research writing.

The tenth chapter is extremely practical. It demonstrates how to write effective *business letters.*

The next part is about the structure and style of your writing. The eleventh chapter focuses on that essential building block of texts, the *paragraph.* And chapters twelve and thirteen will help you improve the *style* of your prose. You will gain instruction and practice in writing readable prose that gives your ideas the proper relationships and emphases.

Finally, the "Reference Guide" at the end of the book will help you proofread your text to remove mechanical errors.

Throughout *The Contemporary Writer,* you will find hints and procedures for *discovering and developing ideas.* These techniques, many of which are regularly used by scientists and social scientists, can help you become a more versatile thinker and problem solver.

WRITING AND THINKING

It is quite possible to write without creating marks on paper (or clay tablets, blackboards, or computer screens). We know that many people whom we call "writers" speak their words into a recorder, for someone else to *transcribe,* and that even though the blind Milton dictated *Paradise Lost* to his daughters, we say that he *wrote* the epic. It seems, then, that the *process* of writing does not necessarily involve *inscription* (making marks); of course, if the writer's words are not finally inscribed by someone in some way, we would not have a text. The point, however, is that it is possible to write without inscribing: writing as a process is not creating marks on a surface. Writing is a way of thinking, and *inscribing*—making marks that a reader can decipher, creating a text—is a way to record and transmit thought.

However, the marks that you or any other writers make on a page are not the thought, not the meaning, just as a map is not the territory that it represents; the marks on the page are instructions through which readers can construct a meaning. If the map lacks such essential data as newly constructed highways, the person using it may well get lost, and if the text does not supply what the reader needs to derive a meaning, the reader too will get lost.

It is the writer's job to give the reader effective instructions. You can view this book as a set of guidelines for giving readers effective instructions.

FACTORS IN THE WRITER-READER TRANSACTION

Before we get down to practical details, let's take an overview of what it means to write anything so that we can relate the details to the whole process.[2] When you write anything—a note to a friend, a scientific report, a legal brief, a novel—you are concerned with *content, structure, style,* and *readers.* Often you may be writing only for yourself: class notes that only you will see, a private diary, scribbles that help you solve a problem. If this kind of writing (for yourself) satisfies you and serves your purposes, it is successful because you are the reader.

Since the purpose of most writing is to communicate with *readers,* the writer must think about the reader's needs, interests, personality, and values. Diagrammatically,

WRITER ⟵—————————————⟶ READER

The fact that you are trying to let a reader know what you mean is one complication of the whole writing process.

A piece of writing conveys meaning; it has *content*. However, in order to communicate effectively the writer must adjust his or her presentation of the content according to the needs of the reader.

Meeting the Needs of Readers

Write two brief explanations of a technical term (for example, "byte," "pronoun," "field goal," "sauté"), first for an eight-year-old child and then for an educated adult who is unfamiliar with the field from which the term comes.

After you have completed the writing, think about the differences between the two pieces. Did you change your word choice? How about examples and analogies? Was your sentence structure less complex in one explanation than in the other?

Thus, we can add another element to our diagram of the writing transaction:

CONTENT

WRITER ⟵—————————————⟶ READER

In conveying the intended meaning, the writer must *structure* the content. Structure organizes information for the reader and helps the writer achieve his or her desired effect. (Mystery stories are structured to keep readers in suspense until the very end. Scientific reports are structured so that readers can learn the results or conclusions immediately, before entering into the details, which are presented in the "body" of the report.) And the diagram gains yet another element:

CONTENT
STRUCTURE

WRITER ⟵—————————————⟶ READER

The *medium* through which the writing is conveyed is also an important consideration. As an extreme example, a letter of application for admittance to law school written with a pencil on blue-lined notebook paper is unlikely to be as effective as the same message neatly typed on bond paper. So we add *medium* to the diagram:

Finally every piece of writing demands language choice or *style*. If your purpose is to explain as clearly as possible how to get to your home, you will use one kind of style, but if you want to describe the beauty along the route, you will choose another style. Therefore,

Writer, readers, content, structure, and style—these elements are not separate and distinct, but are interrelated and influence one another at every point in the writing process. When you are writing, you must be aware of problems of

Content Are my data reliable? Have I provided adequate information for the readers? Is my content up-to-date? Appropriate? Fair? Will it interest my readers? Is it relevant?

Structure Is my text coherent? (Does it have "flow"? Does it hang together?) Have I met special requirements, such as the proper form for a scientific report? Would reorganization make my text more effective?

Style Does my text contain distracting mechanical errors? Is my prose readable, or is it unnecessarily obscure and difficult to understand? Is my style graceful? Does it have "flow"?

Readers   What do they know (or don't they know) about the subject? What are their purposes for reading? What do they expect to get out of the writing? Do they have prejudices that the text must overcome? Does the text square with the readers' value systems?

The writing process is a complicated drama, the writer adjusting his or her text according to the interrelated demands of content, structure, style, and readers. Throughout the rest of this book, you will be reminded that you can use the preceding questions as guides for revising your texts.

THE WRITER-READER CONTRACT

In many ways, writing is a game made up of rules—like chess or football. Without the rules, there would be no game. And without rules, there could be no language. You may not be able to state the rules of language in the way that many fans can precisely explain the rules of football, chess, or hockey, but, as the following examples illustrate, there are rules:

1. (a) The dog bit the man.   [In this sentence, the dog does the biting.]
   (b) The man bit the dog.   [In this sentence, the man does the biting.]
   (c) Man the dog the bit.   [We know that this is not an English sentence.]
2. I promise you I'll punch you in the nose if you step on my petunias.   [Because we know the rules of language, we realize that this sentence is a threat, not a promise, even though it begins "I promise. . . ."]
3. We know that *ungraltimorness* might possibly be a word in English, but that *ptliumx* is almost certainly not an English word.
4. We know that if a person says, "Once upon a time," we can expect a story, probably a fairy tale or folktale.

To be successful in writing instructions that readers can use to get meaning, the writer must play by a set of rules, four of which might be stated as

1. Give readers all they need in order to understand, but no more than they need. (The rule of *quantity*.)
2. Be truthful, and know your subject. (The rule of *quality*.)

3. Do not include irrelevant material. (The rule of *relation.*)
4. Be as clear as possible. (The rule of *manner.*)[3]

If as a writer you unintentionally violate any of the "rules," you will create humor or will merely puzzle your reader. For example, the following violates the rule of *quantity:*

> I'll meet you at my car. It's in slot nine at the east parking lot. It's a yellow Toyota Corolla, with Goodyear tires. On the left fender is a slight dent, where I was hit by a punk rocker riding a moped. The odometer registers 11,281.7 miles.

If the purpose was merely to allow someone to find the automobile, the writer has given far too much information in this note. The opposite extreme would be, "I'll meet you at my car. It's in one of the university parking lots." A reader seeking directions would take these passages to be either ineptness or attempts at humor.

Any time you think a person is lying, you are assuming that he or she has broken the rule of *quality.* And, of course, the great American tall tale intentionally violates the rule of quality to create humor. We know that the author of a tall tale such as the one that follows exaggerates for effect:

> Three cowboys were snowbound at a line camp in the early days. They soon ate up all the food and decided to play poker to see which one would go out for supplies.
>
> The loser took off and was gone for three days. On the fourth day they were excited to hear him pounding on the snow-covered door. He forced the door open, threw a bag of groceries on the bed. The others tore open the bag and found fourteen bottles of whiskey and one loaf of bread.
>
> They stared in amazement, then turned to the exhausted cowboy in disgust. "What in the hell are we going to do with all this bread?"
>
> —*Montana Tall Tales,* compiled by Georgia Nation Carter

The information contained in a message must be *related* (pertinent) to the writer's purpose, a fact that makes the example that follows puzzling:

> I'll meet you at my car. Automobiles are an important part of American history, the symbol of American industrial might, technological proficiency, and individual freedom. The car is a yellow Toyota Corolla, parked in slot nine of the east lot.

If the writer's purpose was to provide the information necessary for the reader to get to the car, the sentence concerning the role of automobiles in American history is irrelevant.

The *manner* in which you give directions is, of course, also an important factor. If your purpose is to enable someone to meet you at your automobile, you should be as direct and clear as possible, which explains why the following is odd:

> The cynosure of our attention at the moment is a vehicle of bilious complexion under the sign of the Ram, in occupancy at the present time of a space in a certain area designated by this institution for the temporary storage of motor vehicles. The courses of our destiny will intersect at the ninth sector of the oriental area set aside for parking.

This text conveys only the following information: "The car is a yellow Aries parked in the ninth space of the east lot. I'll meet you there." That being the case, all the circumlocution is purposeless and merely creates problems for the reader.

No one is likely to violate the rules as flagrantly as these examples do, but it is not uncommon for writers—experienced or novice—to forget the "rules" and thus create unsuccessful texts.

For example, the following essay from English 101 is not convincing, and we can use the "rules" of quantity, quality, relation, and manner to explain some of the problems.

The Influence of Television

Television has been the topic of much controversy recently. Can television be beneficial, or is it strictly an escape for people? Does it project negative aspects which influence the young audience?

Concern for whom? (quantity)

Violence on television has been a major concern because it is believed that young people watching such shows might be badly influenced. For example, a young boy recently was tried for murder, and an investigation was made by a psychologist because they thought he may have watched too much TV and thus obtained a warped perspective on violence. TV is an escape into a dream world and after too much subjection, as in the case of the young boy, it becomes difficult to distinguish the difference between reality and the dream.

Which shows? (quantity)

Source of information about the boy? Is the information accurate? How can the reader check? (quality)

Examples of programs that are escapist? (quantity)

Meaning of the word "subjection" in this context? (manner)

Is the information about little brother relevant? (relation)	In the past, I used to believe that television had one beneficial show, the news. My little brother enjoys "Sesame Street." The news is informative and brings to us, conveniently, up-to-date information on the world situations. Now, I have reassessed my views on this subject and have decided that TV is not worthwhile despite the news broadcasts. The reporter expresses world dilemmas in a prejudiced way, reflecting either his own views or the opinions of the station he works for. If an unbiased presentation were to occur, I am still inclined to believe it is a waste of time. In order to learn and retain information it is necessary to work to learn. When the news is broadcast, it is handed to the viewer on a silver platter. No thought is needed, and therefore, I think we just accept what we hear being told to us, instead of formulating our own ideas and opinions.
Are all reporters prejudiced? Can the reader trust a writer who makes such broad, unsubstantiated claims? (quality)	
What does "it" refer to? Just the news? Television in general? (manner)	
Backing for the conclusion that viewers don't need to think? Can we trust a writer who deals in such broad generalities? (quality)	
Has the argument substantiated the conclusion that TV is virtually useless? If not, then the conclusion does not follow from the body of the essay. (relation)	Television is nicknamed "boob tube," "idiot box," etc. for appropriate reasons as it is virtually useless. People should read more to gain information and resort to watching television as an *occasional* educational device.

If you unintentionally violate one of the terms of the "contract," you have committed an error. Therefore, you might make it a policy to ask yourself questions like the following:

1. *Quantity.* Have I included all the information—examples, data, narratives, details—that my readers need in order to understand my full intention in writing? (If not, what should I add?) Have I included more than my readers need? (If so, what should I cut?)
2. *Quality.* Are my data current? Are my sources reliable? Do my readers know why I am competent to write about my subject?
3. *Relevance.* Does everything relate to the point that I'm trying to make? Is there anything that I should remove from the body of the piece and put into a note?
4. *Manner.* Is my writing as easy to read as I can possibly make it and still convey my full intention?

Critical Thinking: The Language Game

Use the principles of the writer-reader contract—with its "clauses" of quantity, quality, relation, and manner—to explain the "special effects" in the following examples.

1. *Question:* How many Californians does it take to replace a lightbulb? *Answer:* Three—one to screw in the bulb and two to share the experience.

2. From "Spring Bulletin," by Woody Allen, a course description:

> *Economic Theory:* a systematic application and critical evaluation of the basic analytic concepts of economic theory, with an emphasis on money and why it's good. Fixed coefficient production functions, cost and supply curves, and nonconvexity comprise the first semester, with the second semester concentrating on spending, making change, and keeping a neat wallet. The Federal Reserve System is analyzed, and advanced students are coached in the proper method of filling out a deposit slip. Other topics include: Inflation and Depression—how to dress for each. Loans, interest, welching.
>
> *—Getting Even*

3.   I had been confined to my bed for several days with lumbago. My case refused to improve. Finally the doctor said:

   "My remedies have no fair chance. Consider what they have to fight, besides the lumbago. You smoke extravagantly, don't you?"

   "Yes."

   "You take coffee immoderately?"

   "Yes."

   "And some tea?"

   "Yes."

   "You eat all kinds of things that are dissatisfied with each other's company?"

   "Yes."

   "You drink two hot Scotches every night?"

   "Yes."

   "Very well, there you can see what I have to contend against. We can't make progress the way the matter stands. You must make a reduction in these things; you must cut down your consumption of them considerably for some days."

   "I can't, doctor."

   "Why can't you?"

   "I lack the will-power. I can cut them off entirely, but I can't merely moderate them."

   He said that that would answer. . . . I cut off all those things for two days and nights . . . and at the end of the forty-eight hours the lumbago was discouraged and left me. I was a well man; so I gave thanks and took those delicacies again.

   It seemed a valuable medical course, and I recommended it to a lady. She had run down and down and down, and had at last reached a point where medicines no longer had any helpful effect upon her. I said I knew I could put her on her feet in a week. It brightened her up, it filled her with hope, and she said she would do everything I told her to do. So I said she must stop swearing and drinking and smoking . . . for four days, and then she would be all right again . . . but she said she could not stop swearing and smoking and drinking, because she had never done these things. So there it was. She had neglected her habits. . . . She had nothing to fall back on. She was a sinking vessel with no freight in it to throw overboard. . . . Why, even one or two little bad habits could have saved her, but she was a moral pauper.

—Mark Twain, *Following the Equator*

4.

The Purist

I give you now Professor Twist,
A conscientious scientist.
Trustees exclaimed, "He never bungles!"
And sent him off to distant jungles.
Camped on a tropic riverside,
One day he missed his loving bride.
She had, the guide informed him later,
Been eaten by an alligator.
Professor Twist could not but smile.
"You mean," he said, "a crocodile."

—Ogden Nash

5.

Professor Twist's Last Expedition

That was in . . . uh . . . let me see,
The year of 1923.
In '33 he set out on
A journey up the Amazon.
After hardship you can't describe,
He came upon a savage tribe,
Healthy, happy, without disease—
Twist barely reached up to their knees.
Eagerly he told their chief,
"Your followers defy belief.
They get their vigor by what means?"
The chief replied, "We eat-um beans."
"Beans? Beans? What kind?" Poor Twist was wild.
"Yooman beans!" The chief just smiled.

WRITING FOR READERS

Like all games, football is made of rules: no rules, no game, or, to put it another way, the rules are the game. Within the system of rules, however, teams adapt and change their strategies to meet the challenges of various opponents. A team that normally runs the ball play after play will change to a passing game when confronted by opponents with an excellent defensive line.

Strategies (the way one uses the rules) in the writing "game" change, too, depending on who will read the text. For example, here are two explanations of the "GOTO" statement used in BASIC computer language. The first is from a book for beginners who know nothing about computers or programming. The second is from the IBM manual.

The GOTO statement is one way to tell the computer to repeat a sequence of statements. A GOTO statement consists of a statement number, the word "GOTO" (or "GO TO"), and a second statement number. When the computer encounters a GOTO statement, it does not continue to execute statements in numerical order. Instead, it executes next the statement whose number appears in the GOTO statement, and continues from there. Consider the following example (a rather stupid one):

```
10 LET A = 1
20 LET B = 2
30 PRINT A
40 PRINT B
50 GOTO 30
60 END
```

Statements 10 through 40 print the numbers 1 and 2. When the computer gets to statement 50, it goes back to statement 30, where it prints another 1. Then it continues on from statement 30 to statement 40 and prints a 2. When it comes to statement 50, the computer goes back to statement 30 again, where it again prints a 1. Then it prints a 2. When it comes to statement 50 again, it goes back to statement 30. . . .

In fact, this program succeeds a little too well: the computer will continue to print 1's and 2's . . . until the next power failure or the end of the world, whichever comes first.

—David E. Simon, *IBM Basic from the Ground Up*

Purpose: Branches unconditionally out of the normal program sequence to a specified line number.

Versions: Cassette Disk Advanced Compiler

Format: GOTO *line*

Remarks: *line* is the line number of a line in the program.

If *line* is the line number of an executable statement, that statement and those following are executed. If *line* refers to a non-executable statement (such as REM or DATA), the program continues at the first executable statement encountered after *line*.

The GOTO statement can be used in direct mode to reenter a program at a desired point. This can be useful in debugging.

> Use ON . . . GOTO to branch to different lines based on the result of an expression.
>
> —*IBM Basic*, 2nd ed.

For people who are familiar with computers and programming languages, the IBM manual is far superior to *IBM Basic from the Ground Up*, but that book is excellent for novices. A beginner would need the extended example that David Simon provides and would need to be warned about getting into a "tight loop." The writer of the IBM manual assumes that his or her readers will understand the general principles of computer programs and will be familiar with such terms as "executable statement," "REM," and "DATA."

In other words, we can state another of the main principles of writing, perhaps the most important one: *the intended reader determines the writer's strategies.* If you are explaining chess to your five-year-old niece, you will use different methods than you would if you were explaining the game to a friend.

Giving readers the "instructions" that they need to build meanings from texts is perhaps the most important aspect of writing. Different readers, different "instructions."

A Suggestion for Writing

Write an analysis of an audience.

1. Choose a definite audience: the members of an organization to which you belong, the congregation of your church, the students in your college or university, members of a conservative or liberal political organization on campus—any group that you know or can find out about.
2. Now choose an action that you would like to persuade this group to take: voting for a given candidate, banning the use of a substance such as alcohol, donating money to a cause, joining a rally or a boycott—anything that involves a definite action.
3. Finally, discuss the problems and opportunities that the audience gives you in advancing your cause.

Some questions you might ask yourself about the audience are the following: (a) What features set this group off from other groups? (Politics? Religion? Economics? Social class? Other features?) (b) What are the dynamics of the group? (What sorts of things do they do? What have they supported in the past? If they are organized, in what way? If they are not organized, how do they manage to stay together as an identifiable group?) (c) What other groups are they allied with? (d) How have they changed over the years (or months)? (e) How might they change? (f) How much can I expect my readers to know about my subject?

These are only examples of questions that you might ask. You will undoubtedly think of many others.

Critical Thinking: The Writer-Reader Transaction

The four "clauses" of the writer-reader "contract" are excellent guides to reading critically. By applying the principles of quantity, quality, manner, and relation to texts, you can evaluate their strengths and weaknesses.

From your point of view as a reader, what are the strengths and weaknesses of the following essay, "Artificial Music: An Uncertain Future for Many Musicians," by Susan Foster? Carefully read the essay, and be prepared to discuss the following questions:

1. Do you think that the writer knows what she is talking about? Do you trust her information and opinions? Explain why or why not.
2. Do you need or want more information about any aspect of the essay? Explain. In some instances, does the writer give you more information than you need or want? Explain.
3. Is any part of the essay irrelevant to the subject? Explain.
4. Are any parts of the essay hard to understand or ambiguous? Explain.
5. Could the essay be rearranged to make it more effective or more understandable? Explain.
6. Is the writing clear and easy to read or unclear and difficult to read? Explain. Do any "mechanical" errors annoy you? Point them out.
7. In your opinion, is the essay successful or unsuccessful? Explain.

In the recording industry, the future of musicians who play acoustic instruments looks dismal. With the rise in technology of synthesized, computerized, and electronic music, the need for "live" musicians is drastically declining. One by one, musicians who play in the studios for television commercials, television shows, and motion pictures are being replaced by intricate synthesizers and computerized music. Now, a computer or synthesizer can create the different timbres of an entire symphony orchestra. [1-7]

The advent of recording started to put people out of work nearly a century ago. The piano players who accompanied silent movies were the first to see the unemployment line. More recent are the many out of work dance bands who are seeing one person, called a disc jockey, come in to a gig and spin records for an evening. Today, however, something a little different is shoving live performers to the side: the production of synthesized music. [8-13]

Synthesized music is electronically produced. In other words, the source of a pitch is electronic, as opposed to striking a string or exhaling a column [14-15]

of air. With the turning of knobs or the pushing of buttons, sounds can be 16
produced, varying in duration, pitch, timbre, etc. Small studios or second 17
rate motion pictures with low budgets can hire just one keyboardist to play 18
a synthesizer and make up the film's entire soundtrack. Many tracks might 19
be needed to make up the entire range of the score, but nevertheless, only 20
one musician is hired and paid. In 1981, Vangelis won an Oscar for the Best 21
Original Score for the motion picture "Chariots of Fire". He played all the 22
music on synthesizers. 23

Boyde Hood, a trumpet player, and Tommy Johnson, a tuba player, both 24
private instructors at USC, admit to getting fewer studio calls than in the 25
previous decade, attributing it to the demand for synthesized music. Jim 26
Firmston, a keyboardist and studio musician, is getting many calls for studio 27
work. Firmston says, "Amazing things are being done with all this electronic 28
music." He is more than a little concerned about his future since all of this 29
growing technology may one day replace even him. 30

Listening closely to the background music of some television commer- 31
cials, a HIGHLY well trained ear may be able to detect the sounds of a 32
sophisticated digital music system, but for many people, the music sounds 33
just like that of a 90 piece orchestra. I consider myself a well-educated mu- 34
sician, and even I sometimes have trouble distinguishing synthesized sounds. 35
In a digital music system, everything is reproduced and remembered numer- 36
ically: timbres, modulations, keys, dynamics, articulations, tempos, vibrato, 37
chords, and the list goes on and on. 38

The Synclavier is one such system able to produce almost infinite func- 39
tions. A small portion of the pamphlet for the Synclavier reads, "It (the Syn- 40
clavier) combines the power of a computer with unique digital sound gen- 41
erators, put together in an easy to use package, designed for musicians. As a 42
complete system, it offers digital synthesis of sounds with amazing realism, 43
limitless programmable control, and extensive facilities for composition, re- 44
cording, editing, and performing musical pieces." It is capable of expanding 45
from eight to 128 voices. 46

The USC School of Music owns a Synclavier priced around $75,000. In 47
a major studio, however, up to $200,000 can be spent on these sophisticated 48
instruments. The Fairlight is another digital music system of almost endless 49
possibilities. The synthesizers that studio musicians and performers use are 50
the Yamaha DX7 or Roland brands. Elton John and Julian Lennon are the two 51
performers who play on the DX7. These synthesizers range in cost from $1200– 52
$1500. When considering the cost of a very fine violin—$15,000 to $30,000— 53
spending $1500 for a synthesizer, which can produce almost the exact same 54
sound of that expensive violin, seems like a pretty good deal. 55

Home computers can even be used as a musical instrument or teaching 56
device. At a computer software store, one can buy the programmed disk of 57
"The Music Shop" or "The Music Construction Set" for approximately $40. 58
These programs enable the computer user to write his own music, even with 59
little or no previous background in music. Other programs can aid in the 60
development of aural skills, such as interval, melodic, and harmonic recog- 61
nition. These same home computers can also help the experienced com- 62
poser. A synthetic keyboard is hooked up to the computer, making it possible 63
for the composer to experiment with harmonies, melodies, and timbres while 64
storing up any or all of the material. 65

The biggest takeover of electronic music seems to be in the field of drums and percussion. Not too long ago, the Linn drum machine became the first successful machine on the market, but it is already obsolete since more versatile machines have been developed. The drum machine is like a metronome; there is no error in the time that it produces. "Licks" (musical jargon for a passage of notes or rhythms) can be produced by the machine that no human being, no matter how well trained, could ever execute. The radio station KJLH is a prime example of the use of drum machines. The machines lay down funk beats that are heard song after song.

An example of adapting to the uses of electronic music is demonstrated by the tuba player Jim Self, another private instructor at USC. He accepted a studio job to play a piccolo trumpet part, one no other musician in the city could handle. Self owns an EVI (electronic valve instrument) that is different from the normal synthesizer in that it has valves instead of a keyboard. Turning a knob on the side of the instrument gets different octaves and pushing the buttons produces different timbres.

Must every musician accommodate himself like Self? This is a tuba player working on an incredibly high trumpet part, an extremely drastic change. Musicians will always be wanted for the live symphonic performances of works by Beethoven, Brahms, and Mahler. John Williams continues to hire full orchestras for his scores of motion pictures. Live music will last because of its history and its emotional and spiritual effects on audience and performer alike. One thing is almost certain, though, computerized and synthesized music is here to stay, and for those few musicians who are striving for that goal of studio playing, the future looks not too promising.

FROM SUBJECT TO TOPIC

Before ending the chapter, we need to consider one important concept regarding composition: from the general subject that you write about, you must derive a topic.

The *topic* of your writing is the point that you want to make about your subject. You are writing for some purpose (to convince, to inform, to amuse, to persuade, and so on) and for some reader or readers. In other words, you want your text, when it is read by others, to *do* something.

Sometimes the topic is relatively clear-cut and can be stated in one sentence:

1. The two most common printers for computers are dot matrix and daisy wheel.

This straightforward announcement of a topic leads the reader to expect that the text will *inform* him or her about the two kinds of printers.

2. Because she advocates a balanced municipal budget, a clamp-down on pet owners who let their animals run free, and prose-cution of drivers of noisy vehicles, you should support Norma Mandic for the city council.

Readers of a text based on this topic expect to find *persuasive* reasons for supporting the candidate.

3. Carefully administered tests lead to the conclusion that con-sumers cannot tell the difference between Phizzy Cola and Eleven Down Cola.

In order to be *convinced,* the reader wants the details and an explanation of how the tests were conducted.

At times, however, the topic cannot be so easily stated (nor is it necessary to confine the statement of a topic always to one sentence). Sometimes the topic is not stated directly, but the reader can infer it. Whether or not a topic is stated, *most* pieces of writ-ing have a relatively clear-cut topic, for if they did not, readers would see no direction or purpose in the text and, therefore, would become frustrated.

When you write, a clearly stated topic will help you organize and adjust your text for readers, and we will deal with topics more fully as this book develops.

Narrowing a subject down to a useful topic is essentially a two-step process. First, you determine what you want your text to do, and then you decide *for whom.* You ask, "Who are my readers? What do I want my text to do to or for them?" We can illustrate this principle:

1. *Subject*	Football	
Narrowing	America's football mania	
Topic	The Super Bowl is the great American ritual, embodying national values of competitiveness and excellence.	
Purpose	To *inform* readers of my thoughts about the Super Bowl	
Audience	My colleagues in the composition class	

2. *Subject*	Food	
Narrowing	Food additives	
Topic	Food additives such as monosodium glutamate should be banned.	
Purpose	To *convince* readers that some food additives are perilous to health	
Audience	Readers of the magazine supplement to Friday's edition of the college newspaper	

3. *Subject*   Education

Narrowing   A statement of goals in an application for a scholarship to spend a semester studying at the University of Vienna

    Topic   I have three reasons for applying for this scholarship: I am fluent in German; I have begun to study baroque art and architecture, of which Vienna is a center; and my academic record, with a 3.86 GPA, indicates that I am a serious student.

  Purpose   To *persuade* the readers that the writer should receive the scholarship

Audience   Board members who will award the scholarship

4. *Subject*   Automobiles

Narrowing   The most practical car for a college student who needs transportation from home, to school, and to work

    Topic   The most practical car is the Dodge Aries or its Plymouth version, the Reliant.

  Purpose   To *convince* the writer's wife—who prefers a Ford Escort—that the Dodge Aries is the best choice

Audience   The writer's wife

Exercise: Finding a Topic

Narrow the following impossibly broad (and hence boring) subjects; then in one sentence or more write a topic that gives a viewpoint and purpose to the subject. State the purpose, and identify the intended audience. In each case, you should be willing to write a brief essay based on the topic that you formulate.

a. school
b. sports
c. politics
d. food
e. personal relationships

f. a phobia (irrational fear, such as agoraphobia, the fear of open places)
g. honesty
h. a hobby
i. art, music, or literature
j. the weather

REWRITING

Rewriting—or revision—is not the last step in writing but is an ongoing process, as "Becoming a Reader" (pages 38–47) shows. A good writer is always a good *rewriter*, and the techniques of rewriting are not mysterious or terribly complex.

24

Exactly what does "rewriting" imply? It is the process of making *deletions, additions, rearrangements,* and *substitutions.* Rewriting should not be confused with *proofreading* or *editing,* the process whereby the writer "cleans up" the manuscript by catching "mechanical" errors: misspellings, incorrect use of punctuation, and other such problems.

When we rewrite, we can

Delete
Add
Rearrange
Substitute
} words   phrases   sentences   paragraphs   sections

Revising

Try your hand at the following exercises. You will probably discover that you already understand a great deal about rewriting—how to *delete* unnecessary material; *add* details and ideas that are needed; *rearrange* parts of the text to make it more coherent, effective, and logical; and *substitute* more effective words, phrases, sentences, and chunks for those that are less effective.

I. *Delete* unnecessary words from the following sentences, as in these examples:

a. The president who is the head man of our college will resign next year.
   The president of our college will resign next year.
b. We gave a donation of five dollars to the library.
   We gave five dollars to the library.
   We donated five dollars to the library.

Now do it yourself.

1. The boat which was just coming into the harbor listed heavily to the starboard.
2. The last person at the end of the line could not buy a ticket.
3. The news of Alvin's death made me sad and melancholy.
4. The cardiologist doctor who treats my uncle's heart condition told him to lose twenty-five pounds.
5. On a cloudy day with no sunshine, we began our hike up the John Muir Trail.

II. *Add* details to the following sentences. For example:

a. The student's hair hung over his collar.
   The student's greasy hair hung over his frayed collar.
b. The dog loped across the field.
   The dog, an Irish setter, loped easily across the field, stopping occasionally to sniff at a gopher hole, zigzagging his way toward the lake.

Now it's your turn.

1. The man entered the room.
2. The Sears Tower in Chicago is the world's tallest building.
3. Americans are becoming more and more football crazy.
4. My neighbor rebuilt a 1931 Packard.
5. Roses are red.

III. *Rearrange* the following sentences, but do not make them ungrammatical or change their basic meanings. Here are some examples:

a. My family drinks tea for breakfast every morning of the year.
   Every morning of the year, my family drinks tea for breakfast.
   For breakfast, my family drinks tea every morning of the year.
   For breakfast every morning of the year, my family drinks tea.
b. It is strange that bacteria cause disease.
   That bacteria cause disease is strange.
c. I want some chocolate ice cream.
   What I want is some chocolate ice cream.
   Some chocolate ice cream—that's what I want.

Now you try it.

1. The councilperson decided to run for mayor at the very last minute.
2. It is well known that cigarette smoking is unhealthy.
3. I like music.
4. In the afternoon, the Schultzes often take a walk.
5. An expert on nematodes, the professor was often called upon as a consultant by various groups.

IV. Make one or more *substitutions* in the following sentences, but do not change the basic meaning. For example:

a. The young dog barked with pain when I accidentally stepped on it.
   The puppy yelped with pain when I accidentally stepped on it.
b. On his wrist he wore a watch that shows the time by a series of numbers, not by hands that go around a dial.
   He wore a digital wristwatch.

Now you find substitutions.

1. The young cat made a noise when I petted her.
2. When Uncle Charlie kicks the bucket, I will inherit his stamp collection.
3. Matilda uses a little gismo with numbered keys and a lighted dial to figure her bills.
4. "I completely disagree," said Max angrily.
5. Knowing that the class would wait patiently, the professor dawdled.

Many writers do most of their rewriting at the same time they are writing, changing sentences and substituting words, crossing out some paragraphs and putting others in, making notes for rearranging paragraphs and sections of their manuscripts—and the result, of course, is that the first drafts are messy, with crossouts, interlinear insertions, and marginal notations. The first version of "Becoming a Reader," on pages 38–47, is an example of this messiness.

The second chapter of this book concerns both writing and rewriting, and you will also find helpful ideas for rewriting in chapter 11, "Paragraphs." In particular, chapter 12, "Rewriting Sentences," could well be valuable to you.

FINALLY

We can circle back and take another look at what it means to write.

You have a *subject*—something that interests you, that you want to "think about" in writing. And you have a *purpose:* to explain your subject to readers, to learn more about your subject, to figure out your own attitudes, to persuade your readers to take some action—your purpose can be as varied as is the whole range of human goals and motives. You convey your ideas and achieve your purposes through language *structures:* sentences, paragraphs, essays, reports, narratives. . . . But subject, purposes, and structures must be meaningful to their *audience*, the readers that you intend them for. Thus audience influences your writing at every turn. But so does *scene*. Suppose you are writing for a well-defined audience of ten people, fellow students at your college or university. On campus they are one audience, but change the scene, put the ten in a church or temple, and in a sense they become a different audience.

This book is largely about subjects and purposes, structures, audiences, and scenes.

Notes

[1] Paul A. Strassman, "Information Systems and Literacy," in *Literacy for Life,* ed. Richard W. Bailey and Robin Melanie Fosheim (New York: Modern Language Association, 1983), p. 116.

[2] Adapted from Roman Jakobson, "Linguistics and Poetics," in *Style in Language,* ed. Thomas A. Sebeok (Cambridge: MIT Press, 1960).

[3] Adapted from H. P. Grice, "Logic and Conversation," in *Syntax and Semantics, Vol. 3: Speech Acts,* ed. P. Cole and J. L. Morgan (New York: Seminar Press, 1975).

2
Writing and Rewriting: A Case Study

The following advice appears to be sensible: "First think about what you want to say—get your ideas clear and straight—and then choose the best words in which to express those ideas." What, then, do you make of the following quotation from *Writing and Difference,* by Jacques Derrida, who is one of the most important philosophers and language theorists of our time?

> It is because writing is *inaugural,* in the fresh sense of the word, that it is dangerous and anguishing. It does not know where it is going, no knowledge can keep it from the essential precipitation toward meaning that it constitutes and that is, primarily, its future. . . . Meaning is neither before nor after the act.

In other words, Derrida, in part at least, is saying something like this: "We don't know what we think until we have written."

On the other hand, in his *Autobiography*, Bertrand Russell, certainly one of the great minds of the twentieth century and one of our most esteemed writers, seems to contradict Derrida:

Very gradually I have discovered ways of writing with a minimum of worry and anxiety. When I was young each fresh piece of serious work used to seem to me for a time—perhaps a long time—to be beyond my powers. I would fret myself into a nervous state from fear that it was never going to come right. I would make one unsatisfying attempt after another, and in the end have to discard them all. At last I found that such fumbling attempts were a waste of time. It appeared that after first contemplating a book on some subject, I needed a period of subconscious incubation which could not be hurried and was if anything impeded by deliberate thinking. Sometimes I would find, after a time, that I had made a mistake, and that I could not write the book I had had in mind. But often I was more fortunate. Having, by a time of very intense concentration, planted the problem in my subconscious, it would germinate underground until, suddenly, the solution emerged with blinding clarity, so that it only remained to write down what had appeared as if in a revelation.

Writing as the process of thinking, of generating ideas, *or* writing as putting preformed thoughts into words—which view seems more nearly accurate?

Well, certainly most of us do not begin to write without some kind of notion about our subject and our purpose, as the following list of writings commonly produced by such professionals as lawyers and engineers would indicate: reports to clients, business letters, personal letters, interoffice memos, lists (such as agendas and schedules), notes, reminders, legal briefs (in the case of lawyers), proposals.

On the other hand, even the most cut-and-dried sorts of writing almost always bring about surprises for the writer. In the first place, we seldom know *exactly* what we want to convey, but have only a general idea of what we're getting at. We work out the details of our "message" as we go, and in that process we usually make discoveries: find connections that we had not realized existed, come up with data that we had forgotten we knew, discover flaws in our arguments and, sometimes, effective ways of overcoming those flaws.

Without doubt, writing is an instrument of thinking—and if you don't believe that, try to develop a complex line of thought without writing: no paragraphs, no sentences, no phrases, no marks on paper of any kind. You will find it very difficult to "think" without writing. On the other hand, writing is generative; from writing new ideas develop because language to a certain extent has its own momentum and takes its own directions.

Rather than speak about writing in the abstract, let's watch a text grow, from a purpose for writing through the germ of an idea to a focused topic and ultimately to a finished work. Though we could use anything—from a set of instructions to a philosophical argument—as our example, our case study will be an autobiographical account of how one person, this author, developed his interest in reading. You might say that the essay is part of a "literacy biography." The chapter will follow the development of this essay.

Of course, no one would claim that the methods and procedures I use for my essay will be productive for all writers, at all times, doing all sorts of writing, but there is a good deal to be learned from a step-by-step account of one composing process. As you read this chapter, be alert for techniques that you can adopt for your own writing.

Exercise: The Generative Nature of Language

An easy experiment will show you how language tends to generate its own meanings. Here are three columns of apparently unrelated words. At random, choose one word from each column, making a three-word group. Repeat the process until you have five groups.

Do novel meanings arise from any of these groups? Do these meanings give you any ideas for paragraphs or essays? (If so, write the paragraph or essay.)

mate	colt	utopia
break	subdue	hemp
knight	deadpan	lavish
authoritarian	egotist	iron
feudalism	zodiac	jackrabbit
originate	glamour	wacky
noodle	pinch	thought
view	question	xylophone
royal	yacht	munch
crass	unlikely	book
sunshine	holiday	kick
apple	easy	ignorance
felon	zeal	joyful
oblong	gala	walk
nasty	punctuate	thirst
value	quality	xenophobia

rich	yellow	maximum
capable	understand	brick
silly	humble	kite
available	ecstasy	illness

PURPOSE

Every act of writing begins with a purpose, which might be, for example,

to express oneself (as in a private diary)
to explain something to others (a process, an opinion, or a feeling)
to argue for a point of view (in a documented research paper, for example)
to persuade others to do something (as in a political brochure)
to create imaginative works (poems or stories)

The purpose of this chapter and the essay that I am about to write is, of course, *to explain something*.

Most of the writing that you do in college will have a double purpose. For example, an essay that you complete for a history class will explain the concepts and facts of history to the instructor, but it will also demonstrate that you do understand these materials. We can, then, add a further purpose for writing in college:

to demonstrate one's knowledge of facts and concepts and also to show that one can express ideas accurately and coherently in writing.

PREWRITING: THE GERM OF AN IDEA

Usually, purpose and subject matter are inseparable, as the following ridiculous statement indicates: "I want to explain something to someone. I wonder what I can choose to explain." And yet, in the present case, I had a purpose before I had a subject: I wanted to trace the growth of a text, but I didn't know what the text would be about, what its "topic" would be. However, I've found that my students enjoy writing about episodes in their own literacy biographies: one discovered the challenge and exhilaration of writing in a high school class taught by a gifted teacher, another developed a taste for science fiction because an aunt conveyed her enthusiasm for that genre, and yet another became interested in astronomy and thus read widely to learn about that subject.

I remember vividly the period in my life when I became a "chronic" reader: during my last three years of high school in a small Nevada town. As I look back on those three years, I realize how important they were to me, and I know that I would enjoy writing about my experiences. So I have a subject: the experience of reading (and, as a matter of fact, writing) during my last three years at White Pine County High School in Ely, Nevada.

What, then, has happened so far? I have found a subject that is meaningful to me: the development of my interest in reading. I feel that this subject will be interesting to my readers. I have narrowed that subject to a three-year period. I had thought about dealing with *both* reading *and* writing, but to discuss both topics would take more time than I want to spend on this particular writing task; furthermore, I want my essay to be relatively brief.

FINDING SUBJECT MATTER AND PLANNING FOR MY AUDIENCE

Of course, I am the world's foremost expert on my subject: the development of my interest in reading. No one knows more about *that* than I do! Yet I do not merely start to write. I do quite a bit of thinking and planning. I need to dredge ideas up from my memory and my subconscious, and I need to get some notion of how they might go together. Most of the time when I write, finding subject matter and planning the overall form of the text go on concurrently; I don't first gather a pile of ideas and then sort them out.

As I begin to work on this essay, I am keenly aware of my audience: college and university undergraduates, most of them in freshman writing courses. These readers have diverse backgrounds and interests; therefore, it would be unwise for me to write a technical paper, full of unfamiliar terms and details, as I would do if I were writing for scholars in my field. I continually ask myself whether this or that detail will interest my readers.

The first bit of writing that I did is what you see in Figure 1.

White Pine Co.

~~the town~~

~~school~~ Dunc

Dad

events

FIGURE 1

I knew that I wanted to set the scene: White Pine County, Nevada, an isolated mining district in the 1940s. Two people were extremely important to me during these years: Glen A. "Dunc" Duncan, a high school teacher, and my father. And it seemed to me that certain events in my life at that time were so important that I could focus on them to give an account of how my interests developed.

I could, then, have started to write, telling first about White Pine County, then about Dunc and my father, and finally about certain important events. However, I needed to do some more thinking and planning, so I did a bit of *brainstorming*.

With this technique, the writer simply starts recording anything that comes to mind about his or her subject, one word, idea, or image suggesting another. The secret to brainstorming is to turn off the censor; don't try to judge whether an idea is good or bad, for it is easy to discard useless items and, furthermore, sometimes an idea that at first seems useless or even ridiculous turns out to be useful.

As usual at this stage of my writing process, I began to develop a *cluster*. A very useful technique for generating and organizing ideas, clustering is actually a variation on brainstorming, and I find it extremely helpful in much of my writing. (In a moment, we will discuss clustering and its uses. For the present, the figures will allow you to follow what I'm doing.) Figure 2 is the first phase of my cluster.

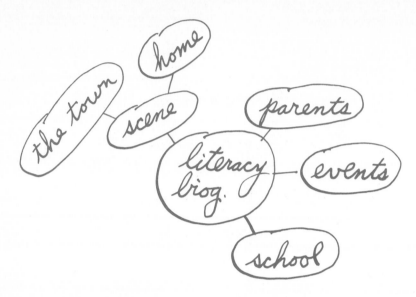

FIGURE 2

As this figure indicates, I had decided not to deal with the whole area in which I lived, but only with my hometown, McGill, and my home within that town. (The high school that I attended was in Ely, thirteen miles from McGill.) I had also decided to write about both of my parents, and Dunc as a single topic had expanded to "school." At this point, I might have begun to write a six-part essay that could be outlined as follows:

 I. Introduction
 II. Scene
     A. Home
     B. The town
III. Parents
     A. Mother
     B. Father
 IV. Events
  V. School
 VI. Conclusion

However, my ideas had not "cooked" long enough; I needed to think some more about details and connections. You can see the results of that "cooking" and thinking in Figure 3. I have added details about my home: the coldness of my bedroom during the winter, the electric blanket that saved me from frostbite, and the

FIGURE 3

cocker spaniel that shared the room with me; the coal stove in the kitchen. These details, I'm certain, will play a part in the text that I am getting ready to produce.

I have also added details about the town: the mill and smelter that dominated it, the dust and smoke that shrouded it, and the drabness that characterized it; I have decided to tell about "cultural" resources available to me: the radio programs that we could receive only at night, the small library, and the movie theater.

A section on my parents is no longer part of my planning, but I am sure that my mother and father will take part in the events that I intend to write about. Those events are three, and they will, I think, give a sense of what my reading experiences were like. (The essay itself will explain some of the items that I

FIGURE 4

have included in the cluster as reminders to myself: "Trelawny," "mint patties," and "green olives.")

But I have a final adjustment to make in my cluster. Initially I had thought of "events" as happenings in my home, but I realized that Dunc's sixth period English class was also an event, so I have added it to the "events" category. Because of Dunc I grew to love the poetry of William Wordsworth and William Blake. Figure 4, the "events" node of my cluster, shows the final planning before I started to write.

My cluster does not capture everything that will go into my essay. In fact, the process of composing the essay will generate ideas that I could not predict before I started to write. However, the planning and generating stage (often called "prewriting") has now ended, and I am ready to begin composing the essay on my IBM computer.

A WORD ABOUT CLUSTERING

As a method of generating ideas and beginning to plan the form of a piece of writing, clustering has many advantages over either the formal outline or random notes. The formal outline imposes a rigidity that oftentimes hinders the organic process of generating ideas and planning how to use them. With the cluster, you can add ideas at any point; formal outlines are never "open" enough to allow the writer to add here, there, and everywhere. In other words, the cluster can grow like a plant, but the formal outline is an inflexible scaffolding.

Unlike random notes, the cluster begins to bring order to a writer's random thoughts. If you will look back at Figure 3, you will discover that the cluster implies an essay with two major parts: "scene" and "events." "Events" has three parts: *Three Musketeers* at Christmas," "Mark Twain over the weekend," and "poetry." (In fact, I could easily use this cluster as the basis for a formal outline.)

The writer can add to the cluster or rearrange it as the text develops. The cluster serves both as a prompt for putting ideas into a text and as a schematic representation of the writer's plans for the text.

The cluster is open-ended and generative. On the basis of almost any of the items in Figure 3, I could develop another extensive cluster.

THE FIRST DRAFT

Note that in this draft crossouts are indicated by strike-throughs (~~crossouts~~); inserts are within brackets [insert] and in color.

I remember the first time my sons saw my hometown. In the old blue Plymouth, we approached from the west, ~~rolling, chugging,~~ lurching down Highway 40, through the mirage puddles on the hot asphalt, watching the dust devils dance across the sagebrush flats. [The smell of sagebrush was heavy in the air blowing into the car through the open windows—for we didn't have air-conditioning.] We could see the ~~cloud of~~ yellow, sulfurous cloud from the smelter, and the giant smokestacks themselves, from perhaps fifty or sixty miles away. A bit nearer, and we could smell the acrid, choking cloud that belched forth from the smokestacks, and we could see the dust beginning to blow on the flat below town as the afternoon wind picked up.

McGill has no outskirts, no suburbs, just sagebrush flats and then town, the sagebrush growing up to the wire fences of the first row of houses. One moment you're in the Great Basin desert, among jackrabbits and rattlesnakes, and the next you're in such civilization as McGill, Nevada, affords.

We drove down Main Street. The post office, a gray sandstone pile, had not changed. Goodman-Tidball, General Mercantile and Service Station, was closed and boarded up, as was the Rexall drugstore. Cononelos Market was still open, in the two-story, dirty-yellow frame building that had once housed, on the first floor, the J. C. Penney store and, on the second, the Winterowd family. At the south end of Main Street, a Dairy Queen had opened.

And the McGill Club was still in operation. My father had dealt roulette in the club during the Second World War, when that institution had served as social center for the community—the kids not allowed behind the partition that separated a soda fountain and ice-cream parlor from the roulette and blackjack tables, the bar, the brass spittoons, the mounted deer heads on three walls, all of this amounting to the "real" McGill Club, the heart and soul of the place.

The frame houses of the town site were as drab as I had remembered, painted shades of brownish yellow, ~~light~~ dirty gray, and stained white. The lawns were still shabby, and the wire fences sagged as badly as they had when I was a boy.

An interesting thing has happened. Searching for a beginning that would interest my readers and get me into my subject, I decided to give an account of the first time my two sons visited my hometown. However, I have become so interested in *that* subject that I have lost sight of my goal. I have begun an essay other than the one I intended to write. Therefore, I back up and start again. As you can see, revising may begin early in the writing process.

I remember the yellow, sulfurous smoke that poured from the stacks of the smelter; the dust cloud that ~~enveloped~~ smothered the town every summer afternoon; the drab houses, painted dirty yellow, gray, and white; Main Street, with its confectionery, ~~gambling hall and saloon,~~ Rexall drugstore, general store, and post office. I can still see the miles of ~~sagebrush flat~~ desert stretching beyond town and smell the almost chemical odor of sagebrush.

[And the McGill Club—my father had dealt roulette there during the Second World War, when that institution had served as social center for the community, the kids not allowed behind the partition that separated a soda fountain and ice-cream parlor from the roulette and blackjack tables, the bar, the brass spittoons, the mounted deer heads on three walls, all of this amounting to the "real" McGill Club, the heart and soul of the place.]

Notice that I have included the passage (slightly revised) about the McGill Club from my original beginning. It seems to me that the club symbolizes the cultural level of the McGill that I knew, and I was unwilling to lose this bit of local color. Particularly if you compose on a computer, it is easy to rearrange, insert, and delete material.

During my high school years, my home was in McGill, Nevada, a town owned by Kennecott Copper Corporation and the site of a mill and smelter to derive copper from the ore mined in Ruth, some twenty miles south of McGill. Between McGill and Ruth was Ely, a town of perhaps five thousand, the seat of White Pine County. I attended high school in Ely.

The town I grew up in was not, then, one of the world's great centers of culture.

The above sentence was unplanned—came as a happy gift from . . . somewhere. However, it is an excellent way to begin a discussion of the "cultural" resources available to me in McGill.

For some reason (my father talked about the lowering of the ionosphere), ~~we were able to~~ we could get radio reception only at night. As a result, I missed all of the legendary radio serials that played on weekdays after school was out: "Jack Armstrong, All-American Boy," "Renfrew of the Royal Mounted," ~~and~~ "Little Orphan ~~Annie.~~" Annie," and others. However, after sundown, the radio became ~~the McGill subst~~ for the residents of McGill during the 1940s what television is for the American family today: a source for news and entertainment. My buddies and I listened without fail to "I Love a Mystery," "The FBI in Peace and War," "The Shadow," ["**The Sixty-four Dollar Question**,"] and "Your Hit Parade." We heard Edward R. Murrow['**s wartime**] broadcast   from London and followed the commentary of Raymond Gram Swing and Gabriel Heatter.

~~My point is that~~
~~We weren't so different, then, from the modern~~
~~The radio generation wasn't so different from the television generation.~~ We did a lot of tramping around the sagebrush flats, hunting rabbits, ~~and in the fall~~ with either our single-shot .22s or our bows and arrows; we sat in the Candy Shoppe, sipping our Cokes and feeling our teenage juices either seep or rush through our systems. Some Friday nights one of us was lucky enough to get the family automobile, and we drove to a dance in the high school gymnasium in Ely. ~~(The 1941 Plymouth that Don Johnson's father caressed and pampered was so elegant that I have never lost my lust for Chrysler products   Because of the 1941 Plymouth that Don Johnson's father caressed and pampered, I still prefer Chrysler products~~ (The classiest auto we had access to was a white 1941 Plymouth, caressed and pampered by Don Johnson's father. I'm still partial to Chrysler products.)

Again, I'm straying. Reliving my past is so intriguing that I begin to write almost by free association. Don Johnson's Plymouth suggests "Dutch" Holland's old Chevy, which leads me to think of Mr. Armstrong's Packard Clipper, the ultimate White Pine County car. I'll let the parenthesis remain, but will reread what I've written so far and then get back on track. I will move on to the second cultural resource in McGill, the library. Writers need to make sure they do not stray from the purpose they have chosen for themselves.

The McGill Public Library was a single room in the Club House, a residence for unmarried male employees of Kennecott Copper—a hulking, three-story, red brick building. How many volumes on those few shelves? I doubt that the total collection was more than, say, ~~five~~ [three] thousand books. I vividly remember the librarian, but can't recall her name. She was not ~~stout~~ [fat], but portly, in a dignified, patrician sort of way. She wore her salt-

and-pepper hair in a bun, and she dressed more primly than any-one else in town—navy-blue tailored suits, white frilly blouses, Red Cross shoes. She should, by all rights, have been a maiden lady, but she was married, to a Kennecott foreman, I think.

The library, open for a couple of hours each weekday eve-ning, did not offer "God's plenty" for a teenager. I vividly re-member checking out *The Magic Mountain*, intrigued by the title. Of course, this massive philosophical novel was light-years beyond my reach. The librarian had told me as much when I checked the book out, but I would not listen to her. Defeated, I returned *The Magic Mountain* to the library after a couple of frustrated attempts to get myself interested in the book, and the librarian, with great generosity, guided me to *Tales of the South Pacific*, then just out and, I suppose, one of the very few new books purchased by the library. Whereas Thomas Mann had baffled me, I found the Michener tales enchanting, far more satisfying than the movie [musical based on them].

I'm now having chronology problems. In this essay, I wanted to show that my serious, "chronic" reading actually began after cer-tain "events." However, the inventory of cultural resources in-cludes the library, and it is inevitable that I tell about my experiences with the library, which actually came after the "events." In other words, I have a structural problem here. I will solve it by giving the reader a straightforward explanation. Readers ex-pect that they will be able to follow the sequence of ideas in a text, and it is the writer's job to keep the readers oriented.

But I am getting ahead of myself. My serious, "chronic" reading began after a series of events that ~~are the real focus of this essay~~ I will relate in due time.

The McGill Theatre—~~the last picture show.~~ ["The Last Pic-ture Show."] The feature started at 7:30 P.M., but the doors opened at 7:00. Christine Constantine, ~~sold the tickets,~~ a stunningly beau-tiful Greek girl, sold the tickets. (Her father had given me a taste of his "peach" wine. It turned out to be retsina, or "pitch" wine.) ~~Yes, she—and her two sisters—made my teenage juices flow.~~

By the time Christine started selling tickets, the first batch of Jolly Time had been popped, and its smell was irresistible. ~~Connie~~ In the lobby, blonde, rosy, well-fed Connie made and vended the popcorn, tinged with the yellow of imitation butter and salted to just the right tang; ~~in the lobby~~ and ~~none~~ no other has ever equaled its crispness, its wholesome aroma. ~~the imitation butter that tinged it with yellow, the salt that gave it just the right tang.~~

At Eastertide, Jim, the irascible old projectionist, always played "White Christmas" as prelude music for the half hour from the opening of the doors until the short subjects began; and at Christmas he played, yes, of course, "Easter Parade." At two or three minutes before 7:30, "The Star-Spangled Banner" rang through the auditorium, and we all stood, hands over our hearts.

~~And that pretty much outlines the cultural resources in McGill: radio at night, the library, and the motion picture theater.~~

The movie that I remember most vividly from this, the archetypical small-town motion picture theater, ~~was~~ is "I Walked with a Zombie."

The section on cultural resources is complete. When I wrote the one-sentence paragraph above, I knew that I was ready to move on—to my home. Notice that I deleted a summary paragraph. It seems to me that the reader does not need to be told that I have now finished my catalog of cultural resources. While the writer is obliged to keep readers oriented, he or she must not insult them by stating the obvious.

There were two scenes for the events that turned me into a compulsive reader: my home and the sixth-period English class of Mr. Glen A. Duncan, "Dunc," as everyone called him.

A couple of things have just happened. In the first place, I have reorganized my essay, changing the structure that I had worked out in the clusters. If you will look back at Figure 3, you will discover that I intended, under "scene," to deal with "home" and "school." Another section of the essay, "events," would tell what happened in these scenes. The first sentence of this new paragraph leads me to realize that I am writing a "drama" and must place my "characters" in the scenes and have them play their "parts" in the "plot." In other words, I am, in effect, eliminating the category "scene," consolidating "scene" material with "events." I also had to check back to determine whether or not I had yet introduced my readers to Dunc.

We lived, during those years, above the J. C. Penney store on Main Street, across from the McGill Club and, ~~next to~~ south of us, Assuras Meat Market, the Oddfellows Hall to the north. We didn't live in a penthouse on Park Avenue, but we resided comfortably in a four-room apartment, with bath, above the J. C. Penney store on Main Street, in the very middle of town, the center of action, if you will.

The comparison between our grubby apartment above the J. C. Penney store and a penthouse on Park Avenue gives the essay a wry tone that I like. I'm saying that we were in the center of the culture of McGill, Nevada. The idea for the comparison simply popped into my mind, and I wrote it down. In fact, the idea of both McGill and New York City as cultural centers is wonderfully ironic. (Yet McGill was *my* cultural center.)

> ~~A coal stove in the kitchen, a coal heater in the living room~~
> My bedroom[, a jerry-built attachment to the main structure,] was beyond the reach of the two sources of heat: a coal range in the kitchen and a coal heating stove in the large room that doubled as our parlor (the north half) and my parents' bedroom (the south half). I shared my bedroom with a cocker spaniel and avoided frostbite by huddling under an electric blanket, certainly one of the first ever manufactured. (The cord to the blanket ran up toward the ceiling, where it joined with a socket dangling by [black] electric ~~cords~~ [wires]. I ~~You~~ turned the socket on first and then set the blanket on "high" and shivered for the first half hour after going to bed.)
> ~~It was Christmas 1943. I was nearly fourteen years old.~~
> In this strange apartment above the J. C. Penney store, in a [Nevada] smelter and mill town, ~~there took place events that would forever change~~ certain events turned me into a compulsive reader.

The above short paragraph is a transition, introducing the section of my essay that will deal with reading experiences in my home.

> It was Christmas 1943. ~~The Second World War was raging in the Pacific, Africa, and Europe.~~ Almost every day there was news of someone from White Pine County dying on ~~alien soil~~ [a Pacific island or in Africa]. Mr. Maw, who ran a gas station in Ely, was never right after he received word of his son's death ~~threatening~~ [and threatened] to incinerate any Japanese who came to his place ~~station.~~ "Where's Davie?" he would say to his old dog, and the dog would search frantically about the premises of the service station [looking for the ~~son~~ [boy] who would never return].
> That Christmas—a somber time in American history—my parents gave me two books: *The Three Musketeers*, by Alexander Dumas, and *Trelawny*, by Margaret Armstrong. The night of the 26th of December Mother and Father were away, and I climbed into their bed, in the well-heated bedroom-living room, and began to read *The Three Musketeers*, the marvelous swashbuckling of Por-

thos, Athos, Aramis, and their noble friend D'Artagnan. ~~Beside me was a box of chocolate mint patties~~ [Beside me was a box of chocolate mint patties left] ~~Left~~ over from Christmas, ~~was a~~ and as I read I sucked on these delicacies.

This was the first time that I had been completely immersed in a book, so deeply taken that time was not a dimension of the experience: just the soft bed in the warm room, with the drama of the tale unfolding and the mint patties melting in my mouth, on a bitterly cold winter night in Nevada.

I still have the book. *The Three Musketeers.* Great Illustrated Classics. Published in the United States of America, 1941, by Dodd, Mead & Company, Inc. A handsome gray book, with dark blue design and gold lettering. [The price, in pencil, is still on the flyleaf: $2.50.]

> Without paying any attention to the sword, Milady endeavoured to clamber onto the bed to strike him, and she did not stop until she felt the sharp point at her throat. She then tried to seize the weapon in her hands, but D'Artagnan eluded her grasp; and presenting the point sometimes to her eyes, sometimes to her bosom, slipped out of the bed, endeavouring to retreat by the door leading into Kitty's room.

The Three Musketeers ~~and their friend D'Artagnan (and the alluring Milady) were first bosom friends in reading~~ was, then, the first book that had completely captured me, that had given me the almost mystic experience of total immersion, and from that time on, I lived an extremely "bookish" life. Sitting in our kitchen, next to the coal stove (to provide warmth in the late night hours), I read Maugham's *Of Human Bondage;* the Horatio Hornblower sea tales; *Tap Roots,* [a Civil War epic after the manner of *Gone with the Wind,*] by (as I recall) James Street; *David Copperfield, Oliver Twist* and *Great Expectations;* a whole string of cowboy stories, which have no individuality for me now.

During that Christmas season of 1943, I also read the other gift book, *Trelawny,* by Margaret Armstrong: bound in crimson cloth with gold lettering, published by the Macmillan Company in 1940 [and sold for $3.50]. "There are no imaginary characters, events, or conversations in this book. It is fact, not fiction. The narrative is based on Trelawny's writings, corrected and amplified from reliable sources."

Trelawny, friend of Byron and Shelley, was himself as romantic and swashbuckling as D'Artagnan.

> Now and then a man is born with a surname that fits him so well it might have been chosen for him by a poet or a painter. Edward

Trelawny was one of those fortunate persons. There is a wild flavor in *Trelawny* that would lend a touch of romance to the most commonplace family; and that the Trelawnys never were. They were courageous, adventurous, full of vitality, eccentric, unreliable, prone to extremes; never, to judge from the family records, commonplace.

As I look back, I think that *The Three Musketeers* and *Trelawny* were just the right books for the right person at the right time. They were guaranteed to provide escape from the **[squalid]** horrid camp in which I lived. In any case, they hooked me. *Trelawny*[,] was the first biography I had ever read, and created for me a lifelong interest in that genre.

Another decision. My essay is extending far beyond the limits that I had envisioned for it. Thus, I will limit my subject to reading at home and will deal with three "events": my Christmas with *The Three Musketeers* and *Trelawny*, a weekend with my father and Mark Twain, and the poetry that the family read aloud. This decision necessitates overhauling the beginning of the essay. You will see the results of this work in the final draft of the essay, which I will include in the chapter.

The second **[noteworthy]** event in the development of my passion for reading came when my mother left town for a weekend, to attend a convention of the Congress of Industrial Organizations, the CIO, of which she was an officer. Father and I were left to our own resources, which turned out to be unconventionally delightful and intensely literary.

Father and I went to the Cononelos market and bought two huge jars of green olives, a stack of salami, a loaf of bread, some cheese, undoubtedly potato chips, and other ready edibles. Father pulled two easy Father arranged a small table between two easy chairs, with a floor lamp just behind the table. On the table, he put a bowl of green olives, potato chips, salami, bread, mustard, and, I'm sure, raw onion. Then from somewhere he produced *The Favorite Works of Mark Twain*, DeLuxe Edition, Garden City Publishing Co., Inc. 1939–1,178 pages in all.

Dad and I would have a weekend of reading.

I don't remember what Dad read on that marvelous weekend, but I had four complete books (in one volume) to choose from: *Life on the Mississippi, The Adventures of Tom Sawyer, The Adventures of Huckleberry Finn,* and *A Connecticut Yankee in King Arthur's Court,* not to mention sixteen other shorter works: excerpts stories and selections from novels stories, excerpts from books, and sketches. At Dad's suggestion, I started with *Tom Sawyer* and then went on to *A Connecticut Yankee*, which Dad particularly liked.

The result of this experience was inevitable. I became an ardent Twain-ite, and I still am one. (In my opinion, *Life on the Mississippi* and the *Autobiography* are his masterpieces.)

My third experience with reading at home—in the apartment above the J. C. Penney store—was not so much one event as an ongoing series of experiences. My father had an eclectic love for poetry, and we read a good deal of verse, particularly on Sunday mornings before the gigantic brunch that my mother always prepared ([grapefruit,] fresh side pork or pork loin, baking powder biscuits, gravy, eggs, pastries, coffee).

Dad, a skeptic, took great glee in *The First Mortgage*, a doggerel verse telling of the Bible story, by a poet named Cook:

> Sometime, and somewhere out in space,
> God felt it was the proper place
> To make a world, as he did claim,
> To bring some honor to his name.

And we read, I think, every word written by Robert Service:

> Men of the High North, the wild sky is blazing,
>   Islands of opal float on silver seas;
> Swift splendors kindle, barbaric, amazing;
>   Pale ports of amber, golden argosies.
> Ringed all around us the proud peaks are glowing;
>   Fierce chiefs in council, their wigwam the sky;
> Far, far below us the big Yukon flowing,
>   Like threaded quicksilver, gleams to the eye.
> —"Men of the High North"

Dad loved to declaim verse from *The Pious Friends and Drunken Companions* (The Macaulay Company, 1936):

> As I walked out in the streets of Laredo,
> As I walked in Laredo one day,
> I spied a poor cowboy wrapped up in white linen,
> Wrapped up in white linen and cold as the clay.

Dad enjoyed both Dorothy Parker (*Enough Rope*) and Shelley. But I don't remember ever hearing him read the American classics: Longfellow, Emerson, Whittier, Dickinson. His taste, with few exceptions, was definitely for the comic and ribald, [though I think probably Dad quoted from his elegantly bound copy of the *Rubaiyat of Omar Khayyam* (translated, of course, by Edward FitzGerald) more often than from any other poet or book. His favorite stanza:

> Some for the Glories of This World; and some
> Sigh for the Prophet's Paradise to come;
>   Ah, take the Cash, and let the Credit go,
> Nor heed the rumble of the distant Drum!]

Though purists might deplore my father's taste for florid or ribald verse, nonetheless poetry became a part of my experience; from my early teens onward, I did not view it as something strange, exotic, with hidden meanings, accessible only to the few. No, poetry (whether written by T. S. Eliot or Robert Service) was to be enjoyed. ~~and, as a matter of fact, in those long gone years, I began to write poetry~~

~~If there~~

What lesson is to be learned from this account of ~~how one young person~~ reading in one home? As I look back on my experiences, I realize that, above all, reading was woven into the fabric of our lives; books were the center of both special occasions and our quotidian existence. They were very much like food: every meal was not an elaborate Sunday brunch, nor was every experience of reading a major occasion. Nonetheless, as we ate three meals a day, so we read books (and magazines, for there was no proper daily newspaper) every day. ~~If, when I was in my early teens, someone had~~

~~I look now at the stack of books that have been part of my life since the~~

The other day my grandson, barely two years old and yet already bookish, was foraging in my library. He pulled Robert Service's *Ballads of a Cheechako* off the shelf and presented it to me to "read" to him. There were no pictures, so he lost interest immediately. But, as I held him close, I said, "You're just a bit too young for that now, Chris, but someday . . . ." And I'm sure that someday Chris and I will read together the books that my father shared with me.

The conclusion—which I must admit I like—came to me, in the form of my grandson, who did exactly what I have said in the above paragraph. And someday, I'm sure, I will share with him the books that my father brought me to.

For Discussion I: Techniques for Writing

What did you learn about the composing process from the "blow-by-blow" account of how my essay on becoming a reader was composed? In what ways will this knowledge be useful to you in your own writing?

A quotation from the writings of the philosopher Jacques Derrida at the beginning of this chapter indicated that writing finds its own way, almost as if the developing ideas control the writer rather than vice versa. On the other hand, Bertrand Russell said that by the time he started to write his works, he had planned them so thoroughly that he knew exactly how they would turn out. How do these statements square with what you have learned from the first draft of my essay?

For Discussion II: The Final Draft

As you read the final draft of "Becoming a Reader," think about answers to the following questions:

1. What changes did I make in the text? Why do you think I made those changes?
2. What changes *should I have made*, but didn't? In other words, what suggestions would you advance for improving the text in yet another revision?

THE FINAL DRAFT

Becoming a Reader

I remember the yellow, sulfurous smoke that poured from the stacks of the smelter; the dust cloud that smothered the town every summer afternoon; the drab houses, painted dirty yellow, gray, and white; and Main Street, with its confectionery, Rexall drugstore, general store, and post office. I can still see the miles of desert stretching beyond town and smell the almost chemical odor of sagebrush.

And the McGill Club—my father had dealt roulette there during the Second World War, when that institution had served as social center for the community, the kids not allowed behind the partition that separated a soda fountain and ice-cream parlor from the roulette and blackjack tables, the bar, the brass spittoons, the mounted deer heads on three walls, all of this amounting to the "real" McGill Club, the heart and soul of the place.

During the 1940s, my home was in McGill, Nevada, a town owned by Kennecott Copper Corporation and the site of a mill and smelter to derive copper from the ore mined in Ruth, some twenty miles south of McGill. Between McGill and Ruth was Ely, a town of perhaps five thousand, the seat of White Pine County. I attended high school in Ely.

The town I grew up in was not, then, one of the world's great centers of culture. We had radio (but only after sundown), a motion picture theater, and a small library—and that was the sum total of our cultural resources.

For some reason (my father talked about the lowering of the ionosphere), we could get radio reception only at night. As a result, I missed all of the legendary radio serials that played on weekday afternoons: "Jack Armstrong, All-American Boy," "Renfrew of the Royal Mounted," "Little Orphan Annie," and others. However, after sundown, the radio became for the residents of McGill what television is for the American family today: a source for news and entertainment. My buddies and I listened without fail to "I Love a Mystery," "The FBI in Peace and War," "The Shadow," "The Sixty-four Dollar Question," and "Your Hit Parade." We heard Edward R. Murrow's wartime broadcasts from London and followed the commentary of Raymond Gram Swing and Gabriel Heatter.

We did a lot of tramping around the sagebrush flats, hunting rabbits, with either our single-shot .22s or our bows and arrows; we sat in the Candy Shoppe, sipping our Cokes and feeling our teenage juices either seep or rush through our systems. Some Friday nights one of us was lucky enough to get the family automobile, and we drove to a dance in the high school gymnasium in Ely. (The classiest auto we had access to was a white 1941 Plymouth, caressed and pampered by Don Johnson's father. I'm still partial to Chrysler products.)

The McGill Public Library was a single room in the Club House, a residence for unmarried male employees of Kennecott Copper—a hulking, three-story, red brick building. How many volumes on those few shelves? I doubt that the total collection was more than, say, three thousand books. I vividly remember the librarian, but can't recall her name. She was not fat, but portly, in a dignified, patrician sort of way. She wore her salt-and-pepper hair in a bun, and she dressed more primly than anyone else in town—navy-blue tailored suits, white frilly blouses, Red Cross shoes. She should, by all rights, have been a maiden lady, but she was married, to a Kennecott foreman, I think.

The library, open for a couple of hours each weekday evening, did not offer "God's plenty" for a teenager. I vividly remember checking out *The Magic Mountain*, intrigued by the title. Of course, this massive philosophical novel was light-years beyond my reach. The librarian had told me as much when I checked the book out, but I would not listen to her. Defeated, I returned *The Magic Mountain* to the library after a couple of frustrated attempts to get myself interested in the book, and the librarian, with great generosity, guided me to *Tales of the South Pacific*, then just out and, I suppose, one of the very few new books purchased by the library. Whereas Thomas Mann had baffled me, I found the Michener tales enchanting, far more satisfying than the movie musical based on them.

But I am getting ahead of myself. My serious, "chronic" reading began after a series of events that I will relate in due time.

The McGill Theatre—"The Last Picture Show." The feature started at 7:30 P.M., but the doors opened at 7:00. Christine Constantine, a stunningly beautiful Greek girl, sold the tickets. (Her father had given me a taste of his "peach" wine. It turned out to be retsina, or "pitch" wine.) By the time Christine started selling tickets, the first batch of Jolly Time had been popped, and its smell was irresistible. In the lobby, blonde, rosy, well-fed Connie made and vended the popcorn, tinged with the yellow of imitation butter and salted to just the right tang; and no other has ever equaled its crispness and its wholesome aroma. At Eastertide, Jim, the irascible old projectionist, always played "White Christmas" as prelude music for the half hour from the opening of the doors until the short subjects began; and at Christmas he played, yes, of course, "Easter Parade." At two or three minutes before 7:30, "The Star-Spangled Banner" rang through the auditorium, and we all stood, hands over our hearts.

The movie that I remember most vividly from this, the archetypical small-town motion picture theater, is "I Walked with a Zombie."

So much, then, for "culture" in McGill, Nevada. Yet I did become an omnivorous reader—largely because my father shared his passion for books with me.

We lived, during those years, above the J. C. Penney store on Main Street, across from the McGill Club, the saloon and gambling hall where my father was a croupier. Next door to us, on the south, was Assuras Meat Market, and the Oddfellows Hall was on the north. We didn't live in a penthouse on Park Avenue, but we resided comfortably in a four-room apartment, with bath, above the J. C. Penney store, in the very middle of town, the center of action, if you will.

My bedroom, a jerry-built attachment to the main structure, was beyond the reach of the two sources of heat: a coal range in the kitchen and a coal heating stove in the large room that doubled as our parlor (the north half) and my parents' bedroom (the south half). I shared my bedroom with a cocker spaniel and avoided frostbite by huddling under an electric blanket, certainly one of the first ever manufactured. (The cord to the blanket ran up toward the ceiling, where it joined with a socket dangling by black electric wires. I turned the socket on first and then set the blanket on "high" and shivered for the first half hour after going to bed.)

It was Christmas 1943. Almost every day there was news of someone from White Pine County dying on a Pacific island or in Africa. Mr. Maw, who ran a gas station in Ely, was never right after he received word of his son's death and threatened to incinerate any Japanese who came to the station. "Where's Davie?" he would say to his old dog, and the dog would search frantically about the premises of the service station looking for the boy who would never return.

That Christmas—a somber time in American history—my parents gave me *The Three Musketeers*, by Alexander Dumas, and *Trelawny*, by Margaret Armstrong, two books that my father had enjoyed. The night of the 26th of December Mother and Father were away, and I climbed into their bed, in the well-heated bedroom-living room, and began to read *The Three Musketeers*: the marvelous swashbuckling of Porthos, Athos, Aramis, and their noble friend D'Artagnan. Beside me was a box of chocolate mint patties left over from Christmas, and as I read I sucked on these delicacies.

This was the first time that I had been completely immersed in a book, so deeply taken that time was not a dimension of the experience: just the soft bed in the warm room, with the drama of the tale unfolding and the mint patties melting in my mouth, on a bitterly cold winter night in Nevada.

I still have the book. *The Three Musketeers*. Great Illustrated Classics. Published in the United States of America, 1941, by Dodd, Mead & Company, Inc. A handsome gray book, with dark blue design and gold lettering. The price, in pencil, is still on the flyleaf: $2.50.

> Without paying any attention to the sword, Milady endeavoured to clamber onto the bed to strike him, and she did not stop until she felt the sharp point at her throat. She then tried to seize the weapon in her hands, but D'Artagnan eluded her grasp; and presenting the point sometimes to her eyes, sometimes to her bosom, slipped out of the bed, endeavouring to retreat by the door leading into Kitty's room.

The Three Musketeers was, then, the first book that had completely captured me, that had given me the almost mystic experience of total immersion, and from that time on, I lived an extremely "bookish" life. Sitting in our kitchen, next to the coal stove (to provide warmth in the late night hours), I read Maugham's *Of Human Bondage*; the Horatio Hornblower sea tales; *Tap Roots*, a Civil War epic after the manner of *Gone with the Wind*, by (as I recall) James Street; *David Copperfield*, *Oliver Twist*, and *Great Expectations*; a whole string of cowboy stories, which have no individuality for me now.

During that Christmas season of 1943, I also read the other gift book, *Trelawny*, by Margaret Armstrong: bound in crimson cloth with gold lettering, published by the Macmillan Company in 1940, and priced at $3.50. "There are no imaginary characters, events, or conversations in this book. It is fact, not fiction. The narrative is based on Trelawny's writings, corrected and amplified from reliable sources."

Trelawny, friend of Byron and Shelley, was himself as romantic and swashbuckling as D'Artagnan.

> Now and then a man is born with a surname that fits him so well it might have been chosen for him by a poet or a painter. Edward Trelawny was one of those fortunate persons. There is a wild flavor in *Trelawny* that would lend a touch of romance to the most commonplace family; and that the Trelawnys never were. They were courageous, adventurous, full of vitality, eccentric, unreliable, prone to extremes; never, to judge from the family records, commonplace.

As I look back, I think that *The Three Musketeers* and *Trelawny* were just the right books for the right person at the right time. They were guaranteed to provide escape from the squalid camp in which I lived. In any case, they hooked me. *Trelawny*, the first biography I had ever read, created for me a lifelong interest in that genre.

The second noteworthy event in the development of my passion for reading came when my mother left town for a weekend, to attend a convention of the Congress of Industrial Organizations, the CIO, of which she was an officer. Father and I were left to our own resources, which turned out to be unconventionally delightful and intensely literary.

Dad and I went to the Cononelos market and bought two huge jars of green olives, a stack of salami, a loaf of bread, some cheese, undoubtedly potato chips, and other ready edibles. Dad arranged a small table between two easy chairs, with a floor lamp just behind the table. On the table, he put a bowl of green olives, potato chips, salami, bread, mustard, and, I'm sure, raw onion. Then from somewhere he produced *The Favorite Works of Mark Twain*, DeLuxe Edition, Garden City Publishing Co., Inc., 1939–1,178 pages in all.

Dad and I would have a weekend of reading.

I don't remember what Dad read on that marvelous weekend, but I had four complete books (in one volume) to choose from: *Life on the Mississippi, The Adventures of Tom Sawyer, The Adventures of Huckleberry Finn,* and *A Connecticut Yankee in King Arthur's Court,* not to mention sixteen other shorter works: stories, excerpts from books, and sketches. At Dad's suggestion, I started with *Tom Sawyer* and then went on to *A Connecticut Yankee,* which Dad particularly liked.

The result of this experience was inevitable. I became an ardent Twain-ite, and I still am one. (In my opinion, *Life on the Mississippi* and the *Autobiography* are his masterpieces.)

My third experience with reading at home—in the apartment above the J. C. Penney store—was not so much one event as an ongoing series of experiences. My father had an eclectic love for poetry, and we read a good deal of verse, particularly on Sunday mornings before the gigantic brunch that my mother always prepared (grapefruit, fresh side pork or pork loin, baking powder biscuits, gravy, eggs, pastries, coffee).

Dad, a skeptic, took great glee in *The First Mortgage,* a doggerel verse telling of the Bible story, by a poet named Cook:

> Sometime, and somewhere out in space,
> God felt it was the proper place
> To make a world, as he did claim,
> To bring some honor to his name.

And we read, I think, every word written by Robert Service:

> Men of the High North, the wild sky is blazing,
>   Islands of opal float on silver seas;
> Swift splendors kindle, barbaric, amazing;
>   Pale ports of amber, golden argosies.
> Ringed all around us the proud peaks are glowing;
>   Fierce chiefs in council, their wigwam the sky;
> Far, far below us the big Yukon flowing,
>   Like threaded quicksilver, gleams to the eye.
>   —"Men of the High North"

Dad loved to declaim verse from *The Pious Friends and Drunken Companions* (The Macaulay Company, 1936):

> As I walked out in the streets of Laredo,
> As I walked in Laredo one day,
> I spied a poor cowboy wrapped up in white linen,
> Wrapped up in white linen and cold as the clay.

Dad enjoyed both Dorothy Parker (*Enough Rope*) and Shelley. But I don't remember ever hearing him read the American classics: Longfellow, Emerson, Whittier, Dickinson. His taste, with few exceptions, was definitely for the comic and ribald, though I think probably Dad quoted from his elegantly bound copy of the *Rubaiyat of Omar Khayyam* (translated, of course, by Edward FitzGerald) more often than from any other poet or book. His favorite stanza:

> Some for the Glories of This World; and some
> Sigh for the Prophet's Paradise to come;
>   Ah, take the Cash, and let the Credit go,
> Nor heed the rumble of the distant Drum!

Though purists might deplore my father's taste for florid or ribald verse, nonetheless poetry became a part of my experience; from my early teens onward, I did not view it as something strange, exotic, with hidden meanings, accessible only to the few. No, poetry (whether written by T. S. Eliot or Robert Service) was to be enjoyed.

What lesson is to be learned from this account of reading in one home? As I look back on my experiences, I realize that, above all, reading was woven into the fabric of our lives; books were the center of both special occasions and our quotidian existence. They were very much like food: every meal was not an elaborate Sunday brunch, nor was every experience of reading a major occasion. Nonetheless, as we ate three meals a day, so we read books (and magazines, for there was no proper daily newspaper) every day.

The other day my grandson, barely two years old and yet already bookish, was foraging in my library. He pulled Robert Service's *Ballads of a Cheechako* off the shelf and presented it to me to "read" to him. There were no pictures, so he lost interest immediately. But, as I held him close, I said, "You're just a bit too young for that now, Chris, but someday . . . ." And I'm sure that someday Chris and I will read together the books that my father shared with me.

THE COMPOSING PROCESS IN SUMMARY

Composing involves four general kinds of activities: prewriting, writing, rewriting, and proofreading. *Prewriting* includes finding subject matter (generating ideas) and planning; in *writing*, one puts ideas into the formal structures of language (the sentences and paragraphs). *Rewriting* is the process of changing text: adding, deleting, rearranging, and substituting. Finally, *proofreading* eliminates "mechanical" errors such as misspellings, lack of verb agreement, mispunctuation, and so on.

As you have seen in this chapter, these operations are not separate and distinct phases in composing, but go on almost simultaneously. I spent considerable time planning and generating ideas before I started to write, but as I was writing, I made changes in my plans and continually generated new ideas. Obviously much of my rewriting took place while I was completing the first draft, and whenever I caught a proofreading error, I corrected it.

Prewriting: Discovering and Developing Ideas

The development of the clusters is the best example of my *prewriting*. But there is nothing sacred about any method of generating ideas and organizing them. Random scratch notes, notes on cards or slips of paper that can be sorted according to topic, outlines, tape recordings of thoughts, marginal notes in books—all of these and many more are commonly used prewriting techniques.

In some cases, prewriting involves research (in the library or elsewhere) to gain essential information, and in a later chapter we will explore methods of research. Interviews with experts on a subject can be an excellent way to gain subject matter. And perhaps most obviously, careful observation of details—colors, sounds, textures, odors, shapes, sizes, tastes—is an important method of prewriting. For example, in the following passage from *Pilgrim at Tinker Creek*, Annie Dillard uses the details of her own observation as well as references to an expert to convey information about the praying mantis.

> She was hanging upside-down, clinging to a horizontal stem of wild rose by her feet which pointed to heaven. Her head was deep in dried grass. Her abdomen was swollen like a smashed finger; it tapered to a fleshy tip out of which bubbled a wet, whipped froth. I couldn't believe my eyes. I lay on the hill this way and that, my knees in thorns and my cheeks in clay, trying to see as well as I could. I poked near the female's head with a grass; she was clearly disturbed, so I settled my nose an inch from that pulsing abdomen. It puffed like a concertina, it throbbed like a bellows; it roved, pumping, over the glistening, clabbered surface of the egg case testing and patting, thrusting and smoothing. It seemed to act so independently that I

forgot the panting brown stick at the other end. The bubble creature seemed to have two eyes, a frantic little brain, and two busy, soft hands. It looked like a hideous, harried mother slicking up a fat daughter for a beauty pageant, touching her up, slobbering over her, patting and hemming and brushing and stroking.

The male was nowhere in sight. The female had probably eaten him. [Jean Henri] Fabre [the French entomologist known for his descriptions of insects] says that, at least in captivity, the female will mate with and devour up to seven males, whether she has laid her egg cases or not. The mating rites of mantises are well known: a chemical produced in the head of the male insect says, in effect, "No, don't go near her, you fool, she'll eat you alive." At the same time a chemical in his abdomen says, "Yes, by all means, now and forever yes."

While the male is making up what passes for his mind, the female tips the balance in her favor by eating his head. He mounts her. Fabre describes the mating, which sometimes lasts six hours, as follows: "The male, absorbed in the performance of his vital functions, holds the female in a tight embrace. But the wretch has no head; he has no neck; he has hardly a body. The other, with her muzzle turned over her shoulder, continues very placidly to gnaw what remains of the gentle swain. And, all the time, that masculine stump, holding on firmly, goes on with the business! . . . I have seen it done with my own eyes and have not yet recovered from my astonishment."

Prewriting: From Subject to Topic

As we saw at the conclusion of the first chapter, the subject of a piece of writing is the broad area with which the writing deals. In the case of "Becoming a Reader," the subject was the way in which I developed my interest in reading. However, that subject covers vast territory: from my first memories of books through my current interest in modern nonfiction. To deal with so much subject matter would demand a book in itself.

Thus, I had to narrow my subject to three years in high school, and then, as you will recall, I narrowed it even further to the events in one year, 1943, and, as the writing progressed, narrowed further yet, to three reading "events" at home.

Writing

Writing is the actual crafting of text. The writer creates *structures*—sentences, paragraphs, sections—that are permeated with meaning. The account of how "Becoming a Reader" developed is an attempt to demonstrate some of the complexity of this operation.

Good writers have mastery over the structures of language, and gaining this mastery comes about through reading and practice in writing. Expert instruction can also be valuable, which is why you are enrolled in a composition class and are studying this book.

Rewriting

In *rewriting*, I changed words, sentences, paragraphs, and whole sections.

Words

She was not ~~stout~~ [fat], but portly . . .
The cord to the blanket ran up toward the ceiling, where it joined with a socket dangling by [black] electric ~~cords~~ [wires].

Sentences

In this strange apartment above the J. C. Penney store, in a [Nevada] smelter and mill town, ~~there took place events that would forever change~~ certain events turned me into a compulsive reader. ~~Father pulled two easy~~ Father arranged a small table between two easy chairs, with a floor lamp just behind the table.

Paragraphs

~~My point is that~~
~~We weren't so different, then, from the modern~~
~~The radio generation wasn't so different from the television generation.~~ We did a lot of tramping around the sagebrush flats, hunting rabbits, ~~and in the fall~~ with either our single-shot .22s or our bows and arrows; we sat in the Candy Shoppe, sipping our Cokes and feeling our teenage juices either seep or rush through our systems. Some Friday nights one of us was lucky enough to get the family automobile, and we drove to a dance in the high school gymnasium in Ely. ~~(The 1941 Plymouth that Don Johnson's father caressed and pampered was so elegant that I have never lost my lust for Chrysler products   Because of the 1941 Plymouth that Don Johnson's father caressed and pampered, I still prefer Chrysler products~~ (The classiest auto we had access to was a white 1941 Plymouth, caressed and pampered by Don Johnson's father. I'm still partial to Chrysler products.)

Suggestion for Writing: An Autobiographical Sketch

Write an autobiographical sketch, either (1) an account of an event (or events) in your own development as a reader or (2) an account of some other event that was meaningful to you, such as discovering a "secret" of nature; developing an interest (in sports or a science, for example); a death in the family; an experience in school. You may, if you want to, use "Becoming a Reader" as a rough model for your own essay.

Remember that autobiography is a story, and stories have vividly depicted scenes, interesting characters, and meaningful actions. To create these scenes, characters, and actions, you must think about and carefully choose your details, for it is details (of sight, sound, taste, touch, smell) that bring stories to life.

As any reader of the Bible knows, stories are excellent vehicles for conveying attitudes, values, and ideas of all sorts to readers. In other words, most stories—like essays—have a gist, a main point. In "Becoming a Reader," this main point is stated directly:

> What lesson is to be learned from this account of reading in one home? As I look back on my experiences, I realize that, above all, reading was woven into the fabric of our lives; books were the center of both special occasions and our quotidian existence. They were very much like food: every meal was not an elaborate Sunday brunch, nor was every experience of reading a major occasion. Nonetheless, as we ate three meals a day, so we read books (and magazines, for there was no proper daily newspaper) every day.

However, the storyteller usually does not state the point directly, but lets the reader derive it through inference and implication. Certainly you won't want to end your story like this:

> And so, from my old dog Rover, I learned the value of loyalty.

or begin it like this:

> In the following story, I will show you how I learned the value of patience from my old cat Flossy.

II
THE
USES OF
WRITING

3
The Writer's Journal

Many writers keep journals, recording in them experiences, impressions, ideas, facts, wishes, and dreams.

Oct. 26

On the way back from Wyoming, I had a discovery: though it's hard for me to read serious stuff on an airplane, I can write, especially if my entries are discontinuous. It's a law of nature, I think, that a writer is compulsive, trailing squiggles everlastingly across the page, if for no other purpose, then to kill time. Real literacy is a compulsion, or, less sinisterly, a way of life: the literate person *must* perpetually read and write.

Nov. 21

VIETNAM MEMORIAL. Pat Ludington took us to see it today. I have seldom been so moved: the austere black wall with its inscribed names; the panorama in one direction, the Washington Monument; in the other, the Lincoln Memorial. Grandeur and grandeur, and black simplicity. Glory and glory, and shame and tragedy. Alabaster and alabaster, and polished anthracite. The Memorial is brilliant. Carnations stuck in the crevices between slabs. Die Namen der Gefallenen! Wreaths on

the lawn before the slabs. I wept. I weep now. How could one stand
the bitterness of seeing a son's name on the black wall?

—From one writer's journal

Thomas Jefferson was a compulsive journal keeper, entering the exact dates of the blossoming and fading of flowers in
his garden, household expenses, passages from books that im-
pressed him, and countless other sorts of items. In 1771, he described a tomb that he planned for his beloved sister Jane, who
had died six years earlier:

> . . . choose out for a Burying place some unfrequented vale in the
> park, where is, 'no sound to break the stillness but a brook, that bub-
> bling winds among the weeds; no mark of any human shape that had
> been there, unless the skeleton of some poor wretch, Who sought that
> place out to despair and die in.'

Here, from his journal, is John Adams's reaction to the Boston Tea Party:

> This Destruction of the Tea is so bold, so daring, so firm, intrepid and
> inflexible, and it must have important Consequences, and so lasting,
> that I can't but consider it an Epocha in History.

THE IDEA OF THE JOURNAL

The journal is like

a photograph album, containing word pictures of what matters to the writer
an idea bank, containing thoughts for future use
a practice field, on which the writer can "scrimmage," perfecting his or
  her technique and experimenting with new "plays"
a private retreat, where the writer can be alone, without interruption or
  criticism
a collection of games, inviting the writer to play for the fun of it
a good listener or therapist, with the writer talking to him- or herself

and, as you will probably discover, much much more.

Samuel Pepys, who lived from 1633 to 1703, kept an elaborate journal (or diary) and, paradoxically, wrote it in code. He
apparently enjoyed keeping a detailed record of his activities,
not intended for others to read. Here, translated from the code,

is an entry from the *Diary,* which seems to have been for Pepys a private retreat and therapist:

> *July 6, 1661*
> Waked this morning with news, brought me by a messenger on purpose, that my uncle Robert is dead, and died yesterday; so I rose sorry in some respect, glad in my expectations in another respect. So I made myself ready, went and told my uncle Wight, my Lady, and some others thereof, and bought me a pair of boots in St. Martin's, and got myself ready; and then to the Post House and set out about eleven and twelve o'clock, taking the messenger with me that came to me. And so we rode and got well by nine o'clock to Brampton, where I found my father well. My uncle's corps in a coffin standing upon joint-stools in the chimney in the hall; but it begun to smell, so I caused it to be set forth in the yard all night, and watched by two men. My aunt I found in bed in a most nasty ugly pickle, made me sick to see it. My father and I lay together to-night, I greedy to see the will, but did not ask to see it till tomorrow.

People often record their travels in journals, in which case the journal has much the same purpose as a photograph album: to preserve the memories of the journey. Here is an example of the journal as "photograph album":

> *Monday, May 13, 1985: Athens*
> The ride from the airport to the hotel: a cabdriver who had been to Los Angeles, his radio playing Greek music, his foot heavy on the gas, his driving, in fact, just as terrifying as that of all other Greek cabbies. And, it turns out, he cheated us: DR800 for a ride that should cost about DR300 (at an exchange rate of DR135 per dollar). But, then, what are cabbies for if not to take advantage of naive tourists? And we had our first glimpse of the Acropolis. There it was, in actual stone fact, not on a postcard or in a history book. When we saw the Parthenon, we knew that we were in Greece.
>
> The Acropolis exceeded our expectations. The Parthenon is not glistening white, but creamy and tan. It is perfect as a ruin, for our imaginations reconstruct it, replace the Elgin marbles, people it with its proper inhabitants.
>
> The Parthenon itself is a temple dedicated to Athena the Virgin; much smaller is the temple of Athena Nike, Athena the victorious. How wonderful: chaste goddess, warrior goddess. Who would dare attack the virginity of the goddess of victory?
>
> The Parthenon, built between 447 and 438 B.C., by the architect Iktinos and sculptor Pheidias, at the behest of Pericles. This structure, more than any other, symbolizes Western civilization. In the shadow of the Acropolis, Socrates, Plato, and Aristotle walked, talked, and taught; our logic was born; our values began to take shape.

We sit and look at the Parthenon; and from the Acropolis, we survey Athens—smoggy, noisy, crowded.

If you look carefully at Greek columns—at least those of the Parthenon—you find that they are slightly convex and smaller in diameter at the top than at the bottom, this part of the design to achieve the harmonious visual effect.

The Acropolis museum is wonderful (as are all the Greek museums): chaste and subdued. In it, we saw the "Picasso" vases that we like so well. The figures looked as if they had been drawn freehand in pen and ink against a creamy background. These vases are much more satisfying to us than the more usual clay red figures against an ebony background. In fact, we bought a reproduction of one of the "Picasso" vases from a young artist named Evi, about whom I shall tell hereafter.

—From one writer's journal

Finally, here is an excerpt from the journal of Dian Fossey, a naturalist who became a leading expert on the African mountain gorilla. Fossey used her journal to record scientific data.

Digit: Silverback [mature male gorilla] of Group 4 approximately 15 years old. Killed by poachers December 31, 1977; body recovered January 3, 1978; autopsy conducted by Dr. Desseaux of Ruhengeri Hospital, Ian Redmond, and the author.

External Examination. Five spear wounds, any one of which could have been fatal, into ventral and dorsal body surfaces; decapitated and hands hacked off. No external parasites found.

Internal Examination. All internal organs appeared healthy except for a 3 cm cyst in spleen. A large trematode parasite found in left lung measuring 3.2 cm in length and 1.9 cm in width. The trematode had a median ventral sucker 1.4 cm long, 0.6 cm wide; its dorsal surface was smooth, coming to a slight point at the anterior symmetrical end; the posterior end was not symmetrical. Consistent with findings of fecal examinations throughout 1977, no cestodes were found in Digit's dung, which, two days prior to death, contained strongyle eggs and nematodes.

—*Gorillas in the Mist*

THE JOURNAL AND THE CREATIVE PROCESS

The journal is useful in preparing to write anything: an essay, a story, a novel, a scientific report.

Recording ideas in your journal starts them "cooking"—so the journal is a stimulus to the creative process. It is also an "idea bank," where you can store your ideas and questions without losing them. Furthermore, in writing your ideas down, you are forced to be more precise in your thinking, and you can use your journal to record further ideas about your subject and to refine and redirect your ideas and hunches.

One successful writer keeps a massive journal, into which he enters all sorts of information about his subject. When he finally gets ready to write, he can often say, "The piece is already written. Now it only needs typing." What he means is this: using his journal, he has done such thorough work in formulation and preparation that he knows quite well what he wants to say. This particular writer spends three-fourths of his time with the journal and one-fourth in the actual writing of the first draft of the piece.

STARTING YOUR JOURNAL

Start your journal right now!

On the first page, write this question: what changes would I make in my present life if changes were possible?

Now begin to jot down ideas, in no particular order or form. These ideas can be words, phrases, sentences (either statements or questions), or paragraphs.

To get a start, you can ask yourself five questions, the answers to which will give you material:

1. What changes would I make in my own personality, appearance, or habits?
2. Where else would I prefer to be? Where would I move to?
3. What would I need in order to make those changes? More money? Plastic surgery? Better will power? More time? Help from others?
4. Why should I want to make the changes?
5. What would be the final result if I made the changes?

FREEWRITING

You can use your journal for freewriting—simply letting words, phrases, and sentences tumble out onto the page, one after another, unplanned, spontaneous, with no obligation to make sense or be coherent, as in the following entry from Allen Ginsberg's *Indian Journals:*

Friday 13 July 1962
Top floor Hotel Amjadia Chandy Chowk & Princep St. Calcutta: looking out the barred window at sunset & the clouds like a movie film
over the sky with cheap red paper kites fluttering over the 4 story
roofs against the mottled green & orange mists of maya—down for a
cup of tea, the sloppy Moslem waiters barefoot and bearded in black-
edged white uniforms—the clang of rickshaw handbells against wooden
pull staves—bells under hand cars—slept all afternoon. . . .

Freewriting can be compared with the warming-up exercises that athletes perform; freewriting limbers up the muscles
of your mind, gets you in the mood, undams the stream of
language.

Here is a bit of practical advice: if you have mental writer's
cramps, merely sit down with your journal and start entering
words in it, just as they pop into your mind; don't think even
about sentences necessarily, but fill a complete page of your journal with spontaneously discovered words. There is a good chance
that this uncontrolled, effortless writing will begin to assume a
direction that you can follow.

FOR YOUR JOURNAL

The following suggestions for journal entries (many adapted
from D. Gordon Rohman and Albert O. Wlecke's book *Pre-Writing*)[1] are largely in the nature of language play, but they also
illustrate some important principles about writing and language
in general.

Abstract-Concrete Sentences

From the comic strip *Peanuts* come such sentences as this
one: "Happiness is a warm blanket." The noun "happiness" is
abstract: one cannot see, touch, taste, smell, or hear "happiness,"
for it is a state of mind, not a physical object. On the other hand,
"blanket" is a *concrete* noun: one can see and touch blankets, or
taste, smell, and even hear them, for that matter. The abstract-
concrete sentence is a sort of *metaphor*. (See pages 416–21 for a
discussion of metaphor.)

The abstract-concrete sentence forces us to jump from one
kind of knowing—that of abstract concepts—into a kind of
knowing based on the senses, and the result can be heightened

awareness, greater interest, and new insights. In any case, such sentences can be surprising and funny.

Here are the rules for composing abstract-concrete sentences in your journal:

First, choose an abstract noun such as *success*.
Second, define it in terms of a concrete noun (with modifiers, if you
so desire).

> Success is *a big red "100" at the top of a midtern exam.*
> Success is *harvesting the first tomato in August.*
> Success is *the contented sighs of your guests after they've finished the
> meal that you spent all day cooking.*

Here are a few more examples of abstract-concrete sentences:

> Laziness is pajamas, B.O., and a two-day beard.
> Vacation is Uncle Eldon, a boat, a fishing rod, and a cold beer.
> Failure is succumbing to the temptation of chocolate cake when
> you're on a diet.
> Failure is a blank page.
> Failure is a crumpled sheet in the wastebasket.

Exercise

I. The following list gives *abstract nouns* on the left and *concrete nouns* on the right. Without advance thought, make random combinations of abstract with concrete nouns and add any modifying words or word groups that you desire. Write these sentences in your journal, and then think about and discuss the questions that follow the list.

ABSTRACT	CONCRETE
authority	zygote
barbarity	YWCA
contentment	xenophobe
diplomacy	whip
efficiency	vegetable
falseness	umiak
greed	tree
health	sonic boom
industry	root
joy	quicksand
knowledge	potato

ABSTRACT	CONCRETE
loneliness	oboe
majesty	nurse
narcosis	mountebank
oligation	lion

1. Some of your combinations probably do not make sense to you—in other words, result in nonsense sentences. (For example, here is a combination that, from my point of view, results in nonsense: "Efficiency is a sonic boom.") Why are these combinations nonsensical?
2. Since everything in the universe is like everything else in some way—though that way might be obscure—finding the points of similarity between "efficiency" and "vegetable" might give at least some minor insights into or understanding of the concept "efficiency." What did you learn, if anything, from the nonsense sentences that this exercise generated? What ideas did the nonsense sentences stir up in your mind?
3. The exercise undoubtedly generated some sentences that you feel are meaningful. What insights did these sentences give you? Explain.

II. Abstract-concrete sentences are good journal material. With practice, you can become a real master at writing these sentences. Start now! In your journal, write ten of them.

Analogy

The analogy, an extremely useful device for thinkers and writers, is simply the comparing of an unknown or imperfectly known thing or concept to something that is known. Suppose that I want to explain the *Reader's Guide to Periodical Literature* to someone who has not used it, but who does understand how to use a card catalog in a library. The analogy would be this:

> The *Reader's Guide* is an index of articles published in generally nontechnical magazines, such as *Time* or the *Atlantic*. It is like the card catalog of a library. The card catalog lists books by (1) their authors or editors, (2) their titles, and (3) their subjects. The *Reader's Guide* has the same listings for magazine articles (in alphabetical order, of course).

When Albert Einstein wanted to explain nuclear fission to nonscientists, he used the analogy of the rich man and his sons:

What takes place can be illustrated with the help of our rich man. The atom M is a rich miser who, during his life, gives away no money (*energy*). But in his will he bequeaths his fortune to his sons M' and M", on condition that they give the community a small amount, less than one thousandth of the whole estate (*energy or mass*). The sons together have somewhat less than the father had (*the mass sum M' + M" is somewhat smaller than the mass M of the radioactive atom*). But the part given to the community, though relatively small, is still so enormously large (*considered as kinetic energy*) that it brings with it a great threat of evil. Averting that threat has become the most urgent problem of our time.

—*Out of My Later Years*

As you can see, analogy is an excellent way to explain things and ideas.

Exercise

In your journal, write an analogy by which you explain something to any person of your choice (a friend, your instructor, a relative, the president of the United States). You must choose a thing to be explained that your intended reader does not yet understand (fully, at least), and you must use the familiar or well known as the basis for your analogy. You can choose a concrete object (such as a complicated instrument), a process (such as registering in college), or a concept (such as honesty).

Outrageous Analogies

When analogies are used either for argumentation or for explanation, writers must be cautious, making sure that the analogy is not false or overextended. (A false analogy compares two things that are not comparable; an overextended analogy carries the comparison too far.) Right now, however, we are not concerned with the validity of analogies, which is why this section is titled "Outrageous Analogies."

In writing outrageous analogies, one describes a common activity in terms of another common activity: driving a car in terms of brushing teeth, keeping a journal in terms of tending a garden, snoozing in terms of chewing gum. For example, the following outrageous analogy describes the activity of *reading* in terms of *fishing*. (Notice that the beginning is an abstract-concrete sentence.)

> Meaning is a trout that keeps the reader ever alert, casting his attention into riffles of words in the hope that meaning will rise for a strike. Warily, meaning sulks beneath a large rock, undulating in the current of the sentences and the paragraphs, ignoring cast after cast by the fisherman. Then suddenly it flashes into view, arcing above the surface and engorging the lure. After a careful battle, the fisherman slips the meaning-trout into his creel, and in the evening he fries the catch in butter and eats it with gusto.

This brief passage, by the way, can stir up many interesting ideas and can make you ask important questions about reading:

1. Where does meaning lurk? In the individual words? In the sentences? In the paragraphs?
2. Which leads to this big question: what is meaning?
3. Why is it that meaning sometimes eludes us?
4. Why is it that meaning sometimes flashes into view, almost as if the reader had received a sudden inspiration?
5. How is meaning stored in memory?
6. How is meaning used?

Exercise

In your journal, write at least two outrageous analogies. If you have trouble, here are some steps toward creating interesting samples:

1. Choose two activities with which you are thoroughly familiar (for example, driving a car and baking a cake).
2. List the steps of each activity.

DRIVING A CAR	BAKING A CAKE
fastening seat belt	reading recipe
starting engine	assembling ingredients
activating left turn signal	heating oven
putting car in gear	mixing ingredients
pulling into traffic . . .	baking . . .

3. Use terms and suggestions from the second column to describe the first process.

> When you drive a car, the best recipe for a safe trip is to fasten the seat belt immediately. You can cook up a successful trip if you'll carefully assemble the ingredients before you start baking. You need a key, a gas

pedal, a gearshift lever, and a steering wheel. First, insert the key into the starter switch and turn, at the same time mixing in carefully a slight depression of the gas pedal so that . . .

Corny? Yes! Certainly! But in writing for the journal—since it is actually writing for oneself—anything goes. And, in fact, it does take some ingenuity to describe driving a car in terms of baking a cake.

The Meditation

The word "meditation" as it is used here has nothing to do with any religion or with any mental discipline such as yoga; it means only the systematic construction of an imaginative experience. For our purposes, then, the meditation is a way of stimulating and guiding the imagination.

For your meditation, find a quiet, comfortable spot at a time when you are calm and relatively at peace.

The kind of meditation that I am suggesting as a stimulus to writing depends heavily on your ability to imagine scenes and actions, for it involves creating or re-creating an event. In this kind of meditation, the meditator is a dramatist, and the meditation itself is a drama that he or she creates.

All forms of drama (stage, television, or film) have certain elements in common.

First, there is a *scene*. All actions take place in a scene that is represented in detail or that the viewer must imagine.

Second, there are *characters:* the hero or heroine and others.

Third, there is a *plot*, and plot consists of the actions that occur and the reasons or motives for those actions. Thus, plot consists of *actions* plus *motives*.

Exercise: Meditation

Through meditation, construct a drama. Create a detailed scene and put yourself into it as the central character, adding other characters if you so desire. Then have the character or characters do something.

The following guidelines might help you.

1. Prepare yourself for fifteen to thirty minutes of meditation. Choose a quiet spot where you won't be disturbed, and make yourself comfortable. Get settled, and then close your eyes.
2. Make your mind as completely blank as possible.

3. Within the empty stage of your mind, construct a scene, not a general scene but one that is specific. What are the three or four most important objects in the scene? What colors appear? What would the textures be if the objects were touched? Are there any sounds? Smells?

4. Put yourself in the scene. What exactly do you look like? How are you dressed? Are you wearing perfume or shaving lotion? How does your skin feel? What is the texture of your clothing? What colors stand out? If you wish, you can add other characters.

5. Have your main character (yourself) do something. If there are other characters, involve them in the actions. Imagine the actions in detail, not in general. If your main character walks across a room, picks up a newspaper, and begins to read, supply all the details: the manner of walking, sounds, hand movements, and so on.

6. Explain the motives for the actions. Why did the characters act as they did?

Your meditation having ended, record it in your journal, capturing as many of the details as possible.

Exercise: The Journal as the Basis for Other Writing

One of the great American classics is Henry David Thoreau's book *Walden*. In a journal entry for July 6, 1846, Thoreau planted the seeds that ultimately grew into one of the most famous passages of his book. Read the journal entry, and then read the selection from Walden that follows it.

How does Thoreau use the ideas in the journal? What methods does he use to develop these ideas?

July 6, 1846
I wish to meet the facts of life—the vital facts, which are the phenomena or actuality the gods meant to show us—face to face, and so I came down here. Life! who knows what it is, what it does? If I am not quite right here, I am less wrong than before; and now let us see what they will have. The preacher, instead of vexing the ears of drowsy farmers on their day of rest at the end of the week,—for Sunday always seemed to me like a fit conclusion of an ill-spent week and not the fresh and brave beginning of a new one,—with this one other draggletail and postponed affair of a sermon, from thirdly to fifteenthly, should teach them with a thundering voice pause and simplicity. "Stop! Avast! Why so fast?" In all studies we go not forward but rather backward with redoubled pauses. We always study *antiques* with silence and reflection. Even time has a depth, and below its surface the waves do not lapse and roar. I wonder men can be so frivolous almost as to attend to the gross form of negro slavery, there are so many keen and subtle masters who subject us both. Self-emancipation in the West Indies of a man's thinking and imagining provinces, which should be more than his island territory,— one emancipated heart and intellect! It would knock off the fetters from a million slaves.

from *Walden*

Henry David Thoreau

I went to the woods because I wished to live deliberately, to front only the essential facts of life, and see if I could not learn what it had to teach, and not, when I came to die, discover that I had not lived. I did not wish to live what was not life, living is so dear; nor did I wish to practice resignation, unless it was quite necessary. I wanted to live deep and suck out all the marrow of life, to live so sturdily and Spartan-like as to put to rout all that was not life, to cut a broad swath and shave close, to drive life into a corner, and reduce it to its lowest terms, and, if it proved to be mean, why then to get the whole and genuine meanness of it, and publish its meanness to the world; or if it were sublime, to know it by experience, and be able to give a true account of it in my next excursion. For most men, it appears to me, are in a strange uncertainty about it, whether it is of the devil or of God, and have *somewhat hastily* concluded that it is the chief end of man here to "glorify God and enjoy him forever."

Still we live meanly, like ants; though the fable tell us that we were long ago changed into men; like pygmies we fight with cranes; it is error upon error, and clout upon clout, and our best virtue has for its occasion a superfluous and evitable wretchedness. Our life is frittered away by detail. An honest man has hardly need to count more than his ten fingers, or in extreme cases he may add his ten toes, and lump the rest. Simplicity, simplicity, simplicity! I say, let your affairs be as two or three, and not a hundred or a thousand; instead of a million count half a dozen, and keep your accounts on your thumb nail. In the midst of this chopping sea of civilized life, such are the clouds and storms and quicksands and thousand-and-one items to be allowed for, that a man has to live, if he would not founder and go to the bottom and not make his port at all, by dead reckoning, and he must be a great calculator indeed who succeeds. Simplify, simplify. Instead of three meals a day, if it be necessary eat but one; instead of a hundred dishes, five; and reduce other things in proportion. Our life is like a German Confederacy, made up of petty states, with its boundary forever fluctuating, so that even a German cannot tell you how it is bounded at any moment. The nation itself, with all its so called internal improvements, which, by the way, are all external and superficial, is just such an unwieldy and overgrown establishment, cluttered with furniture and tripped up by its own traps, ruined by luxury and heedless expense, by want of calculation and a worthy aim, as the million households in the land; and the only cure for it as for them is in a rigid economy, a stern and more than Spartan simplicity of life and elevation of purpose. It lives too fast. Men think that it is essential that the *Nation* have commerce, and export ice, and talk through a telegraph, and ride thirty miles an hour, without a doubt, whether *they* do or not; but whether we should live like baboons or like men, is a little uncertain. If we do not get out sleepers, and forge rails, and devote days and nights to the work, but go to tinkering upon our *lives* to improve *them,* who will build railroads? And if railroads are not built, how shall we get to heaven in season? But if we stay at home and mind our business, who will want railroads? We do not ride on the railroad; it rides upon us. Did you ever think what those sleepers are that underlie the railroad? Each one is a man, an Irishman, or a Yankee man. The rails are laid on them, and they are covered with sand, and the cars run smoothly over them. They are sound sleepers, I assure you. And every few years a new lot is laid down and run over; so that, if some have the pleasure of riding on a rail, others have the misfortune to be ridden upon. And when they run over a man that is walking in his sleep, a supernumerary sleeper in the wrong position, and wake him up, they suddenly stop the cars, and make a hue and cry about it, as if this were an exception. I am glad to know that it takes a gang of men for every five miles to keep the sleepers down and level in their beds as it is, for this is a sign that they may sometime get up again.

Why should we live with such hurry and waste of life? We are determined to be starved before we are hungry. Men say that a stitch in time saves nine, and so they take a thousand stitches today to save nine to-morrow. As for work, we haven't any of any consequence. We have the Saint Vitus' dance, and cannot possibly keep our heads still. If I should only give a few pulls at the parish bell-rope, as for a fire, that is, without setting the bell, there is hardly a man on his farm in the outskirts of Concord, notwithstanding that press of engagements which was his excuse so many times this morning, nor a boy, nor a woman, I might almost say, but would forsake all and follow that sound, not mainly to save property from the flames, but, if we will confess the truth, much more to see it burn, since burn it must, and we, be it known, did not set it on fire,—or to see it put out, and have a hand in it, if that is done as handsomely; yes, even if it were the parish church itself. Hardly a man takes a half hour's nap after dinner, but when he wakes he holds up his head and asks, "What's the news?" as if the rest of mankind had stood his sentinels. Some give directions to be waked every half hour, doubtless for no other purpose; and then, to pay for it, they tell what they have dreamed. After a night's sleep the news is as indispensable as the breakfast. "Pray tell me any thing new that has happened to a man any where on this globe,"—and he reads it over his coffee and rolls, that a man has had his eyes gouged out this morning on the Wachito River; never dreaming the while that he lives in the dark unfathomed mammoth cave of this world, and has but the rudiment of an eye himself.

For my part, I could easily do without the post-office. I think that there are very few important communications made through it. To speak critically, I never received more than one or two letters in my life—I wrote this some years ago—that were worth the postage. The penny-post is, commonly, an institution through which you seriously offer a man that penny for his thoughts which is so often safely offered in jest. And I am sure that I never read any memorable news in a newspaper. If we read of one man robbed, or murdered, or killed by accident, or one house burned, or one vessel wrecked, or one steamboat blown up, or one cow run over on the Western Railroad, or one mad dog killed, or one lot of grasshoppers in the winter,—we never need read of another. One is enough. If you are acquainted with the principle, what do you care for a myriad instances and applications? To a philosopher all news, as it is called, is gossip, and they who edit and read it are old women over their tea. Yet not a few are greedy after this gossip. There was such a rush, as I hear, the other day at one of the offices to learn the foreign news by the last arrival, that several large squares of plate glass belonging to the establishment were broken by the pressure,—news which I seriously think

a ready wit might write a twelvemonth or twelve years beforehand with sufficient accuracy. As for Spain, for instance, if you know how to throw in Don
Carlos and the Infanta, and Don Pedro and Seville and Granada, from time
to time in the right proportions,—they may have changed the names a little
since I saw the papers,—and serve up a bull-fight when other entertainments
fail, it will be true to the letter, and give us as good an idea of the exact state
or ruin of things in Spain as the most succinct and lucid reports under this
head in the newspapers: and as for England, almost the last significant scrap
of news from that quarter was the revolution of 1649; and if you have learned
the history of her crops for an average year, you never need attend to that
thing again, unless your speculations are of a merely pecuniary character. If
one may judge who rarely looks into the newspapers, nothing new does ever
happen in foreign parts, a French revolution not excepted.

What news! how much more important to know what that is which
was never old! "Kieou-he-yu (great dignitary of the state of Wei) sent a man
to Khoung-tseu to know his news. Khoung-tseu caused the messenger to be
seated near him, and questioned him in these terms: What is your master
doing? The messenger answered with respect: My master desires to diminish
the number of his faults, but he cannot accomplish it. The messenger being
gone, the philosopher remarked: What a worthy messenger! What a worthy
messenger!" The preacher, instead of vexing the ears of drowsy farmers on
their day of rest at the end of the week,—for Sunday is the fit conclusion of
an ill-spent week, and not the fresh and brave beginning of a new one,—
with this one other draggletail of a sermon, should shout with thundering
voice,—"Pause! Avast! Why so seeming fast, but deadly slow?"

Shams and delusions are esteemed for soundest truths, while reality is
fabulous. If men would steadily observe realities only, and not allow themselves to be deluded, life, to compare it with such things as we know, would
be like a fairy tale and the Arabian Nights' Entertainments. If we respected
only what is inevitable and has a right to be, music and poetry would re-
sound along the streets. When we are unhurried and wise, we perceive that
only great and worthy things have any permanent and absolute existence—
that petty fears and petty pleasures are but the shadow of the reality. This is
always exhilarating and sublime. By closing the eyes and slumbering, and
consenting to be deceived by shows, men establish and confirm their daily
life of routine and habit every where, which still is built on purely illusory
foundations. Children, who play life, discern its true law and relations more
clearly than men, who fail to live it worthily, but who think that they are
wiser by experience, that is, by failure. I have read in a Hindoo book, that
"there was a king's son, who, being expelled in infancy from his native city,
was brought up by a forester, and, growing up to maturity in that state, imagined himself to belong to the barbarous race with which he lived. One of his
father's ministers having discovered him, revealed to him what he was, and
the misconception of his character was removed, and he knew himself to be
a prince. So soul," continues the Hindoo philosopher, "from the circumstances in which it is placed, mistakes its own character, until the truth is
revealed to it by some holy teacher, and then it knows itself to be *Brahme.*"
I perceive that we inhabitants of New England live this mean life that we do
because our vision does not penetrate the surface of things. We think that *is*

which *appears* to be. If a man should walk through this town and see only the reality, where, think you, would the "Mill-dam" go to? If he should give us an account of the realities he beheld there, we should not recognize the place in his description. Look at a meeting-house, or a court-house, or a jail, or a shop, or a dwelling-house, and say what that thing really is before a true gaze, and they would all go to pieces in your account of them. Men esteem truth remote, in the outskirts of the system, behind the farthest star, before Adam and after the last man. In eternity there is indeed something true and sublime. But all these times and places and occasions are now and here. God himself culminates in the present moment, and will never be more divine in the lapse of all the ages. And we are enabled to apprehend at all what is sublime and noble only by the perpetual instilling and drenching of the reality that surrounds us. The universe constantly and obediently answers to our conceptions; whether we travel fast or slow, the track is laid for us. Let us spend our lives in conceiving them. The poet or the artist never yet had so fair and noble a design but some of his posterity at least could accomplish it.

Let us spend one day as deliberately as Nature, and not be thrown off the track by every nutshell and mosquito's wing that falls on the rails. Let us rise early and fast, or break fast, gently and without perturbation; let company come and let company go, let the bells ring and the children cry,— determined to make a day of it. Why should we knock under and go with the stream? Let us not be upset and overwhelmed in that terrible rapid and whirlpool called a dinner, situated in the meridian shallows. Weather this danger and you are safe, for the rest of the way is down hill. With unrelaxed nerves, with morning vigor, sail by it, looking another way, tied to the mast like Ulysses. If the engine whistles, let it whistle till it is hoarse for its pains. If the bell rings, why should we run? We will consider what kind of music they are like. Let us settle ourselves, and work and wedge our feet downward through the mud and slush of opinion, and prejudice, and tradition, and delusion, and appearance, that alluvion which covers the globe, through Paris and London, through New York and Boston and Concord, through church and state, through poetry and philosophy and religion, till we come to a hard bottom and rocks in place, which we can call *reality*, and say, This is, and no mistake; and then begin, having a *point d'appui*, below freshet and frost and fire, a place where you might found a wall or a state, or set a lamppost safely, or perhaps a gauge, not a Nilometer, but a Realometer, that future ages might know how deep a freshet of shams and appearances had gathered from time to time. If you stand right fronting and face to face to a fact, you will see the sun glimmer on both its surfaces, as if it were a cimeter, and feel its sweet edge dividing you through the heart and marrow, and so you will happily conclude your mortal career. Be it life or death, we crave only reality. If we are really dying, let us hear the rattle in our throats and feel cold in the extremities; if we are alive, let us go about our business.

Time is but the stream I go a-fishing in. I drink at it; but while I drink I see the sandy bottom and detect how shallow it is. Its thin current slides away, but eternity remains. I would drink deeper; fish in the sky, whose bottom is pebbly with stars. I cannot count one. I know not the first letter of the alphabet. I have always been regretting that I was not as wise as the day

I was born. The intellect is a cleaver; it discerns and rifts its way into the secret of things. I do not wish to be any more busy with my hands than is necessary. My head is hands and feet. I feel all my best faculties concentrated in it. My instinct tells me that my head is an organ for burrowing, as some creatures use their snout and fore-paws, and with it I would mine and burrow my way through these hills. I think that the richest vein is somewhere here-abouts; so by the divining rod and thin rising vapors I judge; and here I will begin to mine.

Notes

[1] D. Gordon Rohman and Albert A. Wlecke, *Pre-Writing: The Construction and Application of Models for Concept Formation in Writing* (East Lansing: Michigan State University, 1964).

4
Narration

In this chapter, we will discuss, first, the ways in which skilled writers bring narration to life, making it interesting and believable for readers, and, second, the uses of this kind of writing.

A narrative is nothing more than a story, whether fact or fiction, and stories, as you know, involve *characters*, the *actions* that they perform, the *scenes* in which the actions take place, and the *motives* (reasons, purposes) for the actions.

Autobiographical writing is one of the most common forms of narration. (Some modern autobiographies that would interest you are *The Woman Warrior*, by Maxine Hong Kingston; *Blackberry Winter*, by Margaret Mead; *Off the Court*, by Arthur Ashe; *One Christmas*, by Truman Capote; *Hunger of Memory*, by Richard Rodriguez; *Brothers and Keepers*, by John Edgar Wideman.) Other forms of autobiographical writing are journals and diaries, of which there are examples in chapter 3.

In *Soul on Ice*, Eldridge Cleaver said this about learning to write:

That is why I started to write. To save myself.

I realized that no one could save me but myself. The prison authorities were both uninterested and unable to help me. I had to seek out the truth and unravel the snarled web of my motivations. I had to find out who I am and what I want to be, what type of man I should be, and what I could do to become the best of which I was capable.

Paradoxically, then, one can write to find out who he or she is, not just to reveal that information to the world. Personal narration can be, and frequently is, a way to understand oneself.

However, narration—the story—is essential in both explanations and arguments (see chapters 5 and 6). In *The Art of Readable Writing*, Rudolf Flesch said, "Only stories are really readable." Then he quoted a *Reader's Digest* editor: " 'Whenever we want to draw attention to a problem, we wait until somebody does something about it. Then we print the story of how he did it.' "

It is simply a fact that stories (narratives) are easier for readers to follow than are other types of writing. Let's see how turning an explanation into a narrative can make it easier to understand and more memorable.

In *Desert Solitaire*, a book that almost everyone would enjoy, Edward Abbey uses a story to explain why he loves the desert country in Utah, around Arches National Park:

"This would be good country," a tourist says to me, "if only you had some water."

He's from Cleveland, Ohio.

"If we had water here," I reply, "this country would not be what it is. It would be like Ohio, wet and humid and hydrological, all covered with cabbage farms and golf courses. Instead of the lovely barren desert we would have only another blooming garden state, like New Jersey. You see what I mean?"

"If you had more water more people could live here."

"Yes sir. And where then would the people go when they wanted to see something besides people?"

"I see what you mean. Still, I wouldn't want to live here. So dry and desolate. Nice for pictures but my God I'm glad I don't have to live here."

"I'm glad too, sir. We're in perfect agreement. You wouldn't want to live here, I wouldn't want to live in Cleveland. We're both satisfied with the arrangement as it is. Why change it?"

"Agreed."

We shake hands and the tourist from Ohio goes away pleased, as I am pleased, each of us thinking he has taught the other something new.

If you think about this little story, you'll agree that it conveys many ideas memorably and clearly. It says, and in saying illustrates, among other things, that (1) we should appreciate the desert for what it is; (2) we should preserve such regions as the desert because they *do* provide different perspectives than populated areas do; (3) the land should allow for a diversity of tastes. Embedded in the story also is an argument in favor of diversity and toleration. It is quite remarkable that so much can be said so vividly, concisely, and memorably.

PLOT AND DETAILS

Pilgrim at Tinker Creek, a wonderful autobiographical narrative by Annie Dillard, contains this story:

> I have no intention of inflicting all my childhood memories on anyone. Far less do I want to excoriate my old teachers who, in their bungling, unforgettable way, exposed me to the natural world, a world covered in chitin, where implacable realities hold sway. The Polyphemus moth never made it to the past; it crawls in that crowded, pellucid pool at the lip of the great waterfall. It is as present as this blue desk and brazen lamp, as this blackened window before me in which I can no longer see even the white string that binds the egg case to the hedge, but only my own pale, astonished face.
>
> Once, when I was ten or eleven years old, my friend Judy brought in a Polyphemus moth cocoon. It was January; there were doily snowflakes taped to the schoolroom panes. The teacher kept the cocoon in her desk all morning and brought it out when we were getting restless before recess. In a book we found what the adult moth would look like; it would be beautiful. With a wingspread of up to six inches, the Polyphemus is one of the few huge American silk moths, much larger than, say, a giant or tiger swallowtail butterfly. The moth's enormous wings are velveted in a rich, warm brown, and edged in bands of blue and pink delicate as a watercolor wash. A startling "eyespot," immense, and deep blue melding to an almost translucent yellow, luxuriates in the center of each hind wing. The effect is one of a masculine splendor foreign to the butterflies, a fragility unfurled to strength. The Polyphemus moth in the picture looked like a mighty wraith, a beating essence of the hardwood forest, alien-skinned and brown, with spread, blind eyes. This was the giant moth packed in the faded cocoon. We closed the book and turned to the cocoon. It was an oak leaf sewn into a plump oval bundle; Judy had found it loose in a pile of frozen leaves.
>
> We passed the cocoon around; it was heavy. As we held it in our hands, the creature within warmed and squirmed. We were delighted, and wrapped it tighter in our fists. The pupa began to jerk violently,

in heart-stopping knocks. Who's there? I can still feel those thumps, urgent through a muffling of spun silk and leaf, urgent through the swaddling of many years, against the curve of my palm. We kept passing it around. When it came to me again it was hot as a bun; it jumped half out of my hand. The teacher intervened. She put it, still heaving and banging, in the ubiquitous Mason jar.

It was coming. There was no stopping it now, January or not. One end of the cocoon dampened and gradually frayed in a furious battle. The whole cocoon twisted and slapped around in the bottom of the jar. The teacher fades, the classmates fade, I fade: I don't remember anything but that thing's struggle to be a moth or die trying. It emerged at last, a sodden crumple. It was a male; his long antennae were thickly plumed, as wide as his fat abdomen. His body was very thick, over an inch long, and deeply furred. A gray, furlike plush covered his head; a long, tan furlike hair hung from his wide thorax over his brown-furred, segmented abdomen. His multijointed legs, pale and powerful, were shaggy as a bear's. He stood still, but he breathed.

He couldn't spread his wings. There was no room. The chemical that coated his wings like varnish, stiffening them permanently, dried, and hardened his wings as they were. He was a monster in a Mason jar. Those huge wings stuck on his back in a torture of random pleats and folds, wrinkled as a dirty tissue, rigid as leather. They made a single nightmare clump still wracked with useless, frantic convulsions.

The next thing I remember, it was recess. The school was in Shadyside, a busy residential part of Pittsburgh. Everyone was playing dodgeball in the fenced playground or racing around the concrete schoolyard by the swings. Next to the playground a long delivery drive sloped downhill to the sidewalk and street. Someone—it must have been the teacher—had let the moth out. I was standing in the driveway, alone, stock-still, but shivering. Someone had given the Polyphemus moth his freedom, and he was walking away.

He heaved himself down the asphalt driveway by infinite degrees, unwavering. His hideous crumpled wings lay glued and rucked on his back, perfectly still now, like a collapsed tent. The bell rang twice; I had to go. The moth was receding down the driveway, dragging on. I went; I ran inside. The Polyphemus moth is still crawling down the driveway, crawling down the driveway hunched, crawling down the driveway on six furred feet, forever.

The two questions we will ask about this brief story are "What does it mean?" and "Why is it effective?"

Stories have *plots*, conveying an overall meaning. Stories "add up"; they don't merely ramble on, from one event to the next and the next. If you want, for example, to explain why you decided to go to college, you can tell the story of how your decision came about. The essay in chapter 2, "Becoming a Reader," is a story that explains how the author of this book became "hooked on books." The selection by Annie Dillard is, in one sense, "about" a moth, but in a deeper, more significant way this little tale is about a child's awakening to the mystery of nature and about memory, just as *Moby Dick* is "about" whaling, but, in a more profound sense, about the relationship of God to humankind.

A summary statement of the story by Annie Dillard might go something like this:

> When I was ten or eleven years old, one of my friends brought the cocoon of a Polyphemus moth to school. We children passed it around, and the warmth of our hands stimulated it to hatch. We watched the moth emerge from the cocoon, and then someone freed the moth. I will never forget watching the moth crawl down the school driveway.

The abridged version, of course, doesn't make a very interesting story—because *details* are the lifeblood of stories, and the summary is stripped of all detail.

However, Dillard's narrative is rich in *sense* details. The moth is not "huge" and "colorful"; it has "a wingspread of up to six inches," and these wings "are velveted in a rich, warm brown, and edged in bands of blue and pink delicate as a watercolor wash." The pupa didn't just move in the cocoon; it "squirmed" and "began to jerk violently, in heart-stopping knocks."

Dillard captures the details of actions with verbs. She might have said, "The giant moth *was* in the faded cocoon," but, in fact, she did say, "This was the giant moth *packed* in the faded cocoon." She might have said, "The whole cocoon *moved around* in the bottom of the jar," but, in fact, she did say, "The whole cocoon *twisted* and *slapped* around in the bottom of the jar."

Sometimes narratives emphasize the people performing the actions and sometimes the actions themselves; as we shall discover, scenes—the places where actions take place—are often the most important elements in narration. Skilled writers have mastered the art of using details to bring characters and their actions to life and to portray scenes vividly.

PEOPLE IN NARRATION

In *Dispatches,* a marvelously readable and moving book about the Vietnam War, Michael Herr narrates a brief drama involving a Marine colonel and a "grunt" who had severe heat prostration:

> We could see the colonel approaching, a short, balding man with flinty eyes and a brief black mustache. He was trussed up tightly in his

flak jacket, and as he came toward us small groups of Marines broke and ran to get their flak jackets on too, before the colonel could have the chance to tell them about it. The colonel leaned over and looked hard at the unconscious Marine, who was lying now in the shade of a poncho being held over him by two corpsmen, while a third brushed his chest and face with water from a canteen.

Well hell, the colonel was saying, there's nothing the matter with that man, feed some salt into him, get him up, get him walking, this is the Marines, not the goddamned Girl Scouts, there won't be any chopper coming in *here* today. . . . The corpsmen were trying to tell the colonel that this was no ordinary case of heat exhaustion, excusing themselves but staying firm about it, refusing to let the colonel return to the CP. . . . The Marine looked awful lying there, tying to work his lips a little, and the colonel glared down at the fragile, still form as though it was blackmailing him. When the Marine refused to move anything except his lips for fifteen minutes, the colonel began to relent. He asked the corpsmen if they'd ever heard of a man dying from something like this.

"Oh, yes sir. Oh, wow, I mean he really needs more attention than what we can give him here."

"Mmmmmm . . ." The colonel said. Then he authorized the chopper request and strode with what I'm sure he considered great determination back to his CP.

The colonel is, of course, the central figure in this brief drama, and he is vividly portrayed through a few carefully selected concrete details: he is short and bald, with flinty eyes and a small black mustache. He is "trussed up tightly in his flak jacket." We see that a few carefully chosen details are enough to give readers an image of a character in a narrative.

We also learn what characters say, "hearing" their exact words, not just a paraphrase. Though Herr does not put the colonel's remarks about the ill Marine in quotation marks, we nonetheless have the sense that this is what the officer said: "Well, hell . . . there's nothing the matter with that man, feed some salt into him. . . ." And the remarks of the corpsman are in direct quotes: "Oh, yes sir. Oh, wow, I mean he really needs more attention than what we can give him here."

We also notice this important point: without ever stating his attitude directly, Herr delivers a judgment on the colonel. We know, because of what the colonel does and says, that Herr thinks he is a minor tyrant, a martinet, thoroughly unlikable. In this respect, we feel that Herr chose to mention the black mustache because it inevitably makes us think of Adolf Hitler.

Discussion: Characters in Narration

The following description of a character is from "Gear," by Richard Goldstein. Read the selection, and then discuss these questions:

1. What sort of person is Gear?
2. What techniques does Goldstein use to portray him for the reader?
3. What is the "meaning" of the narrative? That is, what is its main point?

> Too early to get up, especially on Saturday. The sun peeks over his window-sill. Isolated footsteps from the street. Guys who have to work on Saturday. Boy! That's what they'll call you all your life if you don't stay in school. Forty-five definitions, two chapters in *Silas Marner,* and three chem labs. On Sunday night, he will sit in his room with the radio on, bobbing back and forth on his bed, opening the window wide and then closing it, taking a break to eat, to comb his hair, to dance, to hear the Stones—anything. Finally, cursing wildly and making faces at himself in the mirror, he will throw *Silas Marner* under the bed and spend an hour watching his tortoise eat lettuce.
>
> In the bathroom he breaks three screaming pimples. With a toothpick he removes four specks of food from his braces, skirting the barbed wires and week-old rubber bands. Brooklyn Bridge, railroad tracks, they call him. Metal mouth. They said he smiled like someone was forcing him to. Bent fingers with filthy nails. Caved in chest with eight dangling hairs. A face that looks like the end of a watermelon, and curly hair—not like the Stones, not at all like Brian Jones—but muddy curls running down his forehead and over his ears. A bump. Smashed by a bat thrown wildly. When he was eight. Hunchback Quasimodo—Igor—Rodan on his head. A bump. Nobody hip has a bump or braces.

A Suggestion for Writing

Choose a character who interests you, and write a brief character sketch. Involve your character in some kind of "drama" (such as the colonel's confrontation with the medics or Gear's assessment of himself).

SCENES IN NARRATION

In *People of the Deer,* a book about the Ihalmiut eskimos, Farley Mowat gives this description of the inside of one of the people's tents:

All the children, women and old people from the entire camp crowded closely into Ootek's tent behind us, and collectively they produced an overpowering odor—which, however, was cancelled out by the obvious good nature and good feeling which also emanated from these People.

Ootek bade us sit down on the sleeping platform, and while his wife was organizing the other women in preparation for a feast, I had a good look at this home of the Ihalmiut. The tent was not even vaguely weather tight. Great streaks of sky showed along the joints between the skins. Under those portions of the tent which were more or less whole were the belongings of the family, and these possessions were simple almost to the point of nonexistence.

Along one half of the enclosed circle was the low sleeping bench of willow twigs and lichens, covered with a haphazard mattress of tanned deer hides. This was the communal bed where the entire family slept together under a robe or two of softened skins. The rest of the floor space was given over to an amazing litter of half-eaten, ready-to-be-eaten and never-to-be-eaten bits of caribou. I saw an entire boiled head that had been pretty well chewed over, and a pile of leg bones which had been cracked for marrow and then boiled to extract the last precious drop of oil. On one side of the tent was a more or less complete brisket, with skin attached, of a deer that obviously should have been eaten long ago. Later I discovered that this was a sort of snack bar where hungry visitors could slice off a bit of raw, but well tenderized, meat while waiting for mealtime.

Around the inner surface of the tent, suspended from the dozen precious poles, were the odd bits of clothing not required for the moment. A few pairs of *kamik*, stiff and dry and half transparent, waited for their owners' feet. Nearby lay a couple of inner parkas, called *ateegie*, and some children's overalls that are one-piece garments of fawn hide. Pushed under one pole was a huge wad of dried sphagnum moss waiting the needs of the young child Kalak, for diapers are not used in the Barrens, where nature has provided a more efficient sponge.

And that about completed the furnishing of Ootek's tent, except for an ancient wooden chest which held the treasures of the family: the amulet belt of Ootek, the sewing kit of Howmik with its bone needles and hank of caribou sinew thread, half a dozen empty .44-40 brass cartridge cases which someday might ornament the bowls of stone pipes, a bow drill, a musk ox horn comb and some children's toys.

One might call this description a systematic "catalog." Mowat first gives an overall impression of the tent: "The tent was not even vaguely weather tight. Great streaks of sky showed along the joints between the skins. Under those portions of the tent which were more or less whole were the belongings of the family, and these possessions were simple almost to the point of nonexistence." Then he divides his scene into quadrants, or sections, so that the readers can orient themselves: "Along one half of the enclosed circle was the low sleeping bench. . . ."

And now he begins his very specific listing of the contents of the tent: the clutter of meat and bones on the floor, the clothing suspended from the poles, the ancient wooden treasure chest.

The scene, of course, tells us much about the people who inhabit it: their poverty, their simplicity, their hospitality, their lack of sanitation.

Descriptions of scenes can be panoramas as well as close-ups.

> . . . Las Vegas is the only town in the world whose skyline is made up neither of buildings, like New York, nor of trees, like Wilbraham, Massachusetts, but signs. One can look at Las Vegas from a mile away on Route 91 and see no buildings, no trees, only signs. But such signs! They tower. They revolve, they oscillate, they soar in shapes before which the existing vocabulary of art history is helpless. I can only attempt to supply names—Boomerang Modern, Palette Curvilinear, Flash Gordon, Ming-Alert Spiral, McDonald's Hamburger Parabola, Mint Casino Elliptical, Miami Beach Kidney.
>
> —Tom Wolfe, *The Kandy-Kolored Tangerine-Flake Streamline Baby*

> On a winter afternoon—a day without a sunrise, under a moon that had not set for six days—I stand on the frozen ocean 20 miles off Cape Mamen, Mackenzie King Island. The sea of ice of Hazen Strait is not completely featureless, but its surface does not show, either, any evidence of severe torture, such as one would find, for example, in the Lincoln Sea. The currents are relatively calm here. During the nine or ten months the water is frozen, this platform hardly moves.
>
> To the south I can see a thin streak of violet and cobalt sky stretching across 80° of the horizon. But the ice and snow barely reflect these colors. The pervasive light here is the milky blue of the reflected moon. It is possible to see two or three miles in the moonlight; but the pale light gives nothing an edge. Except for the horizon to the south, the color of a bruise, the world is only moonlit ice and black sky.
>
> —Barry Lopez, *Arctic Dreams*

Discussion: Scenes in Narration

When he was twelve years old, Jack Henry Abbott was sent to the Utah State Industrial School for boys—in other words, to what is usually called "reform school." Because of an escape attempt, Abbott was sentenced to sixty days in solitary confinement. Here is the scene of that confinement:

We enter a passageway between rows of heavy steel doors. The passage is narrow; it is only four or five feet wide and is dimly lighted. As soon as we enter, I can smell nervous sweat and feel body warmth in the air.

We stop at one of the doors. [The guard] unlocks it. I enter. Nothing is said. He closes and locks the door, and I can hear his steps as he walks down the dark passageway.

In the cell, there is a barred window with an ancient, heavy mesh-steel screen. It is level with the ground outside. The existing windowpanes are caked with decades of soil, and the screen prevents cleaning them. Through the broken ones I peer, running free again in my mind across the fields.

A sheet of thick plywood, on iron legs bolted to the floor, is my bed. An old-fashioned toilet bowl is in the corner, beside a sink with cold running water. A dim light burns in a dull yellow glow behind the thick iron screening attached to the wall.

The walls are covered with names and dates—some of the dates go back twenty years. They were scratched into the wall. There are ragged hearts pierced with arrows and *pachuco* crosses everywhere. Everywhere are the words: "mom," "love," "god"—the walls sweat and are clammy and cold.

—In the Belly of the Beast

1. Which details convey the feeling of isolation and loneliness?
2. Explain why the following statement is (or is not) valid: Abbott uses the same general method to organize his description as does Mowat.
3. What might Abbott have done to create a more vivid scene? For instance, he does not mention colors or smells.

A Suggestion for Writing

Write a description of a scene that is important to you. In relatively short space, you can create a vivid impression of, for instance, your room, a gymnasium, an artist's studio, a garden, a park. . . .

If you are describing a place such as a room, organize your writing so that the reader will be oriented.

What point do you want your description to make? For instance, Mowat's depiction of the inside of the tent tells us much about the life of the Ihalmiut people, and Abbott's description of the solitary confinement cell gives us a sense of what some prisons must be like. Do you want your description to "say" something about you and your values? Do you want it to be a critique of some institution (as is Abbott's)? Do you want to establish a mood? (Horror movies often involve stormy nights, deserted houses, and so on.)

ACTIONS IN NARRATION

Details bring characters to life and make scenes vivid. Verbs and their modifiers make actions live. For example, "The general *raged* at his troops" is more effective than "The general was *very angry* at his troops" because the verb "raged" expresses both the general's mood and his action.

An easy, but ineffective, way out in writing about actions is to use "be" verbs and general verbs of movement. In describing actions, good writers pay careful attention to the effects of their verbs. For example, in the following pair, "tottered" more specifically describes the action of the baby than does the verb "walked":

> The baby walked from the coffee table to the chair.
> The baby *tottered* from the coffee table to the chair.

Dylan Thomas's use of "bounded" and "laden with" is much more effective than the alternative version:

> We ran into the house, carrying snowballs, and stopped at the
> open door of the smoke-filled room.
> We *bounded* into the house, *laden with* snowballs, and stopped at
> the open door of the smoke-filled room.

Maya Angelou could have written that "echoes of the songs *were in* the air," but in fact here is how she expressed her idea:

> While echoes of the song *shivered* in the air, Henry Reed bowed
> his head, said "Thank you," and returned to his place in the line.

Discussion: Actions in Narration

One of the most widely admired and frequently reprinted essays in the English language is "Shooting an Elephant," by George Orwell. Here is one climactic paragraph from that essay:

> When I pulled the trigger I did not hear the bang or feel the kick—one never does when a shot goes home—but I heard the devilish roar of glee that went up from the crowd. In that instant, in too short a time, one would have thought, even for the bullet to get there, a mysterious, terrible change had come over the elephant. He neither stirred nor fell, but every line of his body had altered. He looked suddenly stricken, shrunken, immensely old, as though the frightful impact of the bullet had paralysed

him without knocking him down. At last, after what seemed a long time—it might have been five seconds, I dare say—he sagged flabbily to his knees. His mouth slobbered. An enormous senility seemed to have settled upon him. One could have imagined him thousands of years old. I fired again into the same spot. At the second shot he did not collapse but climbed with desperate slowness to his feet and stood weakly upright, with legs sagging and head drooping. I fired a third time. That was the shot that did for him. You could see the agony of it jolt his whole body and knock the last remnant of strength from his legs. But in falling he seemed for a moment to rise, for as his hind legs collapsed beneath him he seemed to tower upward like a huge rock toppling, his trunk reaching skywards like a tree. He trumpeted, for the first and only time. And then down he came, his belly towards me, with a crash that seemed to shake the ground even where I lay.

1. What words and word groups contribute to the vividness of this narrative? Explain how they do so.
2. What is Orwell's attitude toward his action? How do you know?

A Suggestion for Writing

Think of an important event that you have witnessed recently or have been involved in: for instance, an automobile collision, an important play in a sporting event, the loss of something valuable, the climactic moment of a ceremony (such as a wedding or funeral). Write a brief narrative of that event, making certain that your verbs and their modifiers convey the drama and the image.

NARRATION AS EXPLANATION

Explanation takes place when an expert tells a novice how to do or understand something. Chapter 5 will develop a thoroughgoing discussion of writing that explains. For the moment, we are concerned with using narration in explanations.

In an essay called "Clever Animals," Lewis Thomas, an eminent scientist and chancellor of the Memorial Sloan-Kettering Cancer Center in New York City, stated that "scientists who work on animal behavior are occupationally obliged to live chancier lives than most of their colleagues, always at risk of being fooled by the animals they are studying or, worse, fooling themselves." Laypersons undoubtedly believe Thomas's claim, but they also find it difficult to understand exactly what he means. Therefore,

Thomas tells a story—supplies a narrative—that gives a concrete illustration of the abstract statement:

> The risks are especially high when the scientist is engaged in training the animal to do something or other and must bank his professional reputation on the integrity of his experimental subject. The most famous case in point is that of Clever Hans, the turn-of-the-century German horse now immortalized in the lexicon of behavioral science by the technical term, the "Clever Hans Error." The horse, owned and trained by Herr von Osten, could not only solve complex arithmetical problems, but even read the instructions on a blackboard and tap out infallibly, with one hoof, the right answer. What is more, he could perform the same computations when total strangers posed questions to him, with his trainer nowhere nearby. For several years Clever Hans was studied intensively by groups of puzzled scientists and taken seriously as a horse with something very like a human brain, quite possibly even better than human. But finally in 1911, it was discovered by Professor O. Pfungst that Hans was not really doing arithmetic at all; he was simply observing the behavior of the human experimenter. Subtle, unconscious gestures—nods of the head, the holding of breath, the cessation of nodding when the correct count was reached—were accurately read by the horse as cues to stop tapping.

The abstract concept of the dangers of animal experimentation is now made concrete in a narrative, and readers will remember the narrative and be able to derive the abstract principle from it.

Discussion: Narration as Explanation

The following selection—"Eclipse," by the American writer John Updike—tells a story in order to explore an aspect of human nature. One might say that "Eclipse" is a philosophical essay. After you have read this piece of writing, answer the following questions:

1. What is the "meaning" of the essay? What point is Updike trying to make?
2. Why did he choose to write a narrative rather than a straightforward explanation? What did he gain (or lose) by choosing to tell a story?

Eclipse
John Updike

I went out into the backyard and the usually roundish spots of dappled sunlight underneath the trees were all shaped like feathers, crescent in the same direction, from left to right. Though it was five o'clock on a summer afternoon, the birds were singing goodbye to the day, and their merged song seemed to soak the strange air in an additional strangeness. A kind of silence prevailed. Few cars were moving on the streets of the town. Of my children only the baby dared come into the yard with me. She wore only underpants, and as she stood beneath a tree, bulging her belly toward me in the mood of jolly flirtation she has grown into at the age of two, her bare skin was awash with pale crescents. It crossed my mind that she might be harmed, but I couldn't think how. *Cancer?*

The eclipse was to be over 90 percent in our latitude and the newspapers and television for days had been warning us not to look at it. I looked up, a split-second Prometheus, and looked away. The bitten silhouette of the sun lingered redly on my retinas. The day was half-cloudy, and my impression had been of the sun struggling, amid a furious knotted huddle of black and silver clouds, with an enemy too dreadful to be seen, with an eater as ghostly and hungry as time. Every blade of grass cast a long bluish-brown shadow, as at dawn.

My wife shouted from behind the kitchen screen door that as long as I was out there I might as well burn the wastepaper. She darted from the house, eyes downcast, with the wastebasket, and darted back again, leaving the naked baby and me to wander up through the strained sunlight to the wire trash barrel. After my forbidden peek at the sun, the flames dancing transparently from the blackening paper—yesterday's Boston *Globe*, a milk carton, a Hi-Ho cracker box—seemed dimmer than shadows, and in the teeth of all the warnings I looked up again. The clouds seemed bunched and twirled as if to plug a hole in the sky, and the burning afterimage was the shape of a near-new moon, horns pointed down. It was gigantically unnatural, and I lingered in the yard under the vague apprehension that in some future life I might be called before a cosmic court to testify to this assault. I seemed to be the sole witness. The town around my yard was hushed, all but the singing of the birds, who were invisible. The feathers under the trees had changed direction, and curved from right to left.

Then I saw my neighbor sitting on her porch. My neighbor is a widow, with white hair and brown skin; she has in her yard an aluminum-and-nylon-net chaise longue on which she lies at every opportunity, head back, arms spread, prostrate under the sun. Now she hunched dismally on her porch steps in the shade, which was scarcely darker than the light. I walked toward her and hailed her as a visitor to the moon might salute a survivor of a previous expedition. "How do you like the eclipse?" I called over the fence that distinguished our holdings on this suddenly insubstantial and lunar earth.

"I don't like it," she answered, shading her face with a hand. "They say you shouldn't go out in it."

"I thought it was just you shouldn't look at it."

"There's something in the rays," she explained, in a voice far louder than it needed to be, for silence framed us. "I shut all the windows on that side of the house and had to come out for some air."

"I think it'll pass," I told her.

"Don't let the baby look up," she warned, and turned away from talking to me, as if the open use of her voice exposed her more fatally to the rays.

Superstition, I thought, walking back through my yard, clutching my child's hand as tightly as a good-luck token. There was no question in her touch. Day, night, twilight, noon were all wonders to her, unscheduled, free from all bondage of prediction. The sun was being restored to itself and soon would radiate influence as brazenly as ever—and in this sense my daughter's blind trust was vindicated. Nevertheless, I was glad that the eclipse had passed, as it were, over her head; for in my own life I felt a certain assurance evaporate forever under the reality of the sun's disgrace.

NARRATION AS ARGUMENTATION

When you *explain* something, you don't try to convince your reader, for the reader accepts your authority and wants to be informed. There is no point of disagreement.

When you argue, however, you are attempting not only to inform your reader, but to change his or her opinion. In chapter 6, the nature and uses of argument will be fully discussed. Right now, the point is that narratives—stories—are useful ways of convincing readers.

A common reason advanced for protecting whales and other animals is that they are like human beings. In "Very Like a Whale," Robert Finch argues *against* this argument. "Whales," he says, "have an inalienable right to exist, not because they resemble man *or* because they are useful to him, but simply because . . . they have a proven fitness to the exactitudes of being on a global scale matched by few other species." In fact, as you will discover, Finch is arguing that whales should be protected because they are *unlike* human beings. This moving and convincing essay is largely narration, a story based on personal experience. It is a perfect example of how narration can be used to *convince* readers of a point.

Very Like a Whale
Robert Finch

One day last week at sunset I went back to Corporation Beach in Dennis to see what traces, if any, might be left of the great, dead finback whale that had washed up there several weeks before. The beach was not as hospitable as it had been that sunny Saturday morning after Thanksgiving when thousands of us streamed over the sand to gaze and look. A few cars were parked in the lot, but these kept their inhabitants. Bundled up against a sharp wind, I set off along the twelve-foot swath of trampled beach grass, a raw highway made in a few hours by ten thousand feet that day.

I came to the spot where the whale had beached and marveled that such a magnitude of flesh could have been there one day and gone the next. But the carcass had been hauled off and the tide had smoothed and licked clean whatever vestiges had remained. The cold, salt wind had lifted from the sands the last trace of that pervasive stench of decay that clung to our clothes for days, and now blew clean and sharp into my nostrils.

The only sign that anything unusual had been there was that the beach was a little too clean, not quite so pebbly and littered as the surrounding areas, as the grass above a new grave is always fresher and greener. What had so manifestly occupied this space a short while ago was now utterly gone. And yet the whale still lay heavily on my mind; a question lingered, like a persistent odor in the air. And its dark shape, though now sunken somewhere beneath the waves, still loomed before me, beckoning, asking something.

What was it? What had we seen? Even the several thousand of us that managed to get down to the beach before it was closed off did not see much. Whales, dead or alive, are protected these days under the Federal Marine Mammals Act, and shortly after we arrived, local police kept anyone from actually touching the whale. I could hardly regret this, since in the past beached whales, still alive, have had cigarettes put out in their eyes and bits of flesh hacked off with pocket knives by souvenir seekers. And so, kept at a distance, we looked on while the specialists worked, white-coated, plastic-gloved autopsists from the New England Aquarium, hacking open the thick hide with carving knives and plumbing its depth for samples to be shipped to Canada for analysis and determination of causes of death. What was it they were pulling out? What fetid mystery would they pluck from the huge coffin of dead flesh? We would have to trust them for the answer.

But as the crowds continued to grow around the whale's body like flies around carrion, the question seemed to me, and still seems, not so much why did the whale die, as why had we come to see it? What made this dark bulk such a human magnet, spilling us over onto private lawns and fields? I watched electricians and oil truck drivers pulling their vehicles off the road and clambering down to the beach. Women in high heels and pearls, on their way to Filene's, stumbled through the loose sand to gaze at a corpse. The normal human pattern was broken and a carnival atmosphere was created, appropriate enough in the literal sense of "a farewell to the flesh." But there was also a sense of pilgrimage in those trekking across the beach, an obligation to view such a thing.

But for what? Are we really such novices to death? Or so reverent toward it?

I could understand my own semiprofessional interest in the whale, but what had drawn these hordes? There are some obvious answers, of course: a break in the dull routine, "something different." An old human desire to associate ourselves with great and extraordinary events. We placed children and sweethearts in front of the corpse and clicked cameras. "Ruthie and the whale." "Having a whale of a time on Cape Cod."

Curiosity, the simplest answer, doesn't really answer anything. What, after all, did we learn by being there? We were more like children at a zoo, pointing and poking, or Indians on a pristine beach, gazing in innocent wonder at strange European ships come ashore. Yet, as the biologists looted it with vials and plastic bags and the press captured it on film, the spectators also tried to *make* something of the whale. Circling around it as though for some hold on its slippery bulk, we grappled it with metaphors, lashed similes around its immense girth. It lay upside down, overturned "like a trailer truck." Its black skin was cracked and peeling, red underneath, "like a used tire." The distended, corrugated lower jaw, "a giant accordion," was afloat with the gas of putrefaction and, when pushed, oscillated slowly "like an enormous waterbed." Like our primitive ancestors, we still tend to make images to try to comprehend the unknown.

But what were we looking at? Or more to the point, from what perspective were we looking at it? What did we see in it that might tell us why we had come? A male finback whale—*Balaenoptera physalus*—a baleen cetacean. The second largest creature ever to live on earth. An intelligent and complex mammal. A cause for conservationists. A remarkably adapted swimming and eating machine. Perfume, pet food, engineering oil. A magnificent scientific specimen. A tourist attraction. A media event, a "day to remember." A health menace, a "possible carrier of a communicable disease." A municipal headache and a navigational hazard. Material for an essay.

On the whale's own hide seemed to be written its life history, which we could remark but not read. The right fluke was almost entirely gone, lost in some distant accident or battle and now healed over with a white scar. The red eye, unexpectedly small and mammalian, gazed out at us with fiery blankness. Like the glacial scratches sometimes found on our boulders, there were strange marks or grooves in the skin around the anal area, perhaps caused by scraping the ocean bottom.

Yet we could not seem to scratch its surface. The whale—dead, immobile, in full view—nonetheless shifted kaleidoscopically before our eyes. The following morning it was gone, efficiently and sanitarily removed, like the week's garbage. What was it we saw? I have a theory, though probably (as they say in New England) it hardly does.

There is a tendency these days to defend whales and other endangered animals by pointing out their similarities to human beings. Cetaceans, we are told, are very intelligent. They possess a highly complex language and have developed sophisticated communications systems that transmit over long distances. They form family groups, develop social structures and personal relationships, and express loyalty and affection toward one another. Much of their behavior seems to be recreational: they sing, they play. And so on.

These are not sentimental claims. Whales apparently do these things, at least as far as our sketchy information about their habits warrants such interpretations. And for my money, any argument that helps to preserve these magnificent creatures can't be all bad.

I take exception to this approach not because it is wrong, but because it is wrongheaded and misleading. It is exclusive, anthropocentric, and does not recognize nature in its own right. It implies that whales and other creatures have value only insofar as they reflect man himself and conform to his ideas of beauty and achievement. This attitude is not really far removed from that of the whalers themselves. To consume whales solely for their nourishment of human values is only a step from consuming them for meat and corset staves. It is not only presumptuous and patronizing, but it is misleading and does both whales and men a grave disservice. Whales have an inalienable right to exist, not because they resemble man *or* because they are useful to him, but simply because they do exist, because they have a proven fitness to the exactitudes of being on a global scale matched by few other species. If they deserve our admiration and respect, it is because, as Henry Beston put it, "They are other nations, caught with ourselves in the net of life and time, fellow prisoners of the splendour and travail of life."

But that still doesn't explain the throngs who came pell-mell to stare and conjecture at the dead whale that washed up at Corporation Beach and dominated it for a day like some extravagant *memento mori*. Surely we were not flattering ourselves, consciously or unconsciously, with any human comparisons to that rotting hulk. Nor was there much, in its degenerate state, that it had to teach us. And yet we came—why?

The answer may be so obvious that we have ceased to recognize it. Man, I believe, has a crying need to confront otherness in the universe. Call it nature, wilderness, the "great outdoors," or what you will—we crave to look out and behold something other than our own human faces staring back at us, expectantly and increasingly frustrated. What the human spirit wants, as Robert Frost said, "Is not its own love back in copy-speech, / But counter-love, original response."

This sense of otherness is, I feel, as necessary a requirement to our personalities as food and warmth are to our bodies. Just as an individual, cut off from human contact and stimulation, may atrophy and die of loneliness and neglect, so mankind is today in a similar, though more subtle, danger of cutting himself off from the natural world he shares with all creatures. If our physical survival depends upon our devising a proper use of earth's materials and produce, our growth as a species depends equally upon our establishing a vital and generative relationship with what surrounds us.

We need plants, animals, weather, unfettered shores and unbroken woodland, not merely for a stable and healthy environment, but as an antidote to introversion, a preventive against human inbreeding. Here in particular, in the splendor of natural life, we have an extraordinary reservoir of the Cape's untapped possibilities and modes of being, ways of experiencing life, of knowing wind and wave. After all, how many neighborhoods have whales wash up in their backyards? To confine this world in zoos or in exclusive human terms does injustice not only to nature, but to ourselves as well.

Ever since his beginnings, when primitive man adopted totems and animal spirits to himself and assumed their shapes in ritual dance, *Home sapiens* has been a superbly imitative animal. He has looked out across the fields and seen and learned. Somewhere along the line, though, he decided that nature was his enemy, not his ally, and needed to be confined and controlled. He abstracted nature and lost sight of it. Only now are we slowly realizing that nature can be confined only by narrowing our own concepts of it, which in turn narrows us. That is why we came to see the whale.

We substitute human myth for natural reality and wonder why we starve for nourishment. "Your Cape" becomes "your Mall," as the local radio jingle has it. Thoreau's "huge and real Cape Cod . . . a wild, rank place with no flattery in it," becomes the Chamber of Commerce's "Rural Seaside Charm"—until forty tons of dead flesh wash ashore and give the lie to such thin, flattering conceptions, flesh whose stench is still the stench of life that stirs us to reaction and response. That is why we came to see the whale.

Its mute, immobile bulk represented that ultimate, unknowable otherness that we both seek and recoil from, and shouted at us louder than the policeman's bullhorn that the universe is fraught, not merely with response or indifference, but incarnate assertion.

Later that day the Dennis Board of Health declared the whale carcass to be a "health menace" and warned us off the beach. A health menace? More likely an intoxicating, if strong, medicine that might literally bring us to our senses.

But if those of us in the crowd failed to grasp the whale that day, others did not have much better luck. Even in death the whale escaped us: the tissue samples taken in the autopsy proved insufficient for analysis and the biologists concluded, "We will never know why the whale died." The carcass, being towed tail-first by a Coast Guard cutter for a final dumping beyond Provincetown, snapped a six-inch hawser. Eluding further attempts to reattach it, it finally sank from sight. Even our powers of disposal, it seemed, were questioned that day.

And so, while we are left on shore with the memory of a deflated and stinking carcass and of bullhorns that blared and scattered us like flies, somewhere out beyond the rolled waters and the shining winter sun, the whale sings its own death in matchless, sirenian strains.

Discussion: Narration as Argument

1. Point out details of characters and scene that bring this writing to life for you.
2. What details concerning the whale are most vivid?
3. The answers to the questions "what had drawn these hordes?" and "what were we looking at?" are the main point of the essay. What are the answers? Explain how you know.
4. What other means might Finch have used to develop his argument?
5. In your opinion, is the argument effective or ineffective? Explain.

DISCOVERING IDEAS FOR NARRATION: THE PENTAD

Among teachers of writing there is a standing joke about the unimaginative instructor who assigns students this topic: "what I did during my summer vacation." The equally unimaginative student sweats and struggles for hours, after which agony he or she is able to write nothing more than

> During my summer vacation, I visited Tibet. It was an interesting trip.
> We saw many strange sights, and we enjoyed the Himalayas.
> I hope to return to Tibet some day.

Every time you take a vacation trip, you are flooded with new experiences—sights, tastes; people, architecture; landscape, climate; customs, art; sounds, smells. And yet it would probably be somewhat difficult for you to write a satisfactory narrative of your trip. First, you would need to "sort out" the experience in your own mind, and you would need to make some effort to recall significant details. Second, there is probably data about the trip that you would need to look up. How much did the trip cost? What is the population of a city that you visited? What is the height of a mountain that you climbed?

There would, then, be two sources for your narrative's content: your own memory and such outside sources as encyclopedias, travel books, people who had visited the places you did, and so on.

Any job of writing begins with the problem of discovering subject matter *that will make your writing successful with your readers.* Even if you know your subject thoroughly, you probably need techniques to retrieve your knowledge and to put it into some kind of structure.

Heuristics, which are techniques for discovering ideas or finding solutions to problems, often help writers overcome "stuckedness," not knowing what to say about a subject. These "devices" force you to "walk around" your subject and view it from various angles.

One of the most useful heuristics is the *Pentad,* developed by the American thinker Kenneth Burke. It is a set of five categories that may at first seem very much like the journalist's questions: Who? What? Where? When? Why? How? But the Pentad, though just as simple as these questions, is much more useful.

Burke explains that in order to understand any human action—anything that people do, say, or think—you need relatively complete answers to the following questions:

Act   What was done? People perform acts. When a rock falls off a cliff, a *motion*, not an act, has occurred. Therefore, the term "act" focuses sharply on the human situation. Furthermore, acts are motivated; there is a human reason for them.

Agent   Who did it? This term names the doer of the action and implies a relationship between the act and the doer.

Agency   By what means or with what was it done? We interpret "agency" very broadly. Here are some possibilities: (1) Agency can be language, as the agency for a warning is the sentence "Look out!" (2) Agency can also be some kind of instrument, as in the case of a murder weapon in a detective story. (3) Agency can be logic, as when I convince you of my point of view through logical argumentation. (4) In the case of an article or book, the agency can be the publisher. In short, agency can be anything whereby acts are brought into being.

Scene   Where and when was it done? You can broaden or narrow this term at will. For instance, the seconds during which you read these words; the week in which you read them; the year; the century. The place where you sit as you read these words; the building; the city; the country. But you need not interpret scene literally. It can also be, for instance, the ethical, economic, or political context of an act, as the scene in which the Constitution of the United States was written was "the Age of Enlightenment" or "the Age of Reason."

Purpose   Why was it done? Apparent purpose is not always real purpose. The real purpose of a patent-medicine ad is to sell products, not cure illness. To understand any speech or writing, you must find out the purpose behind it.

Discussion: The Pentad

Can the Pentad help you understand, analyze, and evaluate a piece of writing?

"Very Like a Whale," by Robert Finch, on pages 91–96, is a rather difficult piece of writing. You can use the Pentad to discover how the essay works.

Answer these questions as fully as possible:

1. *What happened? (Act)*   What can I learn about the Act through considering the Agents, the Scene, the Agencies, and the Purpose?
2. *Who are the characters involved? (Agents)*   What can I learn about

them through considering their Acts, the Scene, the Agencies, and the Purpose?

3. *What was the Scene?*   What can I learn about the Scene through considering the Act, Agents, Agency, and Purpose?

4. *What were the Agencies?*   What can I learn about Agencies through considering Act, Agents, Scene, and Purpose?

5. *What was the Purpose?*   What can I learn about Purpose through considering the Act, Agents, Agencies, and Scene?

A Suggestion for Writing

Write a narrative that either *explains* something or *argues* for some point of view. The essay in chapter 2, "Becoming a Reader," explained how one person became "hooked on books." John Updike's narrative (pages 89–91) is about both the uncertainty of human existence and the lingering of superstition; it is actually an explanation. Robert Finch's narrative (pages 91–96) is an argument for a point of view.

The Pentad will help you get started. Try developing the cluster shown here. In the center circle, write the point that you want your narrative to make, as in the drawing. Here are some examples:

1. Through a backpacking trip in the Bob Marshall Wilderness, I learned the value of protecting some areas from all aspects of modern technology (such as off-road vehicles). [The author of this narrative would tell the story of her trip to the wilderness area and through the

story would explain why she believes that protecting these areas is important.]

2. My experiences with the nursing home that took care of my grandmother convinced me that the state government should more strictly regulate health care facilities. [In the narrative of his experiences, the writer would give his reasons for believing that stricter regulation is needed. The author, of course, wants readers who don't think more regulation is called for to change their opinions.]

3. During my trip to Greece, I learned how to choose economical and comfortable hotels. [By telling his story, the author will give his readers information that will help them choose hotels when they travel.]

5

Exposition

Expository writing conveys information and explains ideas and opinions. For example, here is an expository text giving information and explaining how to get to a certain place:

> The Pecatonica Prairie Path is located in northwestern Illinois between Rockford and Freeport. The trail passes through Winnebago, Pecatonica, and Ridott and ends (or begins) at the eastern edge of Freeport. The western end of the trail begins just south of the East River Road and Illinois Route 75 at the east side of Freeport junction (look for a sign marked *Private Drive, No Trespassing* and a trailboard with the trail name on it). Roadways leading to this westernmost point outside of Freeport include north-south Route 26 to Freeport and east-west Route 20.
>
> —Walter G. Zyznieuski and George S. Zyznieuski,
> *Illinois Hiking and Backpacking Trails*

Exposition is the kind of writing that tells you how to do things. In a book titled *Off and Walking,* Ruth Rudner has a chapter called "How to Deal with a Moose and Other Matters" in which she gives this advice:

If an animal is lying or walking in your path, you get out of *its* way. If a moose (or any of the hooved animals) should charge you, either get up a tree or get some trees between you and it. Do not try to outrun it over open ground. You can't. If an animal is not in the process of charging you, do not move suddenly, but talk to it in a reassuring way as you look around for a tree to climb or move slowly out of its world. I don't know for sure what it does for the animal, but the tone should help you.

Reference sources such as encyclopedias and almanacs are expository, providing the reader with information:

MAJOR VENOMOUS ANIMALS

Lizards

Gila monster—up to 24 inches long with heavy body and tail, in high desert in southwest U.S. and N. Mexico; immediate severe pain followed by vomiting, thirst, difficulty swallowing, weakness approaching paralysis; no recent mortality.

Mexican beaded lizard—similar to Gila monster, Mexican west-coast; reaction and mortality rate similar to Gila monster.

—*The World Almanac 1987*

Definitions are expository, as in the following:

asthenic game plan

Asthenic describes a person suffering from fear, loss of general mental functions, and an inability to act decisively. *Game plan* is a much-loved phrase among big business types, probably because its connotations disguise the often Machiavellian, often cruel practices it describes. The *asthenic game plan* is any method employed by a businessman to intimidate a subordinate (most common), a superior (least common), or a rival in line for the same job promotion.

—Joel Homer, "Big Business Talk"

However, the most important use of exposition is *to explain ideas and opinions,* as in the essay that follows. The author, Charles A. Cerami, explains why gold is the basis for money systems and also why, in his opinion, it is not a good investment. As you read this essay (which appeared in the *Atlantic* magazine in January 1980), notice how Cerami uses facts and definition to convey his ideas, and notice also his use of specific examples. Questions for discussion follow the essay.

Why Almost Everyone Is Wrong About Gold
Charles A. Cerami

Several thousand Americans bought English gold sovereigns for $11 or so in the early 1970s. They now find that each one is worth more than $100. Those who bought and saved the Austrian Corona coin, which has nearly a full ounce of gold, paid $50 or $60 for it at that time and now rejoice that the price is well above $300.

The emotions roused by this price movement are multi-faceted enough to mirror the whole economic trauma of the turbulent 1970s:

■ Many who made these felicitous purchases feel a smug confidence in the contents of their safe-deposit boxes; but others wonder if it is time to take their gains and turn the coins back into paper dollars.

■ The greater number of persons who never bought gold feel left out, and some lie awake nights trying to decide whether they should now start buying this apparently invincible metal.

■ U.S. government officials try to ignore the fact that they sold off billions of dollars worth of their country's gold hoard at giveaway prices just before it soared in value.

■ The "gold bugs," who always considered those government officials idiots deserving of impeachment, now declare that gold has proved itself the perfect risk-free investment, that it will shortly move on to $500, $600, and $1000 per ounce.

They are all wrong—the smug, the eager, the dejected, the anti-gold economists, and the fanatics who think that gold is a magic beanstalk which will grow to the sky.

In the short space of the last twenty years, gold has tried to reteach man a lesson that he keeps refusing to absorb: Precious metal is the only real *money* in the world—the only steady standard of value—and being money, it cannot really be an investment at all. It cannot *for long* go up or down in true value. Distortions lasting weeks or a few months are possible. But over the years, it stands very nearly still while everything else around it bobs up and down. We will all be better investors and citizens when this "news" is more widely understood.

The gold bugs who elevate their admiration for gold to the status of a religion have won—but it is a Pyrrhic victory. They will find that while gold is every bit as special as they have claimed, it is not headed for greater heights. It is not headed anywhere. If its value appears to keep rising, that means only that paper money has fallen further—altering the numbers but not the relative values. The length of a yardstick would not change if officials began to put more line markers on football fields. Neither does tampering with currencies and price tags alter the real value of gold. One ounce of it bought about fifteen barrels of oil years ago, and still does. This relationship could change if, for example, the total supply of oil should suddenly swell enormously; but even then, gold's value in relation to the sum total of all world goods would not—*could* not—change appreciably.

To see why this is so, consider what money really is. It is a store of value, of buying power. It has to be something imperishable, savable, easily transportable, plentiful enough to cover the needs of a growing population, but scarce enough to require quite a lot of effort to acquire. And it must be costly to produce. Otherwise, people would just make more of it and spoil its value.

There is nothing mystical that makes gold the ideal money; it is merely a matter of natural accident. Nothing else meets all the criteria quite so neatly. Silver has often served the purpose, but its supply is potentially too erratic to keep values steady. Diamonds are not as uniform, not as divisible into smaller units or usable for so many things. And as for paper "money," it is not money at all—only a warehouse receipt for the metal that a responsible government should keep in storage. Gold's one shortcoming is a scarcity that frustrates the desire of popularly elected governments to buy more favor from more voters. If they were to increase the amount of paper money that they print in a very orderly way—in line with the productivity of their economies—they could keep these paper receipts viable and respectable indefinitely. It has been done for long periods. (The British pound, and consequently Britain's government securities, were a steady store of value for most of the eighteenth and nineteenth centuries. There were lapses during wars and financial crises; each time the Bank of England resolutely went back to holding 100 percent coin or bullion against all notes it issued, making the banknotes "as good as gold.") But in the end, the desire of major governments to please too many people at once results in too much printing of "money." And then, as Voltaire said, "All paper money eventually returns to its intrinsic value—zero."

Discussion

1. In your own words, briefly sum up the essay. What is its main point?
2. Does Cerami give you all the information you need in order to understand what he is explaining? If not, point out the spots in the essay where the author provides too little information. (Remember the principle of *quantity*, discussed on pages 11–14.)

3. Do you think that Cerami knows what he's talking about? That is, do you think that his information and opinions are reliable? How do you know? (Where was the essay originally published? Does this source of publication have any influence on your judgment concerning Cerami's reliability?) (Remember the principle of *quality,* discussed on pages 11–14.)

4. What do you think Cerami's purpose was in writing the essay? What did he want this piece of writing to *do?*

5. What sort of reader do you think Cerami had in mind when he wrote the piece? (Was he aiming at educated readers? At any economic class? A political group? A religious group?) Explain your opinion.

6. What facts did Cerami present? What purpose did these facts serve?

7. Which term did Cerami define? Why was the definition necessary?

FROM WRITER TO READER

A point that has now been made several times in this book is the obligation that the writer has to the reader—or, to state the matter another way, the expectations that the reader has of the writer. Relying on the work of the philosopher H. P. Grice, we can summarize the writer-reader transaction in this way:

Readers expect the writer to

1. give them all the information that they need in order to understand the text, but no extraneous information
2. know his or her subject and be truthful
3. be as clear as possible
4. stick to the point

It will be useful to keep the terms of this "contract" in mind as we discuss methods of developing ideas in exposition, the writer's credibility, and methods of organization.

DEVELOPING EXPOSITORY WRITING

This section will explain and illustrate some of the ways in which writers develop their ideas for readers. The discussion is not meant to be a "cookbook" of ingredients for exposition, but focuses attention on some of the ways in which expert writers achieve their purposes—how writers give readers the information needed for understanding.

Facts

In chapter 4, we saw that details bring narration to life. For example, this passage from *Pilgrim at Tinker Creek,* by Annie Dillard, "works" because it is packed with detail:

> It [the Polyphemus moth] was a male; his long antennae were thickly plumed, as wide as his fat abdomen. His body was very thick, over an inch long, and deeply furred. A gray, furlike plush covered his head; a long, tan furlike hair hung from his wide thorax over his brown-furred, segmented abdomen. His multijointed legs, pale and powerful, were shaggy as a bear's.

Without the sensory detail, we would have no reason to be interested in the moth.

Facts have at least two uses in writing: to "prove" points and to clarify ideas.

In a book titled *Illiterate America,* Jonathan Kozol portrays the consequences of an inability to read and write, and he does so largely with large bodies of facts concerning unemployment, economic status, family stability, and other indications of success or failure in the American system. In the following paragraph, Kozol uses statistics to back up his argument that when a large proportion of citizens are illiterate, there can be no democracy:

> The number of illiterate adults exceed by 16 million the entire vote cast for the winner in the 1980 presidential contest. If even one third of all illiterates could vote, and read enough and do sufficient math to vote in their self-interest, Ronald Reagan would not likely have been chosen president. There is, of course, no way to know for sure. We do know this: Democracy is a mendacious term when used by those who are prepared to countenance the forced exclusion of one third of our electorate. So long as 60 million people are denied significant participation, the government is neither of, nor for, nor by, the people. It is a government, at best, of those two thirds whose wealth, skin color, or parental privilege allows them opportunity to profit from the provocation and instruction of the written word.

On the other hand, Mark Twain has no need to argue in favor of his statement that "the Mississippi is well worth reading about. It is not a commonplace river, but on the contrary is in all ways remarkable." He goes on to pile up facts to illustrate his statement that the river is "in all ways remarkable":

> Considering the Missouri its main branch, it is the longest river in the world—four thousand three hundred miles. It seems safe to say that

it is the crookedest river in the world, since in one part of its journey it uses up one thousand three hundred miles to cover the same ground that the crow could fly over in six hundred and seventy-five. It discharges three times as much water as the St. Lawrence, twenty-five times as much as the Rhine, and three hundred and thirty-eight times as much as the Thames. No other river has so vast a drainage basin; it draws its water supply from twenty-eight states and territories; from Delaware on the Atlantic seaboard, and from all the country between that and Idaho on the Pacific slope—a spread of forty-five degrees of longitude. The Mississippi receives and carries to the Gulf water from fifty-four subordinate rivers that are navigable by steamboats, and from some hundreds that are navigable by flats and keels. The area of its drainage basin is as great as the combined areas of England, Wales, Scotland, Ireland, France, Spain, Portugal, Germany, Austria, Italy, and Turkey; and almost all this wide region is fertile; the Mississippi valley, proper, is exceptionally so.

—Life on the Mississippi

Facts, then, don't mean grubbiness. In *Life on the Mississippi,* Mark Twain talks about the Mississippi as the mythic central artery of America and about the time he spent on it as the most glorious period of his life; the book is largely prose poetry. But the facts and nothing but the facts contribute to the overall impression that our most American of American authors achieves in this magnificent work.

Examples

Examples clarify ideas and give them concreteness and specificity.

In a book called *Class,* Paul Fussell talks about—and pokes fun at—the class system in the United States. In the following paragraph, he uses an example to illustrate how much one can learn about class at the cocktail hour:

There is hardly a richer single occasion for class revelation than the cocktail hour, since the choice of any drink, and the amount consumed, resonates with status meaning. For example: if you are a middle-aged person and you ask for white wine—the sweeter it is, by the way, the lower your host and hostess—you are giving off a very specific signal identifying yourself as upper- or upper-middle class. You're saying that of course you used to booze a lot on expensive hard liquor, a habit mastered at a socially OK college, but that now, having been brought to the brink of alcoholism by your attractive excesses, you are bright enough to shift your style in midlife and drink something "milder." (The reputation of dry white wine as the lowest calorically of drinks also recommends it to the thin-obsessed.) So many classy people have now forgone hard liquor that there's a whole new large group of upper- and upper-middle-class white-wine drunks who, because they are seen to be knocking back only something light and sensible, hope that their swayings and stammerings will pass unnoticed. One of their favorite tipples is Italian Soave, which is cheap, readily available, and pronounceable, while remaining foreign enough to qualify as a conspicuous import and thus a high-class item. Frascati is another favorite. Asking for Perrier (upper) or club soda (middle), while others are consuming alcohol, delivers a message similar to asking for white wine. It says: "I am grand and desirable for two reasons: first, I used to drink heavily, and thus formerly was funny, careless, and adventuresome, etc.; and second, I had the sense to give it up, and am thus both intelligent and disciplined. Further, I am at the moment your social superior, because, sober, I'm watching you get drunk, and I can assure you that you are a pathetic spectacle."

Of course, Fussell is writing ironically, but examples often advance completely serious arguments. In *Gödel, Escher, Bach,* Douglas R. Hofstadter discusses artificial intelligence (that is, creating programs that allow computers to "think" like human beings). One important concept for artificial intelligence is "almost" situations, which are better exemplifed than explained. In the following passage, note how Hofstadter uses examples to clarify his concept:

> After reading *Contrafactus,* a friend said to me, "My uncle was almost president of the U.S.!" "Really?" I said. "Sure," he replied, "he was skipper of the PT 108." (John F. Kennedy was skipper of the PT 109.)
>
> That is what *Contrafactus* is all about. In everyday thought, we are constantly manufacturing mental variants on situations we face, ideas we have, or events that happen, and we let some features stay exactly the same while others "slip." What features do we let slip? What events are perceived on some deep intuitive level as being close relatives of ones that really happened? What do we think "almost" happened or "could have" happened, even though it unambiguously did not? What alternative versions of events pop without any conscious thought into our minds when we hear a story? Why do some counterfactuals strike as "less counterfactual" than other counterfactuals? After all, it is obvious that anything that didn't happen didn't happen. There aren't degrees of "didn't-happen-ness." And the same goes for "almost" situations. There are times when one plaintively says, "It almost happened," and other times when one says the same thing, full of relief. But the "almost" lies in the mind, not in the external facts.
>
> Driving down a country road, you run into a swarm of bees. You don't just duly take note of it; the whole situation is immediately placed in perspective by a swarm of "replays" that crowd into your mind.

Typically, you think, "Sure am lucky my window wasn't open"—or worse, the reverse: "Too bad my window wasn't closed!" "Lucky I wasn't on my bike!" "Too bad I didn't come along five seconds earlier." Strange but possible replays: "If that had been a deer, I could have been killed!" "I bet those bees would have rather had a collision with a rosebush." Even stranger replays: "Too bad those bees weren't dollar bills!" "Lucky those bees weren't made of cement!" "Too bad it wasn't just one bee instead of a swarm." "Lucky I wasn't the swarm instead of being me." What slips naturally and what doesn't—and why?

In a recent issue of *The New Yorker* magazine, the following excerpt from the "Philadelphia Welcomat" was reprinted:

> If Leonardo da Vinci had been born a female the ceiling of the Sistine Chapel might never have been painted.
>
> [The editors of *The New Yorker* commented:] And if Michelangelo had been Siamese twins, the work would have been completed in half the time.

The point of *The New Yorker's* comments is not that such counterfactuals are *false;* it is more that anyone who would entertain such an idea—anyone who would "slip" the sex or number of a given human being—would have to be a little loony. . . . What is it about the way we classify events and people that makes us know deep down what is "sensible" to slip, and what is "silly"?

And, of course, the point here is that artificially intelligent machines would need to have this same kind of knowledge.

Analogies

In chapter 3, *analogy* was defined like this: "The analogy, an extremely useful device for thinkers and writers, is simply the comparing of an unknown or imperfectly known thing or concept to something that is known." Through this comparison, the unknown is explained to the reader.

In the following discussion, from "If the Weapons Are So Smart, How Come Radar Can Find Them?" by Thomas Amlie, the author uses two analogies to clarify his point—and notice also, by the way, that he uses an example. The analogies are italicized.

> . . . radar is a double-edged sword, and increasingly the use of it endangers the very weapons that depend on it. This issue—the extreme vulnerability of systems that radiate strong and distinctive signals—has been thoroughly understood by specialists since World War II, but largely overlooked by just about everyone else—except the Soviets.
>
> Radars emit powerful and very distinctive pulses of electromagnetic energy. There is a tremendous asymmetry between the distance

at which a radar can detect a target and the distance at which a relatively simple "listening" apparatus can detect the radar.

For instance, a typical fighter aircraft radar might be designed to detect another fighter at 50 miles range but a simple receive-only system can detect and classify radar at, literally, thousands of miles, assuming, of course, that line-of-sight conditions prevail. *Those readers who have "fuzzbusters" in their automobiles will understand this point immediately. The police have changed their tactics in order to defeat the fuzzbusters; the Pentagon has not.*

An exact analogy that might make this difference more understandable is to *imagine a man with a powerful flashlight trying to find another man on a dark night. He might find him at 100 to 200 feet. The other man can see the flashlight at a range of at least one-half mile. To pursue the analogy a bit further, if the second man has an automatic rifle and homicidal tendencies, the fellow with the flashlight could be in deep trouble.*

Norman Mailer was exactly the right person to give the most complete journalistic account of the first flight to the moon. *Of a Fire on the Moon* is a classic in its own day, a wonderfully skillful interpretation of both the technical and the mythic accomplishment of perching three men atop a giant firecracker (as Mailer termed the rocket) and propelling them out into space on a voyage that unbound humanity from earth. Here are two paragraphs in which Mailer uses analogy to explain the command module of *Apollo 11* to the reader:

To speak of a self-contained universe when one is dealing with a vehicle which is self-sustaining for a short period is to trespass on the meaning. A man is a universe by that measure, indeed he is more self-sustained in his ability to adapt and survive than the ship of *Apollo 11*. In fact the Command Module is more like the sort of universe complete in itself one glimpses in a flower cut for a vase. Such an ornament receives food, breathes, exudes, molts, can even preside over a fresh development like the opening of a bud, and presumably this cut flower is capable of sending and receiving messages from other flowers and plants (if such communication is one of the functions of a flower) but still! we know the flower will live only a few days. It is a self-contained universe whose continuation is sealed off from itself.

The same was true of the Command Module. The men in it could live no longer than there were supplies of oxygen for them to breathe, and that was for two weeks. Nonetheless, *Apollo 11* was more a cosmic expression than an ornament. Its vase was space, and through space it traveled, a ship, a species of man-made comet, a minuscule planet with an ability to steer. . . .

One more analogy, this one again from *Life on the Mississippi:*

But I am wandering from what I was intending to do; that is, make plainer than perhaps appears in the previous chapters some of the peculiar requirements of the science of piloting steamboats on the Mississippi. First of all, there is one faculty which a pilot must incessantly cultivate until he has brought it to absolute perfection. Nothing short of perfection will do. That faculty is memory. He cannot stop with merely thinking a thing is so and so; he must *know* it; for this is eminently one of the "exact" sciences. With what scorn a pilot was looked upon, in the old times, if he ever ventured to deal in that feeble phrase "I think," instead of the vigorous one, "I know!" One cannot easily realize what a tremendous thing it is to know every trivial detail of twelve hundred miles of river and know it with absolute exactness. If you will take the longest street in New York, and travel up and down it, conning its features patiently until you know every house and window and lamppost and big and little sign by heart, and know them so accurately that you can instantly name the one you are abreast of when you are set down at random in that street in the middle of the night, you will then have a tolerable notion of the amount and exactness of a pilot's knowledge who carries the Mississippi River in his head. And then, if you will go on until you know every street-crossing, the character, size, and position of the crossing stones, and the varying depth of mud in each of these numberless places, you will have some idea of what the pilot must know in order to keep a Mississippi steamer out of trouble. Next, if you will take half the signs in that long street, and *change their places* once a month, and still manage to know their new positions accurately on dark nights, and keep up with these repeated changes without making any mistakes, you will understand what is required of a pilot's peerless memory by the fickle Mississippi.

Definition

We have seen two examples of definition: (1) of "asthenic game plan," on page 102, and (2) of "money," in "Why Almost Everyone Is Wrong About Gold," page 104.

The reason for defining "asthenic game plan" is obvious: very few readers could be expected to know the meaning of the term. Though every reader could be expected to have a definition for "money," Cerami wanted to give the word a special meaning that most readers would not be aware of ("a store of value, of buying power").

The need for definition—like the need for other kinds of information in writing—depends on the audience. If, for instance, you were reading the program notes for a performance of the American Ballet Theater and found such words as *arabesque, glissade, pas de deux,* you, like many other members of the audience, would need definitions of these technical terms. In the notes, a skillful writer probably would give parenthetical definitions: *arabesque* (a graceful posture in which one leg is raised and extended behind the body); *glissade* (a sliding step performed to the side); *pas de deux* (dance performed by two partners).

Key words in writing often need extended definitions, as in the following example, which gives the meaning and traces the history of "laid-back":

> What is "laid-back" anyway?
>
> The term originated in and derives its only precise meaning from the drug culture. If one was high enough frequently enough, chances are one was not going to be in a state of tension or acceleration or even in a straight-up position but, rather, laid-back. Taking on a broader meaning, it began to describe a mood of being easygoing and convincingly unconcerned with the power-money-fame-success game. The laid-back style crystalized in southern California in the early Seventies. It has since spread across the country and put many young men in a brand-new bind, contending as they must with the new duality problem—of success or personal freedom—while putting themselves through the necessary contortions to hide the old ambition on their sleeves.
>
> —Gail Sheehy, "The Laid-Back Philosophy"

Classification

Classification is the logical process of breaking any set into its component parts and identifying those parts. A wonderful example of this process, its purposes, and its results is *The Audubon Society Field Guide to North American Wildflowers,* in which 666 major species within 99 families are classified and described in such a way that users of the guide can readily identify the wildflowers that they come across in their wanderings. In fact, the book is an 862-page exercise in classification, of which the following is a brief example:

Simple-shaped Flowers:	The individual flowers tend to stand out separately; most flowers are radially symmetrical, usually with 4 or 5 petals (occasionally 3 or 6).
Daisy- and Dandelion-like Flowers:	Flower head with a button-like center and many radiating, strap-like petals (actually ray flowers) or flowers with many rays and no button-like center.
Odd-shaped Flowers:	Flowers or plants with an unusual overall appearance (generally bilaterally symmetrical), often difficult to classify in terms of shape.
Elongated Clusters:	Elongated masses of flowers either tightly or somewhat loosely arranged along the stalk; individual flowers may be symmetrical or asymmetrical.

| Rounded Clusters: | Rounded masses of flowers either tightly or somewhat loosely arranged on a stalk; individual flowers may be symmetrical or asymmetrical. |
| Vines, Shrubs and Trees: | Climbers, and woody plants with one or many stems. |

As you can see, whole pieces of writing—books, reports, essays—can be, and often must be, based on classification. If you are dealing with a set, the way in which you classify the members of the group will determine the organization of your writing.

Comparison and Contrast

Recently my family decided that we desperately need a van so that all of us—from Great Grandmother to little Christopher—can take trips together. Like other car buyers, I wanted the best value for my money, so I purchased the Consumer Guide volume *Rating the 1987 Autos,* which is nothing more than a detailed comparison and contrast of makes and models. Here is some of the useful information that I found:

> Voyager's 4-cylinder engines lack the power and acceleration of V-6 engines available on GM and Ford compact vans and that has been the biggest drawback. The new Mitsubishi V-6 coming next spring should remedy that problem, though we haven't yet driven a Voyager with that engine, so that we can't say how much difference it will make.

Comparison (indicating the similarities of two items) and contrast (indicating differences) are also useful in dealing with abstractions, as does Stephen Jay Gould in an essay that explains two versions of the theory of evolution, that of Lamarck and that of Charles Darwin. In the following paragraphs, notice how Gould points out the main similarity between the two theories and then clarifies the main difference (and also notice, by the way, how he uses definition and examples):

> Darwin's theory of natural selection is more complex than Lamarckism because it requires *two* separate processes, rather than a single force. Both theories are rooted in the concept of *adaptation*—the idea that organisms respond to changing environments by evolving a form, function, or behavior better suited to these new circumstances. Thus, in both theories, information from the environment must be transmitted to organisms. In Lamarckism, the transfer is direct. An organism perceives the environmental change, responds in the "right" way, and passes its appropriate reaction directly to its offspring.

Darwinism, on the other hand, is a two-step process, with different forces responsible for variation and direction. Darwinians speak of genetic variation, the first step, as "random." This is an unfortunate term because we do not mean random in the mathematical sense of equally likely in all directions. We simply mean that variation occurs with no preferred orientation in adaptive directions. If temperatures are dropping and a hairier coat would aid survival, genetic variation for greater hairiness does not begin to arise with increased frequency. Selection, the second step, works upon *unoriented* variation and changes a population by conferring greater reproductive success upon advantageous variants.

This is the essential difference between Lamarckism and Darwinism—for Lamarckism is, fundamentally, a theory of *directed* variation. If hairy coats are better, animals perceive the need, grow them, and pass the potential to offspring. Thus, variation is directed automatically toward adaptation and no second force like natural selection is needed. Many people do not understand the essential role of directed variation in Lamarckism. They often argue: isn't Lamarckism true because environment does influence heredity—chemical and radioactive mutagens increase the mutation rate and enlarge a population's pool of genetic variation. This mechanism increases the *amount* of variation but does not propel it in favored directions. Lamarckism holds that genetic variation originates *preferentially* in adaptive directions.

—"Shades of Lamarck," from *The Panda's Thumb*

Cause and Effect

Expository writing often attempts to answer the question "Why did such and such happen?" In an essay titled "The Ghost Continent," Loren Eiseley, anthropologist and man of letters, advances an explanation (cause) for the violence and chaos of our age (effect). After you have read the selection, in your own words explain the cause and effect that Eiseley advances.

Ours is certainly the most time-conscious generation that has ever lived. Our cameras, our television, our archaeological probings, our C^{14} datings, pollen counts, under-water researches, magnetometer readings have resurrected lost cities, placing them accurately in stratigraphic succession. Each Christmas season the art of ice age Lascaux is placed beside that of Rembrandt on our coffee tables. Views of Pompeii share honors with Chichén Itzá upon the television screen in the living room. We unearth obscure ancestral primates and, in the motion picture "2001," watch a struck fragment of bone fly into the air and become a spaceship drifting among the stars, thus telescoping in an instant the whole technological history of man. We expect the average onlooker to comprehend the symbolism; such a civilization, one must assume, should show a deep veneration for the past.

Strangely the results are quite otherwise. We appear to be living, instead, amidst a meaningless mosaic of fragments. From ape skull to Mayan temple we contemplate the miscellaneous debris of time like sightseers to whom these mighty fragments, fallen gateways, and sunken galleys convey no present instruction.

In our streets and on our campuses there riots an extremist minority dedicated to the now, to the moment, however absurd, degrading, or irrelevant the moment may be. Such an activism deliberately rejects the past and is determined to start life anew—indeed, to reject the very institutions that feed, clothe, and sustain our swarming millions.

A yearning for a life of noble savagery without the accumulated burdens of history seems in danger of engulfing a whole generation, as it did the French *philosophes* and their eighteenth-century followers. Those individuals who persist in pursuing the mind-destroying drug of constant action have not alone confined themselves to an increasingly chaotic present—they are also, by the deliberate abandonment of their past, destroying the conceptual tools and values that are the means of introducing the rational into the oncoming future.

Their world, therefore, becomes increasingly the violent, unpredictable world of the first men simply because, in losing faith in the past, one is inevitably forsaking all that enables man to be a planning animal. For man's story, in brief, is essentially that of a creature who has abandoned instinct and replaced it with cultural tradition and the hard-won increments of contemplative thought. The lessons of the past have been found to be a reasonably secure instruction for proceeding against the unknown future. To hurl oneself recklessly without method upon a future that we ourselves have complicated is a sheer nihilistic rejection of all that history, including the classical world, can teach us.

Suggestions for Writing

1. Write a brief essay that uses facts and data to "fill out" the following statement: *It is not a commonplace _____, but on the contrary is in all ways remarkable.* You, of course, can fill in the blank with anything you choose. For a model, see the passage by Mark Twain on pages 106–07.
2. Write an analogy in which you use something familiar to your readers to explain something that is unfamiliar to them. For models of analogies, see pages 109–11.
3. Write an extended definition of a term that your readers would be unlikely to know—some bit of specialized jargon from your field of study or from a sport; some term that your in-group (family, circle of friends) uses but that would be unfamiliar to your readers.

4. Choose a set or group with which you are familiar and write a classification of the members of the group.
5. Compare and contrast two items, ideas, places, and so on.

STRUCTURE

Writers need to consider not only the subject matter but how it can best be arranged to achieve its purpose.

The Gist

In trying to make sense of a text, readers search for the main idea, the *gist,* and try to find how all the parts of the text relate to that gist. Schematically, the perfectly structured essay could be diagrammed as a "branching tree," like this:

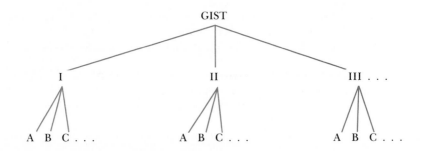

and so on, with points I, II, and III directly relating to and establishing the gist and the A, B, and C points relating to and establishing the I, II, and III points.

This means that IN MOST CASES, *the pivot or center of gravity for a text is its gist.* Whether or not the gist is directly stated, it serves as the hub for organization of the text.

The *gist,* or main point, of "Why Almost Everyone Is Wrong About Gold" is

> The value of precious metal, the only real money, never changes.

Everything else in the essay relates either directly or indirectly to that idea (thesis, topic, or whatever term one chooses to apply). The essay might be "treed" like this:

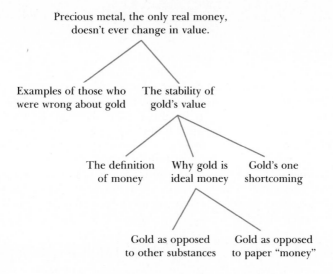

This "tree" does not represent the *sequence* of parts in the essay, but the way they add up to make a coherent whole. For example, we don't find the gist until the eighth paragraph.

When you write exposition, you should be able to state your gist, and you should be able to explain how all the points in your text relate to the gist. In other words, *you should be able to "tree" your text.* You may not be able clearly to define your main point until the writing is well under way, but in revising you should make certain that everything in the text relates to that main point.

Discussion: "Treeing"

Do a tree of "Very Like a Whale," by Robert Finch, in chapter 4, pages 91–96. The tree will begin with a one-sentence statement of Finch's main point.

Beginnings

In expository writing, three sorts of beginnings are common: a statement of the main point of the text immediately; a statement of the main point after a lead-in to gain the reader's interest; and an *abstract.*

The fourth chapter of *The Mind's New Science,* a book by Howard Gardner, about the development of cognitive psychology, is titled "Reason, Experience, and the Status of Philosophy." Gardner begins the chapter by telling his readers what the chapter will contain:

> In this chapter I begin my survey of the cognitive sciences by examining the history and current status of philosophy. This choice is appropriate. Not only is philosophy the oldest of the cognitive sciences, but its epistemological branch has supplied the initial agenda—the list of issues and topics upon which empirically oriented cognitive scientists are working today. Indeed, philosophers have wrestled for centuries with such currently fashionable issues as the nature of mental representation, the extent to which human thought is merely a mechanical (as opposed to a spiritual) process, and the relationship between reason and feeling.

We know, then, that Gardner will deal with the ways in which philosophers have dealt with problems that now concern cognitive scientists, and we have examples of those problems.

However, Gardner begins his seventh chapter quite differently, with this paragraph:

> At first reading, one of the most famous sentences of twentieth-century science makes little everyday sense. This is Noam Chomsky's oxymoronic proposition "Colorless green ideas sleep furiously." After all, ideas don't have colors, ideas don't sleep, something can't be simultaneously colorless and green—and for that matter, what does it mean for any entity to sleep furiously?

This opening paragraph arouses the reader's curiosity. How will Gardner answer the questions that he poses? Why is Chomsky's sentence one of the most famous in twentieth-century science?

In the seventh chapter, Gardner explains the relationship of work in modern linguistics to the field of cognitive science, and the linguist Noam Chomsky used the famous sentence to illustrate some principles about linguistics. Thus, in the chapter, the reader finds the significance of the first paragraph.

An advantage of starting with a statement of your main point is that readers find it easier to understand the details as they read, for they will know how the parts relate to the point that the writer is trying to make.

Technical and scientific papers often begin with *abstracts,* which are simply brief summaries of the contents of the texts. For example, here is the abstract of a paper from *Written Communication,* a scholarly journal:

[1] This essay is an extension of recent research on nonacademic writing and represents an initial effort to explore the contexts for the letters citizens send their legislators. [2] It focuses on only one aspect of this writing—its value. [3] Most of the information in the essay comes from interviews with the author's state and national legislators and/or their staff. [4] This essay suggests why the letters about political issues and personal concerns that citizens send their legislators are of great value to both the writer and the reader, and why the relationship between citizens and their public officials as writers and readers may deserve more intensive exploration.

> —Sandra Stotsky, "Writing in a Political Context"

From the abstract we learn (1) what the study is about, (2) the exact focus of the study, (3) the way in which the study was carried out, and (4) the significance of the study. With this much information, we can decide whether or not the details of the paper will be useful to us, and if we do decide to read the paper we will have a general idea of the contents and therefore will find it easier to understand the details.

Abstracts are important in scholarly writing, for they help readers determine whether or not the detailed contents of the texts will be useful.

Summaries are useful not only in scholarly and scientific writing, but also in other kinds of texts, such as "The Reach of the Imagination," by Jacob Bronowski, which begins thus:

> For three thousand years, poets have been enchanted and moved and perplexed by the power of their own imagination. In a short and summary essay I can hope at most to lift one small corner of that mystery; and yet it is a critical corner. I shall ask, What goes on in the mind when we imagine? You will hear from me that one answer to this question is fairly specific: which is to say, that we can describe the working of the imagination. And when we describe it as I shall do, it becomes plain that imagination is a perfectly *human* gift. To imagine is the characteristic act, not of the poet's mind, or of the painter's, or the scientist's, but of the mind of man.

With that statement, we know the *gist* of Bronowski's text; the text itself gives us the details.

But, of course, efficiency in its narrowest sense isn't always desirable. (Who, after all, wants to read an "efficient" novel or go on an "efficient" picnic?) You may want to capture your reader's interest by starting with a story, an *anecdote*, that leads into the body of the discussion:

> Not long ago I was at work in my study writing, when, as was her custom, the lady across the way burst into song. There was something about that lady's voice which prevented the use of human intelligence, and I called upon the janitor to give her my compliments and then silence her. She replied with a good deal of conviction that this was a free country and she would sing when the spirit moved her; if I did not like it, I could retire to the great open spaces.
>
> —Walter Lippmann, "The Nature of the Battle over Censorship"

In the following example, Susanne K. Langer, author of the important book *Philosophy in a New Key,* briefly outlines a problem and then asks a question that her essay will answer. We might call this the *problem-question beginning.* (Langer is writing about World War II.)

> The world is aflame with man-made public disasters, artificial rains of brimstone and fire, planned earthquakes, cleverly staged famines and floods. The Lord of Creation is destroying himself. He is throwing down the cities he has built, the works of his own hand, the wealth of many thousand years in his frenzy of destruction, as a child knocks down its own handiwork, the whole day's achievement in a tantrum of tears and rage.
>
> What has displeased the royal child? What has incurred his world-shattering tantrum?

It is even possible, but somewhat dangerous, to begin with a brief, but original, *generality* that will be supported in detail by the rest of the essay:

> America appears to be the only country in the world where love is a national problem.
>
> —Raoul de Roussy de Sales, "Love in America"

Shifting our focus a bit, we might ask: What do beginnings *do?* What do they accomplish?

The abstract (as in the case of the scholarly paper by Sandra Stotsky) gives the reader a preview of the body of the text, making it easier to get through a detailed report on research, a utilitarian function. Bronowski's statement of his gist serves much the same function as the abstract, though less formally. Lippmann's anecdote is amusing, catching our interest and establishing a tone of familiarity with the writer; it gets us into his subject obliquely. Langer's grave, ominous beginning not only announces her subject but establishes an almost oracular mood. And de Sales's witty generality leads us to expect a cynical analysis of love American style.

The point is this: *beginnings accomplish two purposes.*

1. They get the discussion under way, and
2. they establish a tone.

And the concept of *tone* leads us to the next phase of our inquiry regarding exposition.

TONE AND DICTION

Tone is the attitude that the writer expresses toward his or her subject. The tone of an essay on, for instance, American funeral customs might be serious, ironic, comic, morbid, straightforward and factual, argumentative, melancholy, joyful. . . .

The main factor in tone is *diction,* the words that the writer chooses. (Diction is discussed in chapter 13, pages 390–400, and in the "Reference Guide," pages 469–85.) For one kind of writing, an author may choose one type of vocabulary, perhaps slang, and for another the same writer may choose an entirely different set of words. Sometimes, to get a special effect, a writer may mix the kinds of words he or she chooses, as Norman Mailer mixes formal and informal language in the following example from *The Armies of the Night:*

> Another student came by, then another. One of them, slight, with a sharp face, wearing a sport shirt and dark glasses, had the appearance of a Hollywood hustler, but that was misleading; he wore the dark glasses because his eyes were still weak from the mace squirted in them by police at Oakland. This student had a Berkeley style which Mailer did not like altogether: it was cocky, knowledgeable, and quick to mock the generations over thirty. Predictably, this was about the first item on which the kid began to scold the multitude. "You want to come along with us," he told the Over-Thirties, "that's okay, that's your thing, but we've got our thing, and we're going to do it alone whether you come with us or not." Mailer always wanted to give a kick into the seat of all reflection when he was told he had his thing—one did not look forward to a revolution which would substitute "thing" for better words.

Notice Mailer's use of such informal or slang words as "hustler" and "kid" alongside words like "appearance" (instead of *look*), "knowledgeable" (instead of *savvy*), or "predictably" (instead of the phrase *as you could've guessed*).

Even such small matters as contractions make a difference in tone, the contracted verbs being less formal:

> *It is* strange that the professor *had not* assigned any papers for three weeks.
>
> *It's* strange that the professor *hadn't* assigned any papers for three weeks.

Specialized jargon is another problem in diction. Often, vocabulary that is perfectly familiar to members of a profession or social group is unknown by outsiders. Thus, if you were an expert on foods of the world and were writing for other experts, the following would be quite acceptable:

> The dinner began with *billi bi,* followed by *maste khiar.* The main course was *moussaka à la grecque,* and for dessert our host served *riz à l'impératrice.*

However, you would need to "translate" if you were writing for nonexperts:

> The dinner began with a rich seafood soup, followed by sliced cucumbers with yogurt. The main course was an eggplant and lamb casserole, and for dessert our host served rice and cherry pudding.

Exercise

Using formal diction, write a paragraph concerning a serious subject, such as marriage or a religious custom. Then substitute informal diction or slang for words in the paragraph, thus creating a comic or ironic tone. (When you handle a serious subject informally or with slang, the result is often comic or ironic.) Here is an example:

> It is a custom in America to have a "viewing" of a body the evening before the funeral. After the corpse has been embalmed, the morticians apply cosmetics to make it appear lifelike. It is then dressed and placed in a coffin. The viewing takes place in what is often called a "slumber room," where friends and relatives come to pay their respects and to bid farewell to the loved one.

> Americans have the custom of "viewing" stiffs before they're planted. The mortician stuffs the corpse and paints it up. It's dressed up in its best

duds and stuck into a coffin, after which it's wheeled to what is called a "slumber room" so that friends and relatives can gawk at it.

For an example of a brilliant handling of tone, read the following selection:

The Kitchen Revolution
Verta Mae Smart-Grosvenor

there is confusion in the kitchen!
we've got to develop kitchen consciousness or we may very well see the end of kitchens as we now know them. kitchens are getting smaller. in some apts the closet is bigger than the kitchen. something that i saw the other day leads me to believe that there may   5
well be a subversive plot to take kitchens out of the home and put them in the street. i was sitting in the park knitting my old man a pair of socks for next winter when a tall well dressed man in his mid thirties sat next to me.
i didnt pay him no mind until he went into his act.   10
he pulled his irish linen hankie from his lapel, spread it on his lap, opened his attache case, took out a box, popped a pill, drank from his thermos jug, and turned and offered the box to me. thank you no said i. "i never eat with strangers."
that would have been all except that i am curious black and i looked   15
at the label on the box, then i screamed. the box said INSTANT LUNCH PILL; (imitation ham and cheese on rye, with diet cola, and apple pie flavor). i sat frozen while he did his next act. he folded his hankie, put it back in his lapel, packed his thermos jug away, and took out a piece of yellow plastic and blew into it. in   20
less than 3 minutes it had turned into a yellow plastic castro convertible couch.
enough is enough i thought to myself. so i dropped the knitting and ran like hell. last i saw of that dude he was stretched out on the couch reading portnoys complaint.   25
the kitchens that are still left in the home are so instant they might as well be out to lunch.
instant milk, instant coffee, instant tea, instant potatoes, instant old fashioned oatmeal, everything is preprepared for the unprepared women in the kitchen. the chicken is pre cut, the flour is   30
pre measured, the rice is minute, the salt is pre seasoned, and the peas are pre buttered. just goes to show you white folks will do anything for their women. they had to invent instant food because the servant problem got so bad that their women had to get in

the kitchen herself with her own two lily white hands. it is no   35
accident that in the old old south where they had slaves that they
was eating fried chicken, coated with batter, biscuits so light they
could have flown across the mason dixon line if they had wanted
to. they was eating pound cake that had to be beat 800 strokes.
who do you think was doing this beating?   40
it sure wasnt missy. missy was beating the upstairs house nigger
for not bringing her mint julep quick enough. massa was out beating the field niggers for not hoeing the cotton fast enough. meanwhile up in the north country where they didnt have no slaves to
speak of they was eating baked beans and so called new england   45
boiled dinner.

In this wonderful piece, there is a subtle shading of tone that is
certainly as important as the overt content.

We know immediately that something is up, if for no other
reason than that the author uses no capitals, but up to line 4, she
is merely stating her thesis—literally, that kitchens are getting
smaller and less important. Beginning with line 4, the tone
changes, and soon we realize that we are dealing with some kind
of satire, for we don't believe that kitchens will literally be moved
out of the home.

Enter the tall, well-dressed man who sits next to the author
as she knits her "old man" a pair of socks. Lines 10 through 14
begin a funny, almost burlesque, sequence, which ends with the
prim statement, "i never eat with strangers"—even though the
man had apparently not eaten, but merely popped a pill. The
comedy grows even more delightfully slapstick in the paragraph
that runs from line 15 to line 22. The climax of the wild humor
comes with the statement (lines 24–25), "last i saw of that dude
he was stretched out on the couch reading portnoys complaint."

Up to this point, then, the tone of the passage is simply
humorous, slapstick, and it contains no trace of bitterness or ill
humor. But an almost violent change takes place from line 26
on, and the piece concludes as a vitriolic condemnation of white
society, which was built on a foundation of black servitude.

The modulations of tone in this passage are quite remarkable, and the author's skill in conveying them constitutes the real
strength of the message.

The writer has conveyed her opinions, to be sure, but she
has given them the tonal quality that imbues them with *affective*
significance. That is, she not only manages to tell us what she

thinks but also expresses her emotional attitude toward what she thinks.

TONE AND THE WRITER'S CREDIBILITY

Since readers want information from the writer, they must have confidence in him or her, must feel that he or she knows the subject and is not withholding crucial information or lying.

To give the reader this confidence, the writer tries to establish his or her credibility in several ways. Perhaps the most obvious method of doing this is the writer's direct statement that he or she is an authority on the subject, that is, the writer presents his or her credentials. Another way to establish credibility is through the skillful use of words common to the subject and appropriate to the writer's audience, or, in the jargon of writing, through the skillful use of diction and tone. Yet another method, closely related to diction and tone, is the writer's adaptation of style or manner to an audience, that is, the writer adopts a rhetorical stance suitable to his or her readers.

Now, let us look a little more closely at these techniques.

Credentials

Writers often need to state their credentials in order to gain the reader's confidence, as does the author of an article on drug use:

> When we at Boston University's Mental Health Clinic were first confronted, five years ago, with the new drug scene we knew very little about it and all pharmacology books were of little help beyond the chemical analysis which they offered. Although we were well-trained psychiatrists, drugs other than for therapeutic purposes were not part of our training. Drugs for the most part had been a ghetto problem and thus neglected and the very hard-core users were being treated in isolated government hospitals, and the results were worse than a dismal failure. But we were trained in the psychoanalytic model so we knew that we could learn, that we could see with sufficient experience how and in what ways drugs affected personality, if at all.
>
> —Alan S. Katz, "The Use of Drugs in America: Toward a Better Understanding of Passivity"

In this passage, Dr. Katz indicates his connection with a major university, tells us that he is a psychiatrist, and outlines his experience with the subject, preparing the reader to accept the information and conclusions in the essay.

An extremely interesting freshman essay on computers begins like this:

> When I was a sophomore in high school, I became interested in computer science. Fortunately, my father, a computer specialist at McDonnell-Douglas, has a terminal in our home, and my math teacher was a genius at programming. Since I had access to a terminal, both at school and at home, and expert help in both places, I soon became "fluent" in two computer languages.
>
> During my senior year in high school, I helped my math teacher design a computerized record-keeping system for the school. Now all registration and class scheduling are done by the computer, saving the staff hundreds of hours and the students the frustration that usually goes along with registration.

Without some knowledge of the writer's background, his readers (classmates and teacher) might well have doubted his ability to discuss so complex a subject.

Project: A Search for Credentials

Look through five or six issues of such magazines as *Harper's,* the *Atlantic, Esquire,* and *Scientific American.* What techniques are used to establish the authors' credentials, their credibility and authority in their subjects? Some of the techniques will undoubtedly be "internal," appearing as parts of the essays, but there are other ways in which journals "validate" their authors. What are some of these ways?

Rhetorical Stance

Closely related to tone is the concept of *rhetorical stance,* which is a fancy term for a simple idea.

Most language transactions are face-to-face: we can see the people we are talking to. In these situations, we all make subtle shifts in our way of talking, depending on the audience, and it is these shifts—some of which are not so subtle—that make up our rhetorical stance in spoken discourse.

As an illustration, think of the many ways in which you adjust to different talk situations. When you're chatting with close friends on campus, you are probably quite at ease, your diction is likely to be slangy, and you probably use speech mannerisms that you would avoid in more formal situations—such as repeatedly interjecting *ya know*. When you talk with your professors about official business, undoubtedly you shift your diction and try to exclude slangy mannerisms. Probably even your posture is more formal; you don't slump or sprawl quite as much.

In short, when you talk, you adjust your rhetorical stance continually, using different techniques for different people in various situations.

In writing, tone is a part of rhetorical stance: seriousness, irony, humor, outrage, and so on. So is purpose: you can explain, explore, or demonstrate; you can attempt to *persuade* someone to take an action or make a decision. And, of course, you can try to rouse emotions with a poem or to amuse people with a fictional tale.

Exercise

Observe a friend or acquaintance in a conversation with another person. What can you discover about rhetorical stance? (Diction? Body language? Tone of voice? Distance between the two speakers?)

Orally or in writing, discuss what you discovered about rhetorical stance from your observations.

EXPOSITION AND THE PROBLEM OF PROBLEMS

In problem situations, things just don't "add up"; there is *dissonance*. Often we sense problems before we fully understand them, but if we are to find solutions we must gain understanding.

If a problem is well defined, we use arithmetic or some other artificial language (such as Basic or Pascal) to solve it. Jerry Nelson, the designer of the largest telescope in the world, now being constructed at Mauna Kea, Hawaii, faced and still faces countless problems:

> At first, Nelson recalls, he didn't know much about the difficulty of building a large telescope. "I was ignorant," he says. " 'Gee, why not make [the Palomar design] bigger?' Well, it doesn't take very long to understand why you can't make the 200-inch design bigger." If all one did was double the dimensions, he explains, the gravitational deformations of such a huge mass of glass would leave you with a critical

optical surface four times less accurate than Palomar's. And even this assumes that you could pour a piece of glass twice as big as Palomar's—which may or may not be possible, since it would weigh something on the order of 150 tons. The expense of making such a massive mirror—and the machinery to support and point it—could easily drive the project's total cost beyond the capability of any university or private donor.

—Paul Ciotti, "Mr. Keck's Bequest," Los Angeles Times Magazine,
May 24, 1987

The problems outlined in this paragraph are mathematical, not the sort that one thinks through with natural language.

However, many problems cannot be solved with mathematics or other artificial languages; they must be "talked through," discussed, argued. Here is the real-world problem that many students face: choosing a major. Career opportunities and students' interests often clash: the student loves literature and wants to major in English, but the job market for English teachers is limited; and anyway, the man the student plans to marry is an engineering major and wants her to major in mechanical engineering. In order to understand the problem of choosing a major, the student must gain answers to a number of questions, such as:

1. What are her own motives? What are the motives of her intended? How might these motives be changed? (Do the motives relate to the backgrounds of the people concerned? How?)
2. What are the relationships of time and place to the problem? The economic scene? Social classes?
3. What about means for accomplishing goals? Finances? Intelligence? Availability of schools?

You have probably discovered that behind these questions lie the five master questions of the Pentad that were discussed in chapter 4, pages 96–100.

Exploring Problems

How does the exploration of problems take place? Although everyone develops his or her own method, there are certain similarities among procedures, certain steps in the process that seem to be common to a great many writers and thinkers. Understanding the process should be useful, and it is certainly interesting; therefore, let's take a look at what might happen when a person encounters a problem and goes about solving it.[1]

In the first place, you must have *a preliminary knowledge of the field.* If you know almost nothing about writing insurance policies or planning the defense in a football game, then you cannot be aware of problems in those fields, at least not in a way that is specific enough to be useful. To define your problem as the need for health insurance or a desire to beat the Oklahoma team will be of little use, for these are general goals; they are not penetrating enough to yield solutions, because in their very broadness they give you nothing to work with.

The next step is known as *cognitive dissonance,* the awareness of a difficulty. Cognitive dissonance reveals itself in wonder (Why should such and such be the case?); in instability (There is a contradiction here that I cannot resolve); in anomaly (On the basis of my current knowledge I cannot explain this phenomenon).

Next comes *focus.* The problem becomes clear. It can be exactly defined.

Fourth is *the search for a new model* that can be tested.

Fifth, *the new model is imposed on the field* to see if it eliminates the cognitive dissonance.

Finally, *a new hypothesis is formed;* a tentative explanation is offered. Here is a thumbnail example:

> Hanson's classic example of the whole exploration process vividly illustrates the use of the model. He uses Kepler's discovery of the elliptical orbit of Mars, for "Kepler typifies all reasoning in physical science" . . . [1. *Preliminary knowledge of field*] The dogma current from Aristotle to Galileo was that planetary orbits were necessarily circular. . . . He says, "Before Kepler, circular motion was to the concept of planet as 'tangibility' is to our concept of 'physical object' " . . . [2. *Cognitive dissonance*] But the circular model did not account for the anomalies in measurements of Mars's varied distances from the sun and of Mars's varied velocities at different points in its orbit. [3. *Focus of problem*] Even inaccuracies in measuring procedures should not have led to such notable departures from what the theory dictated. . . . [4. *Search for new model*] To explain these anomalies Kepler then repudiated the circular orbit model and cast about for another model. . . . He first tried an oval and then an ellipse as models, [5. *Imposition of new model*] settling eventually on the ellipse. . . . [6. *Hypothesis: tentative explanation*] The ellipse offered a plausible explanation of all the anomalies which had been bothering him and suggested other testable hypotheses. These he followed through and the results confirmed the validity of the new model. . . .[2]

This brief example is not meant to imply that problem solving takes place only in the exact sciences. Whenever a critic attempts to explain a poem, he or she goes through the same kind of procedure, and whenever you advance an opinion on any subject, you probably—consciously or not—go through at least some of these steps.

Gaining New Perspectives on Problems

It's the first day of class, English 101, composition. I walk into a room populated by seventeen brand-new freshmen at my university. They glance at me and then at each other. They are, of course, wondering, "What sort of guy is this prof? What can I expect from him?" As usual, I carry my battered old briefcase.

After introducing myself and making some preliminary remarks, I announce: "Since this is a writing class, let's write. See this briefcase? I want you to use it as evidence concerning me. What can you conclude about me on the basis of the briefcase? Think about this question, and in the next half hour write as complete an answer as possible."

Most of the students appear stunned, staring either at the paper before them or at the briefcase, not knowing where to begin. However, one young woman in the back row tentatively raises her hand. I acknowledge her, and she asks, "Can we look at the contents of the briefcase?" "Of course," I respond, and I pass the object to her, for her investigation.

The contents of the briefcase tell her and her classmates a good deal about me, for they find my appointment book, the draft of a poem that I'm working on, my notes for a graduate seminar that I'm teaching, a novel that I'm reading, a receipt from Liquor Barn, a memo from my dean denying my request for funds to travel to a professional meeting, and many more items, including a Scripto mechanical pencil and several BIC bananas.

The point is this: rather than staring at the object and scratching their heads, the students investigated it, taking it apart, searching its innards, gaining new perspectives on it.

Another heuristic, which we will call *shifting perspectives*,[3] helps writers and thinkers "walk around" problems and "take them apart."

Anything—concrete object or abstract concept—can be viewed from five perspectives, each of which will reveal a different aspect of the subject.

The Five Perspectives

The Los Angeles freeway system, for instance, can be viewed as:

1. *An isolated, static entity.* We ask, What features characterize it? We can draw a map of it; we can measure its total length; we can count the number of overpasses and underpasses. We can describe it in great detail. In fact, such a description could well demand a number of thick volumes. But the point is that we can view anything as an isolated, static entity and begin to find those features that characterize it.
2. *One among many of a class.* We ask, How does it differ from others in its class? From this point of view, we would compare the Los Angeles freeway system with others like it. I, for instance, immediately think of the differences between the L.A. freeway system and the turnpikes of the east and midwest.
3. *A part of a larger system.* We ask, How does it fit into larger systems of which it is a part? The L.A. freeway system would be worthless if it did not integrate with national, state, and county highway systems; therefore, its place in these larger systems is crucial.
4. *A process, rather than a static entity.* We ask, How is it changing? In regard to the L.A. freeway system, this question brings up the whole problem of planning for the future, which implies the problem of history, or how the system got to be the way it currently is.
5. *A closed system, rather than an entity.* We ask, What are the parts, and how do they work together? Now we are focusing on the L.A. freeway as a transportation system, each part of which must integrate and function with the whole.

That is one example of how the procedure works. You can ask the questions in any order, starting with any one of the five perspectives.

It might be interesting to see how many ideas the system just outlined will generate concerning so ordinary an object as a ballpoint pen.

Discussion: Shifting Perspectives

Use the five perspectives just explained to gain ideas concerning a common object such as a ballpoint pen or a pair of jogging shoes. Probably you will come up with insights that would not have arisen if you had not used this heuristic.

A Suggestion for Writing

Write an analysis of one of your classes. How is it managed? What are the attitudes of the teacher and students? What are the goals of the class? To develop your analysis, apply the five perspectives to the subject. You may want to do this in group discussion.

Notes

[1] This discussion is adapted from James L. Kinneavy, *A Theory of Discourse* (Englewood Cliffs, N.J.: Prentice-Hall, 1971).

[2] Kinneavy, pp. 103–04.

[3] Based on a concept developed in Richard E. Young, Alton L. Becker, and Kenneth L. Pike, *Rhetoric: Discovery and Change* (New York: Harcourt Brace Jovanovich, 1970).

6

Argumentation and Persuasion

"I'm from Missouri. You'll have to show me. You could well be right, but before I'll accept what you say, you must convince me by giving me your reasons for believing as you do."

In order to convince someone who doesn't agree with you, you must develop an effective *argument.* What works for one audience doesn't work for another. If you are successful with this argument, your reader will assent, granting your premises. However, it is possible to convince a reader without *persuading* him or her, for persuasion results in action of some kind. You read a magazine article that convinces you of the health hazards of a high-cholesterol diet, but you continue to eat saturated fats until your roommate *persuades* you that you should change your life style. Literally millions of people are convinced that cigarette smoking is disastrous for the health, but they have not been persuaded to give up the habit.

The goals of *exposition, argumentation,* and *persuasion* differentiate these kinds of writing:

■ In exposition, the writer wants to *inform* the reader.

■ In argumentation, the writer wants to *convince* the reader.

■ In persuasion, the writer wants to *cause the reader to act.*

Discussion: An Example of Argumentation

In the following essay, Toney Anaya, the governor of New Mexico, argues for his opinion, trying to convince readers that the death penalty is ineffective and immoral. Read this argument, which appeared in the *Los Angeles Times* of December 14, 1986, and then discuss the questions that follow.

A Departing Governor Defies Death Sentence
Toney Anaya

On Nov. 26, I commuted the sentences of five men awaiting execution on New Mexico's "death row." Now, let me review some recent state history.

No one has been executed in New Mexico since David Cooper Nelson died in the gas chamber in January, 1960. Between that time and 1974, seven men were sentenced to death. When the New Mexico death penalty was declared unconstitutional in 1974, these men were given life sentences.

Four of the seven later were found to be innocent, their convictions and death sentences based on perjured testimony. But the death penalty, because of its finality, makes no provision for the falsely accused.

Another seven men have been sentenced to death since the re-enactment of the New Mexico death penalty in 1979; five convictions and death sentences were affirmed by a divided majority of the New Mexico supreme court; the court reversed the sentences of two others who were subsequently sentenced to life imprisonment.

Thus, of the 14 men who have received a death sentence in New Mexico since 1960, four have been found innocent of the crimes charged, five have since received life sentences instead of death and five were, until Nov. 26, on death row awaiting further appeals, delays and uncertainties. The cost to society in economic terms and traumatic consequences of such appeals is intolerable.

Debate about the effectiveness of the death penalty has raged for decades and very likely will for several more. Meanwhile, crime victims continue to mount.

Total elimination of crime will never be achieved. But the vicious cycle of violence in crime must be broken, the rise in crime halted. An effective fight can only be waged through an effective plan declaring war on crime, a plan that must be fair, humane, swift and certain—must also be efficient, rational and realistic.

The United States should:

■ Abolish capital punishment.

■ Replace the death penalty with life imprisonment without parole, where appropriate.

- Offer, until capital punishment is abolished, life imprisonment without parole as an alternative sentence that juries may return.
- Improve its efforts to reform or rehabilitate inmates who are ultimately returned to society.
- Provide more alternatives to sentencing, such as community corrections programs that are more effective, more humane and less costly.
- Improve the quantity and quality of existing resources to police, prosecutors, public defenders, courts and corrections departments.
- Provide victim compensation and assistance programs that are not designed for vengeance but for compassionate and practical financial relief to victims, together with medical and psychological treatment where needed.
- Work on averting or diverting the next generation of criminals, to prevent crime in the first instance. Let us attack and prevent substance abuse, child abuse, domestic violence and the glamorizing of violence in entertainment. Let us improve child care, education and job opportunities. Let us concentrate on breaking the cycle of poverty and injustice.

The death penalty is inhumane, immoral, anti-God and incompatible with an enlightened society.

Despite opposition to the death penalty by virtually every organized religion in this country, the United States stands alone among the so-called civilized and industrialized nations—joining instead with the likes of the Soviet Union, South Africa and Iran—in applying capital punishment.

Beyond considerations of morality and fairness is the cold realization that capital punishment is a false god. People cry out in bloodcurdling unison to "kill the killers," giving themselves a false sense of security—a false sense of accomplishment—a hollow, costly, vengeful outburst of emotions. And, when the killers are killed, we have accomplished none of our crime-fighting goals as an enlightened society. Rather, we have lowered ourselves to the very rabble we have condemned.

The death penalty fails additional tests: it is neither swift nor certain. Rather, because of its finality, the U.S. Supreme Court has established such a maze of protections that ultimately, capital punishment is the slowest, least certain of all our penalties and consequently, the most costly—costly in both human and economic terms. The price of seeking the death penalty far outweighs the cost of incarceration for life.

Capital punishment is applied in an arbitrary and disproportionate manner. National statistics show that if you are young, poor and a minority, you are more likely to be investigated, prosecuted, convicted and sentenced to death than if you are prosperous and white.

My personal beliefs do not allow me to permit the execution of an individual in the name of the state. And while many argue that I could have left office having already fulfilled my commitment that no one would be executed during my term as governor, without the action I have taken, that argument rings hollow. During the recent political campaigns in this state, my opponents were virtually guaranteeing executions. For me to simply walk away would make me as much an accomplice as those who would participate in their execution.

New Mexico's life sentence means a minimum of 30 years behind bars. Each of these convicted felons is serving additional sentences beyond the death sentence. They will never again set foot in society.

Polls show that the majority of Americans support capital punishment but responses to my commutations have been running 5–1 or 6–1 in favor of my actions. In shopping centers, in grocery stores and even on the ski slopes many individuals have stopped to thank me for taking this ostensibly unpopular move and to say they too believe all life is sacred. This is evidence of a deep humanitarianism not reflected in the public-opinion polls.

New Mexico has provided leadership in many areas. One of our achievements, rousing mixed feelings among citizens, was the development of the most destructive weapon known to mankind—the atomic bomb. The most powerful force of all has been defined as an idea whose time has come. It is my prayer that New Mexico will become the birthplace of another idea whose time has come—elimination of the death penalty once and for all. And in its place, the establishment of, and commitment to, a moral, just—and effective—criminal justice system.

1. What is the *gist* of the argument? In a nutshell, what is Anaya's point?
2. In what ways are facts and figures important to this argument?
3. Does Anaya use any emotional appeals? Explain.
4. Would more data, more facts, more explanation strengthen the argument? At which points? (Does Anaya fulfill the requirement of *quantity*? See pages 11–14.)
5. Is Anaya reliable and believable? Does he know what he's talking about? Explain. (Does Anaya fulfill the requirement of *quality*? See pages 11–14.)
6. Does everything in the argument relate to Anaya's point? If not, explain why some parts of the text are irrelevant. (Does Anaya fulfill the requirement of *relation* or *relevance*? See pages 11–14.)
7. Is the argument as clear as it could possibly be? If not, explain. (Does Anaya fulfill the requirement of *manner*? See pages 11–14.)

TWO BASIC PRINCIPLES OF ARGUMENTATION

1. *You can't begin an argument unless you can find a point on which all the parties involved can agree. So you must start an argument on the basis of agreement, not disagreement.*

If two points of view are completely opposed, then there is no way to begin an argument. If Smith, a fundamentalist, is a confirmed believer in the literal creation story in the Bible and Jones, an evolutionist, is equally convinced of the theory of biological evolution, it is unlikely that either will be able to convince the other, and the result of an attempt to do so could well be confrontation and "warfare," not argument. (For an example of such a confrontation, you might like to read about the Scopes "monkey trial.")

However, most points of view are not completely opposed to one another. For example, the firm believer in biological evolution might also believe in a guiding intelligence or in God. In this case, the fundamentalist and the evolutionist would share a belief: that there is a divine reason for creation, whether that creation came about in an instant, in a week, or throughout millions of years. This shared belief could well be the grounds for argument.

Alpha might be violently opposed to socialized medicine, and Beta might be as ardently in favor of it. Beta's argument to convince Alpha might begin something like this:

> A major national goal should be to provide good medical care for all Americans, regardless of their economic status or the region in which they live. About this, everyone can agree. Problems arise, however, when we begin to seek out means for accomplishing this goal. In the pages that follow, I will explain one way in which the health care dilemma might be solved.

With this beginning, Beta has identified herself with Alpha; she does not make him an antagonist. If Beta had begun her essay as follows, she would have created an antagonist:

> Socialized medicine is the only answer to the health care dilemma in America. The free enterprise system has proven its inability to provide decent medicine for all Americans, regardless of economic status or the region in which they live.

A Suggestion for Writing

Choose a current issue—local or national—on which there is a sharp division of opinion, and on which you hold a firm view.

Write an opening paragraph for an essay that argues your point. In the paragraph, outline a facet of the issue on which you and your opponents agree.

2. *You can't argue a point unless it has definition and uncertainty.*

When a proposition lacks definition, it is too broad to be argued. "Some changes in government might be beneficial to the nation" lacks definition. What changes? Beneficial in what ways? The proposition is too unstable to serve as the basis for an argument.

The proposition "Electing honest officials would improve government" is a truism; it does not contain the element of uncertainty. The response to this proposition is "So what else is new?" What we want is "Why do you say that?"

The proposition "Government financing of presidential election campaigns would make America a more democratic nation" is arguable. It has definition and it can be questioned.

Discussion: Arguable Propositions

Some of the following propositions appear not to be arguable; either they are too ill-defined or they lack uncertainty. Which of the propositions do you think are arguable? Which are unarguable? Explain.

1. Development of the Strategic Defense Initiative (the so-called "Star Wars" nuclear defense system) involves significant moral issues.
2. Revision of the general education requirements would benefit most students in this university.
3. Since early predictions about election results probably influence votes, there should be no projection of winners until after the polls have closed.
4. Every driver should know the basics about how a car works.
5. Since the ability to write well is not essential in every profession, the university should exempt certain majors—dental hygienists, computer technologists, and musicians—from the English composition requirement.
6. Most Americans watch too much television.
7. If teachers received better training, public education in America would improve.
8. Since ignorance is bliss, it is folly to be wise.
9. The best government is the least government.
10. In order to conserve energy and reduce pollution, the federal government should impose a substantial horsepower tax on automobiles—the more the horsepower, the higher the tax.
11. Drivers should not be forced by law to wear seat belts.
12. The prices of many commodities are too high.
13. The incidence of lung cancer would decline if no one smoked cigarettes.
14. The United States should not increase its nuclear capability beyond the present level.
15. Both Russia and Iran produce caviar.

BUILDING AN ARGUMENT
Data, Link, Claim

In its most basic form, an argument contains three elements: (1) the *claim,* (2) *data* or *evidence* in support of the claim, and (3) the *link* between the data or evidence and the claim.[1]

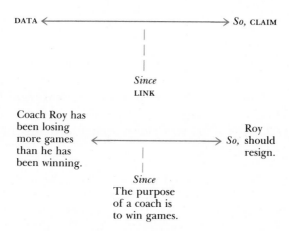

In many arguments, the link (the *Since* element) is not expressed, but the audience knows what it must be and can supply it. So the argument concerning Coach Roy can be expressed this way:

Coach Roy has been losing more games than he has been winning, so he should resign.

Discussion: Data, Link, Claim

1. What is the *claim* of the argument by Toney Anaya on pages 134–36? What are the *data* and the *link*?
2. Write (or roughly outline) a simple data/evidence-link-claim argument.

Support for the Link

The Coach Roy argument is simple enough:

Data/Evidence   This season, Roy has lost more games than he's won.
Link   The purpose of a coach is to win games.
Claim   Roy should resign.

In the argument, however, the link is vulnerable to attack, as in the following counterargument:

Data/Evidence The great coaches of history—Knute Rockne, Ara Parseghian—are remembered because of the effect they had on their players, not especially because their teams won. On the other hand, Woody Hayes will be remembered for his unsportsmanlike conduct.

Link (*Since*) We value character more than winning.

Claim (*So*) The main purpose of a coach should be to build character by teaching sportsmanship and fair play.

This argument against the link in the Roy argument forces the author of the Roy argument to provide *support* or *backing* for the link—reasons for us to believe that the main purpose of a coach is to win games:

> The purpose of a coach is to win games, just as the purpose of a physician is to heal. We remember the great coaches of history as good people with high ethical standards, as people who had great influence on the character of their players, but if they had not been winning coaches, they would have failed in their primary responsibility and thus would not have been remembered or respected enough to influence very many players. No matter how fine a man or woman a physician is, if he or she is not a successful healer, that physician is not worthy of our respect. Those who are not successful at their chosen profession—be it medicine or coaching—should, as a matter of principle, leave it.

Discussion: Backing

What sort of *backing* would be needed to strengthen the *links* in the following arguments?

EVIDENCE	LINK (*Since*)	CLAIM (*So*)
1. Dilligan has served on the city council.	The most experienced candidate is usually the best candidate.	You should vote for Dilligan.
2. The U.S. is the only industrialized nation that retains capital punishment.	In the context of the modern world, capital punishment is cruel and unusual.	Capital punishment should be abolished in the U.S.

3. More and more businesses and charities are doing telephone solicitation.	A telephone in the home is intended for maintaining social contacts.	Telephone solicitation should be abolished in the U.S.
4. Since 1913, the U.S. has had an income tax.	The income tax confiscates private property, which is unconstitutional.	The income tax violates the U.S. Constitution.
5. The courts are giving accused felons too much protection, as in the case where an illegally obtained confession cannot be used as evidence.	The security of its citizens against criminals is the responsibility of the government.	The right to protection against crime must take precedence over an accused person's right to due process between the time of arrest and the time of arraignment.

Reservation and Qualification

Sometimes arguers must state reservations concerning their *links* and qualifications concerning their *claims*. The elements of argument state the conditions under which the links and claims hold—set limits and boundaries. But all this is more easily illustrated than explained. Notice how the *reservation* and *qualification* work in regard to the Coach Roy argument:

Evidence	This season, Roy has lost more games than he's won, five to one.
Link	The purpose of a coach is to win games,
RESERVATION	*unless the players are interested only in killing time and getting some exercise.*
Backing	We might remember the great coaches of history because of their qualities as human beings, but if they had not been winners, they wouldn't have had the chance to display that fine character.
Claim	Roy should resign,
QUALIFICATION	*unless he wins the rest of the games this season.*

The argument that has been used for an example is, of course, simplified and inadequately developed with detail, but the purpose has been to show, in a bare-bones way, how a persuasive essay can be constructed. The following diagram is extremely useful, for it sums up what we have seen about the model for persuasion.[2]

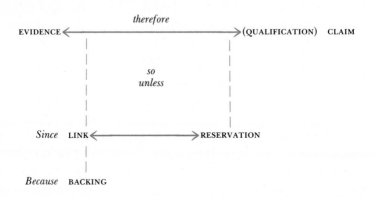

RULES OF THUMB FOR CONSTRUCTING ARGUMENTS

From the model of argumentation that we have constructed in the last few pages, we can derive some very practical rules of thumb. Your argument must:

1. Make a reasonable claim.
2. Contain adequate evidence to support the claim.
3. Provide a *valid* link between the evidence and the claim.
4. Explain valid reservations to the link.
5. Provide adequate backing for the link.
6. Qualify the claim if necessary.

Discussion: Analyzing an Argument

Analyze the following structure for an argument written by a college freshman:

Evidence   California has now legalized some nude beaches. Pornography shops are legal in many cities in the state. Partially clad or nude dancers entertain in some cabarets. (In the essay, the evidence is developed with specific examples and data.)

Link   A decline in morals will bring about a general decline in the quality of life, affecting even the economy of the state. (In the essay, the link is further developed with explanations and examples.)

Backing   It has often been said by historians that the downfall of the Roman Empire was brought about by the moral decay of its citizenry. (This point is elaborated and sources are quoted.)

Claim   If the laws are not changed so that nude beaches, pornography shops, and lewd entertainment are abolished, the state of California will decay, as did the Roman Empire.

An Argument for Analysis

Samuel Johnson, the great eighteenth-century man of letters who compiled the first "modern" dictionary, wrote an argument for freeing a slave, Joseph Knight, who had been kidnapped as a child and sold to a Scottish gentleman. Knight's lawyer used Johnson's argument, and the court did, indeed, set Knight free. Read Samuel Johnson's argument, and answer the discussion questions that follow it.

Freeing a Negro Slave
Samuel Johnson

It must be agreed that in most ages many countries have had part of their inhabitants in a state of slavery; yet it may be doubted whether slavery can ever be supposed the natural condition of man. It is impossible not to conceive that men in their original state were equal, and very difficult to imagine how one would be subjected to another but by violent compulsion. An individual may, indeed, forfeit his liberty by a crime; but he cannot by that crime forfeit the liberty of his children. What is true of a criminal seems true likewise of a captive. A man may accept life from a conquering enemy on condition of perpetual servitude; but it is very doubtful whether he can entail that servitude on his descendants; for no man can stipulate without commission for another. The condition which he himself accepts, his son or grandson perhaps would have rejected. If we should admit, what perhaps may with more reason be denied, that there are certain relations between man and man which may make slavery necessary and just, yet it can never be proved that he who is now suing for his freedom ever stood in any of those relations. He is certainly subject by no law, but that of violence, to his present master; who pretends no claim to his obedience, but that he bought him from a merchant of slaves, whose right to sell him never was examined. It is said that, according to the constitutions of Jamaica, he was legally enslaved; these constitutions are merely positive; and apparently injurious to the rights of mankind, because whoever is exposed to sale is condemned to slavery without appeal; by whatever fraud or violence he might have been originally brought into the merchant's power. In our own time Princes have been sold, by wretches to whose care they were entrusted, that they might have an European education; but when once they were brought to a market in the plantations, little would avail either their dignity or their wrongs. The laws of

Jamaica afford a Negro no redress. His colour is considered as a sufficient testimony against him. It is to be lamented that moral right should ever give way to political convenience. But if temptations of interest are sometimes too strong for human virtue, let us at least retain a virtue where there is no temptation to quit it. In the present case there is apparent right on one side, and no convenience on the other. Inhabitants of this island can neither gain riches nor power by taking away the liberty of any part of the human species. The sum of the argument is this:—No man is by nature the property of another: The defendant is, therefore, by nature free: The rights of nature must be some way forfeited before they can be justly taken away: That the defendant has by any act forfeited the rights of nature we require to be proved; and if no proof of such forfeiture can be given, we doubt not but the justice of the court will declare him free.

1. Briefly state the *claim* of this argument.
2. What *evidence* does Johnson present?
3. What is the *link?*
4. Does Johnson state a *reservation* to the link? If so, what is it?
5. What is the *backing* for the claim?
6. Is the claim *qualified?* If so, explain.
7. Why can we say that this argument is intended as *persuasion?*
8. Do you find the argument convincing or unconvincing? Explain.

LOGIC

At the very least, an argument for or against a position must be consistent. Consistency is a *negative* virtue because no one would praise an argument for possessing it, whereas any reasonable audience would condemn inconsistency. For example, if I argue that all people are created equal, and therefore each is entitled to human dignity, no one will exclaim, "What a consistent argument!" However, if I argue that all people are created equal, but nonetheless some should be deprived of dignity, my audience will be puzzled by my inconsistency.

Formal Truth and Material Truth

Another way of stating that an argument must be consistent is to say that it must be *formally* true. Formal truth concerns the relationship *if–then necessarily. If* you believe such and such, *then necessarily* you must conclude this and that. Of *if* such is the case, *then necessarily* this must follow.

> *If* the moon is made of green cheese, *then necessarily* modern studies of it are misguided.

Material truth concerns the content of statements. Since we have overwhelming evidence that the moon is not made of green cheese, we can say that this argument is materially untrue even though it is formally true.

The following brief argument is formally true in that the statements follow from one another:

> The horoscope is infallible, based as it is on the exact science of astrology. Your horoscope for today reads thus: "You are in the mood to make radical changes, but it is better to count your blessings instead." I know that you are planning to transfer to another college immediately, but since your horoscope advises against radical changes, you should count your present blessings and wait until a more favorable time to make changes.

If the person to whom the argument is addressed believes that astrology is an exact science and hence that the horoscope is infallible, the argument will probably be convincing. However, another person—an astronomer, for instance—might question the material truth of the statement that astrology is an exact science.

Logic is the branch of philosophy that studies the consistency of arguments. We will not, however, go into the details of that subject, for one does not need to be a logician in order to construct formally true arguments, nor does one need a course in logic to recognize inconsistency. But it will be worthwhile to look briefly at one form of logical argumentation, the syllogism, as in the following:

> A coach who is a bad sport should be discharged.
> Coach Roy is a bad sport.
> Therefore, Coach Roy should be discharged.

No one would question the formal truth of this argument, but in order for it to be persuasive, you as the arguer must accomplish a number of things. First, you must define satisfactorily what you mean by "unsportsmanlike" and convince your audience to adhere to this definition. Next, you must argue that being a good sport is necessary for a coach. Then you must establish to your audience's satisfaction that Coach Roy is indeed a bad sport. If you do all this, your audience is then likely to conclude that Coach Roy should be fired. The formal truth of the argument is self-evident. On the basis of how you fill out that formal structure, the audience may conclude that the argument is also materially true.

Deduction and Induction

Traditionally, reasoning is classified as deductive or inductive. Deduction moves from a general statement to a conclusion, and induction first states particulars and then reaches a conclusion on the basis of them. The following syllogism illustrates deduction:

> All human beings are mortal.   [major premise]
> Jones is a human being.   [minor premise]
> Therefore, Jones is mortal.   [conclusion]

If the premises are consistent, then the conclusion is inevitable. An example of induction is the following:

> Apple A is green, feels hard, tastes sour.
> Apple B is green, feels hard, tastes sour.
> Apple C is green, feels hard, tastes sour.
> Apple D is green and feels hard; therefore, it will taste sour (that
>   is, we conclude that hard, green apples are sour).

It has often been said that the scientific method is inductive, but it is both inductive and deductive. It is inconceivable that scientists would work with a set of data unless they felt that the data would establish some general principle (a hypothesis or theory) that they had already formulated on the basis of past knowledge or intuition. In other words, before scientists begin their work, they have a premise that they hope to prove or disprove. Scientists do not examine randomly selected sets of data in the hope that they will accidentally come up with a universal principle.

Whether one is working inductively or deductively, there must be a premise.

Organization of Arguments

Like formal logic, arguments can move from the general to the specific or from the specific to the general. Thus, the argument regarding Coach Roy's sportsmanship could begin like this, with the general principle at the beginning:

Thesis: If a coach is not a good sport, he should be discharged.

   I. Definition of good sportsmanship
     A. Playing by the rules
     B. Being a gracious loser

C. Being a gracious winner
D. Being cheerful.
II. Relationship of good sportsmanship to coaching
  A. Need to teach young men and women the proper values
  B. Duty to uphold the reputation of one's school
  C. Realizing that the good sport always wins in the long run
III. Coach Roy's conduct
  A. Breaking the rules
  B. Losing ungraciously
  C. Winning ungraciously
  D. Constant bad disposition
IV. Conclusion

That same topic handled inductively might look like this in outline:

I. Ideal conduct for coaches [established inductively on the basis of examples]
  A. Coach Y's conduct
  B. Coach Z's conduct
  C. Coach W's conduct
II. Coach Roy's conduct
III. Relationship of morality to a coach's duties
IV. Conclusion [including a statement of thesis and recommendations]

Induction and Deduction

Write a letter to the president of your college persuading him or her to support some action or policy that will improve the quality of student life. Organize the letter so that it moves from the general to the specific, like a deductive argument.

In a second draft of the letter, use the specific-to-general organization, like an inductive argument.

Logical Fallacies

Fallacies are two-edged swords: they are traps into which an unwary arguer can fall, and they are traps into which an immoral persuader can lure an audience. The fallacies that we will be dealing with here are usually called *informal*. Most of them will be familiar to you, for you will have encountered them again and again in advertising (which is not to say that all advertisers are unreliable).

Most of the fallacies that will be discussed fall into the general category of *non sequitur,* a Latin term meaning "it does not follow." A non sequitur is an argument in which the conclusion does not follow from the premises.

Ad Hominem ("Against the Man")

Suppose that the thesis of your argument is that the president should not have vetoed a certain bill; as your argument progresses, you shift from an attack on that particular action by the president to an attack on the president as a person. You have committed the *ad hominem* fallacy.

The ad hominem trick is particularly shoddy, for it confuses issues with those who advocate them, and, needless to say, perfectly valid issues can be supported by reprehensible people. Even Hitler supported some causes that most of us would agree with, such as full employment.

Here is an example of an ad hominem argument: "The city council should not have voted to spend a million and a half dollars on a new library when there are other, more urgent needs; one wonders how much in kickbacks the members of the council will get from the contractors who build the library."

Bandwagon

This common fallacy goes something like this: "Everyone else is doing it, so you should too." For instance, when an advertiser claims, "More people use Brand X than any other," the implication is that you should get on the bandwagon and use Brand X too. But, of course, this argument evades such considerations as price and quality of the product, the very issues a purchaser should take into account.

In politics, the bandwagon effect is of great concern. Voting places in the east close three hours earlier than those in the west; thus, the TV networks can broadcast voting trends before many western voters have gone to the polls. Some think that these broadcasts may create a bandwagon effect, influencing western voters to follow the patterns set by the easterners.

Begging the Question

This is sometimes called arguing in a circle, and it involves using one's premises as conclusions. A simple example: I argue that students at Golden West College are exceptionally intelligent, and you ask me why I think so. I reply, "Because only intelligent students go to Golden West College." I have begged the question by restating my premise in different terms.

Composition

In this fallacy, one assumes that what is valid for each member of a class will be valid for the class as a whole. For instance: "The gross national product of Thailand must be greater than that of Tibet, because individual incomes are higher in Thailand than in Tibet." This argument overlooks the possibility that the population of Tibet is greater than that of Thailand, so Tibet's smaller individual incomes may contribute to a greater gross national product than Thailand's.

Division

This is the opposite of composition. It is the assumption that what holds for the group will also hold for each member. For example, more beer is consumed in West Germany, per capita, than in any other nation. Therefore, it is accurate to say that West Germans drink more beer than, say, Japanese. But it would be inaccurate to conclude on this basis that German X drinks more beer than Japanese Y, for X might be a teetotaler, whereas Y might guzzle the stuff continually. It may be true that the average household in Orange County has two and one-third occupants, but, nonetheless, no single household can possibly have that number.

Equivocation

In equivocation, the sense of a key word is shifted, thus invalidating the argument. For instance, "The dictionary defines *republican* as 'one who favors a republic,' and *republic* is defined as 'a state in which the supreme power rests in the body of citizens entitled to vote.' Therefore, if you believe that the voters should control the government, vote Republican in the next election." The fallacy here lies in the shift of *republican* in its generic use, specifying one who favors a certain form of government, to its specific use as the designation of a political party. An amusing example of the fallacy of equivocation is this: "Blacksmiths are vanishing. Uncle George is a blacksmith. Therefore, Uncle George is vanishing."

Post Hoc, Ergo Propter Hoc

The Latin phrase means "after this, therefore because of this." The *post hoc* fallacy consists in attributing a cause-and-effect relationship to what is merely a time relationship. For example, "After Murgatroyd was elected, property taxes decreased; therefore, Murgatroyd must have lowered property taxes." (Murgatroyd may well have done so, but the mere time relationship does not establish the fact.)

Reification

In this fallacy, an abstraction is treated as if it had concrete reality. Here is the Puritan Thomas Hooker (1586–1647) talking about sin: "We must see it clearly in its own Nature, its Native color and proper hue. . . ." We cannot, of course, "see" sin as a concrete object. In discussing such abstractions as democracy, many arguers reify, talking as if the concept itself were somehow physically embodied by the United States, or as if Russia embodied the concept "communism."

Testimonial

Sports figures endorse breakfast cereals, movie stars speak on behalf of presidential candidates, Jane Fonda and Bill Cosby give pitches for just about everything. These are testimonials— famous people giving their endorsements. But there is no reason why a sports figure should know more about the nutritive qualities of breakfast cereals than you or I do. Nor does the fact that Ed Asner is a good actor give him any particular authority to speak knowledgeably about politics. The testimonial is a mendacious use of well-known people to push products and ideas.

There are other kinds of fallacies, but the point has undoubtedly been made: bad thinking can lead one into bad arguments, and bad thinking can also set one up as a pigeon for immoral arguers. Who, after all, wants to be either a huckster or a pigeon?

Exercise

Read and enjoy the following essay. After you have done so, make an alphabetical list of the fallacies that are explained in it, define each fallacy, and invent an example of each.

Love Is a Fallacy
Max Shulman

Charles Lamb, as merry and enterprising a fellow as you will meet in a month of Sundays, unfettered the informal essay with his memorable *Old China* and *Dream Children*. There follows an informal essay that ventures even beyond Lamb's frontier. Indeed, "informal" may not be quite the right word to describe this essay; "limp" or "flaccid" or possibly "spongy" are perhaps more appropriate.

Vague though its category, it is without doubt an essay. It develops an argument; it cites instances; it reaches a conclusion. Could Carlyle do more? Could Ruskin?

Read, then, the following essay which undertakes to demonstrate that logic, far from being a dry, pedantic discipline, is a living, breathing thing, full of beauty, passion, and trauma.

—Author's Note

Cool was I and logical. Keen, calculating, perspicacious, acute and astute—I was all of these. My brain was as powerful as a dynamo, as precise as a chemist's scales, as penetrating as a scalpel. And—think of it!—I was only eighteen.

It is not often that one so young has such a giant intellect. Take, for example, Petey Burch, my roommate at the University of Minnesota. Same age, same background, but dumb as an ox. A nice enough fellow, you understand, but nothing upstairs. Emotional type. Unstable. Impressionable. Worst of all, a faddist. Fads, I submit, are the very negation of reason. To be swept up in every new craze that comes along, to surrender yourself to idiocy just because everybody else is doing it—this, to me, is the acme of mindlessness. Not, however, to Petey.

One afternoon I found Petey lying on his bed with an expression of such distress on his face that I immediately diagnosed appendicitis. "Don't move," I said. "Don't take a laxative. I'll get a doctor."

"Raccoon," he mumbled thickly.

"Raccoon?" I said, pausing in my flight.

"I want a raccoon coat," he wailed.

I perceived that this trouble was not physical, but mental. "Why do you want a raccoon coat?"

"I should have known it," he cried, pounding his temples. "I should have known they'd come back when the Charleston came back. Like a fool I spent all my money for textbooks, and now I can't get a raccoon coat."

"Can you mean," I said incredulously, "that people are actually wearing raccoon coats again?"

"All the Big Men on Campus are wearing them. Where've you been?"

"In the library," I said, naming a place not frequented by Big Men on Campus.

He leaped from the bed and paced the room. "I've got to have a raccoon coat," he said passionately. "I've got to!"

"Petey, why? Look at it rationally. Raccoon coats are unsanitary. They shed. They smell bad. They weigh too much. They're unsightly. They—"

"You don't understand." he interrupted impatiently. "It's the thing to do. Don't you want to be in the swim?"

"No," I said truthfully.

"Well, I do," he declared. "I'd give anything for a raccoon coat. Anything!"

My brain, that precision instrument, slipped into high gear. "Anything?" I asked, looking at him narrowly.

"Anything," he affirmed in ringing tones.

I stroked my chin thoughtfully. It so happened that I knew where to get my hands on a raccoon coat. My father had had one in his undergraduate days; it lay now in a trunk in the attic back home. It also happened that Petey had something I wanted. He didn't *have* it exactly, but at least he had first rights on it. I refer to this girl, Polly Espy.

I had long coveted Polly Espy. Let me emphasize that my desire for this young woman was not emotional in nature. She was, to be sure, a girl who excited the emotions, but I was not one to let my heart rule my head. I wanted Polly for a shrewdly calculated, entirely cerebral reason.

I was a freshman in law school. In a few years I would be out in practice. I was well aware of the importance of the right kind of wife in furthering a lawyer's career. The successful lawyers I had observed were, almost without exception, married to beautiful, gracious, intelligent women. With one omission, Polly fitted these specifications perfectly.

Beautiful she was. She was not yet of pin-up proportions, but I felt sure that time would supply the lack. She already had the makings.

Gracious she was. By gracious I mean full of graces. She had an erectness of carriage, an ease of bearing, a poise that clearly indicated the best of breeding. At table her manners were exquisite. I had seen her at the Kozy Kampus Korner eating the specialty of the house—a sandwich that contained scraps of pot roast, gravy, chopped nuts, and a dipper of sauerkraut—without even getting her fingers moist.

Intelligent she was not. In fact, she veered in the opposite direction. But I believed that under my guidance she would smarten up. At any rate, it was worth a try. It is, after all, easier to make a beautiful dumb girl smart than to make an ugly smart girl beautiful.

"Petey," I said, "are you in love with Polly Espy?"

"I think she's a keen kid," he replied, "but I don't know if you'd call it love. Why?"

"Do you," I asked, "have any kind of formal arrangement with her? I mean are you going steady or anything like that?"

"No. We see each other quite a bit, but we both have other dates. Why?"

"Is there," I asked, "any other man for whom she has a particular fondness?"

"Not that I know of. Why?"

I nodded with satisfaction. "In other words, if you were out of the picture, the field would be open. Is that right?"

"I guess so. What are you getting at?"

"Nothing, nothing," I said innocently, and took my suitcase out of the closet.

"Where are you going?" asked Petey.

"Home for the weekend." I threw a few things into the bag.

"Listen," he said, clutching my arm eagerly, "while you're home, you couldn't get some money from your old man, could you, and lend it to me so I can buy a raccoon coat?"

"I may do better than that," I said with a mysterious wink and closed my bag and left.

"Look," I said to Petey when I got back Monday morning. I threw open the suitcase and revealed the huge, hairy, gamy object that my father had worn in his Stutz Bearcat in 1925.

"Holy Toledo!" said Petey reverently. He plunged his hands into the raccoon coat and then his face. "Holy Toledo!" he repeated fifteen or twenty times.

"Would you like it?" I asked.

"Oh yes!" he cried, clutching the greasy pelt to him. Then a canny look came into his eyes. "What do you want for it?"

"Your girl," I said, mincing no words.

"Polly?" he said in a horrified whisper. "You want Polly?"

"That's right."

He flung the coat from him. "Never," he said stoutly.

I shrugged. "Okay. If you don't want to be in the swim, I guess it's your business."

I sat down in a chair and pretended to read a book, but out of the corner of my eye I kept watching Petey. He was a torn man. First he looked at the coat with the expression of a waif at a bakery window. Then he turned away and set his jaw resolutely. Then he looked back at the coat, with even more longing in his face. Then he turned away, but with not so much resolution this time. Back and forth his head swiveled, desire waxing, resolution waning. Finally he didn't turn away at all; he just stood and stared with mad lust at the coat.

"It isn't as though I was in love with Polly," he said thickly. "Or going steady or anything like that."

"That's right," I murmured.

"What's Polly to me, or me to Polly?"

"Not a thing," said I.

"It's just been a casual kick—just a few laughs, that's all."

"Try on the coat," said I.

He complied. The coat bunched high over his ears and dropped all the way down to his shoe tops. He looked like a mound of dead raccoons. "Fits fine," he said happily.

I rose from my chair. "Is it a deal?" I asked, extending my hand.
He swallowed. "It's a deal," he said, and shook my hand.

I had my first date with Polly the following evening. This was in the
nature of a survey; I wanted to find out just how much work I had to do to
get her mind up to the standard I required. I took her first to dinner. "Gee,
that was a delish dinner," she said as we left the restaurant. Then I took her
to a movie. "Gee, that was a marvy movie," she said as we left the theater.
And then I took her home. "Gee, I had a sensaysh time," she said as she
bade me good night.

I went back to my room with a heavy heart. I had gravely underesti-
mated the size of my task. This girl's lack of information was terrifying. Nor
would it be enough merely to supply her with information. First she had to
be taught to *think*. This loomed as a project of no small dimension, and
at first I was tempted to give her back to Petey. But then I got to thinking
about her abundant physical charms and about the way she entered a
room and the way she handled a knife and fork, and I decided to make an
effort.

I went about it, as in all things, systematically. I gave her a course in
logic. It happened that I, as a law student, was taking a course in logic myself, so I had all the facts at my finger tips. "Polly," I said to her when I
picked her up on our next date, "tonight we are going over to the Knoll and
talk."

"Oo, terrif," she replied. One thing I will say for this girl: you would
go far to find another so agreeable.

We went to the Knoll, the campus trysting place, and we sat down
under an old oak, and she looked at me expectantly. "What are we going to
talk about?" she asked.

"Logic."

She thought this over for a minute and decided she liked it. "Magnif,"
she said.

"Logic," I said, clearing my throat, "is the science of thinking. Before
we can think correctly, we must first learn to recognize the common fallacies
of logic. These we will take up tonight."

"Wow-dow!" she cried, clapping her hands delightedly.

I winced, but went bravely on. "First let us examine the fallacy called
Dicto Simpliciter."

"By all means," she urged, batting her lashes eagerly.

"Dicto Simpliciter means an argument based on an unqualified generalization. For example: Exercise is good. Therefore everybody should exercise."

"I agree," said Polly earnestly. "I mean exercise is wonderful. I mean
it builds the body and everything."

"Polly," I said gently, "the argument is a fallacy. *Exercise is good* is an
unqualified generalization. For instance, if you have heart disease, exercise
is bad, not good. Many people are ordered by their doctors *not* to exercise.
You must *qualify* the generalization. You must say exercise is *usually* good,
or exercise is good for *most people*. Otherwise you have committed a Dicto
Simpliciter. Do you see?"

"No," she confessed. "But this is marvy. Do more! Do more!"

"It will be better if you stop tugging at my sleeve," I told her, and when she desisted, I continued. "Next we take up a fallacy called Hasty Generalization. Listen carefully: You can't speak French. I can't speak French. Petey Burch can't speak French. I must therefore conclude that nobody at the University of Minnesota can speak French."

"Really?" said Polly, amazed. "Nobody?"

I hid my exasperation. "Polly, it's a fallacy. The generalization is reached too hastily. There are too few instances to support such a conclusion."

"Know any more fallacies?" she asked breathlessly. "This is more fun than dancing even."

I fought off a wave of despair. I was getting nowhere with this girl, absolutely nowhere. Still, I am nothing if not persistent. I continued, "Next comes Post Hoc. Listen to this: Let's not take Bill on our picnic. Every time we take him out with us, it rains."

"I know somebody just like that," she exclaimed. "A girl back home— Eula Becker, her name is. It never fails. Every single time we take her on a picnic—"

"Polly," I said sharply, "it's a fallacy. Eula Becker doesn't *cause* the rain. She has no connection with the rain. You are guilty of Post Hoc if you blame Eula Becker."

"I'll never do it again," she promised contritely. "Are you mad at me?"

I sighed deeply. "No, Polly, I'm not mad."

"Then tell me some more fallacies."

"All right. Let's try Contradictory Premises."

"Yes, let's," she chirped, blinking her eyes happily.

I frowned, but plunged ahead. "Here's an example of Contradictory Premises: If God can do anything, can He make a stone so heavy that He won't be able to lift it?"

"Of course," she replied promptly.

"But if He can do anything, He can lift the stone," I pointed out.

"Yeah," she said thoughtfully. "Well, then I guess He can't make the stone."

"But He can do anything," I reminded her.

She scratched her pretty, empty head. "I'm all confused," she admitted.

"Of course you are. Because when the premises of an argument contradict each other, there can be no argument. If there is an irresistible force, there can be no immovable object. If there is an immovable object, there can be no irresistible force. Get it?"

"Tell me more of this keen stuff," she said eagerly.

I consulted my watch. "I think we'd better call it a night. I'll take you home now, and you go over all the things you've learned. We'll have another session tomorrow night."

I deposited her at the girls' dormitory, where she assured me that she had had a perfectly terrif evening, and I went glumly home to my room. Petey lay snoring in his bed, the raccoon coat huddled like a great hairy beast at his feet. For a moment I considered waking him and telling him that he could have his girl back. It seemed clear that my project was doomed to failure. The girl simply had a logic-proof head.

But then I reconsidered. I had wasted one evening; I might as well waste another. Who knew? Maybe somewhere in the extinct crater of her mind, a few embers still smoldered. Maybe somehow I could fan them into flame. Admittedly, it was not a prospect fraught with hope, but I decided to give it one more try.

Seated under the oak the next evening I said, "Our first fallacy tonight is Ad Misericordiam."

She quivered with delight.

"Listen closely," I said. "A man applies for a job. When the boss asks him what his qualifications are, he replies that he has a wife and six children at home, the wife is a helpless cripple, the children have nothing to eat, no clothes to wear, no shoes on their feet, there are no beds in the house, no coal in the cellar, and winter is coming."

A tear rolled down each of Polly's pink cheeks. "Oh, this is awful, awful," she sobbed.

"Yes, it's awful," I agreed, "but it's no argument. The man never answered the boss's questions about his qualifications. Instead he appealed to the boss's sympathy. He committed the fallacy of Ad Misericordiam. Do you understand?"

"Have you got a handkerchief?" she blubbered.

I handed her a handkerchief and tried to keep from screaming while she wiped her eyes. "Next," I said in a carefully controlled tone, "we will discuss False Analogy. Here is an example: Students should be allowed to look at their textbooks during examinations. After all, surgeons have X-rays to guide them during an operation, lawyers have briefs to guide them during a trial, carpenters have blueprints to guide them when they are building a house. Why, then, shouldn't students be allowed to look at their textbooks during an examination?"

"There now," she said enthusiastically, "is the most marvy idea I've heard in years."

"Polly," I said testily, "the argument is all wrong. Doctors, lawyers, and carpenters aren't taking a test to see how much they have learned, but students are. The situations are altogether different, and you can't make an analogy between them."

"I still think it's a good idea," said Polly.

"Nuts," I muttered. Doggedly I pressed on. "Next we'll try Hypothesis Contrary to Fact."

"Sounds yummy," was Polly's reaction.

"Listen: If Madame Curie had not happened to leave a photographic plate in a drawer with a chunk of pitchblende, the world today would not know about radium."

"True, true," said Polly, nodding her head. "Did you see the movie? Oh, it just knocked me out. That Walter Pidgeon is so dreamy. I mean he fractures me."

"If you can forget Mr. Pidgeon for a moment," I said coldly, "I would like to point out that the statement is a fallacy. Maybe Madame Curie would have discovered radium at some later date. Maybe somebody else would have discovered it. Maybe any number of things would have happened. You can't start with a hypothesis that is not true and then draw any supportable conclusions from it."

"They ought to put Walter Pidgeon in more pictures," said Polly. "I hardly ever see him any more."

One more chance, I decided. But just one more. There is a limit to what flesh and blood can bear. "The next fallacy is called Poisoning the Well."

"How cute," she gurgled.

"Two men are having a debate. The first one gets up and says, 'My opponent is a notorious liar. You can't believe a word that he is going to say.' . . . Now, Polly, think. Think hard. What's wrong?"

I watched her closely as she knit her creamy brow in concentration. Suddenly a glimmer of intelligence—the first I had seen—came into her eyes. "It's not fair," she said with indignation. "It's not a bit fair. What chance has the second man got if the first man calls him a liar before he even begins talking?"

"Right!" I cried exultantly. "One hundred per cent right. It's not fair. The first man has *poisoned the well* before anybody could drink from it. He has hamstrung his opponent before he could even start. . . . Polly, I'm proud of you."

"Pshaw," she murmured, blushing with pleasure.

"You see, my dear, these things aren't so hard. All you have to do is concentrate. Think—examine—evaluate. Come now, let's review everything we have learned."

"Fire away," she said with an airy wave of her hand.

Heartened by the knowledge that Polly was not altogether a cretin, I began a long, patient review of all I had told her. Over and over and over again I cited instances, pointed out flaws, kept hammering away without let-up. It was like digging a tunnel. At first everything was work, sweat, and darkness. I had no idea when I would reach the light, or even *if* I would. But I persisted. I pounded and clawed and scraped, and finally I was rewarded. I saw a chink of light. And then the chink got bigger and the sun came pouring in and all was bright.

Five grueling nights this took, but it was worth it. I had made a logician out of Polly; I had taught her to think. My job was done. She was worthy of me at last. She was a fit wife for me, a proper hostess for my many mansions, a suitable mother for my well-heeled children.

It must not be thought that I was without love for this girl. Quite the contrary. Just as Pygmalion loved the perfect woman he had fashioned, so I loved mine. I determined to acquaint her with my feelings at our very next meeting. The time had come to change our relationship from academic to romantic.

"Polly," I said when next we sat beneath our oak, "tonight we will not discuss fallacies."

"Aw, gee," she said, disappointed.

"My dear," I said, favoring her with a smile, "we have now spent five evenings together. We have gotten along splendidly. It is clear that we are well matched."

"Hasty Generalization," she repeated. "How can you say that we are well matched on the basis of only five dates?"

I chuckled with amusement. The dear child had learned her lessons well. "My dear," I said, patting her hand in a tolerant manner, "five dates is plenty. After all, you don't have to eat a whole cake to know that it's good."

"False Analogy," said Polly promptly. "I'm not a cake. I'm a girl." I chuckled with somewhat less amusement. The dear child had learned her lessons perhaps too well. I decided to change tactics. Obviously the best approach was a simple, strong, direct declaration of love. I paused for a moment while my massive brain chose the proper words. Then I began:

"Polly, I love you. You are the whole world to me, and the moon and the stars and the constellations of outer space. Please, my darling, say that you will go steady with me, for if you will not, life will be meaningless. I will languish. I will refuse my meals. I will wander the face of the earth, a shambling, hollow-eyed hulk."

There, I thought, folding my arms, that ought to do it.

"Ad Misericordiam," said Polly.

I ground my teeth. I was not Pygmalion; I was Frankenstein, and my monster had me by the throat. Frantically I fought back the tide of panic surging through me. At all costs I had to keep cool.

"Well, Polly," I said, forcing a smile, "you have certainly learned your fallacies."

"You're darn right," she said with a vigorous nod.

"And who taught them to you, Polly?"

"You did."

"That's right. So you do owe me something, don't you, my dear? If I hadn't come along you never would have learned about fallacies."

"Hypothesis Contrary to Fact," she said instantly.

I dashed perspiration from my brow. "Polly," I croaked, "you mustn't take all these things so literally. I mean this is just classroom stuff. You know that the things you learn in school don't have anything to do with life."

"Dicto Simpliciter," she said, wagging her finger at me playfully.

That did it. I leaped to my feet, bellowing like a bull. "Will you or will you not go steady with me?"

"I will not," she replied.

"Why not?" I demanded.

"Because this afternoon I promised Petey Burch I would go steady with him."

I reeled back, overcome with the infamy of it. After he promised, after he made a deal, after he shook my hand! "The rat!" I shrieked, kicking up great chunks of turf. "You can't go with him, Polly. He's a liar. He's a cheat. He's a rat."

"Poisoning the Well," said Polly, "and stop shouting. I think shouting must be a fallacy too."

With an immense effort of will, I modulated my voice. "All right," I said. "You're a logician. Let's look at this thing logically. How could you choose Petey Burch over me? Look at me—a brilliant student, a tremendous intellectual, a man with an assured future. Look at Petey—a knothead, a jitterbug, a guy who'll never know where his next meal is coming from. Can you give me one logical reason why you should go steady with Petey Burch?"

"I certainly can," declared Polly. "He's got a raccoon coat."

An Example of Persuasion

The advertisement on page 160 appeared in *Air & Space* for June/July 1987. Carefully read the ad, and then answer the following questions about it.

1. What is the *claim?*
2. What is the *evidence* for the claim?
3. What is the *link?*
4. What is the *backing* for the link?
5. Are there *reservations* or *qualifications?* If so, explain them.
6. How does the advertisement go about *persuading* you to act? (Do you or do you not find the ad persuasive? Explain.)

Notes

[1] The model for argumentation presented in this section is adapted from the work of Stephen Toulmin. See his *The Uses of Argument* (Cambridge: Cambridge University Press, 1969).

[2] The schematic was developed by Erwin P. Bettinghouse, cited in Charles W. Kneupper, "Teaching Argument: An Introduction to the Toulmin Model," *College Composition and Communication*, XXIX (October 1978), 238.

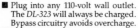
© Haverhills, 1987. Copy by Gerardo Joffe. Reprinted by permission.

A Spectrum of
Student Writing

■■■■■■■■ **These** essays, composed by students in the freshman writing program at a state university in California, vary in quality from *lower-than-average* to *better-than-average* writing for first-year students at this typical four-year institution.

How do these essays compare with your own work and that of your classmates?

If they had been written for your composition class, what grades would they have received? What comments and suggestions would you give the writers?

The following questions should help you judge the essays and formulate comments:

1. Is the essay original and interesting? Explain.
2. Does the essay satisfy your need for details and explanations, or should the author have provided more development at any point? (Be specific in your answer.)
3. Does the essay contain any irrelevant material that should be deleted? (Be specific.)
4. Do you think that the author is a reliable source of information on the subject? (Does the author know what he or she is talking about? Do you trust him or her?) Explain.
5. Is the essay unclear at any point? How could the author improve the hazy passages?
6. Is the style of the essay satisfactory? Are any of the sentences awkward, ambiguous, or difficult to read? How could the author improve these passages?
7. Does the essay contain annoying or glaring mechanical errors, such as misspellings and erroneous punctuation? What is the effect of these errors on you as a reader?

My Town Has Disappeared

Mary Moses

The town I grew up in has disappeared. Don't misunder-
stand me, there is still a town in the same geographical location,
and it is still called Dawes, but it's not the one I grew up in. My
home town didn't disappear in a matter of seconds, as did entire
villages bombed in the Vietnam War; rather, it slowly withdrew
from existence under the onset of progress and multitudes of
people.

A few remnants of my old home town still exist. For instance, the old two-room school house is still there, but it's a new,
remodeled mercantile store. It no longer houses the small cloak
room where I hung my heavy winter coat and placed my snow-
covered boots after walking a half mile to school. And all that remains of the old wooden bridge are two sun-bleached railroad
ties, still snug in the earth, with wild plants sprouting from their
sides, appearing as though they were alive and growing. The new
bridge doesn't shake and tremble like the old one did when the
strong winds blew, and there are no gaps between the boards to
look down and see the rocks at the bottom of the clear blue
water.

Just north of Dawes, the mountains covered with green
pines and speckled with white and pink dogwoods still stand tall
and the small figures of rabbits and squirrels can still be seen
scampering through the green meadows just below. But, a portion of the mountains just west of Dawes has been carved away to

make room for a new four-lane turnpike. The bottom land just below the turnpike where my father used to hunt jack rabbits and ground squirrels until sundown has been leveled and new homes, all built in the same fashion and equally spaced apart, cover what was once tall thick brush.

On the east side of the main highway, apartment buildings now stand where small shanties used to lie hidden in the trees providing shelter to the homeless on cold winter nights. Further down this same highway was a drive-in Dairy Queen where a kid could get a triple-scoop of his favorite ice cream and still have change left over. But now you have to go inside a high-priced shopping mall for an ice cream. Also in this same location there used to be a mom and pop grocery store that extended credit to the less fortunate folks.

To accommodate the influx of visitors to my old town, expensive motels and restaurants now line the river bank where once a kid could go fishing under the shade of a weeping willow on a hot summer day. The railroad tracks still run along the same area of the foothills, but instead of box cars hauling shinning black coal and moving slowly, the cars are bright red and silver and carry passengers as they move at a rapid speed. Not too far from this area, nestled in the background of my town, was a large wooded area filled with wild flowers and trees of every type and size. The trees and flowers have been replaced by campgrounds, gas stations, mini-markets, and weekend people. Here also the four-wheeled vehicles grind a path where the wild flowers bloomed and the trees grew tall, and the roar of engines and the smell of fumes fill the air that once was filed with the scent of honeysuckle and the soft sounds of the birds singing.

Even the main street through Dawes has been widened to four lanes to handle the bustling traffic. As the automobiles go speeding in both directions, the sidewalks are crowded with people rushing in both directions, where not long ago folks strolled along the white picket fences and took time to say hello to their neighbors. I know children are still being born and raised in this new Dawes, but they're not growing up in my home town.

When Anxiety Becomes Fear

Jason Ware

I think everyone has a certain anxiety that he or she feels in a dentist's office. The feeling probably comes from having one's mouth violated with sharp instruments, needles, and foul tasting concoctions. Ever since childhood I have shared that feeling of anxiety in the pit of my stomach with most everyone who reclines in that banana shaped vinyl chair.

For some the feeling is genuine anxiety, for others the feeling is plain <u>fear</u>. What makes the difference between those who feel anxiety, and those who feel fear, is probably the past experiences they have had as patients. It just takes one incident to justify the feeling of anxiety and cause a person to be afraid. For me that incident came in childhood. I'm terrified of dentists and I think I have every right to feel that way!

I was twelve and had been ordered by my orthodontist to see my dentist to have <u>eight</u> teeth pulled to make way for braces. Some were stubborn baby teeth that needed to come out, but four were permanent. "I'll send these forms to your dentist so he knows what teeth need to be pulled," Dr. Hutchings told me after a long session of poking, X-raying, and generally making my mouth uncomfortable.

"O.K.," I managed to mumble from behind the gauze pads packed in my cheeks.

I make an appointment at the dentist for the following

week. My anxiety gnawed at the inside of my ribs more with each passing day until finally, the time had come.

I eased back into the vinyl while watching the nurse preparing the Novacain needle. The doctor came in, pumped my gums full of the foul tasting Novacain, then left me to wait for it to take effect. The next step was listening to the hideous cracking sound my teeth made while being yanked and twisted from my mouth. I was so twisted inside with anxiety that I felt nauseous.

When it was finally over I was so pumped with medicine and emotionally exhausted that I was dizzy. I stumbled out into the waiting room where my grandmother sat waiting to give me a ride home. Just as I thought the nightmare was over, the dentist stepped into the waiting room and pulled me back in. "I'm afraid that I have misread the chart that your 'Ortho' sent. I pulled two of the wrong teeth." Instantly the anxiety metamorphosed into fear.

He sat me back in the clammy, heartless chair and pumped even more Novacain into my already sore jaw. Then he took the two permanent teeth that he had just pulled, and shoved them into the bleeding gaps--I winced from the excruciating pain. Next he put gauze pads between my upper and lower teeth and told me to "bite down." I did so and tears came to my eyes.

"They will probably re-attach in a few weeks and be as good as new," he told me. I heard a little fear in his voice, obviously scared of a malpractice suit. I put the Codine he gave me in my pocket and hurried out the door before anything else could happen to me. I went back regularly for the next few months to have them tested and checked. Now it was fear that I felt when I got close to that office, not anxiety at all--pure <u>fear</u>. At the end of the second month of visits the doctor told me with relief in his voice, "They did turn out to be 'as good as new.'"

I have advice for those of you who share in my past feeling of anxiety. You have good reason to feel that way! At all costs avoid dentists' offices. If you should have to see a dentist always keep an eye on him; he is capable of making mistakes. One little mistake can change your feelings from anxiety to justified fear!

One for All

Diane K. Levy

"Ahhhhhhh!" screams the girl, her popcorn flying into the lap of the person two rows behind her. Her hair is standing straight up in the air, her nails bitten down to the pinks. The screen is filled with the shiny knife, dripping blood. A dark figure is seen raising the knife--for the kill! "AHHH!"

Surprisingly enough, she hasn't seen half of the movie because she is forever covering her eyes with the current issue of Moviegoer whenever that "dark figure" appears on the screen. But she needn't pay another five bucks to see the movie again (this time making her boyfriend hold her hands down and eyes open), that is, if she has seen at least one horror movie straight through. For, you see, there is only one definition of the killer; he is an unhumanlike, immortal monster who has a very selective range of victims to choose from.

One characteristic of the slasher, and perhaps the most obvious, is that he--and it always is a he--is not human in the true sense of the word. Yes, he does have the frame of Homo sapiens, a rather large one of course, and he does have skin, not a thick layer of fur or anything. However, one does not consider something human if it does not have a face--and those horror movie killers never have one, as far as the viewers can tell. This "faceless" theory is derived from the fact that the slasher always wears a mask of some sort. Since he probably doesn't have a nose, he breathes very heavily through his mouth. This sound is easily made audible because of the small holes in his mask. His heavy breathing only meant someone else would stop breathing altogether.

The killer, unlike Manson or some other psychotic killer in the real world, is very limited to who he can and cannot kill. His most popular kills are the party-animal teenagers out with their friends, drinking beer and having sex. However, he does have a lot of trouble with the typical schoolgirl that was forced (by peer pressure) to join the group of wild schoolmates. This girl, usually without the protection of a boyfriend, is the only one who can dodge the slasher's thrust with his butcher knife, and the only one who can find sewing needles or some type of sharp kitchen utensil within reach to stab the monster. Usually by the time the killer gets to the schoolgirl, all the other teenagers are dead. So who's left in the movie? The doctor at the insane asylum, of course. The doctor is the only other person that might give the slasher a problem, because the slasher can only injure him, not kill him.

The slasher is immortal. No matter how many times the schoolgirl stabs him or the doctor shoots him, he always gets up, but only after a few minutes go by, long enough for the person to relax and think he or she is safe. This accounts for the very profitable sequels the horror movies have (like Friday the 13th, Part 100). And each one ends the same way: showing the killer getting up and then cutting to a scene showing that he has disappeared--and to where? The next movie!

More often than not, the killer was once a normal teenager. But something terrible happened to him emotionally and physically. This "something" is usually graphic enough to make it a movie in itself: How the Slasher Came to Be, for instance. Wouldn't that be an interesting psychological standpoint for a movie to take? I guess not, since that would ruin our definition of the killer by making him a three-dimensional character. Ahhh! We can't do that. Else how can we cover our eyes through the scary parts and still know exactly what is going on in the movie?

Well, we needn't worry about the disappearance of the slasher; conformity is a much simpler way to the bank. So, how 'bout it? Want to catch the double-feature downtown? It's Halloween VII and Friday the 13th, Part . . . hmmm . . . I lost track.

Cocaine: The Nonuser

Susan Woolworth

"This is drugs," butter spattering in a frying pan; "this is your brain on drugs," an egg falling into that pan; "get the picture." This is just one of the commercials seen by many of us today. Cocaine is one drug that we have been hearing a lot about in the past few years. We hear how the users of cocaine set out to have a good time and end up losing their jobs, friends, families, and finally, their homes. What we don't hear about are the unfortunate people, both adults and children, that come in contact with the cocaine user. Cocaine is a dangerous drug, not only to the user, but also to the people around the user. The occasional user of cocaine usually won't steal to get cocaine, but the addict, at all costs, will. First he will start off by robbing liquor stores or burglarizing homes of innocent people. If the addict falls too deep into his addiction, he will begin stealing from his loved ones. The rent money will disappear, and often pay checks won't even be seen coming into the household. When personal items start vanishing, family members become hurt and distrustful towards their loved one. The addict will steal anything from anybody just to get "high."

Children can especially be greatly harmed, not only emotionally, but physically as well. When sellers are on the streets pushing cocaine, they usually aim at children. Children are a good target for a pusher, because they are easily influenced to buy. Even worse, small children may find it in their own home. A very small amount of cocaine can be deadly to a child. If the drug doesn't kill them, the paraphernalia most likely will. Razor blades and ether can, most likely, be found laying around the house for a child to pick up and begin playing with. Not only are the drugs and paraphernalia dangerous, the user, when "high," can be dangerous also.

A person using cocaine can become paranoid about the whole world. He thinks everyone is out to destroy him. Strangers seem to be after him, loved ones become enemies, and even the family pet looks like a violent killer. He will often hide in closets or behind doors; striking at anyone that seemingly sneaks up on him. People are in great danger when around a paranoid person, because they never know what he is going to do next.

Through television and newspaper articles, we are always hearing about how we should be helping the users, but what about the victims of the users? Emotionally and physically innocent people are being hurt everyday. There has to be a way to stop this pain. I don't think the memories of our treasured belongings being stolen, children found dead from overdose, or paranoid friends and loved ones looking at us like strangers will ever go away, but if the cocaine addict could see through the nonusers eyes, maybe the pains would slow down. "Say no to drugs," is a well known slogan. I wish every cocaine user, even the occasional one, would "get the picture."

A Firm Swat

Christina Sauppe

The ball that Adam and Lindsley were playing with flew over the bushes and out into the street. Adam found a dirt pile to explore as Lindsley ran to the edge of the curb. She remembered how Mommy had told her never, never to go in the street or Mommy would be very angry. But Mommy wasn't around, so she ran out to grab the ball just as a car screeched to a halt a few yards away. Mommy ran out of the house in panic and apologized to the man in the car as she firmly, very firmly, took Lindsley's hand and pulled her into the house.

As a parent, how would you punish this little 5-year-old? Would you reason with her, send her to her room, or wait until her father came home? Many parents choose one of the oldest and most widely used punishments today: spanking. Through my own observation and experience I have found spanking to be an abusive and unacceptable punishment for children

Of course, many parents would disagree with this standpoint. I have heard phrases such as these time and time again: "Sometimes children just need a good 'whack' to keep them in line," or "the only way to make my toddler obey me is if I threaten her with spanking," or "a spanking scares them out of doing it again," and finally, "How can you call an old-fashioned 'smack' on a child's behind 'abuse'?" The chief argument these people have is that by using spanking as a consistent punishment their children have a constant awareness that if they do something naughty, they will get physically hurt--and this prevents them from doing it. In reality, the reasons that I have found against spanking far out-weigh this common argument.

First, how do we define the term "spanking" and where do we draw the line between "spanking" and "abuse"? We call child abuse anything having to do with physically harming a child. Does spanking not apply? Toddlers are about one-third the size of adults, giving parents complete physical control over them. In the school yards we hear "Why don't you pick on someone your own size!?" We call these "bullies" unfair, and yet when grown, mature adults spank small, defenseless children it is perfectly acceptable. And why is it that our most dangerous criminals are protected from any kind of physical brutality, while spanking our children is permissable? Hitting and spanking are synonymous and are abuse that should not be tolerated.

The use of spanking as a means of deterring a child from doing something naughty can be called a method of fear. The child does become afraid to do certain things, but this leads to a fear of the parent that holds only if the parent is nearby. Here is one example that I encountered while working at a day-care center.

Eric walked in quietly and sat down at the puzzle-table, leaving his mother to sign him in. He quickly saw his favorite puzzle being put together by another child and began a tug-of-war. A towering voice traveled across the room, "Eric! If you don't give back that puzzle you are going to get the spanking of your life tonight!" The playfulness left him and he looked up in fear, dropping the puzzle. His mother shook her finger at him as she walked out of the room. The tug-of-war resumed between the two children. Eric was then confused when I took the puzzle from him and explained why it wasn't fair for him to have it, right then. So, because the fear of his mother had been lifted when she had left, Eric had felt free to act as he pleased. He only knew that his mother wasn't there to hit him, so he wasn't afraid to "do it again."

Yet another important reason why spanking should not be used as a punishment is that it sets a bad example. Most parents will agree that a child learns practically everything he knows by imitating those around him--most of all his parents. Children learn to talk, walk, brush their teeth, tie their shoes, etc., by observing their parents. It is then easy to see how a child will react observing or experiencing spanking. The child learns that when you are angry at someone, you should hit him. Because the parents hit, children learn that this is a way to deal with problems. Therefore, violence produces violence.

While taking care of a 3-year-old baby and his baby sister one afternoon, I noticed that the older, Brendon, was becoming frustrated. Little Sarah had other things in mind and wasn't interested in his fire truck games. In his anger, he hit Sarah hard enough to knock her over on the hard floor. I was shocked at such behavior until I realized that he was following the example his parents had set for him. He had been spanked ever since he could walk. As parents, we should certainly not teach our children how to hit.

Perhaps the most important effect a childhood of spanking could produce is the long-lasting one. Some children are often more violent than others as they are reaching adolesence. There are those that continually start fights in the school yard. If their parents continue to punish them by violence, why shouldn't they feel it acceptable to punish someone else in the same way?

When I was young (perhaps six or seven) I remember being with my family while we stopped at a gas station. Across the street was a shop with the most beautiful, large stuffed animals, and I wanted one. Although I cried for a few minutes and put up a fuss, my Dad explained to me that I had lots of stuffed animals at home and that they were too expensive. I was reasoned with in this way each time I was naughty or unreasonable. Therefore I grew up learning that the way to handle a problem is to reason about it.

I was in a store the other day and saw a 5-year-old in a cart going through the checkout stand with his mother. The child insisted on having a candy bar while the mother repeatedly said "No." The little boy cried louder and louder until finally she picked him up and gave him a firm "swat" on the behind. She then carried out the screaming boy. This child was taught that the way to deal with a problem was to get angry and then hit. Being filled with these examples throughout childhood could lead to a violent person and someone who doesn't know how to deal with a problem effectively. These are not the sorts of problems we as parents want to instill in our children.

The reasons not to use spanking as a form of punishment are clear; it is a form of child abuse, it is founded on fear of the parent, it is setting a bad example for children to follow, and it may cause problems to develop in later childhood or even adulthood. It seems that parents are often saying, "This is for your own good," or "I only want what's best for my child." But is spanking really doing what's best for your child?

III

SPECIAL
USES OF
WRITING

7

Writing About Literature

In one sense, reading the newspaper and reading a short story by Nathaniel Hawthorne are exactly the same. You "process" the page—employing your visual system and your mind—to gain meaning from print. Of course, it might be said that you read with your mind, not your eyes, since it is quite possible for you to see print clearly but not be able to gain the meaning, as, for instance when you look at a page of foreign language, and blind people read with their fingertips, not their eyes.

THE ACT OF READING

Reading is, simply, the act of gaining meaning, not of seeing words and sentences and not of deriving sounds from those words and sentences. (One can learn to pronounce a foreign language without being able to understand the words that are pronounced.)

Reasons for Reading

But even though the *act* of reading—the interpretation of raw visual data by the mind—is essentially the same for all reading, purposes in reading vary widely. If you want to learn how to cultivate roses, you will most probably go to a reference source, such as the *Sunset Book of Gardening,* not to a poem about roses. On the other hand, millions of people do quite frequently read poems (about roses and other subjects). Their purpose in this kind of reading is radically different from their purpose in using a manual, a newspaper, or an encyclopedia.

The point, of course, is that we do not always read for information, to learn directly about the world "out there," but frequently take up a book—a novel, a collection of poems, an anthology of short stories—to gain the *experience* that this kind of reading affords.

It is fair to make a rough cut in the act of reading, dividing it into subcategories that we might call *informational* and *esthetic.* Baldly stated, we read either to gain information or to gain the experience that certain kinds of reading afford. In informational reading, purpose is firmly connected with results in the world "out there": we want to find out what's happening in the Middle East or what the current standings are among college football teams. When our purpose is esthetic, we want to immerse ourselves in the text, lose ourselves in the experience that the poem or story offers. And yet, when we read a novel, poem, story, or play, we gain an extremely complex sort of meaning.

In writing about literature, we can attempt to explain the nature of the experience or, on the other hand, we can try to explain the complex meaning of the work. In other words, we can write about our *response* to the work (what it means to *us*) or about the structure of the work itself and how that structure conveys meaning. The second kind of writing—that which explains how the story, poem, novel, or play "works"—is often called *explication.*

Here is a poem by James Dickey, followed by the poet's account of the "facts" of the events on which the poem is based. After you have carefully read the poem and Dickey's explanation of it, you should understand what the poem is "about."

The Performance
James Dickey

The last time I saw Donald Armstrong
He was staggering oddly off into the sun,
Going down, off the Philippine Islands.
I let my shovel fall, and put that hand
Above my eyes, and moved some way to one side
That his body might pass through the sun,

And I saw how well he was not
Standing there on his hands,
On his spindle-shanked forearms balanced,
Unbalanced, with his big feet looming and waving
In the great, untrustworthy air
He flew in each night, when it darkened.

Dust fanned in scraped puffs from the earth
Between his arms, and blood turned his face inside out,
To demonstrate its suppleness
Of veins, as he perfected his role.
Next day, he toppled his head off
On an island beach to the south,

And the enemy's two-handed sword
Did not fall from anyone's hands
At that miraculous sight,
As the head rolled over upon
Its wide-eyed face, and fell
Into the inadequate grave

He had dug for himself, under pressure.
Yet I put my flat hand to my eyebrows
Months later, to see him again
In the sun, when I learned how he died,
And imagined him, there,
Come, judged, before his small captors,

Doing all his lean tricks to amaze them—
The back somersault, the kip-up—
And at last, the stand on his hands,
Perfect, with his feet together,
His head down, evenly breathing,
As the sun poured up from the sea

And the headsman broke down
In a blaze of tears, in that light
Of the thin, long human frame
Upside down in its own strange joy,

And, if some other one had not told him,
Would have cut off the feet

Instead of the head,
And if Armstrong had not presently risen
In kingly, round-shouldered attendance,
And then knelt down in himself
Beside his hacked, glittering grave, having done
All things in this life that he could.

Almost every word of "The Performance" is literally true, except that the interpretation of the facts is my own. It's a poem about a boy named Donald Armstrong, who came from somewhere in the West. He was in my squadron, the 418th Night Fighter Squadron, during the Second World War. He was probably my best friend in the squadron, a very lovable, ugly fellow. You need somebody like him in a combat situation, someone who sees the humorous side of everything and is happy-go-lucky and daring. He was an awfully good pilot, but he took a lot of unnecessary chances, and the older air crews in the squadron were a bit chary of him. He was always doing crazy things like going to sleep with the airplane on Automatic Pilot. He and his observer—the P61 had a two-man crew—sometimes would both go to sleep and just drone along coming back from convoy cover or wherever they'd been.

Most of our missions were to the north of the island we were on, Mindoro, the island immediately south of Luzon. But we also had missions to the south, to Panay. As nearly as I can remember, some Japanese held the island and were using Filipino labor to build an airstrip. Armstrong and his observer, Jim Lalley, went down to Panay in a P61 one evening on a strafing run. Apparently it was just at dusk, when it's hard to judge distances, and the plane hit the ground. It was damaged and began to come apart, so Armstrong made a crash landing. They were both hurt, according to the reports we got from the Filipino guerrillas, but they were alive. They were taken out of the aircraft by the Japanese, kept in an old schoolhouse, and beheaded the next day at dawn. We found out about this immediately from the guerrilla forces on Panay, but there was nothing we could have done about it.

Don Armstrong was always doing gymnastic tricks in the squadron area. He used to do flips and all kinds of such things, and would work on his handstands. He was a tall fellow, and because his center of gravity was high, it was hard for him to do handstands. I can remember him falling over on his head and back and getting up and trying again. For a long time I tried to write this poem, but the poems I wrote were all official tributes to my old buddy. They didn't have the distinctiveness that I thought the poem really ought to have. So I said to myself, "Goodness, Jim, what is the thing you remember *most* about Don? Do you remember how ugly he was, or how skinny he was, or something that he did?" There was a squadron movie area where we used to have movies when the Japanese weren't bombing us. Don and I saw a movie called *Laura* there, and he was wild about it. I remember sitting in the weeds watching that movie with him; so I put that into the poem, but it wasn't right. Then I remembered that he used to do all those flips and tricks in the squadron area. People would stand around watching him, but sometimes he'd just be out there by himself standing on his hands, or trying to. He never mastered it; I never saw him do a good handstand.

Finally I tried to bring together the unsuccessful handstand, the last trick he was trying to perfect, and the grotesque manner of his death, and I tried to describe the effect these would have on the beholders, the executioners, and on the poet who tells the poem. I thought, "Why not make it *really* crazy?" The poem isn't about the facts of Armstrong's death, because the narrator is trying to imagine them. I said to myself, "I'll bet that damned Armstrong would be crazy enough to throw off a dozen cartwheels before he got his head chopped off! And what would *that* do to the Japanese?"

Since you can make anything you like happen in a poem, I made it happen that way. I wrote the poem in a rather matter-of-fact way with no obvious rhetorical devices, like refrains. I did it straight because I didn't want to write amazingly about ordinary events, but matter-of-factly about extraordinary events. It seemed to be more effective that way, as well as much truer to the kind of experience that it might have been for the narrator. I suppose "The Performance" is the most anthologized of my poems. I've never taken an actual count, but I've come across it in more places than I have any other of my poems, maybe partly because it's been in circulation longer. I wrote it in the first part of 1958, also in an advertising office.

I'm always trying to synthesize, and I thought, "Boy, next week I'm going to try to get these two techniques together. (I had to drop poetry and do some radio commercials.) I'm going to use the crazy approach to subject matter I used in 'The Performance' and some other things, like refrains, and see what happens." As I said, experimentation is very, very important to me. That's what makes poetry so damned much fun! If you ask yourself the fundamental question, "What would happen if.   .?" then the only one thing to do is to see what *would* happen if you did such-and-such a thing. That's always been very much a part of writing poetry for me, and that's the part I enjoy the most.

Response

Informally, in your journal or in a formal essay, explain what "The Performance" means *to you*. In this writing, you will be focusing on your own experiences, interests, and values. To get under way, you might ask yourself the following questions, think about them, and record as many ideas as you can in the form of rough notes.

1. *You as reader.* Your interests? Fears? Attitudes toward war? Toward death? Your values (concerning life, bravery, and the like.)? Your personality? Do you like poetry? (Explain.) What other questions can you think of?
2. *The events in the poem.* Have you had experiences that are in any way similar? (What about the death of a friend or a loved one?) How did you react to the mixture of comedy and tragedy in the poem? How do you feel about executions? What other questions can you think of?
3. *The characters.* Have you ever known anyone like Donald Armstrong? (How is that person like Armstrong?) Have you ever known people like the captors? (Explain.) What other questions can you think of?
4. *Time and place.* In what way is the setting of the poem like (or unlike) places you have known? What does the setting remind you of? Have you ever experienced a time of "war"? (In your imagination? In your family? In your neighborhood?) What does "wartime" mean to you? What other questions can you think of?
5. *The poem itself.* Did you enjoy the language? (Explain.) How about the images? What didn't you like about the poem? What other questions can you think of?
6. *Purposes.* Why did the events happen? Have you know of other events that happened for the same reasons? Have you been involved in such events? Were the events in the poem senseless? (Have you ever been the victim of senseless events?) What other questions can you think of?

Your notes regarding these questions should give you a basis for explaining your reaction to the poem.

Toward Explication

The following questions focus your attention more on the poem itself than on your reaction to it. By making notes of your answers to the questions, you can prepare to do an *explication*, an explanation of how the poem "works."

1. In both the poem and the explanation of how it came into being, the speaker is Dickey himself. (In some imaginative literature, the

speaker, as we shall see, is a character invented by the author.) How does Dickey's attitude toward his subject in the poem differ from his attitude in the explanation?

2. If you want the "facts" about Donald Armstrong, Dickey's explanation is the best source. But what sort of *meaning* do you get from the poem that you can't get from the explanation?

3. The poem is more concrete, specific, visual than the explanation. What does this concreteness contribute to your reading of the poem?

4. Does it make any difference to your understanding of the poem that there was an actual Donald Armstrong? Explain.

5. In what ways does Dickey change the facts in the poem? Why does he do so?

6. What scenes and events does Dickey invent for the poem? Why does he do so?

7. Was your reading of the poem more intense than your reading of the explanation? If so, explain.

8. Explain what the following means in relation to the experience of reading: "The purpose of Dickey's explanation is to give information about the poem, but the purpose of the poem is to re-create an experience for the reader."

9. How do answers to the followng questions help you explain the poem and your reaction to it?

   a. What happens in the poem?
   b. What sort of character is Donald Armstrong?
   c. By what means are the actions in the poem brought about?
   d. When and where do the actions take place?
   e. Why do the actions take place?

10. One of the main images in the poem is that of the sun. It appears in various guises throughout the poem (for example, it is suggested by its very absence in the last line of the second stanza, "He flew in each night, when it [the air, sky] darkened"). How does this image— and its varying appearance—help in understanding what Dickey is saying?

Response and Explication

With response, the focus is on the reader: his or her reaction to the work. With explication, the focus is on the poem or story: its plot, the nature of the characters, the setting, the reasons for the characters' doing what they do. Actually, response involves explication and vice versa. If I asked you to explain your response to "The Performance," and you said that you liked it because it is about the joys and frustrations of playing Frisbee, I would be puzzled, to say the least. I would ask you to show me *in the poem* where you found that subject matter, and you would need to explicate. On the other hand, if I gave you a thorough explication of the poem—plot, characters, structure, style—but nothing more, you would be justified in asking, "But did you like the poem, and if so, why? What did it mean *to you?*"

Exploring your response to a work of literature might be easier than doing an explication, for the simple reason that you don't need a special vocabulary to talk about the work; you know that it made sense and was satisfying, but can't explain why. The discussion that follows will teach you how to make such explanations.

ELEMENTS OF PROSE FICTION

The great storytellers throughout history have taken their places among the most highly honored of the world's heroes: Cervantes, Goethe, Dickens, Tolstoy, Twain, Hemingway. People have always thirsted for stories; their most basic response is the eager question "And then what?" What is so mysterious about our reaction to stories is that we know they are fictions, "untrue," and yet our thirst for this fictional experience drives us from story to story throughout our lives. (Almost without exception, even nonreaders hunger for stories, and to satisfy that hunger watch television or attend movies.) We feel that a person uninterested in stories is slightly less than human, lacking some spark of playfulness and imagination that makes a human being different from the less-than-human creatures that populate science fiction.

It makes no sense, of course, to talk about literature in a vacuum: we need a work to refer to. That work will be a classic American short story.

Young Goodman Brown
Nathaniel Hawthorne

Young Goodman Brown came forth at sunset into the street at Salem village; but put his head back, after crossing the threshold, to exchange a parting kiss with his young wife. And Faith, as the wife was aptly named, thrust her own pretty head into the street, letting the wind play with the pink ribbons of her cap while she called to Goodman Brown.

"Dearest heart," whispered she, softly and rather sadly, when her lips were close to his ear, "prithee put off your journey until sunrise and sleep in your own bed to-night. A lone woman is troubled with such dreams and such thoughts that she's afeard of herself sometimes. Pray tarry with me this night, dear husband, of all nights in the year." 10

"My love and my Faith," replied young Goodman Brown, "of all nights in the year, this one night must I tarry away from thee. My journey, as thou callest it, forth and back again, must needs be done 'twixt now and sunrise. What, my sweet, pretty wife, dost thou doubt me already, and we but three months married?"

"Then God bless you!" said Faith, with the pink ribbons; "and may you find all well when you come back." 20

"Amen!" cried Goodman Brown. "Say thy prayers, dear Faith, and go to bed at dusk, and no harm will come to thee."

So they parted; and the young man pursued his way until, being about to turn the corner by the meeting-house, he looked back and saw the head of Faith still peeping after him with a melancholy air, in spite of her pink ribbons.

"Poor little Faith!" thought he, for his heart smote him. "What a wretch am I to leave her on such an errand! She talks of dreams, too. Methought as she spoke there was trouble in her face, as if a dream had warned her what work is to be done to-night. But no, 30 no; 'twould kill her to think it. Well, she's a blessed angel on earth; and after this one night I'll cling to her skirts and follow her to heaven."

With this excellent resolve for the future, Goodman Brown felt himself justified in making more haste on his present evil purpose. He had taken a dreary road, darkened by all the gloomiest trees of the forest, which barely stood aside to let the narrow path creep through, and closed immediately behind. It was all as lonely as could be; and there is this peculiarity in such a solitude, that the traveller knows not who may be concealed by the innumerable 40 trunks and the thick boughs overhead; so that with lonely footsteps he may yet be passing through an unseen multitude.

"There may be a devilish Indian behind every tree," said Goodman Brown to himself; and he glanced fearfully behind him as he added, "What if the devil himself should be at my very elbow!"

His head being turned back, he passed a crook of the road, and, looking forward again, beheld the figure of a man, in grave and decent attire, seated at the foot of an old tree. He arose at Goodman Brown's approach and walked onward side by side with 50 him.

"You are late, Goodman Brown," said he. "The clock of the Old South was striking as I came through Boston, and that is full fifteen minutes agone."

"Faith kept me back awhile," replied the young man, with a tremor in his voice, caused by the sudden appearance of his companion, though not wholly unexpected.

It was now deep dusk in the forest, and deepest in that part of it where these two were journeying. As nearly as could be discerned, the second traveller was about fifty years old, apparently in the same rank of life as Goodman Brown, and bearing a considerable resemblance to him, though perhaps more in expression than features. Still they might have been taken for father and son. And yet, though the elder person was as simply clad as the younger, and as simple in manner too, he had an indescribable air of one who knew the world, and who would not have felt abashed at the governor's dinner table or in King William's court, were it possible that his affairs should call him thither. But the only thing about him that could be fixed upon as remarkable was his staff, which bore the likeness of a great black snake, so curiously wrought that it might almost be seen to twist and wriggle itself like a living serpent. This, of course, must have been an ocular deception, assisted by the uncertain light.

"Come, Goodman Brown," cried his fellow-traveller, "this is a dull pace for the beginning of a journey. Take my staff, if you are so soon weary."

"Friend," said the other, exchanging his slow pace for a full stop, "having kept convenant by meeting thee here, it is my purpose now to return whence I came. I have scruples touching the matter thou wot'st of."

"Sayest thou so?" replied he of the serpent, smiling apart. "Let us walk on, nevertheless, reasoning as we go; and if I convince thee not thou shalt turn back. We are but a little way in the forest yet."

"Too far! too far!" exclaimed the goodman, unconsicously resuming his walk. "My father never went into the woods on such an errand, nor his father before him. We have been a race of honest men and good Christians since the days of the martyrs; and shall I be the first of the name of Brown that ever took this path and kept"—

"Such company, thou wouldst say," observed the elder person, interpreting his pause. "Well said, Goodman Brown! I have been as well acquainted with your family as with ever a one among the Puritans; and that's no trifle to say. I helped your grandfather, the constable, when he lashed the Quaker woman so smartly through the streets of Salem; and it was I that brought your father a pitchpine knot, kindled at my own hearth, to set fire to an Indian village, in King Philip's war. They were my good friends, both; and many a pleasant walk have we had along this path, and returned merrily after midnight. I would fain be friends with you   100 for their sake."

"If it be as thou sayest," replied Goodman Brown, "I marvel they never spoke of these matters; or, verily, I marvel not, seeing that the least rumor of the sort would have driven them from New England. We are a people of prayer, and good works to boot, and abide no such wickedness."

"Wickedness or not," said the traveller with the twisted staff, "I have a very general acquaintance here in New England. The deacons of many a church have drunk the communion wine with me; the selectmen of divers towns make me their chairman; and   110 a majority of the Great and General Court are firm supporters of my interest. The governor and I, too—But these are state secrets."

"Can this be so?" cried Goodman Brown, with a stare of amazement at his undisturbed companion. "Howbeit, I have nothing to do with the governor and council; they have their own ways, and are no rule for a simple husbandman like me. But, were I to go on with thee, how should I meet the eye of that good old man, our minister, at Salem village? Oh, his voice would make me tremble both Sabbath day and lecture day."   120

Thus far the elder traveller had listened with due gravity; but now burst into a fit of irrepressible mirth, shaking himself so violently that his snake-like staff actually seemed to wriggle in sympathy.

"Ha! ha! ha!" shouted he again and again; then composing himself, "Well, go on, Goodman Brown, go on; but, prithee, don't kill me with laughing."

"Well, then, to end the matter at once," said Goodman Brown, considerably nettled, "there is my wife, Faith. It would break her dear little heart; and I'd rather break my own."   130

"Nay, if that be the case," answered the other, "e'en go thy ways, Goodman Brown. I would not for twenty old women like the one hobbling before us that Faith should come to any harm."

As he spoke he pointed his staff at a female figure on the path, in whom Goodman Brown recognized a very pious and exemplary dame, who had taught him his catechism in youth, and was still his moral and spiritual adviser, jointly with the minister and Deacon Gookin.

"A marvel, truly, that Goody Cloyse should be so far in the wilderness at nightfall," said he. "But with your leave, friend, I   140 shall take a cut through the woods until we have left this Christian woman behind. Being a stranger to you, she might ask whom I was consorting with and wither I was going."

"Be it so," said his fellow-traveller. "Betake you to the woods, and let me keep the path."

Accordingly the young man turned aside, but took care to watch his companion, who advanced softly along the road until he had come within a staff's length of the old dame. She, meanwhile, was making the best of her way, with singular speed for so aged a woman, and mumbling some indistinct words—a prayer, doubtless—as she went. The traveller put forth his staff and touched her withered neck with what seemed the serpent's tail.

"The devil!" screamed the pious old lady.

"Then Goody Cloyse knows her old friend?" observed the traveller, confronting her and leaning on his writhing stick.

"Ah, forsooth, and is it your worship indeed?" cried the good dame. "Yea, truly is it, and in the very image of my old gossip, Goodman Brown, the grandfather of the silly fellow that now is. But—would your worship believe it?—my broomstick hath strangely disappeared, stolen, as I suspect, by that unhanged witch, Goody Cory, and that, too, when I was all anointed with juice of smallage, and cinquefoil, and wolf's bane"—

"Mingled with fine wheat and the fat of a new-born babe," said the shape of old Goodman Brown.

"Ah, your worship knows the recipe," cried the old lady, cackling aloud. "So, as I was saying, being all ready for the meeting, and no horse to ride on, I made up my mind to foot it; for they tell me there is a nice young man to be taken into communion to-night. But now your good worship will lend me your arm, and we shall be there in a twinkling."

"That can hardly be," answered her friend. "I may not spare you my arm, Goody Cloyse; but here is my staff, if you will."

So saying, he threw it down at her feet, where, perhaps, it assumed life, being one of the rods which its owner had formerly lent to the Egyptian magi. Of this fact, however, Goodman Brown could not take cognizance. He had cast up his eyes in astonishment, and, looking down again, beheld neither Goody Cloyse nor the serpentine staff, but his fellow-traveller alone, who waited for him as calmly as if nothing had happened.

"That old woman taught me my catechism," said the young man; and there was a world of meaning in this simple comment.

They continued to walk onward, while the elder traveller exhorted his companion to make good speed and persevere in the path, discoursing so aptly that his arguments seemed rather to spring up in the bosom of his auditor than to be suggested by himself. As they went, he plucked a branch of maple to serve for a walking stick, and began to strip it of the twigs and little boughs, which were wet with evening dew. The moment his fingers touched them they became strangely withered and dried up as with a week's sunshine. Thus the pair proceeded, at a good free pace, until suddenly, in a gloomy hollow of the road, Goodman Brown sat himself down on the stump of a tree and refused to go any farther.

"Friend," said he, stubbornly, "my mind is made up. Not another step will I budge on this errand. What if a wretched old woman do choose to go to the devil when I thought she was going to heaven: is that any reason why I should quit my dear Faith and go after her?"

"You will think better of this by and by," said his acquaintance, composedly. "Sit here and rest yourself a while; and when you feel like moving again, there is my staff to help you along."

Without more words, he threw his companion the maple stick, and was as speedily out of sight as if he had vanished into the deepening gloom. The young man sat a few moments by the roadside, applauding himself greatly, and thinking with how clear a conscience he should meet the minister in his morning walk, nor shrink from the eye of good old Deacon Gookin. And what calm sleep would be his that very night, which was to have been spent so wickedly, but so purely and sweetly now, in the arms of Faith! Amidst these pleasant and praiseworthy meditations, Goodman Brown heard the tramp of horses along the road, and deemed it advisable to conceal himself within the verge of the forest, conscious of the guilty purpose that had brought him thither, though now so happily turned from it.

On came the hoof tramps and the voices of the riders, two grave old voices, conversing soberly as they drew near. These mingled sounds appeared to pass along the road, within a few yards of the young man's hiding-place; but, owing doubtless to the depth of the gloom at that particular spot, neither the travellers nor their steeds were visible. Though their figures brushed the small boughs by the wayside, it could not be seen that they intercepted, even for a moment, the faint gleam from the strip of bright sky athwart which they must have passed. Goodman Brown alternately crouched and stood on tiptoe, pulling aside the branches and thrusting forth his head as far as he durst without discerning so much as a shadow. It vexed him the more, because he could have sworn, were such a thing possible, that he recognized the voices of the minister and Deacon Gookin, jogging along quietly, as they were wont to do, when bound to some ordination or ecclesiastical council. While yet within hearing, one of the riders stopped to pluck a switch.

"Of the two, reverend sir," said the voice like the deacon's, "I had rather miss an ordination dinner than to-night's meeting. They tell me that some of our community are to be here from Falmouth and beyond, and others from Connecticut and Rhode Island, besides several of Indian powwows, who, after their fashion, know almost as much deviltry as the best of us. Moreover, there is a goodly young woman to be taken into communion."

"Mighty well, Deacon Gookin!" replied the solemn old tones of the minister. "Spur up, or we shall be late. Nothing can be done you know until I get on the ground."

240

The hoofs clattered again; and the voices, talking so strangely in the empty air, passed on through the forest, where no church had ever been gathered or solitary Christian prayed. Whither, then, could these holy men be journeying so deep into the heathen wilderness? Young Goodman Brown caught hold of a tree for support, being ready to sink down on the ground, faint and overburdened with the heavy sickness of his heart. He looked up to the sky, doubting whether there really was a heaven above him. Yet there was the blue arch, and the stars brightening in it.

"With heaven above and Faith below, I will yet stand firm against the devil!" cried Goodman Brown.

250

While he still gazed upward into the deep arch of the firmament and had lifted his hands to pray, a cloud, though no wind was stirring, hurried across the zenith and hid the brightening stars. The blue sky was still visible, except directly overhead, where this black mass of cloud was sweeping swiftly northward. Aloft in the air, as if from the depths of the cloud, came a confused and doubtful sound of voices. Once the listener fancied that he could distinguish the accents of towns-people of his own, men, and women, both pious and ungodly, many of whom he had met at the communion table, and had seen others rioting at the tavern. The next moment, so indistinct were the sounds, he doubted whether he had heard aught but the murmur of the old forest, whispering without a wind. Then came a stronger swell of those familiar tones, heard daily in the sunshine at Salem village, but never until now from a cloud of night. There was one voice of a young woman, uttering lamentations, yet with an uncertain sorrow, and entreating for some favor, which, perhaps, it would grieve her to obtain; and all the unseen multitude, both saints and sinners, seemed to encourage her onward.

260

270

"Faith!" shouted Goodman Brown, in a voice of agony and desperation; and the echoes of the forest mocked him, crying, "Faith! Faith!" as if bewildered wretches were seeking her all through the wilderness.

The cry of grief, rage, and terror was yet piercing the night, when the unhappy husband held his breath for a response. There was a scream, drowned immediately in a louder murmur of voices, fading into far-off laughter, as the dark cloud swept away, leaving the clear and silent sky above Goodman Brown. But something fluttered lightly down through the air and caught on the branch of a tree. The young man seized it, and beheld a pink ribbon. 280

"My Faith is gone!" cried he, after one stupefied moment. "There is no good on earth; and sin is but a name. Come, devil; for to thee is this world given."

And, maddened with despair, so that he laughed loud and long, did Goodman Brown grasp his staff and set forth again, at such a rate that he seemed to fly along the forest path rather than to walk or run. The road grew wilder and drearier and more faintly traced; and vanished at length, leaving him in the heart of the dark wilderness, still rushing onward with the instinct that 290 guides mortal man to evil. The whole forest was peopled with frightful sounds—the creaking of the trees, the howling of wild beasts, and the yell of Indians; while sometimes the wind tolled like a distant church bell, and sometimes gave a broad roar around the traveller, as if all Nature were laughing him to scorn. But he was himself the chief horror of the scene, and shrank not from its other horrors.

"Ha! ha! ha!" roared Goodman Brown when the wind laughed at him. "Let us hear which will laugh loudest. Think not to frighten me with your deviltry. Come witch, come wizard, come Indian 300 powwow, come devil himself, and here comes Goodman Brown. You may as well fear him as he fear you."

In truth, all through the haunted forest there could be nothing more frightful than the figure of Goodman Brown. On he flew among the black pines, brandishing his staff with frenzied gestures, now giving vent to an inspiration of horrid blasphemy, and now shouting forth such laughter as set all the echoes of the forest laughing like demons around him. The fiend in his own shape is less hideous than when he rages in the breast of man. Thus sped the demoniac on his course, until, quivering among 310 the trees, he saw a red light before him, as when the felled trunks and branches of a clearing have been set on fire, and throw up their lurid blaze against the sky, at the hour of midnight. He paused, in a lull of the tempest that had driven him onward, and heard the swell of what seemed a hymn, rolling solemnly from a distance with the weight of many voices. He knew the tune; it was a familiar one in the choir of the village meeting-house. The verse died heavily away, and was lengthened by a chorus, not of human voices, but of all the sounds of the benighted wilderness pealing

in awful harmony together. Goodman Brown cried out, and his   320
cry was lost to his own ear by its unison with the cry of the desert.

In the interval of silence he stole forward until the light glared
full upon his eyes. At one extremity of an open space, hemmed
in by the dark wall of the forest, arose a rock, bearing some rude,
natural resemblance either to an altar or a pulpit, and surrounded
by four blazing pines, their tops aflame, their stems untouched,
like candles at an evening meeting. The mass of foliage that had
overgrown the summit of the rock was all on fire, blazing high
into the night and fitfully illuminating the whole field. Each pen-
dant twig and leafy festoon was in a blaze. As the red light arose   330
and fell, a numerous congregation alternately shone forth, then
disappeared in shadow, and again grew, as it were, out of the
darkness, peopling the heart of the solitary woods at once.

"A grave and dark-clad company," quoth Goodman Brown.

In truth they were such. Among them, quivering to and fro
between gloom and splendor, appeared faces that would be seen
next day at the council board of the province, and others which,
Sabbath after Sabbath, looked devoutly heavenward, and benig-
nantly over the crowded pews, from the holiest pulpits in the land.
Some affirm that the lady of the governor was there. At least there   340
were high dames well known to her, and wives of honored hus-
bands, and widows, a great multitude, and ancient maidens, all of
excellent repute, and fair young girls, who trembled lest their
mothers should espy them. Either the sudden gleams of light
flashing over the obscure field bedazzled Goodman Brown, or he
recognized a score of the church members of Salem village famous for their especial sanctity. Good old Deacon Gookin had
arrived, and waited at the skirts of that venerable saint, his revered pastor. But, irreverently consorting with these grave, repu-
table, and pious people, these elders of the church, these chaste   350
dames and dewy virgins, there were men of dissolute lives and
women of spotted fame, wretches given over to all mean and filthy
vice, and suspected even of horrid crimes. It was strange to see
that the good shrank not from the wicked, nor were the sinners
abashed by the saints. Scattered also among their pale-faced enemies were the Indian priests, or powwows, who had often scared
their native forest with more hideous incantations than any known
to English witchcraft.

"But where is Faith?" thought Goodman Brown; and, as hope
came into his heart, he trembled.   360

Another verse of the hymn arose, a slow and mournful strain,
such as the pious love, but joined to words which expressed all
that our nature can conceive of sin, and darkly hinted at far more.
Unfathomable to mere mortals is the lore of fiends. Verse after

verse was sung; and still the chorus of the desert swelled between like the deepest tone of a mighty organ; and with the final peal of that dreadful anthem there came a sound, as if the roaring wind, the rushing streams, the howling beasts, and every other voice of the unconcerted wilderness were mingling and according with the voice of guilty man in homage to the prince of all. The 370 four blazing pines threw up a loftier flame, and obscurely discovered shapes and visages of horror on the smoke wreaths above the impious assembly. At the same moment the fire on the rock shot redly forth and formed a glowing arch above its base, where now appeared a figure. With reverence be it spoken, the figure bore no slight similitude, both in garb and manner, to some grave divine of the New England churches.

"Bring forth the converts!" cried a voice that echoed through the field and rolled into the forest.

At the word, Goodman Brown stepped forth from the shadow 380 of the trees and approached the congregation, with whom he felt a loathful brotherhood by the sympathy of all that was wicked in his heart. He could have well-nigh sworn that the shape of his own dead father beckoned him to advance, looking downward from a smoke wreath, while a woman, with dim features of despair, threw out her hand to warn him back. Was it his mother? But he had no power to retreat one step, nor to resist, even in thought, when the minister and good old Deacon Gookin seized his arms and led him to the blazing rock. Thither came also the slender form of a veiled female, led between Goody Cloyse, that 390 pious teacher of the catechism, and Martha Carrier, who had received the devil's promise to be queen of hell. A rampant hag was she. And there stood the proselytes beneath the canopy of fire.

"Welcome, my children," said the dark figure, "to the communion of your race. Ye have found thus young your nature and your destiny. My children, look behind you!"

They turned; and flashing forth, as it were, in a sheet of flame, the fiend worshippers were seen; the smile of welcome gleamed darkly on every visage.

"There," resumed the sable form, "are all whom ye have rev- 400 erenced from youth. Ye deemed them holier than yourselves, and shrank from your own sin, contrasting it with their lives of righteousness and prayerful aspirations heavenward. Yet here are they all in my worshipping assembly. This night it shall be granted you to know their secret deeds: how hoary-bearded elders of the church have whispered wanton words to the young maids of their households; how many a woman, eager for widows' weeds, has given her husband a drink at bedtime and let him sleep his last sleep in her bosom; how beardless youths have made haste to inherit their fathers' wealth; and how fair damsels—blush not, sweet 410 ones—have dug little graves in the garden, and bidden me, the sole guest to an infant's funeral. By the sympathy of your human hearts for sin ye shall scent out all the places—whether in church, bed-chamber, street, field, or forest—where crime has been committed, and shall exult to behold the whole earth one stain of guilt, one mighty blood spot. Far more than this. It shall be yours to penetrate, in every bosom, the deep mystery of sin, the fountain of all wicked arts, and which inexhaustibly supplies more evil impulses than human power—than my power at its utmost—can make manifest in deeds. And now, my children, look upon each   420 other."

They did so; and, by the blaze of the hell-kindled torches, the wretched man beheld his Faith, and the wife her husband, trembling before that unhallowed altar.

"Lo, there ye stand, my children," said the figure, in a deep and solemn tone, almost sad with its despairing awfulness, as if his once angelic nature could yet mourn for our miserable race. "Depending upon one another's hearts, ye had still hoped that virtue were not all a dream. Now are ye undeceived. Evil is the nature of mankind. Evil must be your only happiness. Welcome   430 again, my children, to the communion of your race."

"Welcome," repeated the fiend worshippers, in one cry of despair and triumph.

And there they stood, the only pair, as it seemed, who were yet hesitating on the verge of wickedness in this dark world. A basin was hollowed, naturally, in the rock. Did it contain water, reddened by the lurid light? or was it blood? or, perchance, a liquid flame? Herein did the shape of evil dip his hand and prepare to lay the mark of baptism upon their foreheads, that they might be partakers of the mystery of sin, more conscious of the   440 secret guilt of others, both in deed and thought, than they could now be of their own. The husband cast one look at his pale wife, and Faith at him. What polluted wretches would the next glance show them to each other, shuddering alike at what they disclosed and what they saw!

"Faith! Faith!" cried the husband, "look up to heaven, and resist the wicked one."

Whether Faith obeyed he knew not. Hardly had he spoken when he found himself amid calm night and solitude, listening to a roar of the wind which died heavily away through the forest.   450 He staggered against the rock, and felt it chill and damp; while a hanging twig, that had been all on fire, besprinkled his cheek with the coldest dew.

The next morning young Goodman Brown came slowly into the street of Salem village, staring around him like a bewildered man. The good old minister was taking a walk along the graveyard to get an appetite for breakfast and meditate his sermon, and bestowed a blessing, as he passed, on Goodman Brown. He shrank from the venerable saint as if to avoid an anathema. Old Deacon Gookin was at domestic worship, and the holy words of his prayer were heard through the open window. "What God doth the wizard pray to?" quoth Goodman Brown. Goody Cloyse, that excellent old Christian, stood in the early sunshine at her own lattice, catechizing a little girl who had brought her a pint of morning's milk. Goodman Brown snatched away the child as from the grasp of the fiend himself. Turning the corner by the meeting-house, he spied the head of Faith, with the pink ribbons, gazing anxiously forth, and bursting into such joy at sight of him that she skipped along the street and almost kissed her husband before the whole village. But Goodman Brown looked sternly and sadly into her face, and passed on without a greeting.

Had Goodman Brown fallen asleep in the forest and only dreamed a wild dream of a witch-meeting?

Be it so if you will; but, alas! it was a dream of evil omen for young Goodman Brown. A stern, a sad, a darkly meditative, a distrustful, if not a desperate man did he become from the night of that fearful dream. On the Sabbath day, when the congregation were singing a holy psalm, he could not listen because an anthem of sin rushed loudly upon his ear and drowned all the blessed strain. When the minister spoke from the pulpit with power and fervid eloquence, and, with his hand on the open Bible, of the sacred truths of our religion, and of saint-like lives and triumphant deaths, and of future bliss or misery unutterable, then did Goodman Brown turn pale, dreading lest the root should thunder down upon the gray blasphemer and his hearers. Often, waking suddenly at midnight, he shrank from the bosom of Faith; and at morning or eventide, when the family knelt down at prayer, he scowled and muttered to himself, and gazed sternly at his wife, and turned away. And when he had lived long, and was borne to his grave a hoary corpse, followed by Faith, an aged woman, and children and grandchildren, a goodly procession, besides neighbors not a few, they carved no hopeful verse upon his tombstone, for his dying hour was gloom.

The Narrator

Who tells the story of "Young Goodman Brown"? The obvious, but misleading, answer would be "Nathaniel Hawthorne." Hawthorne *wrote* the tale, true enough, but we must separate the author from the character that tells the story. This is a simple but very important point. Nathaniel Hawthorne the author is not *omniscient;* that is, he cannot know everything—just as you could not know of two actions that are going on in different parts of the world at the same time, and just as you cannot know all of the secrets of the human heart.

Narrators in fiction, however, can know anything that their authors want them to know. For example, in lines 34–36, the narrator says, "With this excellent resolve for the future, Goodman Brown felt himself justified in making more haste on his present evil purpose." So the narrator knows something that the mere observer could not possibly know, for the narrator can see into the character's mind.

First person narration. When a character *in* a story is also the narrator, we have first person narration. (The pronoun *I* is first person singular.)

Here is the first paragraph of Charles Dickens's *Great Expectations,* in which the main character tells his own story:

> My father's family name being Pirrip, and my Christian name Philip, my infant tongue could make of both names nothing longer or more explicit than Pip. So I called myself Pip, and came to be called Pip.

The first person narrator is limited; he or she cannot read minds or take a godlike view of all that happens everywhere. In first person narration, the story we read is "viewed" through the mind of the narrator.

Third person narration. The third person pronouns are *she, he, it,* and *they,* and we use them to report what others did. In making fictional "reports," the third person narrator can be either a camera, recording the sights and sounds within his or her range, or a godlike being who knows all and sees all—perceiving actions that take place simultaneously on opposite sides of the earth, knowing the innermost thoughts and feelings of the characters. On the other hand, the third person narrator can take a position between these extremes, knowing more than a mere mortal could, but not having a godlike omniscience. The narrator in "Young Goodman Brown" seems to occupy this middle position.

In *The Plumed Serpent,* by D. H. Lawrence, the narrator is omniscient:

> Cipriano sat motionless as a statue. But from his breast came that dark, surging passion of tenderness the Indians are capable of. Perhaps it would pass, leaving him indifferent and fatalistic again. But

at any rate for the moment he sat in a dark, fiery cloud of passionate male tenderness. He looked at her soft, wet white hands over her face, and at the one big emerald on her finger, in a sort of wonder. The wonder, the mystery, the magic that used to flood over him as a boy and a youth, when he kneeled before the babyish figure of the Santa Maria de la Soledad, flooded him again. He was in the presence of the goddess, white-handed, mysterious, gleaming with a moon-like power and the intense potency of grief.

Narrative point of view is one of the major factors in creating the magic of a story. When we hear someone tell a story, face to face, we can easily sense the personality and skill of the teller and understand how these factors permeate and shape the narrative. Though the personality of the teller is not so obvious in stories that we read, nonetheless there is a fictional person who does the telling and who shapes our attitudes and expectations. Sometimes this teller is a hazy, impersonal figure whom we don't get to know very well, as in the case of the narrator of "Young Goodman Brown." Sometimes the teller is vividly realized.

Point of View

1. Characterize the narrators as they appear in the following excerpts. Some questions you might ask yourself are these: (1) Who is the narrator? That is, what is the narrative point of view? Is it a first person or a third person narration? (2) What are the narrator's values and what is the tone of the narration? Cynical? Naive? Sincere? (3) What narrative devices are used to establish contact with the reader? For example, does the narrator address the reader directly? (4) What is the "voice" of the narrator? That of a child? A foreigner? An educated person? An imbecile?

   a.   You don't know about me without you have read a book by the name of the *Adventures of Tom Sawyer;* but that ain't no matter. That book was made by Mr. Mark Twain, and he told the truth mainly. There was things which he stretched, but mainly he told the truth. That is nothing. I never seen anybody but lied one time or another, without it was Aunt Polly, or the Widow, or maybe Mary. Aunt Polly—Tom's Aunt Polly, she is—and Mary, and the Widow Douglas is all told about in that book, which is mostly a true book, with some stretchers, as I said before.

   —Mark Twain, *The Adventures of Huckleberry Finn*

   b.   Krebs went to the war from a Methodist college in Kansas. There is a picture which shows him among his fraternity brothers, all of them wearing exactly the same height and style collar. He enlisted in the Marines in 1917 and did not return to the United States until the second division returned from the Rhine in the summer of 1919.

There is a picture which shows him on the Rhine with two German girls and another corporal. Krebs and the corporal look too big for their uniforms. The German girls are not beautiful. The Rhine does not show in the picture.

—Ernest Hemingway, "Soldier's Home"

c.　　　　To begin with I wish to disclaim the possession of those high gifts of imagination and expression which would have enabled my pen to create for the reader the personality of the man who called himself, after the Russian custom, Cyril son of Isidor—Kirylo Sidorovitch—Razumov.

If I have ever had these gifts in any sort of living form they have been smothered out of existence a long time ago under a wilderness of words. Words, as is well known, are the great foes of reality. I have been for many years a teacher of languages. It is an occupation which at length becomes fatal to whatever share of imagination, observation, and insight an ordinary person may be heir to. To a teacher of languages there comes a time when the world is but a place of many words and man appears a mere talking animal not much more wonderful than a parrot.

This being so, I could not have observed Mr. Razumov or guessed at his reality by the force of insight, much less have imagined him as he was. Even to invent the mere bald facts of his life would have been utterly beyond my powers. But I think that without this declaration the readers of these pages will be able to detect in the story the marks of documentary evidence. And that is perfectly correct. It is based on a document; all I have brought to it is my knowledge of the Russian language, which is sufficient for what is attempted here. The document, of course, is something in the nature of a journal, a diary, yet not exactly that in its actual form. For instance, most of it was not written up from day to day, though all the entries are dated. Some of these entries cover months of time and extend over dozens of pages. All the earlier part is a retrospect, in a narrative form, relating to an event which took place about a year before.

I must mention that I have lived for a long time in Geneva. A whole quarter of that town, on account of many Russians residing there, is called La Petite Russie—Little Russia. I had a rather extensive connexion in little Russia at that time. Yet I confess that I have no comprehension of the Russian character. The illogicality of their attitude, the arbitrariness of their conclusions, the frequency of the exceptional, should present no difficulty to a student of many grammars; but there must be something else in the way, some special human trait—one of those subtle differences that are beyond the ken of mere professors. What must remain striking to a teacher of languages is the Russians' extraordinary love of words. They gather them up; they cherish them, but they don't hoard them in their breasts; on the contrary, they are always ready to pour them out by the hour or by the night with an enthusiasm, a sweeping abundance, with such an aptness of application sometimes that, as in the case of very accomplished parrots, one can't defend oneself from the suspicion that they really understand what they say. There is a generosity in their ardour of speech which removes it as far as possible from common loquacity; and it is ever too disconnected to be classed as eloquence. . . . But I must apologize for this digression.

—Joseph Conrad, *Under Western Eyes*

d.   Alice was beginning to get very tired of sitting by her sister on the bank, and of having nothing to do: once or twice she had peeped into the book her sister was reading, but it had no pictures or conversations in it, "and what is the use of a book," thought Alice, "without pictures or conversations?"

So she was considering in her own mind (as well as she could, for the hot day made her feel very sleepy and stupid), whether the pleasure of making a daisy-chain would be worth the trouble of getting up and picking the daisies, when suddenly a White Rabbit with pink eyes ran close by her.

There was nothing so very remarkable in that; nor did Alice think it so *very* much out of the way to hear the Rabbit say to itself "Oh dear! Oh dear! I shall be too late!" (when she thought it over afterwards, it occurred to her that she ought to have wondered at this, but at the time it all seemed quite natural); but when the Rabbit actually *took a watch out of its waistcoat-pocket,* and looked at it, Alice started to her feet, for it flashed across her mind that she had never before seen a rabbit with either a waistcoat-pocket, or a watch to take out of it, and, burning with curiosity, she ran across the field after it, and was just in time to see it pop down a large rabbit-hole under the hedge.

—Lewis Carroll, *Alice's Adventures in Wonderland*

2. Answer and discuss the following questions about the narrator of "Young Goodman Brown."
   a. In lines 34–36 of the story, the narrative viewpoint changes. Explain that change. What happens? (Compare lines 34–36 with the first 33 lines.)
   b. Perhaps you feel that "Young Goodman Brown" is ambiguous. Was the experience real, or was it a dream? Explain how the narrative viewpoint helps create the ambiguity. (See, for instance, lines 68–73).
   c. The narrator holds certain values. What are they? How do you know? For instance, how do you know that the narrator is a devout Christian? How do these values help shape the story?
   d. Characterize the "voice" of the narrator. What evidence do you have for its characterization?

Make notes of your answers to these questions, for you will have use for your ideas later.

The Theme

Most works of literature have a theme; they are "about" something. The plot of a story is what happens. The *theme* of a story is the deeper meaning, the idea that underlies the narrative. The plot of "Young Goodman Brown" concerns a young man's experience with the Devil. The theme of the story concerns the loss of innocence; it might be stated like this: The loss of innocence through the discovery of humanity's wickedness is one of the great tragedies of life.

When you write about literature, you need an organizational pivot for your essay—a thesis that will allow you to begin, a point of departure, something to work *from*. The theme of the work that you are discussing can well serve as the basis for your essay. For example, if you can state the theme of a work of literature, then you can ask how that theme was developed, and your answer to that question will be your essay.

This is a simple but important point. Which of the following two statements would better serve to get an essay under way?

> "Young Goodman Brown" is about a young man's visit to a witches' sabbath.

> "Young Goodman Brown" is about the tragedy of the loss of innocence.

To demonstrate the first statement, about all one could do would be to retell the story. To discuss the second statement—which is the theme of the story—one would have to analyze and interpret the work. So the second statement will produce more subject matter than the first.

For example, here is one of Aesop's fables:

The Wolf and the Lamb

Once upon a time a Wolf was lapping at a spring on a hillside, when, looking up, what should he see but a Lamb just beginning to drink a little lower down. "There's my supper," thought he, "if only I can find some excuse to seize it." Then he called out to the Lamb, "How dare you muddle the water from which I am drinking?"

"Nay, master, nay," said Lambikin; "if the water be muddy up there, I cannot be the cause of it, for it runs down from you to me."

"Well, then," said the Wolf, "why did you call me bad names this time last year?"

"That cannot be," said the Lamb; "I am only six months old."

"I don't care," snarled the Wolf; "if it was not you it was your father"; and with that he rushed upon the poor little Lamb and—*warra warra warra warra warra*—ate her all up. But before she died she gasped out:

"ANY EXCUSE WILL SERVE A TYRANT."

The fable ends with a moral, some lesson that should be learned from it: "Any excuse will serve a tyrant." This moral is very near to the theme, which might be stated thus: In tyranny there is no law except the whim of the tyrant.

Exercise

1. What are the themes of the following fables?

Androcles

A slave named Androcles once escaped from his master and fled to the forest. As he was wandering about there, he came upon a Lion lying down moaning and groaning. At first he turned to flee, but finding that the Lion did not pursue him, he turned back and went up to him. As he came near, the Lion put out his paw, which was all swollen and bleeding, and Androcles found that a huge thorn had got into it and was causing all the pain. He pulled out the thorn and bound up the paw of the Lion, who was soon able to rise and lick the hand of Androcles like a dog. Then the Lion took Androcles to his cave, and every day used to bring him meat from which to live. But shortly afterward, both Androcles and the Lion were captured, and the slave was sentenced to be thrown to the Lion, after the latter had been kept without food for several days. The Emperor and all his Court came to see the spectacle, and Androcles was led out into the middle of the arena. Soon the Lion was let loose from his den and rushed bounding and roaring toward his victim. But as soon as he came near to Androcles, he recognized his friend and fawned upon him and licked his hands like a friendly dog. The Emperor, surprised at this, summoned Androcles to him, who told him the whole story. Whereupon the slave was pardoned and was set free, and the Lion was let loose to his native forest.

Belling the Cat

Long ago, the mice had a general council to consider what measures they could take to outwit their common enemy, the Cat. Some said this, and some said that; but at last a young mouse got up and said he had a proposal to make which he thought would meet the case. "You will all agree," said he, "that our chief danger consists in the sly and treacherous manner in which the enemy approaches us. Now, if we could receive some signal of her approach, we could easily escape from her. I venture, therefore, to propose that a small bell be procured and attached by a ribbon round the neck of the Cat. By this means we should always know when she was about and could easily retire while she was in the neighborhood."

This proposal met with general applause, until an old mouse got up and said, "That is all very well, but who is to bell the Cat?" The mice looked at one another and nobody spoke. Then the old mouse said. . . .

2. What is the theme of the following tale from Native American lore?

Assemoka, the Singer of Sweet Songs
From the Mississaugas Indian

Long, long ago two brothers lived together in an Indian village on the shore of a great lake. One was a hunter, swift of foot, strong of arm, and keen of eye. Whenever his arrow darted through the air, something fell dead, with the result that there was never any hunger nor cold in the tepee where he lived. The other brother, Assemoka, was a dreamer whose feet never pursued the fleeing deer, whose arm never hurled the deadly club nor let loose the whirring string of the bow. Instead of following the trail where the deer fled, he remained at home, doing all needful things and dreaming strange dreams which were full of high, sweet songs.

As time went by, this quiet dreamer grew discontented. "Alas," said he, "here I stay forever in one spot, dreaming dreams. In my dreams creatures sing. I must go far away into the world and find these singers and sing with them."

"Brother," said Assemoka the next morning, "I am going away on a long journey."

"Foolish fellow," said the brother. "You will be wiser if you stay right here where there is peace and plenty. You would not go far before something or other would lead you astray."

"I am going away just the same," said Assemoka.

"Very well," replied his brother. "When you need me, tell the wind and I shall come to you."

Assemoka had not traveled many miles before he came to two trees that bent over the lake. One tree had been blown down and lay heavily on the trunk of the other. When the wind blew, it rubbed back and forth and chanted a high, shrill song.

"I-iu, I-iu," it sang. "I-iu, I-iu!"

Assemoka listened as if he had fallen under a spell. "It is beautiful," he cried. "I want to be the tree that gives forth such sweet music."

"Oh, no, no," groaned the tree. "Don't say that. I am not happy at all. I am very sad indeed in spite of the shrill, clear song I sing."

Just then the wind blew and the tree began to sing, "I-iu" again in so shrill and clear a voice that Assemoka, in spite of the warning, shoved it aside and took its place, letting the fallen tree rest on his own bosom. Once again the wind blew strongly, but no sound came forth as the heavy trunk sawed back and forth across Assemoka's chest.

"Alas," he cried in his pain, "this song is not for me to sing. Only sorrow has come to me for trying to do another's work."

In his tepee the brother heard Assemoka's cry and came to him. "It is just as I told you," he said as he lifted off the fallen tree and cast it into the brush. "Now you must come back home with me."

"No, no," said Assemoka. "I must go on another journey. I have not seen the other singers in the world."

"Very well," agreed the brother. "If you need me, tell the wind and I shall come to you."

Before long Assemoka came to a swift stream in which a long stick, whose end was driven into the mud, was whirled round and round by the current. As it sped through the water, the stick sang a shrill, clear song. "I-iu!" it sang, "I-iu! I-iu!"

Assemoka stood and listened. "It is beautiful," he cried. "I have heard it in my dreams. I want to be that stick and sing its song there in the swift waters."

"Oh, no, no," begged the stick. "Do not wish that. Although I sing a shrill, clear song I am most unhappy. It is so lonesome here in the swift water. Nothing comes to visit me but the pale blue dragon fly."

"I like the song you sing," cried Assemoka. "I shall take your place." In a second he had plunged into the stream. Round and round he swung with a dull swish, swish, as the swift waters raced by.

"Alas," he cried, half smothered by the white foam, "where is the shrill, clear song of the stick? Can it be that once again I have learned that I cannot sing another's song?"

Assemoka's brother heard the high wail and came and stood on the bank. "Brother," said he, "it is just as I said. Now you see clearly that you must sing your own song. For every song there is a singer and for every singer a song. Come forth, now, and let us sit down here on the bank and take counsel together."

When the brother had drawn Assemoka from the water, the two sat in silence long hours. Below them stretched the reedy margin of the river. "Assemoka," said the brother at last, "listen to the music of the wind among the reeds. What the breath of the wind does, you can do also. It is true that you have a singing soul, but it is I who must give you the means to sing; thus must the mighty hunters and the strong of arm protect the dreamer and the singers of song."

As he spoke, the brother cut off a stout reed and fashioned it with his stone knife. Swiftly he fitted a mouthpiece and a tongue and gave it to Assemoka.

"Blow on it, my brother," said he. "In it is the song that you wish to sing, the song of your sweetest dream."

It was so. No sooner did the lips of Assemoka touch the slender reed than the air was full of song as if a thousand birds fluttered by on happy wings.

"Come now," said the brother, "let the birds sing in the wilderness, for that is their appointed place; but you must sing close to the ears of men in the lodges of the braves and around the camp fires where the old people and the children sit."

Structure

Theme emerges from the imaginative structure of a work of a literature; it is seldom stated directly. The structure of any narrative consists of three elements: *plot* (the actions or events of the story), *characters,* and *scenes.* Our understanding of a work comes about when we discover how these elements of structure—as controlled by the narrator—relate to form a whole.

Plot

In its simplest form, a story is nothing more than a series of events: first this happened, then that, and then the other. But this sort of narrative seldom interests anyone except children, who seem insatiable in their curiosity about "What happened next?" "And then what?"—that's the most basic response to a story.

However, as one matures, another question becomes just as important as "Then what?": the question "Why?" A very simple story—"First the king died, and then the queen died"—can be given a very simple plot through the addition of *motivation,* the reason for the events: "First the king died, and then the queen died *of grief.*" Now we know *why* the queen died.

Most often questions regarding motivations relate to character. However, natural disasters, fate, the will of the gods, or mere chance can provide motivation.

Exercise

Write a plot synopsis of "Young Goodman Brown." In this, you will outline the major episodes (events) in the story and explain *why* they come about.

Character

In the attempt to understand and explain the characters in a story, we can ask questions regarding:

Actions	What do the characters do? Do they have any typical or identifying actions? What parts do the characters play in the plot?
Motivation	Why do the characters do what they do?
Appearance	What does the character look and dress like?
Manner of talking	How does the character talk?
Scene	Does the character appear in or is the character associated with any particular scene?

One of the chief reasons for the effectiveness of literature is the people that we get to know through it. Ahab and Ishmael, Don Quixote, Becky Sharp, Emma Bovary, King Lear, Dorothea Brooke, Walter Mitty—all these characters have entered into the imaginative life of people who have read *Moby Dick, Don Quixote, Vanity Fair, Madame Bovary, King Lear, Middlemarch,* and "The Secret Life of Walter Mitty."

Exercise

Make and *keep* notes regarding the characters in "Young Goodman Brown." Ask yourself about *actions, motivation, appearance, manner of talking, and scene.* Ask yourself, furthermore, if any of these factors influences others. For instance, when the scene changes in the story, does the manner of talking also change?

Scene

In fiction, scene is frequently very important, as it is in "Young Goodman Brown." The forest that Goodman Brown enters is literally a gloomy and dangerous place, but it is also symbolically the "forest of evil." (We will discuss symbols later.)

In real life, tragedy can take place on a sunny spring morning, with the birds chirping and cherry trees in bloom, but in fiction, scene is often symbolic: the place is matched to the action. (Think of the movies: very seldom do the scene and the action clash in emotional content.) Here are the first two paragraphs of *The Return of the Native,* by Thomas Hardy. On the basis of this description of the scene of the novel, one can predict the emotional tone of the book:

A Saturday afternoon in November was approaching the time of twilight, and the vast tract of unenclosed wild known as Egdon Heath embrowned itself moment by moment. Overhead the hollow stretch of whitish cloud shutting out the sky was a tent which had the whole earth for its floor.

The heaven being spread with this pallid screen and the earth with the darkest vegetation, their meeting-line at the horizon was clearly marked. In such contrast the heath wore the appearance of an instalment of night which had taken up its place before its astronomical hour was come: darkness had to a great extent arrived hereon, while day stood distinct in the sky. Looking upwards, a furze-cutter would have been inclined to continue work; looking down, he would have decided to finish his faggot and go home. The distant rims of the world and of the firmament seemed to be a division in time no less than a division in matter. The face of the heath by its mere complexion added half an hour to evening; it could in like manner retard the dawn, sadden noon, anticipate the frowning of storms scarcely generated, and intensify the opacity of a moonless midnight to a cause of shaking and dread.

Writing a Story

You might now want to try your hand at writing a story. If you can't think of anything to write about, try the following exercise, which should get you under way in the process of creating an imaginative universe. The exercise is based on this passage from Ecclesiastes:

> I returned, and saw under the sun, that the race is not to the swift, nor the battle to the strong, neither yet bread to the wise, nor yet riches to men of understanding, nor yet favour to men of skill; but time and chance happeneth to them all.

The theme of this passage will be your theme.

1. Choose an instance from your life that seems to illustrate the theme— an occasion when someone you considered undeserving gained success of some kind. The event should be one that had great meaning to you, that took on great importance in your own life, that caused you bitter disappointment. Briefly narrate that incident "like it was," making no attempt to tell anything but what actually happened as clearly as you can.
2. Choose a narrative viewpoint, and create a narrator for your story. For the purposes of this exercise, don't assume that you are the narrator. Imagine someone else who will tell the story. The speaker might be someone who was involved (excluding yourself) or an onlooker who knew what happened but didn't participate. It might be a good friend or a psychiatrist to whom you told the story. You might have a very wise or a very foolish speaker, and the speaker could be young or old, male or female. In two or three paragraphs, characterize this speaker. Who is he or she? What sort of person? Relationship to you?

Remember that your speaker can be based on some actual person or can be completely imaginary.

3. You have already told your story as it happened. Now make any changes that you feel will make it more dramatic. You have no obligation to stick to the facts of the case; what you want is a plot that will best convey your theme. The result may be almost identical with the actual event or almost completely different. As briefly as you can (without sacrificing pertinent details), write a plot outline. Remember that you can change the actual event as much as you like in order to construct a satisfactory plot.

4. Now sketch the characters who are to play roles in your story. Some of them may be flat, always reacting in exactly the same predictable way. You should be able to present each character in one paragraph. Concentrate on showing the reader those aspects of the character that will be useful to you in the story. For instance, one character may never say a word, but may merely be a threatening presence in the story; in this case, we must know why he or she seems threatening. Another character may have a mannerism that is important. And so on.

5. Now sketch (in words) a scene in which your drama can take place. The scene should contribute to the total effect of your story.

6. You now have all the elements for a story. Write it.

Symbols

Both *signs* and *symbols* convey meanings, but they are different in their functions. Signs stand in lieu of their objects or referents. For example, a red light at an intersection can be either a sign or a symbol. If it causes pedestrians and drivers to stop, it is merely a sign. But if it triggers the idea of "danger" in the minds of drivers and pedestrians, it is a symbol.

As readers, we should realize that characters, actions, and scenes may be taken either literally or symbolically. Faith is literally Goodman Brown's wife, but she is symbolically the principle of faith. At the literal level, Goodman Brown's walk is merely a trip into a forest, but at the symbolic level, the journey is from innocence to the knowledge of human wickedness. And the forest is on the one hand just a forest, but on the other, it is the place deep in the human heart where wickedness lies.

Exercise

Find and explain other symbols in "Young Goodman Brown." In your opinion, which symbols are the most important? Explain.

Metaphors

On pages 416–21, you will find a complete discussion of metaphors, which are essentially comparisons. For example,

> Inside its cocoon of work or social obligation, the human spirit slumbers for the most part, registering the distinction between pleasure and pain, but not nearly as alert as we pretend.
>
> —E. M. Forster, *A Passage to India*

Forster compares the human spirit to a pupa in its cocoon, alive but inert, barely sensible of changes in the environment, but, nonetheless, having the potential to come forth as a butterfly.

Since all writers use metaphor, you must understand this figure of speech if you are to gain meaning from prose (fiction or nonfiction) and poetry. If you have trouble dealing with metaphor in your reading, turn now to pages 416–21 of this book.

Toward the Interpretive Essay

An essay that interprets a work of literature tells first what the work is about, that is, explains the theme. Second, the essay explains how the theme or meaning is developed. The body of an interpretive essay is an *explication* of a piece of literature.

At this point, you have gathered a large number of ideas concerning "Young Goodman Brown." Your notes concern *the narrator* (the teller of the tale), *the theme* (the meaning of the story or the ideas that it is about), *the structure* (including plot, characters, and scene), *symbols,* and *metaphors.* You should be ready to start putting together an interpretation.

A final series of questions will help you understand the story more fully.

1. How do you know the work is what it is? (If you say that the work is a story, then you should be able to "point to" the features that bring you to that conclusion.)
2. What is its meaning? Can you state its theme? How does it convey its meaning? Plot? Scene? Character? Symbols? Direct statements?
3. What is its structure? Does it have parts? What are they?
4. How is it different from other works of literature with which you are familiar? How much could it be changed and still be the same kind of thing?
5. How did you go about gaining your understanding of the work? (Understanding of a complex work does not come in a flash but grows through analysis and thought.) How is your understanding of the work growing?

6. What are the various artistic devices in the different sections of the work?
7. How does the work relate to other kinds of statements concerning its theme? (Theological, sociological, biological, psychological, and philosophic statements concerning the loss of innocence would differ in significant ways from "Young Goodman Brown.")
8. How does the work fit into or square with your understanding of life? Does it contradict or reinforce your value system?

An Interpretation of "Young Goodman Brown"

Now that you have thought about and discussed "Young Goodman Brown," it might interest you to read what a professional critic and scholar has to say about the tale.

Ambiguity and Clarity in Hawthorne's "Young Goodman Brown"
Richard H. Fogle

"Young Goodman Brown" is generally felt to be one of Hawthorne's more difficult tales, from the ambiguity of the conclusions which may be drawn from it. Its hero, a naïve young man who accepts both society in general and his fellowmen as individuals at their own valuation, is in one terrible night presented with the vision of human Evil, and is ever afterwards "A stern, a sad, a darkly meditative, a distrustful, if not a desperate man . . . ," whose "dying hour was gloom." So far we are clear enough, but there are confusing factors. In the first place, are the events of the night merely subjective, a dream; or do they actually occur? Again, at the crucial point in his ordeal Goodman Brown summons the strength to cry to his wife Faith, "look up to heaven, and resist the evil one." It would appear from this that he has successfully resisted the supreme temptation—but evidently he is not therefore saved. Henceforth, "On the Sabbath day, when the congregation were singing a holy psalm, he could not listen because an anthem of sin rushed loudly upon his ear and drowned all the blessed strain." On the other hand, he is not wholly lost, for in the sequel he is only at intervals estranged from "the bosom of Faith." Has Hawthorne himself failed to control the implications of his allegory?

I should say rather that these ambiguities of meaning are intentional, an integral part of his purpose. Hawthorne wishes to propose, not flatly that man is primarily evil, but instead the gnawing doubt lest this should indeed be true. "Come, devil; for to thee is this world given," exclaims Goodman Brown at the height of his agony, but he finds strength to resist the devil, and in the ambiguous conclusion he does not entirely reject his former faith. His trial, then, comes not from the certainty but the dread of Evil. Hawthorne poses the dangerous question of the relations of Good and Evil in man, but withholds his answer. Nor does he permit himself to settle whether the events of the night of trial are real or the mere figment of a dream.

These ambiguities he conveys and fortifies by what Yvor Winters has called "the formula of alternative possibilities,"[1] and F. O. Matthiessen "the device of multiple choice,"[2] in which are suggested two or more interpretations of a single action or event. Perhaps the most striking instance of the use of this device in "Young Goodman Brown" is the final word on the reality of the hero's night experience:

> Had Goodman Brown fallen asleep in the forest and only dreamed a wild dream of a witch-meeting?
> *Be it so if you will;*[3] but alas! it was a dream of evil omen for young Goodman Brown.

This device of multiple choice, or ambiguity, is the very essence of Hawthorne's tale. Nowhere does he permit us a simple meaning, a merely single interpretation. At the outset, young Goodman Brown leaves the arms of his wife Faith and the safe limits of Salem town to keep a mysterious appointment in the forest. Soon he encounters his conductor, a man "in grave and decent attire," commonplace enough save for an indefinable air of acquaintanceship with the great world. ". . . the only thing about him that could be fixed upon as remarkable was his staff, which bore the likeness of a great black snake, so curiously wrought that it might almost be seen to twist and wriggle itself like a living serpent. *This, of course, must have been an ocular deception, assisted by the uncertain light.*"[4]

---

[1] *Maule's Curse* (Norfolk, Connecticut, 1938), 18. Mr. Winters limits his discussion of the device to Hawthorne's novels.

[2] *American Renaissance* (New York, 1941), 276.

[3] These and all subsequent italics are mine.

[4] Hawthorne may have taken this suggestion from the serpent-staff of Mercury. He later uses it for lighter purposes on at least two occasions in *A Wonder Book*. Mercury's staff is described by Epimetheus as "like two serpents twisting around a stick, and . . . carved so naturally that I, at first, thought the serpents were alive" ("The Paradise of Children"). Again, in "The Miraculous Pitcher," "Two snakes, carved in the wood, were represented as twining themselves about the staff, and were so very skilfully executed that old Philemon (whose eyes, you know, were getting rather dim) almost thought them alive, and that he could see them wriggling and twisting."

This man is, of course, the Devil, who seeks to lure the still-reluctant goodman to a witch-meeting. In the process he progressively undermines the young man's faith in the institutions and the men whom he has heretofore revered. First Goody Cloyse, "a very pious and exemplary dame, who had taught him his catechism in youth, and was still his moral and spiritual adviser," is shown to have more than casual acquaintance with the Devil—to be, in fact, a witch. Goodman Brown is shaken, but still minded to turn back and save himself. He is then faced with a still harder test. Just as he is about to return home, filled with self-applause, he hears the tramp of horses along the road:

> On came the hoof tramps and the voices of the riders, two grave old voices, conversing soberly as they drew near. These mingled sounds appeared to pass along the road, within a few yards of the young man's hiding-place; *but, owing doubtless to the depth of the gloom at that particular spot, neither the travellers nor their steeds were visible. Though their figures brushed the small boughs by the wayside, it could not be seen that they intercepted, even for a moment, the faint gleam from the strip of bright sky athwart which they must have passed.* It vexed him the more, because he could have sworn, *were such a thing possible,* that he recognized the voices of the minister and Deacon Gookin, jogging along quietly, as they were wont to do, when bound to some ordination or ecclesiastical council.

The conversation of the minister and the deacon makes it only too clear that they also are in league with the evil one. Yet Goodman Brown, although now even more deeply dismayed, still resolves to stand firm, heartened by the blue arch of the sky and the stars brightening in it.[5] At that moment a cloud, "though no wind was stirring," hides the stars, and he hears a confused babble of voices. *"Once the listener fancied that he could distinguish* the accents of townspeople of his own . . . The next moment, so indistinct were the sounds, *he doubted whether he had heard aught* but the murmur of the old forest, whispering without a wind." But to his horror he believes that he hears the voice of his wife Faith, uttering only weak and insincere objections as she is borne through the air to the witch-meeting.

Now comes a circumstance which at first sight would appear to break the chain of ambiguities, for his suspicions seem concretely verified. A pink ribbon, which he remembers having seen in his wife's hair, comes fluttering down into his grasp. This ribbon, an apparently solid object like the fatal handkerchief in *Othello*, seems out of keeping with the atmosphere of doubt which has

---

[5]Cf. Bosola to the Duchess at a comparably tragic moment in Webster's *Duchess of Malfi*: "Look you, the stars shine still."

enveloped the preceding incidents.[6] Two considerations, however, make it possible to defend it. One is that if Goodman Brown is dreaming, the ribbon like the rest may be taken as part-and-parcel of his dream. It is to be noted that this pink ribbon appears in his wife's hair once more as she meets him at his return to Salem in the morning. The other is that for the moment the ribbon vanishes from the story, melting into its shadowy background. Its impact is merely temporary.

Be it as you will, as Hawthorne would say. At any rate the effect on Goodman Brown is instantaneous and devastating. Casting aside all further scruples, he rages through the wild forest to the meeting of witches, for the time at least fully accepting the domination of Evil. He soon comes upon a "numerous congregation," alternately shadowy and clear in the flickering red light of four blazing pines above a central rock.

> Among them, *quivering to and fro between gloom and splendor,* appeared faces that would be seen next day at the council board of the province, and others which, Sabbath after Sabbath, looked devoutly heavenward, and benignantly over the crowded pews, from the holiest pulpits in the land. *Some affirm that* the lady of the governor was there. . . . *Either the sudden gleams of light flashing over the obscure field bedazzled Goodman Brown, or he recognized* a score of the church members of Salem village famous for their especial sanctity.

Before this company steps out a presiding figure who bears "With reverence be it spoken . . . *no slight similitude,* both in garb and manner, to some grave divine of the New England churches," and calls forth the "converts." At the word young Goodman Brown comes forward. *"He could have well-nigh sworn that* the shape of his own dead father beckoned him to advance, looking downward from a smoke wreath, while a woman, with dim features of despair, threw out her hand to warn him back. *Was it his mother?"* But he is quickly seized and led to the rock, along with a veiled woman whom he dimly discerns to be his wife Faith. The two are welcomed by the dark and ambiguous leader into the fraternity of Evil, and the final, irretrievable step is prepared.

> A basin was hollowed, naturally, in the rock. *Did it contain water, reddened by the lurid light? or was it blood? or, perchance, a liquid flame?* Herein did the shape of evil dip his hand and prepare to lay the mark of

---

[6]"As long as what Brown saw is left wholly in the realm of hallucination, Hawthorne's created illusion is compelling. . . . Only the literal insistence on that damaging pink ribbon obtrudes the labels of a confining allegory, and short-circuits the range of association." Matthiessen, *American Renaissance,* 284.

baptism upon their foreheads, that they might be partakers of the mystery of sin, more conscious of the secret guilt of others, both in deed and thought, than they could now be of their own. The husband cast one look at his pale wife, and Faith at him. What polluted wretches would the next glance show them to each other, shuddering alike at what they disclosed and what they saw!

"Faith! Faith!" cried the husband, "look up to heaven, and resist the wicked one."

Whether Faith obeyed he knew not.

Hawthorne then concludes with the central ambiguity, which we have already noticed, whether the events of the night were actual or a dream? The uses of this device, if so it may be called, are multiple in consonance with its nature. Primarily it offers opportunity for freedom and richness of suggestion. By it Hawthorne is able to suggest something of the density and incalculability of life, the difficulties which clog the interpretation of even the simplest incidents, the impossibility of achieving a single and certain insight into the actions and motives of others. This ambiguity adds depth and tone to Hawthorne's thin and delicate fabric. It covers the bareness of allegory, imparting to its one-to-one equivalence of object and idea a wider range of allusiveness, a hint of rich meaning still untapped. By means of it the thesis of "Young Goodman Brown" is made to inhere firmly in the situation, whence the reader himself must extract it to interpret. Hawthorne the artist refuses to limit himself to a single and doctrinaire conclusion,[7] proceeding instead by indirection. Further, it permits him to make free with the two opposed worlds of actuality and of imagination without incongruity or the need to commit himself entirely to either; while avoiding a frontal attack upon the reader's feeling for everyday verisimilitude, it affords the author licence of fancy. It allows him to draw upon sources of legend and superstition which still strike a responsive chord in us, possessing something of the validity of universal symbols.[8] Hawthorne's own definition of Romance may very aptly be applied to his use of ambiguity: it gives him scope "so [to] manage his atmospherical

---

[7]"For Hawthorne its value consisted in the variety of explanations to which it gave rise." *American Renaissance,* 277. The extent of my indebtedness to Mr. Matthiessen is only inadequately indicated in my documentation.

[8]"It is only by . . . symbols that have numberless meanings beside the one or two the writer lays an emphasis upon, or the half-score he knows of, that any highly subjective art can escape from the barrenness and shallowness of a too conscious arrangement, into the abundance and depth of nature. . . ." W. B. Yeats, "The Philosophy of Shelley's Poetry," *Ideas of Good and Evil* (London, 1914), 90. Thus Hawthorne by drawing upon Puritan superstition and demonology is able to add another dimension to his story.

medium as to bring out or mellow the lights and deepen and enrich the shadows of the picture."[9]

These scanty observations must suffice here for the general importance of Hawthorne's characteristic ambiguity. It remains to describe its immediate significance in "Young Goodman Brown." Above all, the separate instances of this "multiple choice device" organically cohere to reproduce in the reader's mind the feel of the central ambiguity of theme, the horror of the hero's doubt. Goodman Brown, a simple and pious nature, is wrecked as a result of the disappearance of the fixed poles of his belief. His orderly cosmos dissolves into chaos as church and state, the twin pillars of his society, are hinted to be rotten, with their foundations undermined.[10] The yearning for certainty is basic to his spirit—and he is left without the comfort even of a firm reliance in the Devil.[11] His better qualities avail him in his desperation little more than the inner evil which prompted him to court temptation, for they prevent him from seeking the only remaining refuge—the confraternity of Sin. Henceforth he is fated to a dubious battle with shadows, to struggle with limed feet toward a redemption which must forever elude him, since he has lost the vision of Good while rejecting the proffered opportunity to embrace Evil fully. Individual instances of ambiguity, then, merge and coalesce in the theme itself to produce an all-pervading atmosphere of uneasiness and anguished doubt.

Ambiguity alone, however, is not a satisfactory aesthetic principle. Flexibility, suggestiveness, allusiveness, variety—all these are without meaning if there is no pattern from which to vary, no center from which to flee outward. And, indeed, ambiguity of itself will not adequately account for the individual phenomenon of "Young Goodman Brown." The deliberate haziness and multiple implications of its meaning are counterbalanced by the firm clarity of its technique, in structure and in style.

This clarity is embodied in the lucid simplicity of the basic action; in the skilful foreshadowing by which the plot is bound together; in balance of episode and scene; in the continuous use

---

[9]Preface, *The House of the Seven Gables.*

[10]Goodman Brown is disillusioned with the church in the persons of Goody Cloyse, the minister, and Deacon Gookin, and it will be recalled that the figure of Satan at the meeting "bore no slight similitude . . . to some grave divine of the New England churches." As to the secular power, the devil tells Brown that ". . . the selectmen of divers towns make me their chairman; and a majority of the Great and General Court are firm supporters of my interest. The governor and I, too—But these are state secrets."

[11]The story could conceivably be read as intellectual satire, showing the pitfalls that lie in wait for a too-shallow and unquestioning faith. Tone and emphasis clearly show, however, a more tragic intention.

of contrast; in the firmness and selectivity of Hawthorne's pictorial composition; in the carefully arranged climatic order of incident and tone; in the detachment and irony of Hawthorne's attitude; and finally in the purity, the grave formality, and the rhetorical balance of the style. His amalgamation of these elements achieves an effect of totality, of exquisite craftsmanship, of consummate artistic economy in fitting the means to the attempted ends.

The general framework of the story has a large simplicity. Goodman Brown leaves his wife Faith and the safe confines of Salem town at sunset, spends the night in the forest, and at dawn returns a changed man. Within this simple pattern plot and allegory unfold symmetrically and simultaneously. The movement of "Young Goodman Brown" is the single revolution of a wheel, which turns full-circle upon itself. As by this basic structure, the action is likewise given form by the device of foreshadowing, through which the entire development of the plot is already implicit in the opening paragraph. Thus Faith is troubled by her husband's expedition, and begs him to put it off till sunrise. "A lone woman is troubled with such dreams and such thoughts that she's afeard of herself sometimes," says she, hinting the ominous sequel of her own baptism in sin. " 'My love and my Faith,' replied young Goodman Brown, 'of all nights in the year, this one night must I tarry away from thee. My journey . . . forth and back again, must needs be done 'twixt now and sunrise.' " They part, but Brown looking back sees "the head of Faith still peeping after him with a melancholy air, in spite of her pink ribbons."

> "Poor little Faith!" thought he, for his heart smote him. "What a wretch am I to leave her on such an errand! She talks of dreams, too. Methought as she spoke there was trouble in her face, as if a dream had warned her what work is to be done to-night. But no, no; 'twould kill her to think of it. Well, she's a blessed angel on earth; and after this one night I'll cling to her skirts and follow her to heaven."

This speech, it must be confessed, is in several respects clumsy, obvious, and melodramatic;[12] but beneath the surface lurks a deeper layer. The pervasive ambiguity of the story is foreshadowed in the subtle emphasizing of the dream-motif, which paves the way for the ultimate uncertainty whether the incidents of the night are dream or reality; and in his simple-minded aspiration to

---

[12]It has the earmarks of the set dramatic soliloquy, serving in this case to provide both information about the plot and revelation of character. Mr. Matthiessen attributes Hawthorne's general use of theatrical devices to the influence of Scott, who leads in turn to Shakespeare. *American Renaissance,* 203.

"cling to her skirts and follow her to heaven," Goodman Brown is laying an ironic foundation for his later horror of doubt. A broader irony is apparent, in the light of future events, in the general emphasis upon Faith's angelic goodness.

Hawthorne's seemingly casual references to Faith's pink ribbons, which are mentioned three times in the opening paragraphs, are likewise far from artless. These ribbons, as we have seen, are in important factor in the plot; and as an emblem of heavenly Faith their color gradually deepens into the liquid flame or blood of the baptism into sin.[13]

Another instance of Hawthorne's careful workmanship is his architectural balance of episodes or scenes. The encounter with Goody Cloyse, the female hypocrite and sinner, is set off against the conversation of the minister and Deacon Gookin immediately afterward. The exact correspondence of the two episodes is brought into high relief by two balancing speeches. Goody Cloyse has lost her broomstick, and must perforce walk to the witch-meeting—a sacrifice she is willing to make since "they tell me there is a nice young man to be taken into communion to-night." A few minutes later Deacon Gookin, in high anticipation, remarks that "there is a goodly young woman to be taken into communion." A still more significant example of this balance is contained in the full swing of the wheel—in the departure at sunset and the return at sunrise. At the beginning of the story Brown takes leave of "Faith with the pink ribbons," turns the corner by the meeting-house and leaves the town; in the conclusion

> . . . Young Goodman Brown came slowly into the street of Salem village, staring around him like a bewildered man. The good old minister was taking a walk along the graveyard to get an appetite for breakfast and meditate his sermon, and bestowed a blessing, as he passed, on Goodman Brown. He shrank from the venerable saint as if to avoid an anathema. Old Deacon Gookin was at domestic worship, and the holy words of his prayer were heard through the open window. "What God doth the wizard pray to?" quoth Goodman Brown. Goody Cloyse, that excellent old Christian, stood in the early sunshine at her own lattice, catechizing a little girl who had brought her a pint of morning's milk.[14] Goodman Brown snatched the child away as from

---

[13]Further, in welcoming the two candidates to the communion of Evil, the Devil says, "By the sympathy of your human hearts for sin ye shall scent out all the places . . . where crime has been committed, and shall exult to behold the whole earth one stain of guilt, *one mighty blood spot.*" For this discussion of the pink ribbons I am largely indebted to Leland Schubert, *Hawthorne, the Artist* (Chapel Hill, 1944), 79–80.

[14]This touch takes on an ironic and ominous significance if it is noticed that Goody Cloyse has that night been Faith's sponsor, along with the "rampant hag" Martha Carrier, at the baptism into sin by blood and flame.

the grasp of the fiend himself. Turning the corner by the meeting-house, he spied the head of Faith, with the pink ribbons, gazing anxiously forth, and bursting into such joy at the sight of him that she skipped along the street and almost kissed her husband before the whole village. But Goodman Brown looked sternly and sadly into her face, and passed on without a greeting.

The exact parallel between the earlier and the later situation serves to dramatize intensely the change which the real or fancied happenings of the night have brought about in Goodman Brown.[15]

Contrast, a form of balance, is still more prominent in "Young Goodman Brown" than the kind of analogy of scene and episode which I have mentioned. The broad antitheses of day against night, the town against the forest, which signify in general a sharp dualism of Good and Evil, are supplemented by a color-contrast of red-and-black at the witch-meeting, by the swift transition of the forest scene from leaping flame to damp and chill, and by the consistent cleavage between outward decorum and inner corruption in the characters.[16]

The symbols of Day and Night, of Town and Forest, are almost indistinguishable in meaning. Goodman Brown leaves the limits of Salem at dusk and reenters them at sunrise; the night he spends in the forest. Day and the Town are clearly emblematic of Good, of the seemly outward appearance of human convention and society. They stand for the safety of an unquestioning and unspeculative faith. Oddly enough, Goodman Brown in the daylight of the Salem streets is a young man too simple and straightforward to be interesting, and a little distasteful in his boundless reverence for such unspectacular worthies as the minister, the deacon, and Goody Cloyse. Night and the Forest are the domains of the Evil One, symbols of doubt and wandering, where the dark subterranean forces of the human spirit riot unchecked.[17] By the dramatic necessities of the plot Brown is a larger figure in the

---

[15]Here we may anticipate a little in order to point out the steady and premeditated irony arising from the locutions "good old minister," "venerable saint," and "excellent old Christian"; and the climactic effect produced by the balance and repetition of the encounters, which are duplicated in the sentence-structure and the repetition of "Goodman Brown."

[16]Epitomized by Brown's description of the assemblage at the meeting as "a grave and dark-clad company."

[17]"The conception of the dark and evil-haunted wilderness came to him [Hawthorne] from the days of Cotton Mather who held that 'the New Englanders are a people of God settled in those which were once the devil's territories.' " Matthiessen, *American Renaissance,* 282–283. See also Matthiessen's remark of *The Scarlet Letter* that ". . . the forest itself, with its straggling path, images to Hester 'the moral wilderness in which she had so long been wandering'; and while describing it Hawthorne may have taken a glance back at Spenser's Wood of Errour." *American Renaissance,* 279–280. This reference to Spenser may as fitly be applied to the path of Young Goodman Brown, "darkened by the gloomiest trees of the forest, which barely stood aside to let the narrow path creep through, and closed immediately behind."

Forest of Evil,[18] and as a chief actor at the witch-meeting, than within the safe bounds of the town.

The contrast of the red of fire and blood against the black of night and the forest at the witch-meeting has a different import. As the flames rise and fall, the faces of the worshippers of Evil are alternately seen in clear outline and deep shadow, and all the details of the scene are at one moment revealed, the next obscured. It seems, then, that the red is Sin or Evil, plain and unequivocal; the black is that doubt of the reality either of Evil or Good which tortures Goodman Brown and is the central ambiguity of Hawthorne's story.[19]

A further contrast follows in the swift transformation of scene when young Goodman Brown finds himself "amid calm night and solitude. . . . He staggered against the rock, and felt it chill and damp; while a hanging twig, that had been all on fire, besprinkled his cheek with the coldest dew."[20]

Most pervasive of the contrasts in "Young Goodman Brown" is the consistent discrepancy between appearance and reality,[21] which helps to produce its heavy atmosphere of doubt and shadow. The church is represented by the highly respectable figures of Goody Cloyse, the minister, and Deacon Gookin, who in the forest are witch and wizards. The devil appears to Brown in the guise of his grandfather, "in grave and decent attire." As the goodman approaches the meeting, his ears are greeted by "the swell of what seemed a hymn, rolling solemnly from a distance with the weight of many voices. He knew the tune; it was a familiar one in the choir of the village meeting-house." The Communion of Sin is, in fact, the faithful counterpart of a grave and pious ceremony at a Puritan meeting-house. "At one extremity of an open space, hemmed in by the dark wall of the forest, arose a rock, bearing some rude, natural resemblance either to an altar or a pulpit, and surrounded by four blazing pines, their tops aflame, their stems untouched, like candles at an evening meeting." The worshippers are "a numerous congregation," Satan resembles some grave divine, and the initiation into sin takes the form of a baptism.[22]

---

[18]"But he was himself the chief horror of the scene, and shrank not from its other horrors."

[19]Hawthorne not infrequently uses color for symbol. See such familiar instances as *The Scarlet Letter* and "The Minister's Black Veil."

[20]See Schubert, *Hawthorne, the Artist*, 63. One would presume this device to be traditional in the story of the supernatural, where a return to actuality must eventually be made. An obvious example is the vanishing at cockcrow of the Ghost in *Hamlet*. See also the conclusion of Hawthorne's own "Ethan Brand."

[21]Evil must provisionally be taken for reality during the night in the forest, in spite of the ambiguity of the ending.

[22]The hint of the perverse desecration of the Black Mass adds powerfully here to the connotative scope of the allegory.

Along with this steady use of contrast at the Sabbath should be noticed its firmly composed pictorial quality. The rock, the center of the picture, is lighted by the blazing pines. The chief actors are as it were spotlighted in turn as they advance to the rock, while the congregation is generalized in the dimmer light at the outer edges. The whole composition is simple and definite, in contrast with the ambiguity occasioned by the rise and fall of the flame, in which the mass of the worshippers alternately shines forth and disappears in shadow.[23]

The clarity and simple structural solidity of "Young Goodman Brown" evinces itself in its tight dramatic framework. Within the basic form of the turning wheel it further divides into four separate scenes, the first and last of which, of course, are the balancing departure from and return to Salem. The night in the forest falls naturally into two parts: the temptation by the Devil and the witch-meeting. These two scenes, particularly the first, make full and careful use of the dramatic devices of suspense and climactic arrangement; and Hawthorne so manipulates his materials as to divide them as sharply as by a dropped curtain.

The temptation at first has the stylized and abstract delicacy of Restoration Comedy, or of the formalized seductions of Molière's *Don Juan*. The simple goodman, half-eager and half-reluctant, is wholly at the mercy of Satan, who leads him step by step to the inevitable end. The tone of the earlier part of this scene is lightly ironic: an irony reinforced by the inherent irony of the situation, which elicits a double meaning at every turn.

> "Come, Goodman Brown," cried his fellow-traveller, "this is a dull pace for the beginning of a journey. Take my staff, if you are so soon weary."
>
> "Friend," said the other, exchanging his slow pace for a full stop, "having kept convenant by meeting thee here, it is my purpose now to return whence I came. I have scruples touching the matter thou wot'st of."
>
> "Sayest thou so?" replied he of the serpent, smiling apart. "Let us walk on, nevertheless, reasoning as we go; and if I convince thee not thou shalt turn back. We are but a little way in the forest yet."

Then begins a skilful and relentless attack upon all the values which Goodman Brown has lived by. His reverence for his Puritan ancestors, "a people of prayer, and good works to boot," is speedily turned against him as the Devil claims them for tried

---

[23]The general effect is very like that of the famous Balinese Monkey Dance, which is performed at night, usually in a clearing of the forest, by the light of a single torch. The chief figures, the Monkey King and the King of the Demons, advance in turn to this central torch, while the chorus of dancers remains in the semi-obscurity of the background. This dancing is allegorical, the Monkeys, as helpers of the Balinese, representing Good against the Evil of the Demons.

and dear companions. Next comes the episode of Goody Cloyse, who taught the young man his catechism. Brown is sorely cast down, but at length sturdily concludes: "What if a wretched old woman do choose to go to the devil when I thought she was going to heaven: is that any reason why I should quit my dear Faith and go after her?" But no sooner has he rallied from this blow than he is beset by another, still more shrewdly placed: he hears the voices of the minister and Deacon Gookin, and from their conversation gathers that they are bound for the meeting, and eagerly anticipating it. This is nearly final, but he still holds out. " 'With heaven above, and Faith below, I will yet stand firm against the devil!' cried Goodman Brown"; only to be utterly overthrown by the sound of his wife's voice in the air, and the crushing evidence of the fatal pink ribbon.

The style has gradually deepened and intensified along with the carefully graduated intensity of the action, and now Hawthorne calls upon all his resources to seize and represent the immense significance of the moment. Nature itself is made at once to sympathize with and to mock the anguished chaos of the young man's breast; in his rage he is both at one with and opposed to the forest and the wind.[24] The symphony of sound, which began with the confused babble of voices in the sky as Faith and her witch-attendants swept overhead, rises to a wild crescendo.[25]

> And, maddened with despair, so that he laughed loud and long, did Goodman Brown grasp his staff and set forth again, at such a rate that he seemed to fly along the forest path rather than to walk or run. The road grew wilder and drearier and more faintly traced, and vanished at length, leaving him in the heart of the dark wilderness, still rushing onward with the instinct that guides mortal man to evil. The whole forest was peopled with frightful sounds—the creaking of the trees, the howling of wild beasts, and the yell of Indians; while sometimes the wind tolled like a distant church bell, and sometimes gave a broad roar around the traveller, as if all Nature were laughing him to scorn. But he was himself the chief horror of the scene, and shrank not from its other horrors.

After ascending to this climax, Hawthorne disengages himself and separates his scenes with the definiteness of the dropping

[24]"The intensity of the situation is sustained by all the devices Hawthorne had learned from the seventeenth century, for just as the heavens groaned in Milton's fall of the angels, the winds are made to whisper sadly at the loss of this man's faith." Matthiessen, *American Renaissance*, 284. The winds, however, roar rather than "whisper sadly."
[25]Cf. Schubert's account of the sound-effects in "Young Goodman Brown," *Hawthorne, the Artist*, 114–117. Mr. Schubert distorts the effect and purpose of Hawthorne's use of sound in the story by comparing it to "the last movement of Beethoven's Ninth Symphony"—description of sound is not the sound itself—but his perception is extremely valuable.

of a curtain—by the simple expedient of shifting his view from the hero to his surroundings. Goodman Brown coming upon the witch-meeting is a mere onlooker until the moment comes for him to step forward for his baptism into sin. Up to that moment Satan usurps the stage. The eye is first directed to the central rock-altar, then to the four blazing pines which light it. Next there is the sense of a numerous assembly, vaguely seen in the fitful firelight. Finally the figure of Satan appears at the base of the rock, framed in an arch of flame. Only when he is summoned are we once more fully aware of Goodman Brown, as he stands at the altar by his wife Faith. Then, a moment later, comes the second crashing climax when Brown calls upon his wife to "look up to heaven, and resist the wicked one"—cut off abruptly by anticlimax as the meeting vanishes in a roaring wind, and Brown leaning against the rock finds it chill and damp to his touch.

The satisfaction one feels in the clean line of the structure of the story is enhanced by Hawthorne's steady detachment from his materials: an attitude which deepens the impression of classic balance, which in turn stands against the painful ambiguity of the theme. Even the full tone of the intensest scenes, as Goodman Brown rushing through the forest, is tempered by restraint. The participant is overweighted by the calm, impartial (though not unfeeling) spectator; Hawthorne does not permit himself to become identified with his hero. He displays young Goodman Brown not in and for himself, but always in relation to the whole situation and set of circumstances. This detachment of attitude is plainest in the almost continuous irony, unemphatic but nonetheless relentless: an irony organically related to the ever-present ambiguities of the situation, but most evident in sustained tone. Thus, after recording Goodman Brown's aspiration to "cling to Faith's skirts and follow her to heaven," the author adds with deadly calm, "With this excellent resolve for the future, Goodman Brown felt himself justified in making more haste on his present evil purpose."

This detachment is implicit in the quiet, the abstractness, and the exquisite gravity of Hawthorne's style, everywhere formal and exactly though subtly cadenced. It throws a light and idealizing veil over the action,[26] and as it were maintains as aesthetic dis-

---

[26]Hawthorne's notion of the ideality which art should lend to nature is apparent in his comment in the introductory essay to *Mosses from an Old Manse* upon the reflection of a natural scene in water: "Each tree and rock, and every blade of grass, is distinctly imaged, and however unsightly in reality, assumes ideal beauty in the reflection." And a few pages later—"Of all this scene, the slumbering river has a dream picture in its bosom. Which, after all was the most real—the picture, or the original? the objects palpable to our grosser senses, or their apotheosis in the stream beneath? Surely the disembodied images stand in closer relation to the soul."

tance from it, while hinting at the ugliness it mercifully covers. The difference between the saying and the thing said, at times provides dramatic tension and a kind of ironic fillip. Note, for example, the grave decorum and eighteenth-century stateliness, the perverted courtliness, of Satan's welcome to young Brown and Faith:

> This night it shall be granted you to know their secret deeds: how hoary-bearded elders of the church have whispered wanton words to the young maids of their households; how many a woman, eager for widows' weeds, has given her husband a drink at bedtime and let him sleep his last sleep in her bosom; how beardless youths have made haste to inherit their fathers' wealth; and how fair damsels—blush not, sweet ones—have dug little graves in the garden, and bidden me, the sole guest, to an infant's funeral.

The steady procession of measured, ceremonious generalizations—"hoary-bearded elders," "wanton words," "beardless youths," and "fair damsels," is in radical contrast with the implication of the meaning; and the grisly archness of "blush not, sweet ones" is deeply suggestive in its incongruity.[27]

In "Young Goodman Brown," then, Hawthorne has achieved that reconciliation of opposites which Coleridge deemed the highest art. The combination of clarity of technique, embodied in simplicity and balance of structure, in firm pictorial composition, in contrast and climactic arrangement, in irony and detachment, with ambiguity of meaning as signalized by the "device of multiple choice," in its interrelationships produces the story's characteristic effect. By means of these two elements Hawthorne reconciles oneness of action with multiplicity of suggestion, and enriches the bareness of systematic allegory. Contrarily, by them he holds in check the danger of lapsing into mere speculation without substance or form. The phantasmagoric light-and-shadow of the rising and falling fire, obscuring and softening the clear, hard outline of the witch-meeting, is an image which will stand for the essential effect of the story itself, compact of ambiguity and clarity harmoniously interfused.

---

[27]I would not be understood to affirm that this adaptation of the eighteenth-century mock-heroic is the sole effect of Hawthorne's style in "Young Goodman Brown." The seventeenth century plays its part too. The agony of the goodman in the forest, and the sympathy of the elements, is Miltonic. And in this same scene of the witch-meeting Hawthorne twice touches upon Miltonic tenderness and sublimity: " 'Lo, there ye stand, my children,' said the figure, in a deep and solemn tone, almost sad with its despairing awfulness, as if his once angelic nature could yet mourn for our miserable race. . . . And there they stood, the only pair, as it seemed, who were yet hesitating on the verge of wickedness in this dark world."

WRITING ABOUT POETRY

Some poems are narrative, telling a story. To interpret a narrative poem, you employ the same principles as those for a prose story. After all, a narrative poem is nothing but a story with the addition, often, of meter and rhyme (about which we will talk in a moment).

Lyric poetry, however, does not tell a story; it uses symbol, image, metaphor, and other figures of speech to convey a meaning and the emotional charge appropriate to that meaning.

Here, for example, is a well-known lyric poem:

The Lake Isle of Innisfree
William Butler Yeats

I will arise and go now, and go to Innisfree,
And a small cabin build there, of clay and wattles made;
Nine bean rows will I have there, a hive for the honey bee,
And live alone in the bee-loud glade.

And I shall have some peace there, for peace comes dropping slow,
Dropping from the veils of the morning to where the cricket sings;
There midnight's all a glimmer, and noon a purple glow,
And evening full of the linnet's wings.

I will arise and go now, for always night and day
I hear lake water lapping with low sounds by the shore;
While I stand on the roadway, or on the pavements grey,
I hear it in the deep heart's core.

In this poem, Innisfree stands for (symbolizes) the peace that can be found only away from the city, and the poet's theme is the longing to get away from the busyness of life and retire to a beautiful, peaceful, and remote spot. We find metaphor in the poem: "for peace comes dropping slow, / Dropping from the veils of the morning to where the cricket sings." And, of course, the poem is full of images.

The language of the poem has special features, such as *rhyme:* Innisfree-bee, made-glade, slow-glow, sings-wings, day-grey, shore-core.

To interpret a lyric poem, we must see how all of its features work together to create a meaning and an emotional response.

Literal Meaning

The first step in interpretation is to see if we can state the literal meaning of the poem in our own words. This kind of statement is known as a *paraphrase*. For example, here is one of the most popular poems in English, followed by a paraphrase:

To His Coy Mistress
Andrew Marvell

Had we but world enough, and time,
This coyness, lady, were no crime.
We would sit down, and think which way
To walk, and pass our long love's day.
Thou by the Indian Ganges' side   5
Shouldst rubies find; I by the tide
Of Humber would complain. I would
Love you ten years before the Flood,
And you should, if you please, refuse
Till the conversion of the Jews.   10
My vegetable love should grow
Vaster than empires, and more slow;
An hundred years should go to praise
Thine eyes, and on thy forehead gaze;
Two hundred to adore each breast,   15
But thirty thousand to the rest;
An age at least to every part,
And the last age should show your heart.
For, lady, you deserve this state,
Nor would I love at lower rate.   20
   But at my back I always hear
Time's wingèd chariot hurrying near;
And yonder all before us lie
Deserts of vast eternity.
Thy beauty shall no more be found,   25
Nor, in thy marble vault, shall sound
My echoing song; then worms shall try
That long-preserved virginity,

Mistress: not kept woman, but sweetheart or beloved.   **2. coyness:** shyness, modesty.   **5. Ganges:** a river in India, a distant and exotic place, at least from the standpoint of a seventeenth-century Englishman.   **7. Humber:** a humble English stream, on the banks of which stood Marvell's family home.   **8. the Flood:** the biblical deluge.   **10. the conversion of the Jews:** not supposed to occur until the Last Judgment.   **26. thy marble vault:** your marble tomb.

And your quaint honor turn to dust,
And into ashes all my lust: 30
The grave's a fine and private place,
But none, I think, do there embrace.
   Now therefore, while the youthful hue
Sits on thy skin like morning dew,
And while thy willing soul transpires   35
At every pore with instant fires,
Now let us sport us while we may,
And now, like amorous birds of prey,
Rather at once our time devour
Than languish in his slow-chapped power.   40
Let us roll all our strength and all
Our sweetness up into one ball,
And tear our pleasure with rough strife
Thorough the iron gates of life.
Thus, though we cannot make our sun   45
Stand still, yet we will make him run.

The paraphrase might be:

If we had enough time, lady, I wouldn't be in any hurry. We could plan, and think, and travel, and wait. I would love you for the whole age of the earth. I'd be willing to spend hundreds of years on preliminaries, such as praising your beauty. For you're such a wonderful person that you deserve all the honor and dignity that I could bestow upon you, and, furthermore, I'm not a piker; I'm willing to give you everything that is your due.

However, I'm always aware of the brevity of life, and I know that before us lies the eternity of death. In the grave, we'll have no chance for love.

Therefore, while we're young and passionate, let's make love. We can't stop time, but we can fill every moment that we have.

Now, then, if all that we wanted from a work of literature were its literal meaning, we would like the paraphrase just as well as we do the poem. Obviously, a work of literature gives us something more than bare meaning, something more than information or opinion.

---

29. quaint: possessing a strange but charming oddness.   **40. slow-chapped:** slow-jawed; we get the image of Time slowly but systematically chewing up the poet and his mistress.   **44. thorough:** simply a version of *through*.

Formal Structure

Works of literature have structure. For instance, plays are divided into acts, which break the movement into segments; novels are divided into chapters and sometimes sections; poems often have clearly defined, formal patterns of stanzas. There is no need for you to be able to name these patterns, but you should be aware of them, for at least some of the enjoyment of poetry comes from the skill with which the poet embodies ideas in strictly defined patterns. For instance, the *sonnet* follows a pattern of just fourteen lines of ten syllables each (with some little room for variation in the number of syllables). As an example, here is Shakespeare's Sonnet 129, about lust:

> Th' expense of spirit in a waste of shame
> Is lust in action; and, till action, lust
> Is perjured, murd'rous, bloody, full of blame,
> Savage, extreme, rude, cruel, not to trust;
> Enjoyed no sooner but despisèd straight;
> Past reason hunted, and no sooner had,
> Past reason hated as a swallowed bait
> On purpose laid to make the taker mad;
> Mad in pursuit, and in possession so;
> Had, having, and in quest to have, extreme;
> A bliss in proof, and proved, a very woe,
> Before, a joy proposed; behind, a dream.
>   All this the world well knows, yet none knows well
>   To shun the heaven that leads men to this hell.

Readers take pleasure in the forms of poems; after all, it is an accomplishment to fit one's ideas and language into a form as strictly defined as a sonnet. When we read for information, we are normally unaware of form—unless the piece is disorganized or in some other way flawed or atypical—but the form of poems is one feature that contributes to our enjoyment of them.

Form

The following poem has an extremely intricate structure. After reading the poem, describe its form, *paying special attention to word repetitions*. In order to do this, you need no fancy terminology. Merely describe what you see on the page.

Here in Katmandu
Donald Justice

We have climbed the mountain,
There's nothing more to do.
It is terrible to come down
To the valley
Where, amidst many flowers,
One thinks of snow.

As, formerly, amidst snow,
Climbing the mountain,
One thought of flowers,
Tremulous, ruddy with dew,
In the valley,
One caught their scent coming down.

It is difficult to adjust, once down,
To the absence of snow.
Clear days, from the valley,
One looks up at the mountain.
What else is there to do?
Prayerwheels, flowers!

Let the flowers
Fade, the prayerwheels run down.
What have these to do
With us who have stood atop the snow
Atop the mountain,
Flags seen from the valley?

It might be possible to live in the valley,
To bury oneself among flowers,
If one could forget the mountain,
How, setting out before dawn,
Blinded with snow,
One knew what to do.

Meanwhile it is not easy here in Katmandu,
Especially when to the valley
That wind which means snow
Elsewhere, but here means flowers,
Comes down,
As soon it must, from the mountain.

The Language of Poetry

The language of poetry often, but not always, contains features that are not found in prose—for instance, meter and rhyme.

As we have seen, rhyme is the soundalike words that end lines of poetry (and that sometimes occur within lines):

> Above the pines the moon was slowly *drifting,*
>   The river sang *below;*
> The dim Sierras, far beyond, *uplifting*
>   Their minarets of *snow.*
>
> —Bret Harte

Thus: drifting-uplifting, below-snow.

Meter is the regular alternation of stressed and unstressed syllables in poetry, creating a definite rhythm.

Iambic meter consists of an unstressed and a stressed syllable.

> Had WE but WORLD eNOUGH and TIME,
> This COYness, LAdy, WERE no CRIME.

Trochaic meter consists of a stressed syllable followed by an unstressed syllable:

> DOUble, DOUble, TOIL and TROUble,
> FIre BURN and CAULdron BUBble.

Anapestic meter consists of two unstressed syllables followed by a stressed syllable:

> Like a CHILD from the WOMB, like a GHOST from the TOMB,
> I aRISE and unBUILD it aGAIN.

Another meter, not often used in English, is *dactylic:* a stressed syllable followed by two unstressed, as in the word *MANikin.*

Poetic language also tends to be more *connotative* than that of prose. (For a discussion of *connotation* and *denotation,* see pages 392–94.) Think, for instance, of the connotations that the word *love* takes on in "To His Coy Mistress." It means, first of all, a tender emotion, but it soon comes to mean "sexual union," as in "to make love." In short, the language of poetry is likely to have more shades of meaning than is the case in prose.

Most poetry is imagistic, it is metaphoric, and it is intense. For instance, here's an anonymous medieval lyric:

Western Wind

> Western wind, when wilt thou blow?
> The small rain down can rain.
> Christ, that my love were in my arms,
> And I in my bed again.

Now, I'm not at all sure what this simple little poem means. But it has strong images; that is, it gives me a visual experience: I see rain, and I see two lovers snuggled close in a warm bed. I interpret "western wind" as a metaphor for autumn, simply because I have at the back of my mind Shelley's "Ode to the West Wind," the first line of which is "O wild West Wind, thou breath of Autumn's being." So "western wind" is imagistic and metaphoric. What about its intensity? The intensity arises, I think, from those other two qualities.

Images are based on observation. As a rule, the closer the observation, the more vivid the image. In writing, this results in focusing on the particulars of an experience and representing that experience through the use of concrete words rather than abstract ones. Here are two very different poems that project striking visual experiences through vivid images.

The Red Wheelbarrow
William Carlos Williams

so much depends
upon

a red wheel
barrow

glazed with rain
water

beside the white
chickens

In a Station of the Metro
Ezra Pound

The apparition of these faces in the crowd;
Petals on a wet, black bough.

In Williams's poem, the image is clear and entirely descriptive; it fulfills his demand that a poem should possess "no ideas but in things." From these few lines we can easily visualize the red wheelbarrow, so important to a farmer, sitting under the rain in a farmyard. The poem by Ezra Pound is a little more complex. Here, the second line is a metaphor of the first and serves to convey, in Pound's words, "the precise instant when a thing outward and objective transforms itself, or darts into a thing inward and subjective." The "thing outward and objective," in this case, is the crowd in a subway station.

Above all other literary artists, poets don't *tell;* they *show,* through their use of images and metaphors. There follows one more example of how poets show.

Here is merely a statement. It tells:

> Once I saw some beautiful daffodils. They still live in my memory. The beauty that we experience stays with us as an inner resource that we can call on for pleasure and solace.

Here is the familiar poem in which William Wordsworth *shows* us what that statement meant to him:

> I wandered lonely as a cloud
> That floats on high o'er vales and hills,
> When all at once I saw a crowd,
> A host, of golden daffodils;
> Beside the lake, beneath the trees,
> Fluttering and dancing in the breeze.
>
> Continuous as the stars that shine
> And twinkle on the milky way,
> They stretched in never-ending line
> Along the margin of a bay;
> Ten thousand saw I at a glance,
> Tossing their heads in sprightly dance.
>
> The waves beside them danced; but they
> Out-did the sparkling waves in glee:
> A poet could not but be gay,
> In such a jocund company:
> I gazed—and gazed—but little thought
> What wealth the show to me had brought:
>
> For oft, when on my couch I lie
> In vacant or in pensive mood,
> They flash upon that inward eye
> Which is the bliss of solitude;
> And then my heart with pleasure fills,
> And dances with the daffodils.

The poem is not really about the uses of beauty in life, but concerns an experience of beauty and conveys that experience to the reader. The poem is not a philosophical statement, but a small chunk of experience vividly conveyed.

One of the devices of writing poetry is to use the specific in order to evoke the general—which is what we've been saying all along. Notice how specific and imagistic proverbs are:

Don't count your chickens before they're hatched.
A bird in the hand is worth two in the bush.
That's water under the bridge.
The squeaking wheel gets the grease.
Birds of a feather flock together.
When in Rome, do as the Romans do.

Looking at the Language of Poetry

1. You have now become somewhat familiar with the way language is used in poetry. Study the five poems that follow and describe the use the rhyme, image, and metaphor. What patterns of language can you see in each of the poems? Read them aloud, to yourself or to a friend. What patterns of sound do you hear?

Richard Cory
Edwin Arlington Robinson

Whenever Richard Cory went down town,
We people on the pavement looked at him:
He was a gentleman from sole to crown,
Clean favored, and imperially slim.

And he was always quietly arrayed,
And he was always human when he talked;
But still he fluttered pulses when he said,
"Good-morning," and he glittered when he walked.

And he was rich—yes, richer than a king—
And admirably schooled in every grace:
In fine, we thought that he was everything
To make us wish that we were in his place.

So on we worked, and waited for the light,
And went without the meat, and cursed the bread;
And Richard Cory, one calm summer night,
Went home and put a bullet through his head.

Elegy
Chidiock Tichborne

My prime of youth is but a frost of cares,
My feast of joy is but a dish of pain,
My crop of corn is but a field of tares,
And all my good is but vain hope of gain;
The day is past, and yet I saw no sun,
And now I live, and now my life is done.

My tale was heard and yet it was not told,
My fruit is fallen and yet my leaves are green,
My youth is spent and yet I am not old,
I saw the world and yet I was not seen;
My thread is cut and yet it not spun,
And now I live, and now my life is done.

I sought my death and found it in my womb,
I looked for life and saw it was a shade,
I trod the earth and knew it was my tomb,
And now I die, and now I was but made;
My glass is full, and now my glass is run,
And now I live, and now my life is done.

The Tyger
William Blake

Tyger, Tyger, burning bright,
In the forests of the night:
What immortal hand or eye
Could frame thy fearful symmetry?

In what distant deeps or skies
Burnt the fire of thine eyes!
On what wings dare he aspire?
What the hand, dare seize the fire?

And what shoulder, and what art,
Could twist the sinews of thy heart?
And when thy heart began to beat,
What dread hand? and what dread feet?

What the hammer? what the chain,
In what furnace was thy brain?
What the anvil? what dread gasp,
Dare its deadly terrors clasp?

When the stars threw down their spears
And watered heaven with their tears:
Did he smile his work to see?
Did he who made the Lamb make thee?

Tyger, Tyger, burning bright,
In the forests of the night:
What immortal hand or eye
Dare frame thy fearful symmetry?

Dream Deferred
Langston Hughes

What happens to a dream deferred?

Does it dry up
like a raisin in the sun?
Or fester like a sore—
And then run?
Does it stink like rotten meat?
Or crust and sugar over—
like a syrupy sweet?

Maybe it just sags
like a heavy load.

Or does it explode?

The Rhodora
Ralph Waldo Emerson

In May, when sea-winds pierced our solitudes,
I found the fresh Rhodora in the woods,
Spreading its leafless blooms in a damp nook,
To please the desert and the sluggish brook.
The purple petals, fallen in the pool,
Made the black water with their beauty gay;
Here might the red-bird come his plumes to cool,
And court the flower that cheapens his array.
Rhodora! if the sages ask thee why
This charm is wasted on the earth and sky,
Tell them, dear, that if eyes were made for seeing,
Then Beauty is its own excuse for being;
Why thou wert there, O rival of the rose!
I never thought to ask, I never knew;
But, in my simple ignorance, suppose
The self-same Power that brought me there brought you.

2. Write a paper discussing the meaning of the following poem. What is
   your reaction to the poem? Do you think it is good? If so, why? Do
   you think it bad? Why? What is the quality of language in the poem?
   For example, what is the quality of the rhyme? Are the rhyming words
   unusual or obvious? What about the images? Can you visualize the
   garden mentioned in the poem? What are the connotations of the

word "gloat"? Do they fit the poem? In other words, explain your reactions by responding to the poem in detail.

A Garden of Love and Beauty
Silas Pennypacker

There's a garden, as named above,
A garden of beauty and love;
Gardeners, toiling all the year round,
Go there as if Paradise-bound!

Clime without frost to fear, all year
Plants from over the earth brought here;
Folks over so much beauty gloat;
In the warm breeze, butterflies float!

Many paths here for lovers' feet.
Loves here walk and loves here meet.
My feet come here as of duty
To spend the day with love and beauty.

SUMMARY AND SUGGESTIONS FOR WRITING

In this chapter, we could not discuss all the possible kinds of writing about literature. It goes without saying, however, that understanding the work precedes any response or written commentary. For this reason the chapter has focused on the interpretive essay, which is an attempt to explain the complex meaning of a work of literature and to demonstrate how the author conveys that meaning through his or her work. Therefore, most of the chapter has dealt with technical matters, such as plot, character, form, metaphor, symbol, image, and so on.

But you should keep in mind the other kind of essay that was discussed at the beginning of this chapter—the kind in which you explain the relationship of a work—its plot, theme, characters—to your life.

Some other possibilities are:

1. A comparison of one work with others like it, or a comparison of a novel with a dramatic version of the book, as in film or television.
2. A critique of the ethics or values that the work expresses.
3. An explanation of why you did or did not enjoy the work.

It is even possible that you would respond to a poem by writing a poem or to a story by writing a story.

8
Writing Essay Examinations

██████████ A chapter on the essay examination is really an addendum to the chapters on exposition and on argumentation and persuasion, for the response to an essay question is nothing more than an expository essay or an argument.

An essay examination invites you to demonstrate that you (1) have an overall understanding of a subject or concept and (2) know significant details, and these are the keys to writing a successful essay examination response: you should organize your answer so that it presents an overview of the subject, and you should "texture" your answer with significant details.

More about these two principles later. Right now, some advice about reading to learn.

READING TO LEARN

Your purpose for reading should determine the way you read. When you read a novel for pleasure, there is no particular reason for trying to be efficient; many of the techniques for reading to learn, which we are about to discuss, would be inappropriate when you want to experience the imaginative world of fiction. But when you want to learn as much as possible in as short a time as possible, you should employ reading methods that will get you through the material rapidly and will help you comprehend and retain what you have read.

The basic principle is this: *first get a general idea of what the material is about, and then fill in the details.*

A widely used and effective reading *and reviewing* strategy is called SQ3R (Survey, Question, Read, Recite, Review). It works like this:

1. *Survey* the material, trying to get an overview of the subject: its main concepts and how they relate to one another.
   a. Read introductions and summaries.
   b. Pay attention to subheadings (especially in textbooks), for they often represent an outline of the subject matter, as do the subheadings in this book. For example, the first part of chapter 13, "Words" (pages 390–99), has the following subheadings:

   DICTION AND USAGE

   > Denotation and Connotation
   > Levels of Usage
   > > Formal and Informal Usage
   > > Nonstandard Usage
   > > A Word About Slang
   > > Jargon
   > > Gobbledygook
   > > Abstractness

   In other words, the section called "Diction and Usage" deals with two main subtopics, "Denotation and Connotation" and "Levels of Usage," and "Levels of Usage" is divided into six sub-subtopics.
   c. Read the first sentences of paragraphs.
   d. Look at the material printed in **boldface** and *italics,* for those print conventions are intended to call attention to important aspects of the subject.
   e. Pay attention to charts and graphs.
2. Using your knowledge of the subject, your class notes, and the chapter titles and subheadings in your book (if you are studying a book), formulate *questions* regarding your subject.
3. *Reread* the material, seeking answers to your questions.
4. *Recite:* explain the questions and the answers to yourself. It will

probably be valuable to write your answers. (If you find that you can't explain both the questions and the answers in writing, you undoubtedly need to study further in order to gain a better understanding of the subject.)

You can use the SQ3R strategy both for the first reading of material that you want to learn and for reviewing that material in preparation for an examination.

Practice: SQ3R

1. Based on a survey of the following headings and subheadings, what questions would you try to answer in your reading?

WHAT ARE DIALECTS?

  Development of Dialects
    Prestige Dialects
    A Look at a Nonstandard Dialect
  Dialect and Social Mobility
  Switching Dialects

After you have posed your questions, read pages 408–13 in this book to see if you asked the right questions and whether or not you can find answers to them.

2. What do you learn from charts and graphs in the section on dialects?

USING ESSAY QUESTIONS AS GUIDES

Good essay questions are designed to guide the test taker toward the sort of answer that the tester wants. *You can find the purpose of the question in key words and phrases* such as "explain," "compare and contrast," "defend," "criticize," "analyze," and so on. The following question is typical:

> *Compare and contrast* the theories of evolution of Charles Darwin and Alfred Russell Wallace.

This question is really asking: in what ways are the theories similar, and in what ways are they different? The implication is that your essay will have two main parts, one discussing similarities and the other differences.

When the key word in a question is "defend," the tester is asking you to put forth the arguments in favor of a point of view:

> *Defend* the argument that slavery was not the main cause of the Civil War.

If the key word is "defend," but you write an essay that merely explains, you have obviously missed the point. Make sure that you respond to the purpose of the question as expressed in the key words.

Essay questions can be, and often are, based on brief quotations from sources:

> Speaking of *Nineteen Eighty-Four,* the critic Irving Howe says,
>
> > Orwell's profoundest insight is that in a totalitarian world man's life is shorn of dynamic possibilities. The end of life is completely predictable in its beginning, the beginning merely a manipulated preparation for the end. There is no opening for surprise, for that spontaneous animation which is the token of and justification for freedom.
>
> Explain how the novel develops this idea through its plot.

In responding to this question, you must first understand what Irving Howe says, and then you must relate his idea to the novel itself: its plot, characters, and scenes.

Frequently, essay questions have more than one part:

1. Outline the events that led up to President Truman's removal of General Douglas MacArthur from command in Korea.
2. Explain why you agree or disagree with Truman's action.

The first part of this question asks for a chronology (a sequence of events), and the second asks you to argue for or against a point.

Read essay questions carefully. Make your response appropriate to the purpose of the question.

PREPARING TO WRITE

1. Roughly schedule your time for writing. Suppose you have a two-hour examination period and two questions to respond to: you must determine whether you should divide your time equally between them or give more time to one than to the other.

Often the instructions will contain suggested times:

I. (30 minutes) Explain the General Assembly and the Security Council of the United Nations.

II. (90 minutes) Has the United Nations been effective as an international tribunal? In arguing for your point of view, cite specific examples.

Obviously, the first question of these two will count only one-third as much as the second; therefore, it is unwise to go beyond half an hour or so in answering—though many students get so caught up in their own thought processes that they forget to divide their time.

2. Make notes. Keep a sheet of paper handy so that you can jot down ideas as they come to you.

STARTING AND ORGANIZING

The most deadly pitfall in taking essay exams is *wandering*. You have limited time for your essay, and you must decide quickly where you want it to go and then remain steadily on the trail. Therefore, a beginning that outlines the complete essay is very useful. It sets up constraints and holds you to your purpose. Here is a typical essay prompt:

One of the most famous events in American history is the Boston Tea Party. Explain the reasons for this act of rebellion.

Of the following beginnings of essay reponses to the prompt, the first is right on target; the second is too skimpy; the third seems to ignore the purpose of the question:

1. The Boston Tea Party resulted from the miscalculation of King George III, Parliament, and Prime Minister Frederick, Lord North, regarding the colonists' feelings about independence as opposed to economic advantage.

This beginning has direction. The reader expects to learn what the miscalculation was and how it brought about the Boston Tea Party. We assume that the essay will outline the historical facts and interpret their significance.

2. The Boston Tea Party came about because King George III, Parliament, and the prime minister miscalculated.

Not as useful as the first beginning, since this one does not imply an argument, as does the first.

> 3. Every schoolchild has heard about the Boston Tea Party. This great event has become a part of American legend, like the surrender at Appomattox. No event in our history is more colorful or more representative of the American spirit of independence.

But the prompt asked for an explanation of why the Boston Tea Party occurred. This beginning implies that the writer will never arrive at the purpose of the prompt.

Advice: Sometimes you will think of a beginning that is stunningly interesting, brilliantly witty, or utterly engaging. Short of such inspiration, however, use the beginning of your response to tell your reader, in a nutshell, what you intend to do in the essay. In other words, use the beginning to state the *gist* of your response. (For a discussion of *gist,* see pages 21–23.)

DETAILS

A sentence toward the beginning of this chapter went as follows: "An essay examination invites you to demonstrate that you (1) have an overall understanding of a subject or concept and (2) know significant details. . . ." Thus, in the essay on the Boston Tea Party, the test taker would want to identify King George III, not merely "the king"; it is more impressive to write about Prime Minister Frederick, Lord North, than merely "the prime minister"; and it is well to know that the event took place in 1773.

An essay response that is merely a spewing forth of details—facts, data—is unsuccessful, but a response that is *only* the big picture, generalities, is also unsuccessful. Thus, when you are studying for the exam, and when you are writing it, you must incorporate the significant details. You might know that Lord North entered Parliament in 1754 and became a junior lord of the treasury in 1759, a privy councilor in 1766, and chancellor of the exchequer in 1767, but these details have nothing to do with the question and would only clutter your answer.

Resist the temptation to set forth everything that you know about a subject. Choose significant detail—texture that will advance your argument *and* show that you're an expert on the subject.

THE ESSAY RESPONSE: AN EXAMPLE

The following is an example of a well-structured essay response that contains significant detail.

The question: One of the most famous events in American history is the Boston Tea Party. Explain the reasons for this act of rebellion.

The first paragraph: the gist of the response.
Detail: the king and the prime minister specifically named.

Detail: dates. Note the mention of the Boston Massacre.

The Boston Tea Party resulted from the miscalculation of King George III, Parliament, and Prime Minister Frederick, Lord North, regarding the colonists' feelings about independence as opposed to economic advantage.

From 1770, the year of the Boston Massacre, to 1773, relative calm had prevailed in the American colonies, but when Parliament passed the Tea Act in 1773, another storm broke.

The explanation: shows that the writer understands the Tea Act and the historical reasons behind it.
Detail: date of founding of the East India Company.

The Tea Act was an attempt on the part of the king and Parliament to revive the fortunes of the financially troubled East India Company. From the time of its founding in 1690, the East India Company had a virtual monopoly on the tea trade, selling the tea at auction to wholesale merchants in London. These wholesalers then sold the tea to American wholesalers, who imported it to the colonies and sold it to retailers. This tea was taxed twice, first in England and then again (by the so-called Townshend duty) in the colonies.

Detail: the name of the duty.

The Tea Act permitted the East India Company to sell tea directly to the colonies, thus eliminating the English wholesalers and their profits, and the act also abolished the English tax on tea, leaving only the Townshend duty.

Frederick, Lord North, the British prime minister, assumed, along with the king and Parliament, that the colonists would not protest the Tea Act, for, after all, the cost of tea was reduced. Therefore, the East India Company promptly shipped about 500,000 pounds of tea to its agents in Boston, New York, Philadelphia, and Charleston.

Detail: amount of tea shipped.

Interpretation: the colonists' reaction.

Contrary to expectations in the British Isles, the colonists were outraged. Even though tea would be cheaper, they deeply resented the fact that Parliament had given an English company a virtual monopoly on tea. In fact, the Tea Act threatened commerce in America. If Parliament could give the East India Company a monopoly on tea, might not other English companies gain similar concessions?

In short, the colonists viewed the Tea Act as part of a plot completely to subordinate the colonies to England.

Detail: date.

Detail: name of leader.

Detail: value of tea.

On the night of December 16, Sam Adams gave the signal, and a group of Bostonians, disguised as Mohawks, boarded the tea ship Dartmouth and pitched some £15,000 worth of tea into the harbor.

Practice

Which of the following beginnings for essay responses seem effective and which seem ineffective? Explain your judgments.

1. It is claimed that some apes—including the gorilla Koko and the chimpanzee Washoe—have learned to "talk," using various symbol systems, such as American Sign Language in the case of Koko. For three reasons, I would argue that apes can "talk." First, they don't merely learn words and phrases and repeat them again and again, but actually make up new words and phrases, just as humans do. Second, they talk to themselves, using language, as do humans, for pleasure and as a problem-solving tool. Third, their talk is "grammatical," that is, rule governed.

2. In the century after Muhammad's death in A.D. 632, Islam spread rapidly through North Africa and into Egypt and Persia. Because of this rapid expansion and because the Arabic people had no significant artistic heritage up to that time, the Muslims developed their unique style by synthesizing the arts of the Byzantines, the Copts, the Romans, and the Sassanids.

3. Isogamy is a biological condition in which the sexual cells or gametes are of the same size and are indistinguishable from one another.

4. In their pure definitions, socialism and capitalism are direct opposites, but in practice and in historical fact, socialism and capitalism share certain basic characteristics.

5. In this essay I will argue that (1) all higher education should be free to those capable of taking advantage of it; (2) rigorous admission tests should eliminate all but the most competent from higher education; (3) those who are not accepted for higher education should be trained for gainful employment at government expense.

9

A Guide to Research Writing

The research paper is a common feature in English classes, both in high schools and in colleges and universities, a part of the tradition, but sometimes it may seem to be another meaningless hurdle that students must leap in order to complete their educations.

THE WHY OF THE RESEARCH PAPER

Of what use is the ability to put together a research paper? To complete a successful research paper, one must (1) assemble information through research, (2) evaluate that information, and (3) synthesize the information so that it is a whole, not just a collection of fragments. In short, completing a research paper gives the student invaluable practice in *finding information and using it.*

Do people in the "real world" write research papers? Yes, as a matter of fact. Any kind of writing might call for research. A report on the financial future of a business demands research, as does an argument in favor of or against a political candidate. Funding proposals, so important to nonprofit institutions such as universities, can be viewed as research papers, as can proposals made by businesses to clients. In short, yes: people in the "real world" do write research papers, very frequently.

There are, of course, many kinds of research: a chemist might well do most of his or hers in the laboratory, while anthropologists frequently use whole cultures as their "laboratories." Public opinion polls are another kind of research, as are personal interviews of the kind published in newspapers and magazines. But this chapter will concern library research. It discusses gathering information from library resources, evaluating that information, putting it together (synthesizing it), and providing documentation (letting your reader know what your sources are).

For Discussion: Research Writing Is Writing

Research writing is not a category separate from all other kinds of writing, but, depending on the author's purpose, can be an explanation, an argument, or a piece of persuasion. Biographies, which are essentially narration, usually involve massive amounts of research, and even autobiographies can demand that the writer do some research. All the principles that you have read and thought about in the other chapters of this book apply to research writing.

As you look back at the chapters you have read and thought about so far, what principles stand out as the most important in regard to research writing? Explain why you think these principles are important.

SOME COMMON-SENSE ADVICE ABOUT RESEARCH WRITING

Begin early! Don't postpone until the last minute! First, define your topic as soon as you can so that your ideas can begin to germinate. If you have a topic in mind, almost certainly you will get ideas and run into sources when you least expect them. Second, begin the actual research as soon as possible. Survey the resources available in your school's library and in the public library. Begin to read so that you will gain familiarity with the ins and outs of your topic.

Keep accurate records! Be orderly! When you find a source that you think you can use, record the bibliographic information at once so that you won't have to make hurried, last-minute trips to the library while you are writing the paper. When you take notes, make sure that you record the page number or numbers of the source from which the information comes. Be certain that you spell names correctly.

Think about assembling, evaluating, and synthesizing the information before you begin to pay attention to such details as the exact form for notes or footnotes. In other words, write before you edit or proofread.

Once you have the paper written, at least in draft form, pay careful attention to such details as bibliographic form.

Above all, enjoy the process of becoming an expert on the subject you choose.

QUOTING, PARAPHRASING, AND SUMMARIZING

When you use the exact words of a source, you are quoting, and quotations must appear either (a) in quotation marks or (b) if the quotation is five typewritten lines or longer, as indented extracts.

For example, the following quotation from *Arctic Dreams*, by Barry Lopez, is not set off as an extract because it will not be five typed lines long: "Like other landscapes that initially appear barren, the arctic tundra can open suddenly, like the corolla of a flower, when any intimacy with it is sought." But the following (a continuation of the quote from *Arctic Dreams*), which will take more than five lines, is put in a block by itself. (You will also indent extracts eleven spaces when you type the final version of your paper.)

> One begins to notice spots of brilliant red, orange, and green, for example, among the monotonic browns of a tundra tussock. A wolf spider lunges at a glistening beetle. A shred of muskox wool lies inert in the lavender blooms of a saxifrage. When Alwin Pederson, a Danish naturalist, first arrived on the northeast coast of Greenland, he wrote, "I must admit to strange feelings at the sight of this godforsaken desert of stone." Before he left, however, he was writing of muskoxen grazing in lush grass that grew higher than the animals' heads on Jameson Land, and of the stark beauty of nunataks, the ice-free spires of rock that pierce the Pleistocene stillness of the Greenland ice cap. I, like Pederson, when stopping to pick up the gracile rib bone of an arctic hare, would catch sudden and unexpected sight of the silken cocoon of an arctic caterpillar.

However, you would seldom want to quote such a long passage, but you might want to *paraphrase* it, giving its meaning in your own words. Here is such a paraphrase:

> Barry Lopez says that at first the arctic tundra appears barren, but if you look closely you will see that it has both color and life. A tussock that appeared merely brown reveals bright red, orange, and green upon closer examination. A wolf spider pounces on a beetle. A bit of muskox hair and an arctic hare's rib bone are to be discovered. Once you learn to look, the arctic becomes beautiful, as it did for Alwin Pederson, the Danish naturalist, who at first called the tundra "this godforsaken desert of stone."

Often you will want to do a summary of a source, getting the main points but not the details. The first chapter of this book contains a summary of the whole thing (pages 6–7). You can turn to this section for an example of a summary.

CHOOSING A TOPIC

Chapter 6, "Argumentation and Persuasion," points out that the topic of an argument must have two characteristics: definition and uncertainty. For example, *religion improves society* lacks definition; it is far too broad. (What kind of religion? Which aspects of religion? Improves society in what respects?) On the other hand, *religious people go to church more frequently than nonbelievers do* lacks uncertainty; since the conclusion is obvious, there is no argument.

Your research topic must also have these two characteristics. It must be well defined, and it must concern a question or problem to which the answer or solution is not obvious.

How do you go about finding a productive topic for research writing? Suppose you are taking a class in American history, and one of the requirements for the course is a research paper. From the first day of the course, you should be alert for a question that interests you and that might be answered through research. You could perhaps find such question in the instructor's lectures or in your textbook or in the other reading that you do for the class.

In a moment you will be reading a paper that I wrote on gasohol, a subject that began to interest me when I saw an advertisement on the subject during a television public affairs broadcast.

THE RESEARCH SITUATION

Much of this book has been a discussion of problem solving, and this chapter will not repeat what has been treated in detail elsewhere, but will attempt to provide some guidance on the kinds of problems that research can solve.

Notice how common it is to encounter a problematic situation that demands research. In your reading, you come across a word that you don't know the meaning of, so you go to the dictionary. That is research of a sort. Your old car finally gives out. Now you have a problem: what kind of car should you buy to replace the old one? You decide that you want a compact, but you don't know which make or model, so you go to *Consumer Reports* for evaluations, you visit dealers and take test drives, you talk with people who own the various kinds of compacts. You have done research that could well provide the basis for a useful paper, which in outline might look like this:

    I. Background of problem
       A. Reason for needing a new car
       B. Factors affecting the choice of a new car
          1. Need for a four-passenger car
          2. Financial restrictions, limiting purchase price
          3. Considerations of fuel economy
    II. Formulation of problem [Taking into consideration passenger space, purchase price, and fuel economy, you decide to buy a compact. Thus the problem is: which compact should you choose?]
   III. Investigation of problem
       A. *Consumer Reports*
       B. Opinions of current owners
       C. Test drives of various makes
   IV. Conclusion based on investigation

The third section of the paper is the one that embodies the results of your research, and the reader will be asking, "Where did the writer get this information? Are the sources reliable? Does the writer let me know what the sources are so that I can verify the paper's accuracy?" You would need some way of referring your reader to the proper issue of *Consumer Reports,* you probably would need to give some background about the owners whose opinions you cited, and you would want to report fully on the results of your test drives. All this amounts to *documentation,* about which we will be talking as the chapter progresses.

WRITING A RESEARCH PAPER

Enough warm-up. Now is the time to get down to cases.

In the following pages, I will give a step-by-step account of doing a research paper, and in this discussion I will try to set forth and explain useful tactics and strategies. As you follow this discussion, you will see an actual research paper come into being.

The system that I use for documenting my paper—parentheses in the text identifying my sources and at the end a list of those sources in "Works Cited"—is taken from *The MLA Handbook for Writers of Research Papers,* 2nd ed., published in 1984 by the Modern Language Association of America. This is an easy system to use, but it is not the preferred system in every field. If you do a research paper in the social sciences, for instance, you will use not the MLA system but one similar to it, very likely the one described in the *Publication Manual of the American Psychological Association* (1983). However, if you understand the general principles about documenting your research, it will be easy for you to change the details to conform to the systems used in various fields. If you want all the nuts and bolts concerning notes, footnotes, in-text citations (such as I use in the paper that follows), bibliography, and so on, you can consult the latest editions of *The MLA Handbook* or *The Chicago Manual of Style.*

The Research Problem

The problem that I want to understand, if not solve, through research can be stated as a question:

Why hasn't ethanol come into wider use as a substitute for gasoline?

I know for a fact that ethanol works in internal combustion engines and that it does not pollute, at least not to the extent that fossil fuels do. I know also that the world reserves of petroleum are rapidly being used up and that the United States, in its need for oil, is at the mercy of other nations, particularly those making up OPEC—the Organization of Petroleum Exporting Countries.

Perhaps through research I can begin to understand the ins and outs of this problem.

1. Getting an Overview of the Subject

So far, I have told you virtually all that I know about ethanol. Oh, I know that it is made from organic products such as corn and that in some areas of the country "gasohol," a mixture of ethanol and gasoline, is obtainable. But that's about all. Therefore, my first stop is the library, to consult the *Encyclopedia Americana*, from which I hope to get a general knowledge of my subject. (The *Encyclopedia Americana* is known for the excellence of its articles on science and technology.)

However, in this case the 1985 edition of the *Americana* doesn't give me much help. Looking under "ethanol," I find that it "is an alcohol widely used in beverages and as an industrial chemical. See *ethyl alcohol*." The article on ethyl alcohol contains the chemical formula for ethanol (C_2H_5OH), which is of no use to me, and the information that ethyl alcohol is the chemical in liquor, that it can be denatured (with such chemicals as methyl isobutyl ketone or kerosene) to make it undrinkable, and that "in some countries where the cost of petroleum is very high, ethyl alcohol is added to motor gasoline as an extender."

So I haven't gained much from the encyclopedia, but checking it took only a few minutes.

2. Checking the Card Catalog

Most libraries today have computerized their card catalogs, the listings by author's name, title, and subject of all the books a library has. (For example, the University of California uses a computer system called "Melvyl.") For my paper on gasohol, I begin in the public library, and a computer search of its holdings reveals nothing under the general subjects "ethanol" or "gasohol," so I search under the more general heading "fuel" and find a number of books, including *Fuel and Energy* (1975); *Fuel and Power* (1968); *An Introduction to the Study of Fuel,* by John Campbell Macrae (no date); *Future Sources,* by James Strachan (1984); *The Quest for Fuel,* by John A. Thomas (1978); *Alternative Fuels for Aviation: Hearings Before the Subcommittee on Aerospace Technology and National Needs,* a government document (1976); *The Whole Earth Energy Crisis: Our Dwindling Sources of Energy,* by John H.

Brown, A. S. ①

Fuel Resources ②

New York: F. Watts, 1985
③   ④   ⑤

333.79
Bro ⑥

1. Name of author, last name first
2. Title of book
3. Place of publication
4. Publisher
5. Date of publication
6. Dewey decimal call number. (Probably your college or university library uses the Library of Congress system of call numbers, rather than the Dewey decimal.)

Bibliography Card for a Book

Woodburn (1973); *Fuel Resources,* by A. S. Brown (1985); and *Economics of Energy,* edited by Leslie E. Grayson (1975).

I enter each of these books on a separate index card, as illustrated on the accompanying Bibliography Card for a Book.

The important point is to enter all the necessary information concerning the book and to do so accurately. The nature of the information you need and your reason for needing it will become clearer as this discussion progresses.

I also do a search of the card catalog at my university library, and under "gasohol" I find three books that, it turns out, will be very important to me: *Gasohol for Energy Production,* by Nicholas P. Cheremisinoff; *Gasohol Sourcebook,* by Nicholas P. Cheremisinoff and Paul N. Cheremisinoff; and *The Gasohol Handbook,* by V. Daniel Hunt. I enter them, too, on bibliography cards.

3. Checking Periodical Indexes

Of course, I also want to find any magazine articles that discuss ethanol, and to do so I go to two periodical indexes, the *Magazine Index,* which is on microfilm, and the *Reader's Guide to*

Fumento, Michael ①

"Some Dare Call Them... Robber Barons" ②

National Review: 13 March 1987: 32-38
     ③   ④   ⑤

1. Name of author, last name first
2. Title of article
3. Name of magazine or journal
4. Date of the issue
5. Pages on which the article appears

Bibliography Card for a Magazine

Periodical Literature. Like the card catalog, these indexes have subject, author, and title entries. (The details concerning indexes and other standard reference works are in a later section of this chapter, titled "A Brief Survey of Library Resources," starting on page 262.) Beginning with the latest issue of *Reader's Guide* and working back to 1983, I find thirteen sources under "ethanol" or "alcohol as fuel," including articles in *Science Digest* (May 1984); *National Review* (March 13, 1987); *Natural History* (April 1985); *World Press Review* (June 31, 1984); *The New Yorker* (October 10, 1983); and *Farm Journal* (October 1983).

Clearly I have hit pay dirt in the magazine indexes.

The illustration shows the form for a bibliography card for a magazine article.

4. Surveying the New York Times Index

The *New York Times Index* is an invaluable resource for topics that are or have been in the news, and I check it under the headings "ethanol" and "alcohol." The most useful aspect of this index is that it gives brief abstracts of articles. Thus, in the 1985 volume I find the following under "alcohol":

> Brazil's alcohol fuel program, long heralded for its success in reducing Brazil's dependence on imported oil, is suddenly being scrutinized in more critical light as result of recent declines in world oil prices; new administration of President Jose Sarney has decided to continue program, but is under growing pressure to raise domestic price of fuel and cut subsidies to alcohol-distilling industry (M), Jl 29, IV, 4:5
>
> Lummis Crest unit of Combustion Engineering and Hagbert Corp receive $104 million contracted from Agrifuels Refining Corp to design and build plan [*sic*] to convert molasses into ethanol for blending into gasoline (S), N 5, IV, 4:4

The newspaper contained a medium-length (M) article on gasohol in Brazil in the issue of July 29, Section IV, page 4, column 5, and another article on converting molasses into ethanol.

The information about Brazil is particularly important to me, for I had not known that a major nation had implemented a large-scale program of producing and using ethanol, and I make index cards for both articles.

5. Scanning and Reading

Now it is time to begin sifting through the sources that my *bibliographic* search has turned up. I will start with the books, then go to the magazines, and finally read the articles in the *New York Times*.

I do not attempt to read the books from cover to cover, one after another, but I scan all of them, to find which are likely to be most useful. In this case, I find that *The Gasohol Handbook* and *Gasohol for Energy Production* seem to be comprehensive and not so technical that I cannot understand them.

6. Planning

By this time, I have begun to get a sense of the issues involved in my subject. In fact, I know that I will want to discuss four topics: the history of gasohol, its effect on environmental pollution, its economic aspects, and the problems involved with its use. Thus, I am ready to zero in on the information that I need, and I return to my sources to answer the questions that I have posed: What is the history of gasohol? How will the use of gasohol affect environmental pollution? What will be the economic effects of the widespread use of gasohol? What problems keep gasohol from being adopted immediately?

> *economics*   *Hunt*
>
> *As of the writing of the Hunt book (pub. 1981), imported oil created cash outflow in U.S. of $10 million per hour. (3)*

The key word "economics" at the top of the card tells me what topic the note concerns. The word "Hunt" on the right-hand side tells me that the information is from *The Gasohol Handbook,* by V. Daniel Hunt. And the numeral 3 in parentheses gives the page in the book on which the information was found.

> *Brazil*   *Cheremisinoff*
>
> *According to Ch, there were three reasons for the development of gasohol in Brazil: An abundance of sugarcane as a base for ethanol, the desire of the government to develop an energy industry that would encourage people to stay in rural areas rather than migrating to the city, and availability of uncultivated lands that could be used to grow manioc (a sugar-bearing tuber similar to the sugar beet). These factors led the government to institute a program aimed at making ethanol a major source of energy. (53-54)*

Key word: "Brazil." Author: Cheremisinoff. Pages on which the information was found: 53-54.

> *pollution, lead*   *Commoner*
>
> *Commoner says, "The new high-compression engines spewed lead - a highly toxic metal - from their exhausts into the air. Lead began to accumulate in living things exposed to exhaust fumes. Soon, roadside plants contained more lead than plants in the wild; the bones of city pigeons contained more lead than the bones of country pigeons; the blood of traffic policemen contained more lead than the blood of other city residents. Children tend to absorb more lead from the environment than adults do, and they are therefore more likely to suffer from lead poisoning, which can damage the brain and the nervous system." (135)*

Key words: "pollution, lead." Author: Commoner. Page number: 135. Since the entry is an exact quotation from the source, I have put it in quotation marks.

Sample Note Cards

7. Gathering Information for Writing

Now that I know what I'm looking for, I go back to my sources to find what I need. Since I have a portable computer, I keep my notes on 3.5-inch disks, not on cards, but if you don't have a portable computer, 3-by-5 or 4-by-6 cards work well. The

Sample Note Cards on page 254 show some of the material that I gathered in my reading.

And here are two pieces of advice about note taking:

1. Double-check to make sure that you have all the information and that you have not been inaccurate.
2. Unless you plan to use a direct quotation in your paper, summarize or paraphrase; don't copy the exact words of the source. If you summarize, the facts and ideas will go through your mind, not simply in your eyes and out your pen.

Writing the Paper

In learning about your subject and gathering material concerning it, you inevitably did a great deal of planning. Your note cards will reflect that planning, and you can work directly from them, arranging them in stacks according to the subdivisions of your subject, as I did for my paper on gasohol. I might have labeled the stacks *history, pollution, economics,* and *problems,* and you will notice that these are the concerns of the major sections of my paper.

Thus your note cards not only contain vital information and ideas; they also imply a structure for your paper.

As you read the paper, you will see that the material in brackets ([ ]) printed in color explains the system I use to inform the reader of my sources.

Gas + Alcohol = Gasohol

In 1980, one-half of all the crude oil used in the United States was imported from such regions as the Persian Gulf and South America. This inflow of oil created an outflow of cash amounting to $10 million per hour (Hunt 3)! [Refers to page 3 of a book by Hunt, listed in the "Works Cited" at the end of the paper. This book is the source for the data about oil imports.] For the year, this added up to more than $87.5 *billion,* and we can assume that, if anything, the flood of capital going out of the United States for oil has increased. The American hunger for oil is obviously a disaster for the economy.

Our reliance on oil contributes not only to the nation's economic problems: fossil fuel (primarily oil) is *the* major source of air pollution. This year, eighty-one American cities failed to meet the standards of the Clean Air Act, exceeding defined levels for both ozone and carbon monoxide ("Ozoned"). [The data about pollution was found in a very short article called "Ozone" in *California* magazine, on page 52. The date and other information about the article are in "Works Cited" under "Ozoned."] Even if the world price of oil sagged and technology solved the pollution problem, we would be faced with the inescapable fact that oil is a rapidly diminishing, nonrenewable resource. Ultimately, we must find alternatives to the "black gold" that has powered American automobiles and industry for nearly a century now.

A Brief History of Ethanol

The most promising alternative energy source is alcohol, technically *ethanol* and *methanol* though the following discussion will concentrate primarily on ethanol. Knowledge of how to produce ethanol is hardly a recent discovery, for the Egyptians and Mesopotamians were brewing beer as early as 2500 B.C., and ethanol is the alcoholic content of beers, wines, whiskey, and other liquors (Cheremisinoff 49). [I discovered the fact about the early production of ethanol in the book by Cheremisinoff, on page 49.] V. Daniel Hunt's *The Gasohol Handbook* (9–12) [I discovered the general outline of the history of ethanol in the book by Hunt, on pages 9–12. Since I am more or less summarizing these pages, I do not try to give a citation for every single item.] outlines the history of alcohol fuels. By the middle of the 1800s, alcohol was replacing whale oil as a fuel in lamps because it was both clean and odorless, and toward the end of the century alcohol was being used as a fuel in internal combustion engines. "The first modern internal combustion engine, the Otto cycle of 1876, ran on alcohol as well as gasoline" (9). [I have used a direct quotation from my source. Therefore, I give the page number. Since I have already indicated that Hunt is my source, I do not need to repeat that information.]

Apparently the first automobile to run on alcohol was a German vehicle built in 1894 by an engineer who worked for the German Agricultural Society (Commoner 130). [I found this fact in an article by Commoner, listed, of course, in "Works Cited."] If automobiles could run on ethanol, distilled from grain, German farmers would have a burgeoning new market for their crops. Henry Ford was a great proponent of alcohol as a motor fuel, and his Model A, the famed "Tin Lizzy," had an adjustable carburetor that allowed the auto to burn either alcohol or gasoline. As Barry Commoner points out, Ford was convinced that farmers could supply industry with many essential products (150). [Since this fact is also from the Commoner article, I cite only the page number.] Thus, Ford (along with Harvey Firestone) was on the side of agriculture in a conflict between that industry and the oil barons that would determine the future of energy use in the United States.

After the First World War, manufacturers began to increase the size and weight of automobiles, necessitating more powerful engines than those that had propelled the light, buggylike earlier autos. If the automakers could increase the compression ratio from four-to-one to eight-to-one, the efficiency of the engine would be doubled; however, "when gasoline was used as the fuel and an engine's compression ratio was gradually increased, the engine's power failed to rise correspondingly; in fact, it eventually fell, accompanied by a noisy metallic ring—'engine knock' " (Commoner 133). [**The citation identifies the exact page of the quotation from Commoner.**] In a study published in 1923, British engineer Harry Ricardo set forth his findings that ethanol and another alcohol, methanol, solved the knock problem (Commoner 133–34). [**The facts concerning Ricardo were on pages 133–34 in Commoner.**] Thus, it appeared that the fuel of the future would be alcohol.

However, by the 1920s the oil boom was on, and entrepreneurs such as J. Paul Getty, Bill Skelly, and the Rockefellers were making vast fortunes from the forests of oil wells that were growing in Oklahoma, California, and elsewhere—a story that Robert Lenzner tells vividly in *The Great Getty*. [**It so happened that I was reading a biography of J. Paul Getty, and what I learned in that book helped me with my discussion of gasohol. Since I got this idea from the whole book, I do not cite specific pages. Other pertinent information about the book is entered in "Works Cited."**] If American automobiles were manufactured to operate on alcohol, the oil industry would collapse. When two General Motors scientists, Thomas Midgley, Jr., and T. A. Boyd, discovered that tetraethyl lead added to gasoline would also suppress the knock, the oil industry was saved (Commoner 134–35). [**I found the information about Midgley and Boyd in the Commoner article, on pages 134–35.**]

The year 1923 was a real turning point in American history. If alcohol had become the national fuel, many of the problems that now beset us would have been either alleviated or avoided— for example, the current highly unfavorable balance in international trade, the farm problem (since there would be a steady demand for the vegetable products—primarily grain—from which ethanol is made), and environmental pollution.

Pollution and Gasohol

The triumph of gasoline with a lead additive over alcohol as the fuel for automobiles meant that millions of tons of lead particulates would be pumped into the atmosphere.

The new high-compression engines spewed lead—a highly toxic metal—from their exhausts into the air. Lead began to accumulate in living things exposed to exhaust fumes. Soon, roadside plants contained more lead than plants in the wild; the bones of city pigeons contained more lead than the bones of country pigeons; the blood of traffic policemen contained more lead than the blood of other city residents. Children tend to absorb more lead from the environment than adults do, and they are therefore more likely to suffer from lead poisoning, which can damage the brain and the nervous system (Commoner 135). **[The quotation is from the Commoner article, page 135.]**

Gasohol emits approximately the same amount of carbon monoxide and hydrocarbons as gasoline does. It generates less nitrogen oxide and more aldehydes (which are currently unregulated) than straight gasoline does. Most important, ethanol contains no sulfur; hence, gasohol cuts down on the amount of brown "guck" in smog (Hunt 395). **[I found this data in Hunt, on page 395.]**

All in all, the widespread use of gasohol would benefit the environment significantly.

Economic Considerations

Figure 1 shows Hunt's breakdown of the cost to the consumer of one gallon of ethanol. The thing to notice particularly in this chart is that the producer receives a 32-cent credit, and the source of this dividend is one of the most interesting aspects of the gasohol story (5). **[At the beginning of this paragraph, I have indicated that the data is from Hunt; therefore, I need only to give the page number.]**

Ethanol, of course, is distilled from the carbohydrate portions of a crop such as grain. The grain is cooked, then fermented, and the alcohol is distilled off; the process is essentially the same whether carried out by a moonshiner in the backwoods or a giant agricultural corporation. **[Up to this point, I am relying on common knowledge and need no citation.]** The residue of this process is known as "distiller's dried grain," which is sold as cattle feed containing all the grain's original protein and about a third of its carbohydrates, accounting for the 32-cent dividend shown in Figure 1 (Commoner 144). **[I found the facts about distiller's dried grain in the Commoner article.]**

In the long run, if not at present, ethanol could have the economic edge over gasoline, since crude oil is becoming increasingly scarce and hence, according to the inevitable laws of supply and demand, will grow ever more expensive, whereas ethanol, deriving from a renewable source, will increase or decrease in price

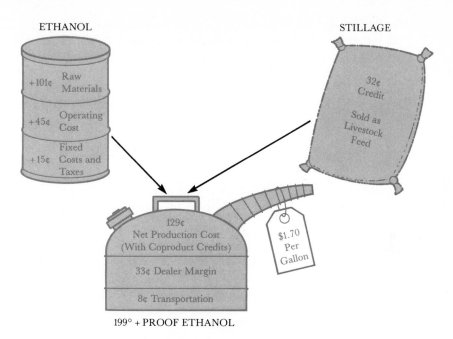

FIGURE 1.   **Breakout of production costs for fermentation ethanol (Hunt 5)**

as inflation grows or decreases, which is to say that in real dollars
the cost of ethanol will remain stable (Commoner 136–37). [**I found
this** *idea* **or** *opinion* **in Commoner.**]

Commoner estimates that by 1995 midwestern farms could
grow enough grain and other raw materials to produce about 30
billion gallons of ethanol per year, about one-third of the predicted demand for gasoline (146). [**The datum is from Commoner.**] But what would be the economic impact on the farmers
who raised the vegetable crops for use as ethanol?

> One computation showed that if a four-hundred-acre beef farm
> operated conventionally, producing corn and soybeans and raising cattle
> but not producing crops for conversion to ethanol, it would make a
> net profit in 1995 of seventy-nine thousand dollars from the sale of
> beef and grain. In contrast, if the farm raised as much livestock as the
> conventional farm but also produced crops—corn and sugar beets—
> for conversion to ethanol, it would make a net profit of a hundred
> and thirty-four thousand dollars from the sale of livestock feed and
> ethanol-yielding crops, and the production of beef (Commoner 146).
> [**The quotation is from Commoner.**]

There is, however, a dark other side to this rosy picture.
Writing in *National Review* (March 13, 1987), Michael Fumento [**I
identify the author, publication, and date of the article from which**

the following opinions come.] claims that gasohol is a mighty boondoggle, providing government subsidies for giants in the agribusiness and doing nothing for the small farmers who are currently in such disastrous straits. Archer-Daniels-Midland, the nation's largest agricultural processing business, made an estimated $36 million on ethanol from July 1985 to July 1986, a profit that, according to Fumento, would have been impossible without heavy government subsidies (33). [**The exact page of the article from which the datum comes.**]

Problems with Gasohol in Brazil—and Elsewhere

It is clear that the *technical* problems of producing and using gasohol have been solved (Cheremisinoff; Cheremisinoff and Cheremisinoff; Hunt). [**I have based my opinion on three sources, which I cite. Note that the second source has two authors, both named Cheremisinoff.**] Yet other problems make it unlikely that gasohol will be a major source of energy for Americans in the near future. Brazil is a case study of the difficulties in weaning an economy from its reliance on oil.

An abundance of sugarcane as a base for ethanol, the desire of the government to develop an energy industry that would encourage people to stay in rural areas rather than migrating to the city, and the availability of uncultivated lands that could be used to grow manioc (a sugar-bearing tuber similar to the sugar beet) led the government of Brazil to institute a massive program aimed at making ethanol a major source of energy. By 1977, all service stations in Rio were selling a 20-percent ethanol-gasoline blend, and the government intended to increase the ratio (Cheremisinoff 53–54). [**This information came from Cheremisinoff's** *Gasohol for Energy Production,* **pages 53–54.**] All seemed to be going well—until 1980, when a strike delayed the production of new cars, and the demand for ethanol fell. Much of the excess was exported to the United States. As Commoner tells the rest of the story,

> Then, with the developing world recession, oil supplies improved and the price differential between ethanol and gasoline diminished. With the economy declining, the demand for automobiles fell, and, given the uncertainties about the supply and price of ethanol, the ethanol-fueled cars were particularly hard to sell (149). [**The quotation is from the Commoner article, page 149.**]

In a 1985 article, the *New York Times* explained that a decline in world oil prices had brought Brazil's gasohol project under scrutiny. The new administration of President Jose Sarney continued the program, but was under pressure to cut subsidies to the distillers (Riding IV, 4). [The article was by Riding. To learn the exact date of the article, see "Works Cited."]

In other words, there is no reason why the United States could not immediately start using significant amounts of ethanol— except that the world is such a complicated place.

In summary, as Commoner says, from the Brazilian experience we learn how difficult it is to make "coordinated changes" in three major industries: oil, automobile, and agriculture (149). [I have not quoted Commoner, but I have paraphrased him and used his ideas; therefore, I must give him credit. I found this idea on page 149 of his article.] The problem, too, is magnified when it is put into the international context, for changes in basic American industries will affect the rest of the world.

Conclusion

This discussion has focused on ethanol, but methanol is also a plentiful and efficient source of energy. It can be derived from urban refuse, crop residues, manures, industrial wastes, logging wastes, sewage, and other miscellaneous wastes (Cheremisinoff 3). Furthermore, methanol can be derived from cellulose—that is, from wood and paper (Commoner 147). As Figure 2 shows, it is perfectly clear that the resources for gasohol are ready and available and equally clear that both methanol and ethanol in their pure form can serve as efficient fuels.

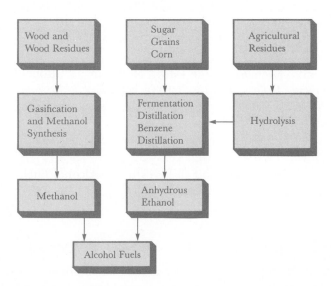

FIGURE 2.   General approaches to the production of methanol and ethanol (Cheremisinoff 6)

Our slowness in switching from fossil fuels to alcohol is explicable in terms of the human tendency to inertia, which only disaster overcomes. During the fuel crisis of 1973, Americans switched from their gas-guzzling monsters to smaller, more fuel-efficient cars, and they cut down on the amount of driving they did. However, as soon as the crisis was over, the gas guzzlers and "muscle" cars began to sell again, and the freeways were as clogged as ever.

The crisis that forces the alcohol fuel issue may not be one dramatic event, but could result from the inevitable gradual increase in gasoline prices. At some point—two dollars a gallon? three? four?—the public will demand relief, and then the government and the industries involved will act.

One thing, however, does seem certain: first gasohol and then pure alcohol fuel are part of our fairly immediate future.

Works Cited

[This is an alphabetical list of all of the sources that I used in the paper. When the reader wants to follow up on one of my citations—such as "(Commoner 147)"—he or she can turn to the listing for the work here to find all the information concerning the article by Barry Commoner.]

Cheremisinoff, Nicholas P. *Gasohol for Energy Production.* Ann Arbor: Ann Arbor Science, 1979.

Cheremisinoff, Nicholas P., and Paul N. Cheremisinoff. *Gasohol Sourcebook.* Ann Arbor: Ann Arbor Science, 1981.

Commoner, Barry. "Ethanol." *The New Yorker.* 10 Oct. 1983: 124–53.

Fumento, Michael. "Some Dare Call Them . . . Robber Barons." *National Review.* 13 March 1987: 32–38.

Hunt, V. Daniel. *The Gasohol Handbook.* New York: Industrial Press, 1981.

Lenzner, Robert. *The Great Getty.* New York: Signet, 1987.

"Ozoned." *California.* Aug. 1987: 52.

Riding, Alan. "Oil Price Fall Perils Brazil Alcohol Fuel." *New York Times* 29 July 1985, IV:4.

A BRIEF SURVEY OF LIBRARY RESOURCES

If you are unfamiliar with your college library, you should inquire about the possibility of receiving an orientation, and probably the library has prepared a pamphlet explaining how to locate and use its resources. The following brief overview will give you an idea of the kinds of sources that you can find in your library.

General Encyclopedias

When you must do research in a field that is unfamiliar, you need some kind of introduction, or overview. The best source for this is a general encyclopedia. The five standard encyclopedias are:

Encyclopaedia Britannica. Noted for the excellence of its articles concerning the humanities. Contains selected bibliographies that can be useful to a person who is just beginning to do research on a given topic.

Encyclopedia Americana. Usually considered the best source for articles concerning the sciences. References will lead the researcher to other standard discussions of topics.

Chambers's Encyclopedia. Provides standard references on topics. A British publication.

Collier's Encyclopedia. The bibliography is centralized in the twenty-fourth volume.

Columbia Encyclopedia. A one-volume work, with articles not as extensive as those in the other encyclopedias. Useful for quick reference.

Unabridged Dictionaries

If the research in question involves the meanings of words, the unabridged dictionaries are invaluable sources. The three that you ought to be aware of are these:

A Dictionary of American English on Historical Principles. This four-volume work, edited by Sir William A. Craigie and James R. Hulbert, gives the histories of meanings of words in American English.

The Oxford English Dictionary. Available as a thirteen-volume work or in a two-volume, reduced-print edition that must be read with a magnifying glass. A reissue of *A New English Dictionary. on Historical Principles,* this work is the most complete source for the histories of word meanings in English.

Webster's Third New International Dictionary. This is the most widely used unabridged dictionary of English, the huge book that you find in the reading rooms of most libraries.

Other unabridged dictionaries are *The American Heritage Dictionary of the English Language, Funk & Wagnall's New "Standard" Dictionary of the English Language, The Random House Dictionary of the English Language,* and *Webster's New Twentieth Century Dictionary.*

General Indexes

Suppose your research involved a specific current event such as the merger of two giant corporations. Your library would contain books about corporations and mergers, but not about your specific subject. Your primary source would be magazines and newspapers. Fortunately, a variety of general indexes direct you to specific newspaper and magazine articles. Most of these indexes are arranged like the card catalog in your library; that is, each entry is listed by author, title, and subject:

Book Review Digest. Appears monthly (except February and July). As its name indicates, it is a guide to reviews of books.

Humanities Index. See *International Index.*

International Index. In April of 1965, the title was changed to *Social Sciences and Humanities Index,* and beginning in April of 1974, the volume was split so that *Social Sciences Index* and *Humanities Index* appear separately. Both of these now appear quarterly, with yearly cumulative issues. As the names imply, they are indexes to journals that publish articles in the social sciences and the humanities.

Magazine Index. Like the *Reader's Guide to Periodical Literature,* an author-title-subject listing of articles in periodicals of general interest. *Magazine Index,* which begins with September of 1983, is on microfilm.

New York Times Index. An author-subject-title listing of articles in the *New York Times.* Since newspapers all over the country deal with the same national and international news events, this index also serves as a rough index to other newspapers.

Nineteenth Century Readers' Guide to Periodical Literature, 1890–1899. An author-subject index covering some fifty periodicals that were published during the period concerned.

Poole's Index to Periodical Literature, 1802–1881. Index to British and American periodicals of the period covered.

Reader's Guide to Periodical Literature. An author-subject-title listing of articles in about 125 periodicals of general interest. Issued semimonthly, with annual and five-year cumulative editions.

Social Sciences Index. See *International Index.*

Biographical Sources

Should your research involve biographical questions, you can go to:

Biography Index: A Cumulative Index to Biographical Material in Books and Magazines.

Current Biography: Who's News and Why. Fairly extensive biographies of people in the news.

Who's Who. Brief biographies of notable living people, chiefly in the British Commonwealth.

Who's Who in America. American counterpart of *Who's Who.*

Dictionary of American Biography. Excellent and fairly extensive biographies of dead Americans.

Dictionary of National Biography. British counterpart of *Dictionary of American Biography.*

Specialized Sources

Our purpose is to survey the kinds of sources available to the researcher, not to provide a complete bibliographical list of everything that a good library contains. Therefore, it is enough to say that there are specialized reference works (including indexes) for virtually every subject. For example, if your question involves mythology, you will find help in the *Larousse Encyclopedia of Mythology,* or if your question concerns physics, you may want to turn to *International Dictionary of Physics and Electronics.* To get some idea of the range of sources that are available, just glance through the following list: *Dictionary of Modern Ballet, Art Index, Cambridge Bibliography of English Literature, Encyclopedia of the Social Sciences, The New Schaff-Herzog Encyclopedia of Religious Knowledge, Van Nostrand's Scientific Encyclopedia, Education Index.* And the list could go on and on.

Your college or public library undoubtedly has trained people in its reference room who can guide you to exactly the sources that you need.

EVALUATING SOURCES

As you know, some sources are more trustworthy than others. The *New York Times* has a reputation for completeness and accuracy, whereas the *National Enquirer* is generally considered sensationalistic and unreliable. However, in some instances the *Enquirer* may be a better source for information than the *Times.*

As a researcher, you must constantly evaluate your sources, questioning reliability, judging one against another when contradictions arise, and considering the qualifications of the authors of the material.

Here are some questions you should ask yourself concerning your sources:

1. Is the *author* (are the authors) qualified? How can I find out?
2. Is the *publication* (book, magazine, newspaper) reliable? In regard to medicine, the *Journal of the American Medical Association* is more reliable than, say, *Reader's Digest,* and, as we have said, the *New York Times* is in general more trustworthy than the *National Enquirer.*
3. Should the *time* and *place* of publication affect my judgment? If you were interested in superconductivity, an article published in 1984 would be outdated, since great breakthroughs started to occur only during the last months of 1986 and the first part of 1987. An article on apartheid published in South Africa would be suspect, since that nation imposes censorship.
4. What is the *purpose* of the source? Since the purpose of an advertisement is to sell products, the information that it contains will probably be incomplete, all unfavorable aspects of the product being excluded.

Exercise

Regarding the current situation in AIDS research, find the following:

1. One source that you distrust because of its author.
2. One source with an author whom you trust.
3. One source in a dubious publication.
4. One source in a reliable publication.
5. One source that you distrust because of either its time or its place of publication, or both.
6. One source that you distrust because of its purpose.

Be prepared to discuss the reasons for your judgments.

DOCUMENTING YOUR SOURCES

In the research paper on pages 255–62, you saw examples of documentation: the parenthetical notations that indicated where the author found his information. You also saw an example of

"Works Cited" (page 262). On page 257 of the paper, this passage appears:

> In a study published in 1923, British engineer Harry Ricardo set forth his findings that ethanol and another alcohol, methanol, solved the knock problem (Commoner 133–34).

The parenthetical information means that I found the datum about Harry Ricardo in a work by Commoner, on pages 133–34.

In the "Works Cited," you found this reference:

> Commoner, Barry. "Ethanol." *The New Yorker.* 10 Oct. 1983: 124–53.

This is the complete information about the source by Commoner: an article titled "Ethanol," published by *The New Yorker* magazine in its issue of October 10, 1983, on pages 124–53.

Through the references in the text and the list of "Works Cited," the reader is able to check the accuracy of statements in the paper and to consult a source to learn more about its subject.

What Should Be Documented?

In your research writing, you should document *specific facts* that you find in your sources:

> This year, eighty-one American cities failed to meet the standards of the Clean Air Act, exceeding defined levels for both ozone and carbon monoxide ("Ozoned").

The "Works Cited" entry for this source is:

> "Ozoned." *California.* Aug. 1987: 52.
> [I found the datum in an anonymous article published by *California* magazine in its issue for August of 1987, on page 52.]

You should also document *direct quotations* from your source:

> . . . "when gasoline was used as the fuel and an engine's compression ratio was gradually increased, the engine's power failed to rise correspondingly; in fact, it eventually fell, accompanied by a noisy metallic ring—'engine knock' " (Commoner 133).
> [The quotation is from page 133 of the article by Barry Commoner.]

When you use the *opinions* of others you should document:

> In the long run, if not at present, ethanol could have the economic edge over gasoline, since crude oil is becoming increasingly scarce and hence, according to the inevitable laws of supply and demand, will grow ever more expensive, whereas ethanol, deriving from a renewable source, will increase or decrease in price as inflation grows or decreases, which is to say that in real dollars the cost of ethanol will remain stable (Commoner 136–37).
>
> [I derived this idea or opinion from the article by Barry Commoner, pages 136–37.]

If a fact or idea in your paper is *common knowledge*, you do not need to document it:

> Ethanol, of course, is distilled from the carbohydrate portions of a crop such as grain. The grain is cooked, then fermented, and the alcohol is distilled off; the process is essentially the same whether carried out by a moonshiner in the backwoods or a giant agricultural corporation.

The system of documentation explained here is adapted from:

> Gibaldi, Joseph, and Walter S. Achtert. *MLA Handbook for Writers of Research Papers*. 2nd ed. New York: The Modern Language Association of America, 1984.

You can refer to this book for a discussion of research, writing, and the format of your paper as well as for a thoroughgoing explanation of the mechanics of documentation.

The MLA system of documentation is widely used in the humanities. The social sciences and many of the sciences use other, though similar, systems. If you are doing a research paper for a class outside the humanities and must use a special system of documentation, you should ask your librarian to help you find the style manual for the field in which you are writing.

The Forms for Documentation

If the author's name is in the text, give only the page number(s) in parentheses:

> As Barry Commoner points out, Ford was convinced that farmers could supply industry with many essential products (150).

If the author's name is not in the text, give both the name and the page number(s) in parentheses:

Most important, ethanol contains no sulfur; hence, gasohol cuts down on the amount of brown "guck" in smog (Hunt 395).

If you are referring to an entire work, not to certain pages, give the author and title in the text.

Writing in *National Review* (March 13, 1987), Michael Fumento claims that gasohol is a mighty boondoggle, providing government subsidies for giants in the agribusiness and doing nothing for the small farmers who are currently in such disastrous straits.

If your "Works Cited" contains two or more titles by the same author, either identify which one you are referring to by mentioning the title in your text:

In *Anatomy of Criticism,* Frye argues for an inductive study of literature (7).

or put the title in the parentheses:

Frye also states the need for what he calls the literary anthropologist (*Fables of Identity* 13).

Forms for Entries in the "Works Cited" List

A Book by a Single Author

Cheremisinoff, Nicholas P. [1] *Gasohol for Energy Production.* [2] Ann Arbor [3]: Ann Arbor Science [4], 1979 [5].
1. Author's name, last name first, followed by a period.
2. Title of book, italicized—or in a typed paper underlined to indicate *italics*—followed by a period.
3. Place of publication, followed by a colon.
4. Name of publisher, followed by a comma.
5. Date of publication.

An Anthology or Collection Edited by One Person

Weber, Ronald, ed. [*] *The Reporter as Artist.* New York: Hastings House, 1974.

*The abbreviation "ed." indicates that Weber is the editor of the book, not the author of its contents. The book is a collection of essays by twenty-six authors.

Two or More Books by the Same Person

Frye, Northrop. *Anatomy of Criticism.* Princeton: Princeton University Press, 1957.
———. [*]*Fables of Identity.* New York: Harcourt, Brace & World, 1963.

*The books are listed alphabetically by title, but after the first entry, the long dash—typed as three hyphens—substitutes for the author's name.

A Book by Two or More Persons

Taylor, Insup, and M. Martin Taylor. [*] *The Psychology of Reading.* New York: Academic Press, 1983.

*Only the first author's name is listed with the last name first, or inverted.

An Article from a Collection

Balz, Daniel J. "Bad Writing and New Journalism." [1] *The Reporter as Artist.* [2] Ed. Ronald Weber. [3] New York: Hastings House, 1974. 288–93. [4]

1. The name of the article in quotation marks.
2. The title of the collection in which the article appears.
3. The editor of the collection. (The abbreviation "Ed." means "editor" or "edited by.")
4. The numbers of the pages on which the article appears.

A Work Consisting of More Than One Volume

Churchill, Winston S. *The Age of Revolution.* New York: Dodd, 1957. Vol. 3 of *A History of the English-Speaking Peoples.* [1] 4 vols. [2] 1956–58. [3]

1. Indicates that *The Age of Revolution* is volume 3 of a multivolume work titled *A History of the English-Speaking Peoples.*
2. The complete work consists of four volumes.
3. They were published between 1956 and 1958.

An Edition

Tate, Gary, ed. *Teaching Composition: Twelve Bibliographic Essays.* Rev. and enl. ed. [*] Fort Worth: Texas Christian University, 1987.

*Means "revised and enlarged edition," indicating that the work cited is not the first edition. More commonly, the editions will be numbered: "2nd ed.," "3rd ed."

An Article in a Reference Book

"Aristotle." [1] *The New Columbia Encyclopedia.* [2] 1975 ed. [3]

1. Title of article.
2. Title of reference source.
3. Edition of reference source.

A Government Publication

California Advisory Committee for an English Language Framework. [1] *English Language Framework for the Public Schools, Kindergarten Through Grade Twelve.* [2] California State Board of Education [3], 1968.

1. The government agency directly responsible for compiling or writing the document.
2. The title of the document.
3. The government agency that published the document.

An Article in a Scholarly Journal with Continuous Pagination

Some scholarly journals number the pages of a whole year's issues (a whole volume) continuously; therefore, the first issue of the volume might, for instance, run from page 1 to page 95; the second issue of that volume would begin with page 96, and so on.

> Myers, Greg. "The Social Construction of Two Biologists' Proposals." *Written Communication* [1] 2 [2] (1985) [3]: 219–45 [4].

1. The name of the journal in which the article by Myers appeared.
2. The *volume* number of the journal.
3. The year in which the journal issue was printed.
4. The page numbers of the article.

An Article in a Journal That Does Not Have Continuous Page Numbers for the Whole Volume

> Warnock, John. "The Writing Process." *Rhetoric Review* 2.1 [1] (1983): 4–27 [2].

1. The volume number (2), and the issue number (1), with a period between them.
2. The pages on which the article appears.

An Article from a Weekly or Biweekly Periodical

> Commoner, Barry. "Ethanol." *The New Yorker.* 10 Oct. 1983: 124–53.

An Article from a Monthly or Bimonthly Periodical

> Schneider, Peter. "Hitler's Shadow: On Being a Self-Conscious German." *Harper's.* [1] Sept. 1987 [2]: 49–54 [3].

1. Name of magazine or periodical.
2. Date of magazine, followed by a colon.
3. Pages on which the article appears.

An Article from a Daily Newspaper

> Jones, Lanie. [1] "A High-Tech 'Miracle' Saves Baby Miguel." [2] *Los Angeles Times.* [3] 15 Aug. 1987 [4], Orange County ed. [5], Part II [6]: 1+ [7].

1. Writer's name, last name first.
2. Title of article.

3. Name of newspaper.
4. Date of issue: day (15), month (Aug.), and year.
5. Particular edition in which the article appeared. Many newspapers have several editions: "late edition," "early edition," "metropolitan edition," and so on.
6. The section of the newspaper in which the article appeared.
7. Page or pages on which the article appeared. In this case, the article begins on the first page of the section and is continued to later pages, as indicated by "1 + ."

When You Lack Bibliographic Information for a Book

Sometimes your source will not provide all the information that is generally required in the "Works Cited." For example, you may use a book that does not contain the date of publication, or perhaps the place of publication is not given. You can use the following abbreviations to show that the information is not available.

No Date of Publication: n.d.

Smith, Alvin. *Catching Catfish.* St. Louis: Sports Publishing, n.d.

No Place of Publication: n.p.

Jones, Phyllis. *The Amateur's Guide to Snorkeling.* N.p.: Waters Publishing, 1984.

No Publisher: n.p.

Brown, George. *Growing Earthworms for Profit.* Salt Lake City: n.p., 1887.

Sources Other Than Books

The following are examples of bibliography entries for sources other than books, magazines, journals, reference works, and such. Obviously it would be impossible to give exact formats for all of the many print and nonprint sources and their multiple versions, but you can use these forms as guides that you can adapt to your own needs.

Radio and Television Programs

Bradbury, Ray. [1] "The One Who Waits." [2] Adapted by Brad Schreiber. [3] KCRW, Los Angeles. [4] 22 June 1988. [5]

1. Name of the author of the story from which the radio version was adapted.

2. Title of the program.
3. Name of the adapter.
4. The radio station and its location.
5. The date of the program.

(If your source is a television or radio program, give your reader as much information as you can—at the very least, the name of the program, the station and its location, and the date.)

Computer Software

PFS: Professional File. [1] Computer software. [2] Software Publishing Corp., 1986. [3]

1. Name of the software program.
2. Identification of the entry as software.
3. Publisher and date of publication.

Recordings

Beethoven, Ludwig van. [1] Symphony no. 7 in A, op. 92. [2] Cond. Herbert von Karajan. [3] Vienna Philharmonic Orch. [4] London, STS 15107, 1966. [5]

1. Name of the composer.
2. Title of the work.
3. Name of the conductor.
4. Name of the orchestra.
5. Recording company, serial number, and date.

Personal Letters

Cranston, Senator Alan. [1] Personal letter to the author of this paper. [2] 22 June 1988. [3]

1. Author of letter.
2. Identification of source.
3. Date of source.

Personal Interviews

Nute, J. Boyce, Jr. [1] Interview with the author of this paper. [2] 22 June 1988. [3]

1. Person interviewed.
2. Identification of source.
3. Date of source.

10
Writing
Business Letters
Betty P. Pytlik,
University of Southern California

Writing business letters, like every writing task, involves a series of problems to be solved, and the best approach to solving them is common sense. Consider, for example, the purpose, the reader, and the tone of the following letter to an inspection supervisor at the Department of Motor Vehicles. The letter was prompted by the refusal of a Department of Motor Vehicles inspector to approve registration for on-the-road use of a student's 1937 Packard. Because the student was angered by the refusal, the inspector suggested the student write to the supervisor. Here is the student's letter.

Dear Mr. Harris:

On June 15, 1988, Inspector Grey declined to approve registration for on-the-road use of my 1937 Packard. When I pointed out that the car is a part of the American tradition, is constructed better than any newer models, and creates less pollution than a high compression engine does, he suggested that I explain his assessment to you and request a new inspection.

Inspector Grey cited three problems with the car: the Packard achieves a top speed of 55 miles per hour. Since that is the legal speed limit, I am puzzled by the requirement that it be capable of exceeding the speed limit. Second, the car does not have seal-beam headlights, although the Packard's lights do emit well above the standard candle-power required for auto headlights. Could brightness tests be conducted? Third, the brakes are mechanical rather than hydraulic. Aren't hydraulic brakes more a matter of convenience than safety?

Because I have driven the car in city traffic and on freeways across the country without any mechanical problems, I believe you will find my request for a new inspection justifiable. May I bring my car to the Inspection Center for you to inspect it personally? Any weekday between nine and noon that is convenient for you would be fine.

The three least effective arguments—the car is a part of the American tradition, it is constructed better than today's cars, and it creates less pollution—are presented in the opening paragraph as an introduction and explanation of the student's request. The more convincing arguments for a new inspection—those about the maximum speed, headlights, and brakes—are couched in the form of questions.

Exercise

1. Discuss the words and phrases that help create the tone in the student's letter to the Department of Motor Vehicles supervisor.
2. Write a response to the following "Last Notice" letter. The purpose of your letter is to clear your account immediately, so you must provide all the information the reader needs in order to do that.

LAST NOTICE

You now have 48 hours to settle your winter-quarter fee bill. If there is some reason you cannot settle it, you must contact the Financial Audit Office, Stone Hall 121, *now*. If you are a CCC student, and wish to remain one, you must respond today.

Sincerely,

Marjorie Anton, Bursar
Financial Audit Office
Stone Hall 121
Phone 233-2369

3. The purpose of the following letter to the CCC bursar from a student is not clear. Analyze the letter by discussing these questions:
   a. What does the student want the bursar to do?
   b. How can the writer's ideas be organized so that his or her purpose is clear?

c. What comments should be omitted to make the tone less offensive and thus increase the chances that the bursar will consider the student's suggestions rather than discount the letter as coming from a crank?

> Gentlemen:
>
> I have just wasted an hour and a half of my time trying to pay my summer fee bill. All of the problems stem from the fact that my classes ended several weeks ago and my financial award letter arrived after those classes ended. Furthermore, I could not pay the bill on time because I was out of town on school business when my award letter came in. That problem, fortunately, has been straightened out.
>
> Nevertheless, I feel it my duty to inform you of the inefficiency that pervades the entire bureaucratic structure of Financial Services, including Tuition Audit and the Department of Collections. Not one person seems to know what he is speaking about. Matters seem to get more confused instead of being resolved. Furthermore, students seem to suffer the consequences of the inefficiency of your personnel. I hope you will not take this letter personally. I am writing not only because I am angry, but also because I hope you can do something to make dealing with your office staff an easy task, instead of a painful one.
>
> Sincerely,

TONE

Tone, as we have seen earlier, reflects the writer's attitude toward the reader. Because the tone you use in business communications is determined by your purpose in writing, it is essential to consider what the reader already knows and what he or she needs to learn in order for your letter to be effective.

So far, the comments on tone and consideration of the reader have been very general. However, there are specific ways to adapt your tone to the reader. The following suggestions assume that you know you must always consider two primary questions: (1) What do you want the reader to do (the purpose of the communication)? (2) What does the reader need to know in order to do it (the information you will include in the letter)? Tone, then, becomes important when you answer a third question: (3) What would encourage the reader to do what you want him or her to do?

Here are some suggestions to guide you in answering this last question:

1. Tell the reader only what he or she needs to know. Put negatively, that means don't waste the reader's time by saying something he or she already knows.

2. Emphasize the reader's interests, not yours or those of your company or organization. Put yourself in the reader's place; compose your letters with a "you" attitude. Notice how the first sentence from a sales letter focuses on the benefits for a potential customer:

> As a Culver Community College student, you can open a Twain Bank and Trust Company checking account with no monthly service charge and no monthly minimum balance required.

3. Emphasize the positive, not the negative. Tell the reader what you can do, not what you can't do, as in the response of a student who has had no experience directly related to the job of collecting signatures for getting candidates on the ballot:

> I have helped my fraternity brothers raise money for scholarships and have assisted my neighborhood council in collecting money for block parties to send inner-city children to summer camp.

4. Be confident that your ideas will be accepted. If something is worth asking for, it is worth asking for with confidence. Similarly, if something is worth reporting, it is worth reporting with confidence. For example:

> Is there a convenient time during the week of October 10–17 that eleven of my Culver Community College classmates and I may visit your office so that we can learn how your computerized purchasing system operates?

5. Eliminate deadwood. It is a courtesy to your reader to save his or her time by presenting your message clearly and concisely. If you want information, ask for it. If you want to order something, get right to the order. Phrases like "I would like to know if . . ." and "I am interested in . . ." are time wasters. Use a direct approach, as in the following example:

> Does Apex make carbon ribbons for its portable typewriters?

6. Avoid criticizing the reader. Three points to remember when you are inclined to criticize a reader: (a) the inconvenience you have suffered was not intentional, (b) the reader of your

letter probably was not responsible for your annoyance, and (c) your chances of getting a favorable response are greater if you present your case concisely and objectively. The following sentences illustrate courtesy to the reader:

> The twelve looseleaf binders that I ordered on January 10 have still not arrived. Please let me know if they have been shipped.

7. Proofread your letters. While most of our errors in business letters are typographical ones, they are often seen as carelessness and must be eliminated if the reader is to respond favorably. Using the proofreader's technique of reading lines backward may help you find typos. Because grammar, punctuation, and spelling errors are so various, and because each of us knows by now the kinds of errors he or she is apt to make, they won't be discussed here.

8. Follow the conventions in setting up your letters. The sample letters throughout this chapter illustrate a variety of acceptable formats for letters. A form that deviates from custom is distracting, that is, it draws the reader's attention away from what is said in the same way that typos and other errors do. Check the sample letters for the placement of the following required parts of a standard business letter: the return address and date; the inside address; the salutation; the body; the complimentary close; and the typed signature. On page 292, you can see an illustration of a subject line; on page 308, attachments; and on pages 282, 283, and 299, enclosures.

Exercise

1. Collect business correspondence that you and your friends have received and evaluate the tone of several of the letters.
2. Reexamine the irate student's letter to the bursar (in the preceding exercise) in terms of the suggestions about tone.
3. Discuss the tone of the following refusal of an order. Be specific about what makes this letter a reader-oriented one.

> Your August 21 order for filing cabinets, office desks, and lamps indicates an optimistic outlook for Samson's Office Supplies. We are proud to have been part of your financial success for the past ten years.
>
> In July 1970, when you made your first purchase from us, you agreed to a balance limit of $10,000. Since then, because of your company's

rapid growth and your excellent credit record, the balance limit has risen until you now have a $25,000 balance limit.

Because your recent order would exceed your limit by $5,000, may we send you one half of your order now and the other half soon, when your balance has reached $25,000? That way your credit rating remains excellent and you can continue to provide your customers with the superior office furniture they have come to expect from Samson's.

Will you call us collect so that the furniture can be shipped soon?

JOB SEARCH LETTERS

Perhaps the most important letters you will write are those seeking employment. To apply for a job that has been advertised is easier than to apply for one that you are not sure exists. For one thing, when you apply for an advertised position, you often know the name of the person to whom you can write, and letters directed to individuals usually receive more attention than letters directed to "Sir or Madam" or "To Whom It May Concern." Also, the job requirements are often stated in the advertisement so that you can match them with your qualifications for the position. However, applying for a position that has not been announced may offer you more advantages. For example, you will face less competition from students seeking summer employment if you apply for a job that has not been advertised. A second advantage is that you are forced to consider carefully how your skills, temperament, experience, and education relate specifically to the company and its needs. What kinds of positions might the company have that you would fit? Third, if you have limited your job search to one area—your hometown or your campus town, for example—you can blanket the town with applications, and thus increase your chances of getting summer or part-time employment. Fourth, when you do get an interview, you may find that other jobs than those you expected are available in the company, and that these tap your skills as well.

Because the unsolicited letter may produce more job choices for you, the rest of this section discusses that kind of letter. Moreover, when you have mastered the more difficult task of selling your qualifications for a position that has not been advertised, it will be easier to write a solicited letter.

In addition to discussing how to compose an unsolicited letter seeking employment, this section will deal with a request for a recommendation, a thank-you for an interview, and a résumé.

Letters of Application

Three considerations are important in writing letters for employment: your purpose in writing the letter, the employer's needs and expectations, the qualities you possess that can satisfy those needs. Each requires the application of common sense.

The purpose of the application letter is, of course, to persuade the employer that your qualifications match the requirements of the company or a specific position; the immediate goal is to get an interview with the employer so that you can elaborate on the qualifications you have mentioned in your letter.

What does the person reading your letter need to know in order to arrange an interview? First, he or she needs to know exactly what kind of position you are interested in. Second, do you want a part-time or a full-time job? Do you want one for the summer only? Obviously, "summer employment" is not specific enough: the employer needs to know what date you will be available to begin work, what date you will have to leave the job, and what date or dates you will be available for an interview. Third, he or she must know your qualifications for the position you have identified. Finally, the reader of your letter must know the names of several respected people who can support your claims.

Clearly, those four reader-oriented considerations reflect common sense. Some additional common-sense procedures to follow when you are composing your letter of application are these:

1. Direct your letter to the person in the company who is responsible for arranging interviews, usually the personnel director, but not always. It is a simple matter to call the company to learn the name of this person; the call is worth your time and money because, as we have already said, letters that are addressed to individuals usually receive more attention than those that aren't.
2. If you are not sure about the requirements of the job—those that you must match with your qualifications—check the want ads. The following ad, for example, could give you information on which to base an application even though you are not applying for the specific position advertised:

WANTED

Security Guard—full-time/part-time, evenings and nights; must be willing and able to prevent unlawful entry or intrusion, check employee and visitor identification, and apply for pistol license. Please write letter stating educational background and previous experience. XYZ Manufacturing Company, Inc., P.O. Box 543, Tucson.

3. Because the impression that your letter makes is the only basis the reader has for deciding whether to grant you an interview, the appearance of the letter and the care you take in editing and proofreading it are important factors. Typographical errors, for example, reflect a carelessness that the reader may assume you have about all your work.

This last instance of common sense leads to the third consideration in writing your letter. Your letter should convey to the reader those qualities you think he or she would want in an employee. Neatness and carefulness are, of course, among the chief requirements for any job. But intelligence and confidence are also generally required. These qualities will be strongly implied in your letter if you assume that you will get the job and if you relate some previous experience to the position you are interested in. Imagine that you are interested in a position as an office clerk in an insurance company. The following sentences indicate related previous experience and confidence in the writer's qualifications:

> I worked as a stock clerk for Mr. John Ackerman of Home-Builders Emporium in the evenings and on weekends during my senior year in high school. He can tell you about my dependability and sense of responsibility. You will find his address and telephone number on the attached résumé.

Notice that the second of these sentences points to two other very important qualities that most employers demand of their employees: dependability and sense of responsibility.

On page 282 is a letter of application from a student who is applying for an unadvertised position as a security guard, although he has had no previous experience directly connected to the job. Note the information that reflects the common-sense items we have just listed.

Now consider another unsolicited letter, from a student who has had a different background from that of Robert Altman. Mary Hymes brings to her letter experience as a dietitian's aide for a hospital. The purpose of the letter is to persuade Mrs. Watkins, whose name Mary obtained by calling the hospital, that the skills she learned as dietitian's aide at Queensbury Hospital match the requirements for a position as a supervisor of aides at Hanover Convalescent Home. Mary believes her personal qualities justify Mrs. Watkins's considering her for this position. Her immediate goal is to obtain an interview so that she can discuss her qualifications further. See her letter on page 283.

3271 Ash Drive
Evansville, Indiana 46015
March 2, 19—

Ms. Marsha Bennett
Personnel Director
Anderson Building Supplies
South Bend, Indiana 47901

Dear Ms. Bennett:

Please consider my qualifications for a position with Anderson
Building Supplies as a full-time security guard from June 1 until
September 4.

While I attended Henry Morrison High School, I played on both the
football and baseball teams. Currently, as a freshman at Culver
Community College, I am on the soccer and baseball intramural
teams. Thus, I would be able to meet the physical requirements for a
position as a security guard.

During my junior and senior years in high school, I worked as an
usher at Grant's Movie Theatre on weekends. This position required
the discreet and responsible exercise of authority. Mr. Harold Rusk,
Manager of Grant's, can tell you about my performance in this
position. You will find his address and telephone number on the
enclosed résumé.

During Easter vacation, April 1 to 5, I will be in South Bend. May I
call for an appointment within this period so that I can discuss the
possibility of working for Anderson Building Supplies during the
summer?

Sincerely,

Robert R. Altman

Résumé Enclosed

6610 Milford Street, Apt. 2B
Somerset, Pennsylvania 15501
April 1, 19—

Mrs. Alicia Watkins
Chief Dietitian
Hanover Convalescent Home
Somerset, Pennsylvania 15501

Dear Mrs. Watkins:

Will Hanover Convalescent Home need a supervisor of dietitian's aides during the summer and on weekends and evenings during the year? If so, please consider my qualifications.

During my senior year at Eddington High School, I worked on the weekends and in the evenings as a dietitian's aide at Queensbury Hospital. Last summer, before I entered Culver Community College, I worked full-time in the same position. My responsibilities were to check that all patients had correct menus, to write salt-free diets, to prepare tube feedings and special cold foods like juice, salads, and special requests, and to keep the menu file up-to-date.

Mrs. Harriet Ohms, Head Dietitian at Queensbury Hospital, can tell you that I was quick to learn the procedures and that I was willing to do more than my job required. For example, I helped train new dietitian's aides and met with aides during meals to discuss problems. Also, Mr. Samuel Scott, Director of Personnel, will tell you that I was always prompt and dependable, and that I adapted well to the hospital's need for flexibility in scheduling hours.

Could you arrange a time when I may come in to talk with you about the possibility of supervising dietitian's aides from June 1 through September 4 and part-time during the school year? I can be reached at 929-9113 any weekday from nine until noon.

Sincerely,

Mary Hymes

Résumé Enclosed

In what ways does Mary Hymes demonstrate an awareness of her reader? First, she makes the purpose of the letter clear in the first paragraph. Second, she summarizes the skills she would bring to a supervisory position. The third paragraph achieves two things: it names references who can and will attest to Mary's strengths, and it lists personal attributes that Mary knows from experience to be essential to a supervisory position. In addition to stating what actions Mary wants Mrs. Watkins to take, the last paragraph makes it easy for the reader to respond to Mary's request for an interview by establishing convenient times for Mrs. Watkins to call her and by giving her the phone number at which Mary can be reached.

Beginning writers of such letters sometimes include irrelevant information. Notice that Mary does *not* say that she is a botany major, a Methodist, and five feet six inches tall. Those facts will not help Mrs. Watkins make her decision about whether to interview Mary; thus, it makes no sense to include them in the letter. What else in the letter demonstrates Mary's common sense?

Now that you have a general notion of what is involved in composing your letter and recognize that you have skills other than those of Robert and Mary, consider how your skills, temperament, experience, and education relate to a temporary summer position you would like to have in your hometown.

If you want a position that will combine past work experience with your career goals—say you have baby-sat since you were fourteen, have worked two summers in a city-sponsored recreation program, and are studying to be an elementary teacher—you can check the Yellow Pages for recreational programs, camps, nurseries, and so on. Even though you are applying for an unannounced position, you can get some ideas about jobs that fall within your area of interest by checking state employment offices, college placement offices, campus newspapers, and local newspapers.

Collecting the Material for the Application Letter

By way of summarizing what has been said about the job search process, here is a list of questions that will help you compose your letter of application. Answer each of the questions.

1. What kinds of temporary positions are you qualified for?
2. What are the skills required for those positions?

3. What kinds of skills do you have? Which skills match the skills required for the position in which you are interested?
4. What personality traits and habits—for example, the ability to get along with others, dependability—do you have that will match the needs of the position?
5. What courses or training have you had that would help you perform well on the job?
6. What work experience have you had that relates either directly or indirectly to the position you want?
7. Who can and will vouch for those qualifications you have listed?
8. When will you be available for interviews?
9. To whom should you write your letter of application?
10. When can you start working? When will you have to stop?

Now write a letter to an imagined employer. Take into consideration the following items:

1. What is the purpose of the letter? In the first paragraph be sure to state the specific position for which you are applying, when you want to begin, and what kind of employment you want, for example, evenings only, full time for the summer.
2. How can you relate the skills, education, personality traits, and job experience that you listed above to the job requirements? Use one or two paragraphs to discuss the qualifications.
3. Who will recommend you? In one paragraph name one or two references who have agreed to provide evidence that your qualifications match the job requirements.
4. When would you like an interview? How can the reader contact you? In the final paragraph make it convenient for the reader to contact you.

Requests for Recommendations

Robert Altman and Mary Hymes name people whom Ms. Bennett and Mrs. Watkins can contact to learn more about their respective qualifications. They know it makes no sense to name people who will perhaps give them bad recommendations, or even weak ones; they also know that no one can be certain about a supervisor's assessment of his or her work, so they ask their former supervisors for permission to use their names as references before they actually use them. Then, Mr. Rusk, Mrs. Ohms, and Mr. Scott have a chance to tell Robert or Mary if they don't feel confident about recommending them or if they don't believe

Robert's or Mary's qualifications match the requirements of the jobs for which they are applying.

If you are more comfortable calling to ask permission to use names as references, or if calling is more convenient, there is no harm in using that approach. But a letter is always appropriate. The purpose of the letter is to ask permission to use the reader's name. The reader needs to know the kind of job you are applying for and with whom, and when he or she should expect to hear from the company, in order to be available at the time of the request.

If your reference agrees to recommend you, one of three things could happen. The personnel director may simply call the reference you listed (thus, you must include the phone number of the reference on your résumé). Second, the company may write directly to the reference for information about your qualifications. Third, the company may ask you to have the reference send a recommendation. In that case, you will need to provide the reference with a stamped envelope addressed to the personnel director. Here are examples of the last two cases:

> Dear Mr. Rusk:
>
> I am applying for a position as a security guard with Anderson Building Supplies in South Bend for the summer. May I please tell Ms. Bennett, the Personnel Director, that she may contact you within the next month to ask about my qualifications for that position?

> Dear Mr. Rusk:
>
> In March you wrote that Anderson Building Supplies could contact you to discuss my qualifications for a summer position as a security guard. Would you please write to Ms. Bennett, the Personnel Director for Anderson's? She is especially interested in knowing how you assess my dependability and sense of responsibility. I have enclosed a stamped, addressed envelope for your convenience.

Exercise

Compose a request for permission to use the name of a former supervisor or an acquaintance who can vouch for your qualifications for the position for which you applied in your letter. Here are some questions that will help you compose the request:

1. What is your professional or personal relationship with the person you will ask for a recommendation?

2. What kind of support of your qualifications can the reader give?
3. When will the company contact the reference?

Writing Thank-you Letters for Interviews

Let us say that Ms. Bennett responded to Robert Altman's letter by saying that there will be no security guard positions open for the summer, but that Anderson's usually hires four or five college students for the summer to replace vacationing employees in other jobs. She suggested that Robert call her when he is in South Bend at Easter so that she can arrange interviews with Mrs. Harvey, the sales manager, and Mr. Jackson, the purchasing agent. Robert does call her, and within a week after his interviews with Mrs. Harvey and Mr. Jackson he writes to thank Ms. Bennett. In addition to showing courtesy, a thank-you letter also reminds the reader that Robert has been there.

> Dear Ms. Bennett:
>
> Thank you for arranging the appointments with Mrs. Harvey and Mr. Jackson last week. I will call again in late May, as you suggested, to find out if you plan to hire students for the summer.
>
> In the meantime, please thank Mrs. Harvey for her explanation of the summer openings and Mr. Jackson for the tour of the buildings.

There are several points to remember about a thank-you letter for an interview. First, if someone has been especially helpful to you, you should direct special thanks to him or her. Second, you need to confirm whatever instructions you were given regarding your next step, in this case to call again in May.

Preparing a Résumé

The résumé that will accompany your letter has been mentioned several times. The purpose of the résumé, as you have already inferred, is to give the reader information about your work experience, your skills, your personal qualities, and your education that will help him or her assess your potential as an employee. When you analyzed your qualifications by answering the questions on pages 284–85, you completed the most difficult task in writing a résumé. Now the easiest steps remain. Consider the process Mary Hymes used in composing her résumé:

1. What is my job objective? A full-time summer job that I can continue on weekends and evenings during the school year.
2. To whom am I applying? Hanover Convalescent Home, Mrs. Watkins, Chief Dietitian.
3. What work experience have I had? Weekends and evenings as dietitian's aide at Queensbury Hospital; full-time last summer.
4. What skills did I acquire in this position? Checked menus, wrote salt-free diets, prepared tube feedings and cold foods, and kept menu file up-to-date.
5. What personality traits will help me do the job well? I'm quick to learn, I get along well with others, I'm prompt, dependable, flexible.
6. What education have I had to prepare me for this job? Nothing directly related.
7. Who can and will recommend me? Mrs. Harriet Ohms, Head Dietitian, Queensbury Hospital; Mr. Samuel Scott, Director of Personnel, Queensbury Hospital; Mr. Frank Sullivan, Guidance Counselor, Eddington High School; Mrs. Helen Burrows, English Instructor, Culver Community College.
8. How can Mrs. Watkins contact me? Call 929-9113 any weekday from nine until noon.
9. What is the best order in which to present the information?

The importance of neatness and correctness cannot be stressed enough. A résumé, along with the application letter, is the first contact the reader will have with you. A second consideration is conciseness. Perhaps it would help you to think of the résumé as an ordered summary of all the information you presented in your letter. Then, your letter gives the reader more details about the qualifications you have listed on your résumé.

Once you have composed your résumé and set it up on the page in such a way as to make your qualifications and personal information clear and concise, you can use the résumé for all the companies to which you write. Simply have the résumé duplicated without the title, and, using the same typewriter you used to type the résumé, rewrite the title each time so that it mentions the name of the company you are sending it to.

On page 289 is a form of a résumé. You have probably seen other forms that are also acceptable. If you decide to use another format, the important thing is to be consistent in your use of headings. For example, if one major heading is typed in capital letters, then you must type all the other major headings in capital letters.

MARY HYMES'S QUALIFICATIONS FOR A POSITION AS
A SUPERVISOR OF DIETITIAN'S AIDES
AT HANOVER CONVALESCENT HOME

6610 Milford Street, Apt. 2B   Born May 23, 1969
Somerset, Pennsylvania 15510   Excellent Health
929-9113

Professional Experience

    Dietitian's Aide. Queensbury Hospital. Weekends and evenings
       during school year, full-time during summer, September
       1986-August 1987

    Responsibilities: Checked patients' menus, wrote salt-free diets,
       prepared tube feedings and special cold foods, kept menu file
       up-to-date

Education

    Attend Culver Community College, September 1987-
    Graduated from Eddington High School, Somerset,
       Pennsylvania, June 1987

References

Mrs. Harriet Ohms   Mr. Samuel Scott
Head Dietitian   Director of Personnel
Queensbury Hospital   Queensbury Hospital
Somerset, Pennsylvania 15501   Somerset, Pennsylvania 15501
932-7751   932-7754

Mr. Frank Sullivan   Mrs. Helen Burrows
Guidance Counselor   English Instructor
Eddington High School   Department of English
Somerset, Pennsylvania 15501   Culver Community College
933-8900   Somerset, Pennsylvania 15501
                                      955-6767

Exercise

1. After reviewing the questions on pages 284–85, prepare a résumé to accompany the letter to the employer that you wrote.
2. Examine the sample résumé on page 289, and then answer the following questions:

   a. What are the principal elements in the résumé?
   b. How are they organized? What comes first and what comes afterward? Why?
   c. What has been omitted from the résumé? What has been included? What is the basis of selection?
   d. What is the verbal style of the résumé? In contrast to the letter? In contrast to other kinds of writing?

   We mentioned earlier that there are various ways of organizing résumés. Now that you have answered the questions here, reorganize Mary Hymes's résumé. Remember that as with all other forms of business writing, the résumé will be read by someone who is very busy.

WRITING REQUESTS

The success of a *request for information*, a *request for an adjustment* (sometimes called a claim)—for example, a refund or an exchange of merchandise—or an *appeal to a reader to do something that he or she may not be inclined to do* depends on telling the reader what he or she needs to know in order to satisfy the request. In these three kinds of requests, *clarity* and *conciseness* are important.

Requesting Information

Requests for information should be clear, complete, and to the point. Imagine, for example, the task that faces the employee of the Environmental Protection Agency who must fill this request for information:

> Please send me information about government regulation of industrial emissions.

Because the request lacks clarity, the EPA employee has two choices: Should he or she send a packet of printed materials, knowing that much of it will be irrelevant to the writer's needs? Or should the employee request that the writer be more specific about what is wanted? In both cases, time is wasted, and both the EPA employee and the writer are frustrated. If the writer had named the industry or industries he or she needed information about and explained the need for the EPA material, the reader could have satisfied the request quickly and efficiently. And a request that is clear and concise is a courteous one, for it makes the reader's job easier.

Subject lines, typed below or in place of the salutation, also make the reader's job easier. The following subject line not only directs the EPA employee to specific printed material but also makes the request more concise:

> SUBJECT A Request for Information about Government Regulation of Emission Control in the Aluminum and Asbestos Industries

Even if you use a subject line, an inquiry should still begin with a clear announcement of the subject, perhaps in question form. If possible, the request or question should be phrased so that it elicits yes or no answers. Sometimes questions require elaboration, as the following one does:

> Where can I learn which aluminum and asbestos companies have consistently complied with government emission standards? The information will be part of a class report on pollution in the Southwest, so I am especially interested in companies in that region.

If you need the information you are requesting by a specific date, it is courteous to let the reader know that. Indicating the date, plus adding a courteous comment, is an effective way to make a favorable impression on your reader.

The letter on page 292 illustrates the elements that make up an effective request for information: a subject line; a clear, concise announcement of the subject; a list of questions, with explanations if they will help the reader answer the questions adequately; a courteous, reader-oriented ending.

Exercise

Your class has decided to have a weekend outing at a mountain inn. There are several inns in your area that you are considering. Using a subject line and itemizing your questions, compose an inquiry about group rates, rec-

202 Harrison Hall
7321 Hoover Avenue
Somerset, Pennsylvania 15501
April 2, 19—

Mr. Jack Holmes, Director
Financial Services Office
Stone Hall 402
Culver Community College
Somerset, Pennsylvania 15501

Dear Mr. Holmes:

SUBJECT: Inquiry about Work-Study Program

As a second-semester freshman at Culver Community College, am I
eligible for the Work-Study Program? If so, may I please have an
application and answers to the following questions:

1. What are the maximum hours I could work?
2. Is there summer work that would continue through the regular
   academic year?
3. Would I have a choice of work-study positions? Because I have
   spent two summers living in Korea, I would especially like to work
   with foreign students.
4. Would my pay be deducted from my tuition, or would I be paid
   directly?

I would appreciate having the application and the information in
time to apply for summer work.

Sincerely,

John McDowell

reational facilities, check-in time, transportation (by car and by bus), and whatever additional information you need to have in order to decide which inn to go to. Consider first, however, what the reader needs to know in order to satisfy your request.

Requesting Adjustments

In your personal or academic life you have probably had occasion to explain to someone that a service you had paid for was unsatisfactory or that merchandise you had purchased was damaged or the wrong item was shipped. Perhaps the Campus Parking Office issued you a nontransferable parking permit instead of the transferable one you requested; or you were overcharged for work on your car; or a shirt you ordered was sent in the wrong size. To call a letter in which you request an adjustment a "complaint" letter—as many people do—is to assign the wrong purpose to the letter. The purpose of such a letter is not to complain, but rather to ask the reader to remedy a situation that you believe merits correction. Moreover, businesses generally welcome adjustment letters because such letters offer these organizations feedback on their products and services. In short, requests for adjustments help control quality, so everyone benefits from them.

This positive view of requests for adjustments will help you remain objective when you write. It will also encourage you to provide all the information the reader needs in order to remedy the situation. Keep in mind that the purpose of your letter is not to relieve your frustration and anger but to get the problem solved.

When you request an adjustment, the specific action you want the reader to take determines the details of the letter. Therefore, before you begin to write, you must formulate your reason for writing. For example, do you want an item replaced? Your money refunded? A damaged article repaired free? Parts of an incomplete order shipped?

Here is an example of a request for an adjustment that makes clear what the writer wants the reader to do:

SUBJECT: Request for Shipment of Second Bookcase in May 12 Order

Thank you for your prompt shipment of my fiberboard bookcase. My check for $42.29 was for two bookcases, plus shipping charges, and only one bookcase was delivered on June 10. Please ship the second one immediately.

Some requested adjustments are not so simple for the company as that one, however. For instance, another unhappy customer who had purchased five bookcases wrote the following letter:

> On May 12 I ordered five fiberboard bookcases, four for $17.95 each, and one for $22.95. My check for $109.75 included $15.00 for shipping. On June 10, only three bookcases were delivered. Although I am pleased with two of them, the $22.95 case had four one-eighth-inch-deep scratches on the top.
>
> Because I have thirty unpacked boxes of books, I cannot wait for the replacement and the other bookcases to be shipped. Therefore, I have returned the damaged one and would appreciate a speedy refund so that I can buy cases at a nearby store. Please send your check for $58.85 representing $22.95 for the bookcase I have returned and $35.90 for the two bookcases you have not shipped.

As with the first letter, the action the writer wants the reader to take is clear: in this case, he or she wants a refund for the damaged bookcase and the two not shipped. This courteous letter gives the date of the order, the method and amount of the payment, the problem with the products, the justification for the request, and the exact amount of the expected refund with an explanation of the figure. Notice, too, that the writer blames no one for the inconvenience.

Exercise

You paid for a three-year subscription to a monthly magazine. When the first issue arrived, the address sticker showed that your subscription expires in one year. Request that the circulation department correct the error.

Special Requests

A special request may require persuasion to get the reader to do something. Requests to contribute time or money, to complete a questionnaire, or to speak to a special interest group are a few examples. Assume, for purposes of discussion, that you want a representative of a business firm to hold practice interviews with your class in preparation for your summer job search. You know that to ask such a person to sacrifice a morning out of his or her busy schedule is an imposition. However, if you approach the letter-writing task with the attitude that the interviewer will benefit from the visit to your class, your special request can be effective. It is, first of all, good public relations for a company representative to perform a public service. Second, interviewing you and your classmates can give the representative a chance to assess the caliber of students who may be applying for part-time positions with the company. The interviews will also reveal what kinds of questions and job interests students have. Finally, mock interviews give students practice for the real thing, and the genuine interviews that the representative conducts later will be all the more productive because he or she has participated in the mock interviews.

From this discussion we can see that there are basically two important prewriting considerations for a special request: deciding how the reader will benefit from satisfying your request, and approaching the request with confidence that the reader will do what you want. Both of these can be seen in the illustration of a special request on page 296. Notice, too, that the beginning of the letter captures the reader's attention. Next, the writer is persuasive by pointing out the benefits to the reader. Then, he includes details that the reader must know in order to satisfy the request. Finally, the writer makes it easy for the reader to respond to the request.

Exercise

1. Assume that you want to invite a staff member of your college administration office to speak to your class. Before you begin to write your request, discuss these questions:
   a. How would a visit to your class benefit the reader of your letter?
   b. How can you capture the reader's attention?
   c. What does the reader need to know in order to agree to your request?
   d. How can you make it easy for the reader to respond?
   Now, write your request.
2. As an annual project, an organization to which you belong is collecting toys and money to buy toys to distribute to children in a nearby children's hospital. Write a special request to local businesses asking for their contributions.

English Department
Elkton College
Henderson, Kentucky 42420
March 24, 19—

Ms. Ellen Walters
Personnel Director
Hudson Chemical Company
Henderson, Kentucky 42420

Dear Ms. Walters:

In April and May, approximately two thousand Henderson area
college students will be seeking summer employment. Because
Hudson Chemical Company is known to fill summer positions by
hiring students, many will be applying to your company. To prepare
for our summer job search, my freshman English class is inviting
several personnel directors from companies with policies similar to
yours to come to campus and conduct practice interviews. The
interviews will give us experience with interview techniques and
would give you a chance to learn what kinds of skills and aptitudes
Hudson's potential applicants have.

Can you interview three of us in front of our class on Monday,
Wednesday, or Friday, April 21, 23, or 25? Our class meets from 9:00
until 10:20 a.m. in 302 Stover Hall.

As soon as we hear from you, we will send you our application letters
and résumés so that you can select the people you want to interview.
Our instructor, Professor Janet Green, can be reached in her office
from 9:00 until noon on Tuesdays and Thursdays. Her number is
727-4556.

Respectfully,

John Hamilton
Coordinator of Student Interviews

ANSWERING REQUESTS

Responding to Requests for Information

Some replies to requests for information need only a pre-printed postcard or form letter that either says that the material requested is on its way or answers a question that is frequently asked. In those instances when unusual questions are asked, however, a personalized business letter may be required, such as the response on pages 298–99 to John McDowell's inquiry about his school's work-study program (page 292).

Mr. Holmes's reply illustrates several elements that are characteristic of effective responses to inquiries. First, he opened his reply with the answer John was most interested in, the one John needed in order for the following answers to make sense. He did not waste John's time by beginning with an empty comment like "Thank you for your interest in CCC's Work-Study Program." Instead, Mr. Holmes showed his appreciation for John's interest by telling him what was most important immediately: "Yes, you are eligible." Second, he answered all of John's questions clearly, concisely, and thoroughly. If one answer had been omitted, John might have thought the writer intended to mislead him or had not read his inquiry carefully. Third, Mr. Holmes combined answers to John's questions. For example, the first paragraph answers John's first and third questions: "Am I eligible?" and "Is there summer employment?" Finally, the letter closes with clear instructions for John.

Mr. Holmes's response was limited to answering the questions in John's inquiry. There are occasions, however, when an inquiry offers a company an opportunity to sell its service or product. Besides answering the questions posed in the inquiry, that kind of response should include incentives for the reader to buy the product or use the service he or she has inquired about. The purpose of such a response is twofold: to answer the questions and to convince the reader to do business with the company.

As an example, let us say that a student has requested information about group rates for theater tickets. Although this request is not a ticket order, it has the potential of becoming an order if the response is effective. Therefore, the ticket manager must not only answer the questions but encourage the student to buy tickets. In the following reply to a request for information about twenty tickets for a Saturday matinee, the italicized parts

The Financial Services Office
CULVER COMMUNITY COLLEGE
Somerset, Pennsylvania 15501

April 15, 19—

Mr. John McDowell
202 Harrison Hall
7321 Hoover Avenue
Somerset, Pennsylvania 15501

Dear John:

As a second-semester freshman, you are eligible to apply for a
position in the Work-Study Program at Culver Community College.
The enclosed application and a financial statement from your
parents or legal guardian must be submitted by May 10 in order for
you to be considered for summer employment. As Item 21 on the
application explains, to be eligible for summer employment, you must
commit yourself to fall employment also.

After the Financial Services Office notifies you of your eligibility for
work-study employment, you will find job lists posted in the Work-
Study Center, Stone Hall 301. You then apply directly to the office or
department that has announced a position you are interested in and
for which you are qualified. Once you have accepted a position, you
and your supervisor determine your weekly schedule. Although there
is a maximum limit of forty hours a month and no minimum limit,
Financial Services will specify the maximum number of hours you
will be permitted to work. This decision is based on your course load
and your financial needs.

Salaries for work-study positions range from $3.50 to $5.00 an hour,
depending upon the position you apply for, and checks are issued
directly to you every two weeks.

Since you are interested in working with foreign students, you may
want to contact Dr. Jayne Hansen, Director of the English Language
and Orientation Institute, in Washington Hall, Room 2. Each
semester ELOI employs twenty students to assist instructors in
conversation classes and to supervise the audio-visual laboratory
sections for foreign students.

We look forward to receiving your application and financial statement before May 10.

Sincerely,

Jack Holmes, Director

Application and Financial
Statement Enclosed

---

do not answer questions asked in the inquiry, but the information is included to encourage the reader to order tickets and to make ordering easy.

> You and your nineteen classmates can purchase tickets at group rate for the June 7, 14, 21, and 28 matinees of "Annie," *which begin at 2:30.* Individual tickets for all seats are $7.50, and prices for groups larger than ten are $6.50 per individual. As students, you will also receive an additional $1.00 discount, provided you order the tickets two weeks in advance of the performance.
>
> *So that you can take advantage of the student group rates, an order form is enclosed, along with reviews and order forms for the July and August performances of Tom Stoppard's "Rosencrantz and Guildenstern Are Dead" and George Bernard Shaw's "Major Barbara."*
>
> We look forward to receiving your ticket order soon so that you and your class can enjoy a delightful production of "Annie" for only $5.50 a person.

Like Mr. Holmes's response to John McDowell's inquiry, the ticket manager's reply begins with an answer to the question the student is most interested in: "Yes, group rates are available." And the letter ends with a courteous comment that combines praise of the play and a reminder of the deadline for ordering discount tickets. In addition, the ticket manager included information that might encourage the class to get tickets for "Annie" and perhaps for the Stoppard and Shaw plays.

Some correspondents think that providing information beyond what has been asked for is overly aggressive. On the contrary, it is a courteous touch, as in the case of the mention of the Stoppard and Shaw plays. If the class cannot make the "Annie" shows, it may want to see one of the other shows, especially after having read the reviews. To guard against having your promotional information seem aggressive, add only information that is directly related to the questions asked in the inquiry. Another guide to adding details is this: If you don't add it, will the reader need to write again? Will you save both yourself and the reader time by adding it?

Requests for information cannot always be satisfied. If the information is no longer available, rather than saying "I'm sorry,

---

MeCo
Public Relations Division
130278 Gateway Boulevard
Chicago, Illinois 60646

May 10, 19—

Ms. Sarah Smalley
9201 Quebec Street
Granston, Ohio 44057

Dear Ms. Smalley:

The road maps and lists of camping sites that MeCo customers have used for over twenty years to plan their trips continue to make vacation planning more pleasant for hundreds of thousands of travelers.

In order to make the maps and lists available to as many MeCo customers as possible—and as quickly as possible—your local MeCo dealer now distributes them for fifty cents each. Your Yellow Pages will tell you where you can pick up the maps and lists so that you can plan your trips with confidence and ease.

Sincerely,

Jason M. Smith, Director
Public Relations Division

we don't have that information," the writer of the response should attempt to retain the reader's good will by offering an alternative. The guide for handling negative responses is this: tell the reader what you *can* do, not what you *cannot* do.

While all letters require careful planning to be effective, planning is crucial in a negative letter. The purpose is to refuse the request and at the same time retain the good will of the reader. But the message doesn't say "No." Nor does it say "No . . . however." Instead, it implies the "No" by emphasizing the reasons behind the "however," as the example on page 300 illustrates. In this case, the person receiving the negative response had asked for free road maps and lists of camping sites from an oil company.

Exercise

1. Compose a refusal of a request based on the following situation: A customer of long standing, the owner of a retail furniture store, has requested two hundred free copies of your annual catalog of home furnishings to distribute to his customers. Your wholesale company has decided the service is too expensive to continue, but the catalogs are available for $2.50 each if the retailer's customers would like to order them directly from your company. With your letter, include several dozen order forms and six catalogs for the retailer's use in his showrooms.
2. Working in several groups, compose lists of four or five questions about a product or service that everyone in your class knows something about (or can make up details about). Exchange the lists with other groups and write responses. Consider the following questions before you begin composing the response:
   a. What is the best order in which to answer the questions?
   b. Do you have answers to *all* the questions?
   c. What additional information will you include?
   d. What means of response will you include? A phone number to be called collect? An order form?
   e. Can you combine some of the answers?

Responding to Requests for Adjustments

When customers ask for adjustments—refunds, exchanges, replacements, shipment of items missing from an order—most companies try to do exactly what the customer has requested.

They think of the customer as a potential buyer and, therefore, will do what he or she asks in the hope of making future sales. Whatever loss they may take, they make up in creating good will for the company. Any effective favorable response to a disappointed customer convinces that customer that he or she comes first with the company.

Apologizing for the source of displeasure is not effective in convincing the customer that he or she comes first with the company. Thus, using words like "damaged," "broken," or "malfunction" defeats the purpose of the letter: to keep the customer. You can do this by promoting a service or product related to the one for which he or she has sought an adjustment or by announcing a forthcoming sale, as is the method used in the following example. The four throw pillows Mrs. Jones charged to her account do not match the shades of brown in her living room, and thus she has returned them to the store. The policy of the company is to accept all reasonable requests for adjustments.

> The four 18-inch by 24-inch throw pillows have arrived, and $49.80 has been credited to your account.
> Your announcement of Hancock's annual household furnishings sale is enclosed. The prices of three thousand cushions and other decorator items have been reduced twenty percent. Calling us collect at (800) 777-6263, or ordering with the form on page 3, can save you time and money on attractive May and June shower gifts.

It is relatively easy to write an adjustment letter when the company's policy is that "the customer is always right." However, many companies do not have such a policy. The alternative is to handle each adjustment request on its own merits.

Like a negative response to a request for information, a rejection of an adjustment request has a twofold purpose: to refuse the adjustment while holding the customer's positive attitude toward the company's product or service. Again, the strategy is to prepare the reader for the refusal by establishing the writer's reasonableness. An effective beginning avoids hints of either acceptance or rejection, and it avoids negative reminders of the reader's annoyance. Yet, the opening sentence or two that the writer is confident the reader will agree to must be related to the product or service about which the request was made. The second part of the letter gives a reason that should be so sound, so logical, that the implied refusal will be obvious to the reader, perhaps before he or she reads it. The next step is to offer an alternative to the requested adjustment. It is essential to make the alternative attractive and thereby retain the reader's favorable attitude. The final step is to make it easy for the reader to respond favorably to the counterproposal. This can be done with a specific suggestion about how to respond and a final reminder of the reader's positive attitude toward the product or service.

Emphasis on the benefits the reader will gain from the alternative is important. One of the most successful ways to emphasize these benefits is to make the reader see, hear, feel, or smell the product in his or her own environment. The first and last sentences of the letter on page 304 illustrate the effective application of this principle. The request for an adjustment was from a woman who had paid $175 for an Egyptian tray. After several unsuccessful attempts to hang it on her wall by using adhesive mounts, she wanted to return the tray and get her money back.

Exercise

1. A customer has requested that your leather goods store exchange a brown pigskin wallet for a black pigskin one or else give him a refund. Because the manufacturer of the wallet no longer produces it in black pigskin, you send the customer a refund. However, you also send him advertisements for new designs in wallets that you will be receiving in a month. Suggest he apply the refund to one of the new designs. Send him an order form.

2. As the manager of an office furniture store, you must refuse a request for a refund on a four-drawer legal-size filing cabinet ($198.95). The buyer, Mr. Smith, was pleased with the cabinet, but it does not fit under the window of his den, the only space he has for it. Rather than refund his money, you suggest he take instead two two-drawer cabinets, which are on sale for $69.95 each. You will send the two for a shipping charge of $15.00.

    Before you begin composing the letter, consider the following:

    a. What do you both agree on—something related to the filing cabinets that you can discuss in the opening paragraph to indicate you are reasonable?

    b. Why would it benefit the reader to accept your offer?

    c. How can you create a vivid picture of the two cabinets situated under the window in his den?

    d. How can you make it easy for him to respond?

EVERETT'S IMPORTS, LTD.
1202 Lincolnshire Boulevard
Des Moines, Iowa 50316

August 12, 19—

Mrs. Cherly Gibbs
7261 Granville Road
Harriston, Minnesota 55102

Dear Mrs. Gibbs:

You are certainly correct in expecting that the thirty-six-inch copper Egyptian tray which you purchased from Everett's on July 20 can be hung securely on the wall.

Your experience with adhesive mounts is a common one for owners of trays that weigh from eight to ten pounds. Adhesive mounts usually do not sustain that much weight for more than a week or so. That is why we recommend a three-quarter-inch metal loop be soldered to the back of the tray approximately three inches above the center.

Because you are pleased with the compliments your tray has received, may we arrange to have the soldering done for you by the company that has done our work for the past ten years? Their charge to retailers is $15.00, nearly $7.00 less than you would probably pay if you had the soldering done locally. Ten days after we receive the enclosed postcard indicating your decision, your copper tray can be securely hung again, and you will be receiving compliments on the unique tray.

Sincerely,

Marjorie Goode
Sales Manager

WRITING MEMORANDUMS

Communication within an organization, such as between members of a university department or employees in different divisions of a company, is usually in the form of an interdepartmental or interoffice memorandum. Memo forms are generally available within the organization; however, there may be times when you will need to create your own form. In that case, you simply type MEMORANDUM at the top of the page; then, type the reader's name and position, your name and position, the date, and the subject of the memo, which tells the reader at a glance what the memo is about. Although placement of this information can take several forms, the following is the most commonly used one:

MEMORANDUM

TO: Sandra Simpson, Office Manager

FROM: Quentin Green, Shipping Department

DATE: September 12, 19—

RE: My Absence from Work on September 18, 19—

A memorandum, then, is a way to transmit a message to someone who is a member of your group. It can explain an event, report information, summarize progress on a project, or recommend improvements, to name just a few of its purposes. Because the purpose and the reader determine the language you use in any writing, it is difficult to generalize about the level of formality appropriate to a memorandum. If you are, for example, handwriting (not typing) a memo to your immediate supervisor, who has asked for a list of equipment needed for a project, you can simply write "Here's the list of equipment you asked for." On the other hand, a memo may transmit technical or specialized information to a group of executives and thus requires highly formal language. Perhaps the only generalization that can be made is this: the language should be appropriate to both the purpose of the message and the reader.

Here is the brief, informal memo Quentin Green wrote to his boss:

MEMORANDUM

TO: Sandra Simpson, Office Manager

FROM: Quentin Green, Shipping Department

DATE: September 12, 19—

RE: My Absence from Work on September 18, 19—

The guidance counselor at Eddington High School in Somerset wants me to participate in my high school's Career Day on September 18, so I'll be missing work that day. I've spoken to my supervisor, Mr. Trainor, about this and he said that he can cover for me, if you have no objection. I hope you will give your approval.

Memorandums that are long or have complex messages often require headings—captions that tell the reader the gist of the information grouped below each heading. Headings help the writer organize the information in the memorandum, but they also are especially helpful to the reader. For example, a lengthy memo may contain sections of information that is of interest only to specific individuals, who can then skim the facts dealing with other areas and concentrate on those sections that are relevant to their own interests. The memo on pages 307–08 illustrates the value of headings.

Exercise

1. Imagine that you are a clerk in the credit office of a large manufacturer. On November 10 you were assigned the task of alphabetizing the company's accounts-receivable records, which had been organized numerically; on November 15 you completed the job. Write a memo to the credit manager, Robert Green, describing the reorganization and telling him that it has been completed. Your task involved not only alphabetizing the records but also developing a cross-reference index organized by account numbers. The credit manager requires this information so that he and his staff can quickly find the record of an individual account.
2. Ask a local business person to describe the company's written communications. Then write a memorandum to your English instructor describing the correspondence the business uses, both within the company and to its patrons. Perhaps you can attach samples of forms the company uses, such as memorandums or postcards telling customers their orders have arrived or reminders of overdue payments. Before you start, however, be sure to plan your interview so that you use the business person's time effectively.

TO: Virginia Patton, Communications Coordinator,
Corporate Headquarters

FROM: Steve Henderson, District Manager

DATE: April 17, 19—

SUBJECT: Communication System at Southwestern Life Insurance
Company in Hendrix

Here is the information you requested about the communication
system within the Hendrix office and with other Southwestern
offices.

Within the Office
Agent to Prospect:
Graphs and charts to explain prospect's insurance needs
Telephones to call prospect to set up and confirm
appointment
Letters and reply cards with small free gift to attract
new prospects
Reply cards (Form 21–330) to request additional information
from agent
Agent to Agent:
Verbal agreements on best sales methods to use
Weekly conferences to discuss problems and set weekly goals
Discussion among agents to solve individual insurance
problems
Agent to Secretary:
Messages from clients to agents relayed on three-copy memo
(Form 44–348) or note card
Tape-recorded messages to be typed when agent is out
Daily log of what was done and what is to be done
Secretary to Client:
Appointment verification
Greeting of prospects when they come for appointments
Letters to clients when agent's assistance not required

2

April 17, 19—
Virginia Patton
Communication System at Southwestern Life Insurance Company
in Hendrix

<u>To Other Offices</u>
    District Agency to General Agency:
        Three-copy memos, applications for insurance, and home
           office inquiries to general agency
        Telephone when immediate answer needed
        Three-copy memos to send short messages between agencies
        Weekly news bulletins to explain agents' weekly sales status
        Quarterly business conferences to summarize sales and set
           sales goals
    District Agency to Home Office:
        Direct mailing information for fast response to questions
        Telephone to home office personnel about applications
        Transmittal letters to inform main office of changes in clients'
           payments or policies (Forms 37–541, 26–771, and 68–990)
        Notification of policy changes and daily status of applications
           being processed
        Monthly reports of agents' sales

Attachments (5)

WRITING PROGRESS REPORTS

You may on occasion be required to give a report on the progress of a project you are working on. For example, your adviser may ask you to report on your progress toward fulfilling the requirements of your undergraduate degree. Or you are on the fund-raising committee of an organization and must report on how close the committee is to attaining its goal. Or, on the job, you may be asked to report your sales progress, as in the case of the sales report on page 309, written by a student whose summer job was selling hospital supplies.

The purpose of the student's report is to document his progress on sales; thus, it involves an account of his visits, the

NATIONAL HOSPITAL SUPPLIES, INC.
MEMORANDUM

SUBJECT: Weekly Progress Report No. 7 on Sales Activities in Iowa
District 17
To: Margaret Weintraub, Iowa District Sales Manager
FROM: Ronald Symms, District 17 Sales Representative
DATE: August 9, 19—

Following are a summary of sales for District 17, a list of my visits and
sales for August 4 in the Sioux City area, and a list of visits planned
for August 11–15.

Summary of Sales

August 4–8 sales were $1778.00. Sales for District 17 are higher than
sales at this time last year. August and September sales projections
are 15% above last August and September's sales.

Visits and Sales for August 4–8

Date	Place	Sales
August 4	Maryville Hospital	$247.00
5	Harrison Hospital	865.00
6	St. Andrews Medical Center	327.00
7	Johnson Memorial Hospital	144.00
	Doctors Clinic	75.00
8	Campbell Professional Center	$120.00
		Total = $1778.00

Visits for August 11–14

Date	Place
August 11	Memorial Hospital, Mill Creek
12	Huntingdon and Jackson
13	Wilson and Manning
14	Manning Rehabilitation Center
15	Mesa Memorial Hospital, Mesa

sales he made, the potential sales, a comparison with last year's sales in the same area, and a projection of sales. The report includes all the information the reader needs to be brought up to date on the progress of one of her representatives. Realizing that the important information, if presented in the form of a letter, would be buried in many unnecessary words and would not be organized so that the reader could immediately see the information most useful to her—the summary of sales for the area—the student has written the report in the form of a memo. In the memo he has supplied headings, eliminated words, and organized the information so that it can be understood quickly.

Because Ronald Symms knows that Ms. Weintraub will prepare a summary report to *her* supervisor using the information from him and other sales representatives, he has placed a summary at the beginning of his memorandum. Usually, progress reports, which often are required at set intervals, tell the reader what has been done, what is being done, and what remains to be done—in that order. If the progress report is a second report on a project, tie the current report to the earlier one to show continuity in the work. The second part, the most important section, discusses the work in progress, that is, the problems that have arisen or the fact that the work is on schedule. The final section summarizes what remains to be done.

So that are you not left with the impression that all progress reports are as brief as Ronald Symms's, consider the volumes of progress reports that will likely be written about a long-term defense project or a new automobile model still in the design stages.

Exercise

1. Assume that an instructor has requested three progress reports, to be submitted at two-week intervals, on a class project. If you are currently working on a project, write the second progress report. Otherwise, create a situation about which you can write a second report.
2. In an earlier exercise (page 295), you requested local businesses to contribute toys and money for a children's hospital. Assume that it is a month before the toy drive is to end. As the chairperson of the toy drive, report on your committee's progress in a memo that will be read at the next executive meeting of the organization.

IV
STRUCTURE AND STYLE

11
Paragraphs

■■■■■■ **As** marks of punctuation signal the structure of the sentences in a piece of writing, so paragraphing signals the structure of the whole subject—grouping the ideas in the way intended by the writer. The way in which paragraphing helps one read an extended piece of writing is illustrated in the exercise on pages 313–18.

THE REALITY OF THE PARAGRAPH

It is very difficult to define "sentence," and yet all of us can recognize sentences; that is to say, we know what a sentence is even though we cannot propose an adequate definition.

in fact I can easily demonstrate to you that you can recognize sentences this paragraph should give you such a demonstration put an X or a check mark before each word that begins a sentence now compare your sentencing with your classmates' almost certainly everyone is in agreement about the sentences in this paragraph

This paragraph demonstrates that the sentence has what might be called "psychological reality"; a sentence cannot be just any string of words but must have certain characteristics, the nature of which we recognize since we can mark off sentence boundaries. (Again, we may not be able to explain the features that make a string of words a sentence, but we must recognize those features since, even in unpunctuated passages, we can agree pretty much on where the sentences begin and end.)

For experienced readers and writers, the paragraph has just such reality also. Take a well-structured expository essay, and reprint it so that all paragraph indentations are removed, and then submit the essay to a group of readers, asking them to indicate the points at which they believe paragraphs should begin. This experiment has been tried again and again, and the results are uniform: experienced readers overwhelmingly agree on the paragraphing, with only a small number of disputed or ambiguous cases.

Exercise

This exercise should demonstrate two points: the paragraph is "psychologically" real, and paragraphing is important for readers.

The following brief essay is printed first without paragraphs and then is reprinted twice, each time with different paragraphing.

1. By making check marks in your book, indicate how you think the essay should be paragraphed.
2. Discuss the paragraphing in the second and third versions of the essay. Which is more effective? Why? Does the paragraphing in either of the versions create confusion and make reading more difficult? Explain.

And Now, the Ultramarathon . . .
Mark N. Grant

Just as the edge of the universe is beyond comprehension, so the distance humans can run seems to have no limits. Mere jogging has given way to the glamorous marathon, which may soon be outmoded by something even more exotic—the ultramarathon, of which Bruce Maxwell and Ken Crutchlow are exemplars. The ultramarathon, an ordeal fit for masochists and other pioneers in pain, is any race longer than the marathon's 26 miles, 385 yards. Its varieties thus far include 50 kilometers (31 miles), 50 miles, the double marathon, 100 kilometers (62 miles), 100 miles, the 24-hour race, and whatever else its slightly mad enthusiasts think of next. These races make Frank Shorter seem appropriately surnamed. The 24-hour record, for instance, is 160 miles. England's Ron Bentley set it in 1973, when he was 43 years old. (Bentley has also done 400 laps on a quarter-mile track in 12½ hours, but that's an hour slower than the world record for 100 miles.) If this seems outlandish, consider that several *thousand* runners routinely finish the Comrades' Double Marathon in South Africa every year. In addition to public ultraraces, such as the 52½-miler from London to Brighton, many ultrarunners pursue even longer solo jaunts. Siegfried Bauer ran the length of New Zealand—1,321 miles—in 18 days, 12 hours. Tom McGrath ran from New York to San Francisco in exactly 53 days, averaging 57 miles per day. A Canadian is now training to run the length of the Alaskan pipeline. And Patty Wilson jogged from her home in La Palma, California to Portland, Oregon—1,310 miles— in 41 days. She was then 15 years old. Ultras are not unique to our epoch. In the 1880s there was a craze for six-day races in which the runners covered 100 miles a day, largely through walking (some of the runners suffered mental derangements from sleep deprivation). The Tarahumara Indians of Mexico's Chihuahua province are known to run 50 to 100 miles in village games. But today's ultramarathoner is unlikely to get much attention or competition. World-class marathoners like Shorter and Bill Rodgers shun ultras. If it takes one month to recover from a marathon, it may take two months after a 50-miler. Running ultras would ruin their training season and prevent them from competing in the shorter races they prefer. On the other hand, some runners seem to have unlimited stamina—among them Park Barner, a 33-year-old computer operator in Harrisburg, Pennsylvania. He once ran a marathon *and* a 50-mile race in the same weekend. Barner talks of such feats as his recent traversal of 187 miles in 36 hours (including a four-hour catnap) with an aw-shucks, nothing-to-it bravado. "I started jogging at 24, and the fifth time out I did 18 miles. I've read that everybody's born with the ability to run a 2:40 marathon. In winter I can go 50 miles without a drink of water." Barner trains by running four miles to work, four miles during his lunch hour, then four miles home again. But the marathon, he says, is actually too fast a race for him. "It cuts up my legs." With near-comic understatement he adds, "I don't go overboard for this running." The secret is pace: the average Boston Marathon pace is seven and a half minutes a mile, the average ultra pace is eight. "If you go two minutes a mile slower than your racing pace, you can run practically indefinitely," asserts Dr. George Sheehan, the medical guru of modern running. "The ultra is an ordinary event for the human body." Most ultrarunners train 75 to 100 miles or more a week, and if it takes one and a half years for a novice to get in shape for a marathon, he may need four years for an ultra. Fritz Mueller, 41, a Manhattan chemist who started jogging in 1972, finished his first 50-miler in 1977. "It's really not as bad as it's made out to be. In a way it's less painful than a shorter race, because you don't run as fast." What happens to a long-distance runner's body? Even in cool weather, for example, a normal marathon runner's core body temperature can rise to 104 degrees or more. But with proper water replacement, there's a minimal danger. Biochemical data on ultrarunners suggest that this rule holds true for them as well. And what of the "wall," that much-discussed shorting-out of the body at approximately 20 miles, when a runner's normal glycogen reserves are exhausted? According to Tom Osler, a 37-year-old ultrarunner from Glassboro, New Jersey, "It's like a car running out of gas. You just keep refilling the tank as you run by drinking liquids high in sugar." Also, extreme distances allow enough time for the body to gear up its slow process of converting stored fat into energy—if the runner can hold out mentally. But the question left dangling is: Why attempt an ultra? Tom Osler, who's run over 50 marathons, ultimately found them boring. "After a while, they're not so exciting. You've had the good days and the bad days. With the ultra, the pacing problems are far more difficult. Walking becomes a part of it. It has incredible new dimensions. The longer races involve unknowns." Finally, the ultraquestion: Do ultrarunners ever tire of ultras? Says Ted Corbitt, who at 53 set the American record for the 24-hour run: "Psychologically, it becomes easier. After the first time, it's never as hard again. Some days it's enjoyable. But it never becomes completely easy, and the joy never lasts. So you keep on trying to find the perfect balance between pain and pleasure."

And Now, the Ultramarathon . . .
Mark N. Grant

Just as the edge of the universe is beyond comprehension, so the distance humans can run seems to have no limits. Mere jogging has given way to the glamorous marathon, which may soon be outmoded by something even more exotic—the ultramarathon, of which Bruce Maxwell and Ken Crutchlow are exemplars. The ultramarathon, an ordeal fit for masochists and other pioneers in pain, is any race longer than the marathon's 26 miles, 385 yards. Its varieties thus far include 50 kilometers (31 miles), 50 miles, the double marathon, 100 kilometers (62 miles), 100 miles, the 24-hour race, and whatever else its slightly mad enthusiasts think of next.

These races make Frank Shorter seem appropriately surnamed. The 24-hour record, for instance, is 160 miles. England's Ron Bentley set it in 1973, when he was 43 years old. (Bentley has also done 400 laps on a quarter-mile track in 12½ hours, but that's an hour slower than the world record for 100 miles.) If this seems outlandish, consider that several *thousand* runners routinely finish the Comrades' Double Marathon in South Africa every year. In addition to public ultraraces, such as the 52½-miler from London to Brighton, many ultrarunners pursue even longer solo jaunts. Siegfried Bauer ran the length of New Zealand—1,321 miles—in 18 days, 12 hours. Tom McGrath ran from New York to San Francisco in exactly 53 days, averaging 57 miles per day. A Canadian is now training to run the length of the Alaskan pipeline. And Patty Wilson jogged from her home in La Palma, California to Portland, Oregon—1,310 miles—in 41 days. She was then 15 years old.

Ultras are not unique to our epoch. In the 1880s there was a craze for six-day races in which the runners covered 100 miles a day, largely through walking (some of the runners suffered mental derangements from sleep deprivation). The Tarahumara Indians of Mexico's Chihuahua province are known to run 50 to 100 miles in village games.

But today's ultramarathoner is unlikely to get much attention or competition. World-class marathoners like Shorter and Bill Rodgers shun ultras. If it takes one month to recover from a marathon, it may take two months after a 50-miler. Running ultras would ruin their training season and prevent them from competing in the shorter races they prefer.

On the other hand, some runners seem to have unlimited stamina—among them Park Barner, a 33-year-old computer operator in Harrisburg, Pennsylvania. He once ran a marathon *and* a 50-mile race in the same weekend. Barner talks of such feats as his recent traversal of 187 miles in 36 hours (including a four-hour catnap) with an aw-shucks, nothing-to-it bravado. "I started jogging at 24, and the fifth time out I did 18 miles. I've read that everybody's born with the ability to run a 2:40 marathon. In winter I can go 50 miles without a drink of water." Barner trains by running four miles to work, four miles during his lunch hour, then four miles home again. But the marathon, he says, is actually too fast a race for him. "It cuts up my legs." With near-comic understatement he adds, "I don't go overboard for this running."

The secret is pace: the average Boston Marathon pace is seven and a half minutes a mile, the average ultra pace is eight. "If you go two minutes a mile slower than your racing pace, you can run practically indefinitely," asserts Dr. George Sheehan, the medical guru of modern running. "The ultra is an ordinary event for the human body." Most ultrarunners train 75 to 100 miles or more a week, and if it takes one and a half years for a novice to get in shape for a marathon, he may need four years for an ultra. Fritz Mueller, 41, a Manhattan chemist who started jogging in 1972, finished his first 50-miler in 1977. "It's really not as bad as it's made out to be. In a way it's less painful than a shorter race, because you don't run as fast."

What happens to a long-distance runner's body? Even in cool weather, for example, a normal marathon runner's core body temperature can rise to 104 degrees or more. But with proper water replacement, there's a minimal danger. Biochemical data on ultrarunners suggest that this rule holds true for them as well. And what of the "wall," that much-discussed shorting-out of the body at approximately 20 miles, when a runner's normal glycogen reserves are exhausted? According to Tom Osler, a 37-year-old ultrarunner from Glassboro, New Jersey, "It's like a car running out of gas. You just keep refilling the tank as you run by drinking liquids high in sugar." Also, extreme distances allow enough time for the body to gear up its slow process of converting stored fat into energy—if the runner can hold out mentally.

But the question left dangling is: Why attempt an ultra? Tom Osler, who's run over 50 marathons, ultimately found them boring. "After a while, they're not so exciting. You've had the good days and the bad days. With the ultra, the pacing problems are far more difficult. Walking becomes a part of it. It has incredible new dimensions. The longer races involve unknowns."

Finally, the ultraquestion: Do ultrarunners ever tire of ultras? Says Ted Corbitt, who at 53 set the American record for the 24-hour run: "Psychologically, it becomes easier. After the first time, it's never as hard again. Some days it's enjoyable. But it never becomes completely easy, and the joy never lasts. So you keep on trying to find the perfect balance between pain and pleasure."

And Now, the Ultramarathon . . .
Mark N. Grant

Just as the edge of the universe is beyond comprehension, so the distance humans can run seems to have no limits. Mere jogging has given way to the glamorous marathon, which may soon be outmoded by something even more exotic—the ultramarathon, of which Bruce Maxwell and Ken Crutchlow are exemplars. The ultramarathon, an ordeal fit for masochists and other pioneers in pain, is any race longer than the marathon's 26 miles, 385 yards.

Its varieties thus far include 50 kilometers (31 miles), 50 miles, the double marathon, 100 kilometers (62 miles), 100 miles, the 24-hour race, and whatever else its slightly mad enthusiasts think of next. These races make Frank Shorter seem appropriately surnamed. The 24-hour record, for instance, is 160 miles. England's Ron Bentley set it in 1973, when he was 43 years old. (Bentley has also done 400 laps on a quarter-mile track in 12½ hours, but that's an hour slower than the world record for 100 miles.)

If this seems outlandish, consider that several *thousand* runners routinely finish the Comrades' Double Marathon in South Africa every year. In addition to public ultraraces, such as the 52½-miler from London to Brighton, many ultrarunners pursue even longer solo jaunts. Siegfried Bauer ran the length of New Zealand—1,321 miles—in 18 days, 12 hours. Tom McGrath ran from New York to San Francisco in exactly 53 days, averaging 57 miles per day. A Canadian is now training to run the length of the Alaskan pipeline. And Patty Wilson jogged from her home in La Palma, California to Portland, Oregon—1,310 miles—in 41 days. She was then 15 years old. Ultras are not unique to our epoch.

In the 1880s there was a craze for six-day races in which the runners covered 100 miles a day, largely through walking (some of the runners suffered mental derangements from sleep deprivation). The Tarahumara Indians of Mexico's Chihuahua province are known to run 50 to 100 miles in village games. But today's ultramarathoner is unlikely to get much attention or competition. World-class marathoners like Shorter and Bill Rodgers shun ultras. If it takes one month to recover from a marathon, it may take two months after a 50-miler. Running ultras would ruin their training season and prevent them from competing in the shorter races they prefer. On the other hand, some runners seem to have unlimited stamina—among them Park Barner, a 33-year-old computer operator in Harrisburg, Pennsylvania.

He once ran a marathon *and* a 50-mile race in the same weekend. Barner talks of such feats as his recent traversal of 187 miles in 36 hours (including a four-hour catnap) with an aw-shucks, nothing-to-it bravado. "I started jogging at 24, and the fifth time out I did 18 miles. I've read that everybody's born with the ability to run a 2:40 marathon. In winter I can go 50 miles without a drink of water." Barner trains by running four miles to work, four miles during his lunch hour, then four miles home again. But the marathon, he says, is actually too fast a race for him. "It cuts up my legs." With near-comic understatement he adds, "I don't go overboard for this running." The secret is pace: the average Boston Marathon pace is seven and a half minutes a mile, the average ultra pace is eight. "If you go two minutes a mile slower than your racing pace, you can run practically indefinitely," asserts Dr. George Sheehan, the medical guru of modern running. "The ultra is an ordinary event for the human body."

Most ultrarunners train 75 to 100 miles or more a week, and if it takes one and a half years for a novice to get in shape for a marathon, he may need four years for an ultra.

Fritz Mueller, 41, a Manhattan chemist who started jogging in 1972, finished his first 50-miler in 1977.

"It's really not as bad as it's made out to be. In a way it's less painful than a shorter race, because you don't run as fast."

What happens to a long-distance runner's body?

Even in cool weather, for example, a normal marathon runner's core body temperature can rise to 104 degrees or more. But with proper water replacement, there's a minimal danger. Biochemical data on ultrarunners suggest that this rule holds true for them as well. And what of the "wall," that much-discussed shorting-out of the body at approximately 20 miles, when a runner's normal glycogen reserves are exhausted? According to Tom Osler, a 37-year-old ultrarunner from Glassboro, New Jersey, "It's like a car running out of gas. You just keep refilling the tank as you run by drinking liquids high in sugar." Also, extreme distances allow enough time for the body to gear up its slow process of converting stored fat into energy—if the runner can hold out mentally. But the question left dangling is: Why attempt an ultra? Tom Osler, who's run over 50 marathons, ultimately found them boring. "After a while, they're not so exciting. You've had the good days and the bad days. With the ultra, the pacing problems are far more difficult. Walking becomes a part of it. It has incredible new dimensions. The longer races involve unknowns." Finally, the ultraquestion: Do ultrarunners ever tire of ultras?

Says Ted Corbitt, who at 53 set the American record for the 24-hour run: "Psychologically, it becomes easier. After the first time, it's never as hard again. Some days it's enjoyable. But it never becomes completely easy, and the joy never lasts. So you keep on trying to find the perfect balance between pain and pleasure."

The paragraph, like the sentence, then, is a *real* structure. Just as punctuation or its lack does not change the basic nature of the sentence, so the indentation that you employ does not change the basic nature of the paragraph—and this is an important enough point to be underscored and illustrated.

We can identify the sentences in the following passage:

a. Rain was gently falling dripping off the eaves and the leaves it was fresh fresh and cool we enjoyed it after the heat of the August day
   1. Rain was gently falling, dripping off the eaves and the leaves.
   2. It was fresh, fresh and cool.
   3. We enjoyed it after the heat of the August day.

If we have good reason, we can violate the rules of edited standard English and punctuate this passage in a variety of ways (the purpose being, of course, to create a variety of effects):

  b. The rain was gently falling. Dripping off the eaves and the leaves. It was fresh. Fresh and cool. We enjoyed it after the heat of the August day.

  c. The rain was gently falling, dripping off the eaves—and the leaves. It was fresh, fresh and cool. We enjoyed it. After the heat of the August day.

Versions *b* and *c* may or may not be effective, depending on the writer's *purpose* and *audience,* but the point is this: even though we violate the rules of punctuation for some reason, we do not change the nature of the sentence; "beneath" the surface of the different punctuations, we can find the sentences, as we can also in an unpunctuated passage. One might say that there are *real* sentences and a variety of *pseudo* sentences created by punctuation.

This is exactly the case with paragraphs. We can break "real" paragraphs up into pseudo paragraphs for many reasons, including *emphasis:*

  d.   There is little to say about choosing a theme or topic from a group that are assigned. You have some latitude, but not very much, and you must work as best you can within the limits of the assignment. It is important to remember, though, that an essay results from the writer's encounter with the subject; if the subject does not come to you, you must bring yourself to the subject. Therefore, you ask yourself, "What do I know about this subject? What can I find out about it? How do I feel about it?" And so on. More about this later.

  e.   There is little to say about choosing a theme or topic from a group that are assigned. You have some latitude, but not very much, and you must work as best you can within the limits of the assignment.
         It is important to remember, though, that an essay results from the writer's encounter with the subject; if the subject does not come to you, you must bring yourself to the subject.
         Therefore, you ask yourself, "What do I know about this subject? What can I find out about it? How do I feel about it?" And so on.
         More about this later.

In example *e,* the original paragraph *d* has been broken up into four shorter paragraphs. These choices of indentation have placed emphasis on the second shorter paragraph ("It is important to remember . . .") by isolating it and thus making it stand out. The final indentation ("More about this later") signals a transition to another subject.

Neither one is "better" or "worse" out of context, but one would probably be more effective than the other for some *purposes* with some *audiences*.

To end this section, a couple of brief comments. Throughout the section I have repeatedly mentioned *purpose* and *audience*, as I have done throughout this book. In the exercise on pages 313–18, the second version of the essay on the ultramarathon represents the original paragraphing.

PARAGRAPH COHERENCE

The following group of sentences does not seem like a paragraph:

> The albacore are beginning to run. In Montana, it often snows in August. Freud created a revolution in the way we view the human mind. Grammar seems to be a dull subject.

But the next example, though it is extremely strange, does seem a bit more like a real paragraph (a paragraph written by a mad person, perhaps):

> The albacore are beginning to run. However, in Montana it often snows in August. That is why Freud created a revolution in the way we view the human mind. Therefore, grammar seems to be a dull subject.

In the second example, words and phrases such as *however, that is why*, and *therefore* make us feel that the writer of the paragraph was trying to make us see connections even though we remain puzzled.

In fact, *transitional* words and phrases (such as *however, thus, moreover, on the other hand, therefore*, and others) help create paragraph coherence. And so do *pointing words* such as *this* and *that, here* and *there, these* and *those*, and others.

> The members of the class seemed puzzled and frustrated. *Therefore*, the teacher stopped the lecture and asked if there were any questions. *This* brief pause was enough to allow everyone to become oriented so that the explanation could continue.

> In order to make a fortune, one might plan a spectacular robbery or perhaps blackmail a millionaire. *On the other hand*, some bright people have made great wealth with simple inventions. *For example*, Robert Abplanalp became a multimillionaire with his invention of the

aerosol valve. *That* is the device that enables one to spray the contents from a can of deodorant or paint.

Wine consumed in moderate quantities can enhance the quality of one's life. *In the first place,* a fine wine always makes dining more pleasurable. *In the second place,* a glass of wine acts as a safe and effective tranquilizer. *These,* among others, are the reasons for wine's popularity.

Another reason for coherence is that paragraphs contain strings of words that relate to one another—which is only a way of saying that paragraphs deal with a limited number of subjects.

In the following paragraph from *The Bern Book,* by Vincent O. Carter, "chains" of words and phrases refer to the same subjects. Those in rectangles refer to *the United States of America,* and those in ovals refer to the *citizens of the United States.*

The United States of America may be described, among other things, as a land of great dynamic tensions. It is a land in which practically all of its citizens are emigrants. Most of the people who emigrated to America went as nobodies and their subsequent history, and therefore the history of America, is the history of their attempts to become somebodies. As to what ideas and culture those criminals, prostitutes, fortune-hunters, speculators, religiously oppressed and land-hungry folk possessed, they brought with them from England and France and Germany and Russia and Spain and Armenia and Ireland and Italy and anywhere else in the world one would wish to name. Are you surprised? Are you astonished to discover that they are your relations, only a few generations removed from the old country? You need not be surprised: grandchildren, look at grandparents! All of those European nobodies trying hard to become somebodies in a land that belonged to the Indian and the Eskimo—that's America!

So transitional words—like *however, therefore, thus,* and *then*—are part of the glue that keeps paragraphs together, and chains of words that refer to the same things are another part.

To get a sense of how transitional words and chains of words function to bring about paragraph coherence, let's look at one more interesting paragraph. In this paragraph, *transitional* words (such as *however, but,* and *thus*) are underlined; words and phrases that give the reader the necessary *time orientation* are in rectangles; and words and phrases relating to *plows* and *plowing* are in ovals.

Until recently, agriculture has been the chief occupation even in "advanced" societies; hence, any change in methods of tillage has much importance. Early plows, drawn by two oxen, did not normally turn the sod but merely scratched it. Thus, cross-plowing was needed and fields tended to be squarish. In the fairly light soils and semi-arid climates of the Near East and Mediterranean, this worked well. But such a plow was inappropriate to the wet climate and often sticky soils of northern Europe. By the latter part of the seventh century after Christ, however, following obscure beginnings, certain northern peasants were using an entirely new kind of plow, equipped with a vertical knife to cut the line of the furrow, a horizontal share to slice under the sod, and a moldboard to turn it over. The friction of this plow with the soil was so great that it normally required not two but eight oxen. It attacked the land with such violence that cross-plowing was not needed, and fields tended to be shaped in long strips.

—Lynn White, Jr., "The Historical Roots of Our Ecological Crisis"

Paragraphs hang together, then, because the words in them form chains of meaning, as in the series of words referring to plows and plowing; because time and space relationships are made clear ("until recently," "by the latter part of the seventh century after Christ," and so on); and because transitional words establish logical relationships.

However, there is no particular reason for you to explain all of these technicalities. *The ability to write coherent paragraphs does not depend on the ability to explain why paragraphs are coherent.* Anyone who can write coherent paragraphs *knows* what makes for coherence, even though he or she cannot explain that knowledge, just as anyone who writes sentences knows what a sentence is even though no one can give a really adequate definition of "sentence."

In summary, you can create coherent paragraphs (1) if you do not shift subjects, that is, if you establish clear-cut chains of related words in your paragraphs, and (2) if you give the reader the necessary relationships by the appropriate use of transitions (*however, moreover, thus,* and so on), adverbs (*now, then, here, there, last year, at present*), and pointing words (*this, that, such, these, those*).

Paragraphs in an Essay

The following exercise has several purposes. In the first place, the essay you will read, think about, analyze, and discuss is a good piece of writing that will, I believe, interest you. In the second place, the essay is about keeping a journal (which the author calls a "notebook"), and, as you have discovered, *The Contemporary Writer* urges all writers to maintain journals. And, third, you will discover that you know a great deal that you did not think you knew; the questions concerning the essay will help you discover some important ideas about coherence and also about the nature of paragraphs.

When you have finished reading the essay, begin to ask yourself these questions:

1. Why did the author choose these particular spots for paragraph indentations? What purposes does the paragraphing serve?
2. What ties the paragraphs together? Words or phrases? Related subjects? Other devices? (For example, the first sentence of paragraph 11 is "And so we do." How does that sentence help tie paragraph 11 to paragraph 10?)
3. What makes for the coherence within the paragraphs? Chains of words? Adverbs? Transitional words and phrases?

In short, do as thorough a job as you can of analyzing the coherence of the essay—but don't, if you can help it, let the analysis interfere with your enjoyment of this lovely piece of writing.

On Keeping a Notebook
Joan Didion

" 'That woman Estelle,' " the note reads, " 'is partly the reason why George Sharp and I are separated today.' *Dirty crepe-de-Chine wrapper, hotel bar, Wilmington RR, 9:45 a.m. August Monday morning.*" [1]

Since the note is in my notebook, it presumably has some meaning to me. I study it for a long while. At first I have only the most general notion of what I was doing on an August Monday morning in the bar of the hotel across from the Pennsylvania Railroad station in Wilmington, Delaware (waiting for a train? missing one? 1960? 1961? why Wilmington?), but I do remember being there. The woman in the dirty crepe-de-Chine wrapper had come down from her room for a beer, and the bartender had heard before the reason why George Sharp and she were separated today. "Sure," he said, and went on mopping the floor. "You told me." At the other end of the bar is a girl. She is talking, pointedly, not to the man beside her but to a cat lying in the triangle of sunlight cast through the open door. She is wearing a plaid silk dress from Peck & Peck, and the hem is coming down. [2]

Here is what it is: the girl has been on the Eastern Shore, and now she is going back to the city, leaving the man beside her, and all she can see ahead are the viscous summer sidewalks and the 3 a.m. long-distance calls [3] that will make her lie awake and then sleep drugged through all the steaming mornings left in August (1960? 1961?). Because she must go directly from the train to lunch in New York, she wishes that she had a safety pin for the hem of the plaid silk dress, and she also wishes that she could forget about the hem and the lunch and stay in the cool bar that smells of disinfectant and malt and make friends with the woman in the crepe-de-Chine wrapper. She is afflicted by a little self-pity, and she wants to compare Estelles. That is what that was all about.

Why did I write it down? In order to remember, of course, but exactly   4 what was it I wanted to remember? How much of it actually happened? Did any of it? Why do I keep a notebook at all? It is easy to deceive oneself on all those scores. The impulse to write things down is a peculiarly compulsive one, inexplicable to those who do not share it, useful only accidentally, only secondarily, in the way that any compulsion tries to justify itself. I suppose that it begins or does not begin in the cradle. Although I have felt compelled to write things down since I was five years old, I doubt that my daughter ever will, for she is a singularly blessed and accepting child, delighted with life exactly as life presents itself to her, unafraid to go to sleep and unafraid to wake up. Keepers of private notebooks are a different breed altogether, lonely and resistant rearrangers of things, anxious malcontents, children afflicted apparently at birth with some presentiment of loss.

My first notebook was a Big Five tablet, given to me by my mother   5 with the sensible suggestion that I stop whining and learn to amuse myself by writing down my thoughts. She returned the tablet to me a few years ago; the first entry is an account of a woman who believed herself to be freezing to death in the Arctic night, only to find, when day broke, that she had stumbled onto the Sahara Desert, where she would die of the heat before lunch. I have no idea what turn of a five-year-old's mind could have prompted so insistently "ironic" and exotic a story, but it does reveal a certain predilection for the extreme which has dogged me into adult life; perhaps if I were analytically inclined I would find it a truer story than any I might have told about Donald Johnson's birthday party or the day my cousin Brenda put Kitty Litter in the aquarium.

So the point of my keeping a notebook has never been, nor is it now,   6 to have an accurate factual record of what I have been doing or thinking. That would be a different impulse entirely, an instinct for reality which I sometimes envy but do not possess. At no point have I ever been able successfully to keep a diary; my approach to daily life ranges from the grossly negligent to the merely absent, and on those few occasions when I have tried dutifully to record a day's events, boredom has so overcome me that the results are mysterious at best. What is this business about "shopping, typing piece, dinner with E, depressed"? Shopping for what? Typing what piece? Who is E? Was this "E" depressed, or was I depressed? Who cares?

In fact I have abandoned altogether that kind of pointless entry; instead   7 I tell what some would call lies. "That's simply not true," the members of my family frequently tell me when they come up against my memory of a shared event. "The party was *not* for you, the spider was *not* a black widow, *it wasn't that way at all*." Very likely they are right, for not only have I always had trouble distinguishing between what happened and what merely might have happened, but I remain unconvinced that the distinction, for my purposes, matters. The cracked crab that I recall having for lunch the day my father came home from Detroit in 1945 must certainly be embroidery, worked into the day's pattern to lend verisimilitude; I was ten years old and would not now remember the cracked crab. The day's events did not turn on cracked crab. And yet it is precisely that fictitious crab that makes me see the afternoon all over again, a home movie run all too often, the father bearing gifts, the child weeping, an exercise in family love and guilt. Or that is what it was to me. Similarly, perhaps it never did snow that August in Vermont; perhaps there never were flurries in the night wind, and maybe no one else felt the ground hardening and summer already dead even as we pretended to bask in it, but that was how it felt to me, and it might as well have snowed, could have snowed, did snow.

How it felt to me: that is getting closer to the truth about a notebook. 8 I sometimes delude myself about why I keep a notebook, imagine that some thrifty virtue derives from preserving everything observed. See enough and write it down, I tell myself, and then some morning when the world seems drained of wonder, some day when I am only going through the motions of doing what I am supposed to do, which is write—on that bankrupt morning I will simply open my notebook and there it will all be, a forgotten account with accumulated interest, paid passage back to the world out there: dialogue overheard in hotels and elevators and at the hat-check counter in Pavillon (one middle-aged man shows his hat check to another and says, "That's my old football number"); impressions of Bettina Aptheker and Benjamin Sonnenberg and Teddy ("Mr. Acapulco") Stauffer; careful *aperçus* about tennis bums and failed fashion models and Greek shipping heiresses, one of whom taught me a significant lesson (a lesson I could have learned from F. Scott Fitzgerald, but perhaps we all must meet the very rich for ourselves) by asking, when I arrived to interview her in her orchid-filled sitting room on the second day of a paralyzing New York blizzard, whether it was snowing outside.

I imagine, in other words, that the notebook is about other people. But 9 of course it is not. I have no real business with what one stranger said to another at the hat-check counter in Pavillon; in fact I suspect that the line "That's my old football number" touched not my own imagination at all, but merely some memory of something once read, probably "The Eighty-Yard Run." Nor is my concern with a woman in a dirty crepe-de-Chine wrapper in a Wilmington bar. My stake is always, of course, in the unmentioned girl in the plaid silk dress. *Remember what it was to be me:* that is always the point.

It is a difficult point to admit. We are brought up in the ethic that 10 others, any others, all others, are by definition more interesting than ourselves; taught to be diffident, just this side of self-effacing. ("You're the least important person in the room and don't forget it," Jessica Mitford's governess would hiss in her ear on the advent of any social occasion; I copied that into my notebook because it is only recently that I have been able to enter a room without hearing some such phrase in my inner ear.) Only the very young and the very old may recount their dreams at breakfast, dwell upon self, interrupt with memories of beach picnics and favorite Liberty lawn dresses and the rainbow trout in a creek near Colorado Springs. The rest of us are expected, rightly, to affect absorption in other people's favorite dresses, other people's trout.

And so we do. But our notebooks give us away, for however dutifully   11
we record what we see around us, the common denominator of all we see is always, transparently, shamelessly, the implacable "I." We are not talking here about the kind of notebook that is patently for public consumption, a structural conceit for binding together a series of graceful *pensées;* we are talking about something private, about bits of the mind's string too short to use, an indiscriminate and erratic assemblage with meaning only for its maker.

And sometimes even the maker has difficulty with the meaning. There   12
does not seem to be, for example, any point in my knowing for the rest of my life that, during 1964, 720 tons of soot fell on every square mile of New York City, yet there it is in my notebook, labeled "FACT." Nor do I really need to remember that Ambrose Bierce liked to spell Leland Stanford's name "£eland $tanford" or that "smart women most always wear black in Cuba," a fashion hint without much potential for practical application. And does not the relevance of these notes seem marginal at best?:

> In the basement museum of the Inyo County Courthouse in Indepen-
> dence, California, sign pinned to a mandarin coat: "This MANDARIN COAT
> was often worn by Mrs. Minnie S. Brooks when giving lectures on her
> TEAPOT COLLECTION."
>
> Redhead getting out of car in front of Beverly Wilshire Hotel, chinchilla
> stole, Vuitton bags with tags reading:
>
> > MRS LOU FOX
> >
> > HOTEL SAHARA
> >
> > VEGAS

Well, perhaps not entirely marginal. As a matter of fact, Mrs. Minnie   13
S. Brooks and her MANDARIN COAT pull me back into my own childhood, for although I never knew Mrs. Brooks and did not visit Inyo County until I was thirty, I grew up in just such a world, in houses cluttered with Indian relics and bits of gold ore and ambergris and the souvenirs my Aunt Mercy Farns-worth brought back from the Orient. It is a long way from that world to Mrs. Lou Fox's world, where we all live now, and is it not just as well to remem-ber that? Might not Mrs. Minnie S. Brooks help me to remember what I am? Might not Mrs. Lou Fox help me to remember what I am not?

But sometimes the point is harder to discern. What exactly did I have   14
in mind when I noted down that it cost the father of someone I know $650 a month to light the place on the Hudson in which he lived before the Crash? What use was I planning to make of this line by Jimmy Hoffa: "I may have my faults, but being wrong ain't one of them"? And although I think it inter-esting to know where the girls who travel with the Syndicate have their hair done when they find themselves on the West Coast, will I ever make suitable

use of it? Might I not be better off just passing it on to John O'Hara? What is a recipe for sauerkraut doing in my notebook? What kind of magpie keeps this notebook? *"He was born the night the Titanic went down."* That seems a nice enough line, and I even recall who said it, but is it not really a better line in life than it could ever be in fiction?

But of course that is exactly it: not that I should ever use the line, but   15
that I should remember the woman who said it and the afternoon I heard it. We were on her terrace by the sea, and we were finishing the wine left from lunch, trying to get what sun there was, a California winter sun. The woman whose husband was born the night the *Titanic* went down wanted to rent her house, wanted to go back to her children in Paris. I remember wishing that I could afford the house, which cost $1,000 a month. "Someday you will," she said lazily. "Someday it all comes." There in the sun on her terrace it seemed easy to believe in someday, but later I had a low-grade afternoon hangover and ran over a black snake on the way to the supermarket and was flooded with inexplicable fear when I heard the checkout clerk explaining to the man ahead of me why she was finally divorcing her husband. "He left me no choice," she said over and over as she punched the register. "He has a little seven-month-old baby by her, he left me no choice." I would like to believe that my dread then was for the human condition, but of course it was for me, because I wanted a baby and did not then have one and because I wanted to own the house that cost $1,000 a month to rent and because I had a hangover.

It all comes back. Perhaps it is difficult to see the value in having one's   16
self back in that kind of mood, but I do see it; I think we are well advised to keep on nodding terms with the people we used to be, whether we find them attractive company or not. Otherwise they turn up unannounced and surprise us, come hammering on the mind's door at 4 a.m. of a bad night and demand to know who deserted them, who betrayed them, who is going to make amends. We forget all too soon the things we thought we could never forget. We forget the loves and the betrayals alike, forget what we whispered and what we screamed, forget who we were. I have already lost touch with a couple of people I used to be; one of them, a seventeen-year-old, presents little threat, although it would be of some interest to me to know again what it feels like to sit on a river levee drinking vodka-and-orange-juice and listening to Les Paul and Mary Ford and their echoes sing "How High the Moon" on the car radio. (You see I still have the scenes, but I no longer perceive myself among those present, no longer could even improvise the dialogue.) The other one, a twenty-three-year-old, bothers me more. She was always a good deal of trouble, and I suspect she will reappear when I least want to see her, skirts too long, shy to the point of aggravation, always the injured party, full of recriminations and little hurts and stories I do not want to hear again, at once saddening me and angering me with her vulnerability and ignorance, an apparition all the more insistent for being so long banished.

It is a good idea, then, to keep in touch, and I suppose that keeping in   17
touch is what notebooks are all about. And we are all on our own when it comes to keeping those lines open to ourselves: your notebook will never help me, nor mine you. *"So what's new in the whiskey business?"* What could that possibly mean to you? To me it means a blonde in a Pucci bathing

suit sitting with a couple of fat men by the pool at the Beverly Hills Hotel. Another man approaches, and they all regard one another in silence for a while. "So what's new in the whiskey business?" one of the fat men finally says by way of welcome, and the blonde stands up, arches one foot and dips it in the pool, looking all the while at the cabaña where Baby Pignatari is talking on the telephone. That is all there is to that, except that several years later I saw the blonde coming out of Saks Fifth Avenue in New York with her California complexion and a voluminous mink coat. In the harsh wind that day she looked old and irrevocably tired to me, and even the skins in the mink coat were not worked the way they were doing them that year, not the way she would have wanted them done, and there is the point of the story. For a while after that I did not like to look in the mirror, and my eyes would skim the newspapers and pick out only the deaths, the cancer victims, the premature coronaries, the suicides, and I stopped riding the Lexington Avenue IRT because I noticed for the first time that all the strangers I had seen for years—the man with the seeing-eye dog, the spinster who read the classified pages every day, the fat girl who always got off with me at Grand Central!—looked older than they once had.

It all comes back. Even that recipe for sauerkraut: even that brings it back. I was on Fire Island when I first made that sauerkraut, and it was raining, and we drank a lot of bourbon and ate the sauerkraut and went to bed at ten, and I listened to the rain and the Atlantic and felt safe. I made the sauerkraut again last night and it did not make me feel any safer, but that is, as they say, another story. 18

FORMULA PARAGRAPHS

It would be difficult if not impossible to give specific instructions for writing most of the paragraphs that we have read so far. But there are some kinds of useful paragraphs that are not so difficult to explain, and for which one can give specific instructions. These are certainly not the *only* kinds of paragraphs that you will need or want to write, but they are commonly used by all writers, and they have this advantage: *anyone can produce them by following a clearly stated set of rules.* Thus, one might call them "formula" paragraphs.

These paragraphs have the following parts: (1) a *topic;* (2) a *restriction* of that topic or sometimes more than one restriction; (3) one or more *illustrations.* We will call this the *TRI* paragraph. The topic is a general statement at the beginning; the restriction is a clarification or qualification; and the illustration is an example or instance.

> *Topic*   Like almost every professional football player, I'm simply not a one-dimensional figure.

Restriction	I'm a businessman much of the time.
Illustration	I own part of the American Archery Company in Wisconsin and part of the Packer Diving Company in Louisiana.
Illustration	I'm the host of a syndicated TV show once a week during the football season, and I'm involved in half a dozen advertising ventures.
Illustration	I follow the stock market.
Illustration	I keep looking for new opportunities for investments.

—Jerry Kramer, *Instant Replay*

In the example paragraph, Jerry Kramer makes a general statement with his topic. He then qualifies and explains the topic with his restriction. Finally, he gives four illustrations.

The instructions for writing such a TRI paragraph are obvious:

1. Provide a topic.
2. Restrict (qualify, explain) it one or more times.
3. Illustrate it one or more times by giving *specific examples.*

Here is another, somewhat more complex, example of the basic TRI pattern. (Notice that the author has added a *summary* or *conclusion* to the basic pattern.)

Topic	Every generation makes mistakes, always has and always will.
Restriction	We have made our share.
Restriction	But my generation has made America the most affluent country on earth.
Illustration	It has tackled, head-on, a racial problem which no nation on earth in the history of mankind has dared to do.
Illustration	It has publicly declared war on poverty.
Illustration	and it has gone to the moon;
Illustration	it has desegregated schools and abolished polio;
Illustration	it has presided over what is probably the greatest social and economic revolution in man's history.
Summary	It has begun these things, not finished them. It has declared itself, and committed itself, and taxed itself, and damn near run itself into the ground in the cause of social justice and reform.

—K. Ross Toole, "I Am Tired of the Tyranny of Spoiled Brats," Billings, Montana, *Gazette*

Paragraph Practice

1. Choose one of the following *topics,* and by supplying one *restriction* and three *illustrations* develop a TRI paragraph.
   a. Most people are guided by the principle of self-interest, looking out for themselves before they think of others.
   b. In theory, at least, classrooms should be democratic.
   c. Television programs often appeal to our lurid interest in violence.
   d. Team sports develop the character of the players.
   e. Arguments concerning capital punishment are often based on emotion, not reason.
2. Choose another one of the preceding topics. Develop it with two restrictions and one or more illustrations. Supply a summary or conclusion.
3. Write your own topic. Restrict it with a sentence that begins with *but* or *however.* Illustrate it one or more times. For example:

Topic	The formula paragraph is easy to write.
Restriction	*However,* in the real world of writing, not all paragraphs are of this kind, though many are.
Illustration	Some paragraphs are examples in and of themselves.
Illustration	Others serve as transitions and are very brief.
Illustration	As a glance at any essay will reveal, most paragraphs do not contain illustrations.

4. Write your own topic. Restrict it with a sentence that begins with *but* or *however.* Illustrate it one or more times. Finally, provide a summary sentence or conclusion. For example:

Topic	In most cases, correct punctuation and spelling are not essential to meaning.
Restriction	*But* there are excellent reasons for spelling and punctuating correctly in much of your writing.
Illustration	Most readers will simply expect you to follow the "rules" and will be offended if you do not.
Illustration	Even though readers can gain the meaning of error-riddled texts, these errors call attention to themselves and therefore make reading for meaning more difficult.
Summary	In general, a writer who violates the obvious norms of edited standard English runs the risk of losing effectiveness with readers.

Variations on Formula Paragraphs

We have seen that some paragraphs have the parts topic, restriction(s), illustration(s): TRI. Writers can use these "building blocks" in a great variety of ways. For example, some paragraphs consist merely of a topic and a restriction or two:

Topic   Most people who are considered mentally sick (especially those confined involuntarily) are defined by their relatives, friends, employers, or perhaps the police—*not* by themselves.

Restriction   These people have upset the social order—by disregarding the conventions of polite society or by violating laws—so we label them "mentally ill" and punish them by commitment to a mental institution.

—Thomas S. Szasz, "What Psychiatry Can and Cannot Do," *Harper's Magazine*

Topic   Obedience is as basic an element in the structure of social life as one can point to.

Restriction   Some system of authority is a requirement of all communal living, and it is only the person dwelling in isolation who is not forced to respond, with defiance or submission, to the commands of others.

Restriction   For many people, obedience is a deeply ingrained behavior tendency, indeed a potent impulse overriding training in ethics, sympathy, and moral conduct.

—Stanley Milgram, *Obedience to Authority*

Other paragraphs consist of a topic and illustrations, with no restriction:

Topic   The reasons for depression are not so interesting as the way one handles it, simply to stay alive.

Illustration   This morning I woke at four and lay awake for an hour or so in a bad state. It is raining again. I got up finally and went about the daily chores, waiting for the sense of doom to lift—and what did it was watering the house plants. Suddenly joy came back because I was fulfilling a simple need, a living one.

Illustration   Dusting never has this effect (and that may be why I am such a poor housekeeper!), but feeding the cats when they are hungry, giving Punch clean water, makes me suddenly feel calm and happy.

—May Sarton, *Journal of Solitude*

In this paragraph, May Sarton tells us that the ways of handling depression are interesting, and then she illustrates two of those ways: watering her plants and feeding her cats.

Indeed, we can do all sorts of things with the Topic-Restriction-Illustration building blocks.

Notice how we can rearrange the paragraph by Jerry Kramer on pages 328–29, thereby achieving different emphasis but still having a coherent paragraph:

Illustration	I own part of the American Archery Company in Wisconsin and part of the Packer Diving Company in Louisiana.
Illustration	I'm the host of a syndicated TV show once a week during football season.
Illustration	and I'm involved in half a dozen advertising ventures.
Illustration	I follow the stock market.
Illustration	I keeping looking for new opportunities for investments.
Topic	Like almost every professional football player, I'm simply not a one-dimensional figure.
Restriction	I'm a businessman much of the time.

It would appear, then, that our handy and simple TRI formula has a great deal of versatility: (1) we can create paragraphs that contain only TR; (2) we can also create paragraphs that contain only TI; (3) we can rearrange the parts in many ways. What started out as a series of rules that appeared restrictive has become a versatile guide to the creation of paragraphs.

Varying the Formula

1. Write a paragraph containing a topic, a restriction, and two illustrations: TRII. Next, *making whatever adjustments are necessary for coherence,* rearrange the TRII form so that the paragraph is IITR.
2. Write a paragraph containing a topic and two restrictions.
3. Write a paragraph containing a topic and two illustrations. Making the adjustments necessary for coherence, change it to the form IIT.
4. Write a paragraph containing a topic, two restrictions, and one illustration: TRRI. Making the adjustments necessary for coherence, change it to the form ITRR.
5. Explain why you would be unlikely to write a paragraph containing two topics.

6. If you are using a collection of essays in your class (a "reader"), look through it to find paragraphs that use the TRI formula and its variations.

7. Following are three formula paragraphs. Use these for the body of an essay, for which you supply a *beginning* and a *concluding* paragraph. In addition to writing an introductory paragraph that will explain what is to come and a final paragraph that draws a conclusion, identify the TRI pattern in the formula paragraphs.

> Because of its wide range of subjects, *Harper's* is currently one of the most interesting magazines published in America. Its articles range from the serious to the frivolous. The June 1988 issue contains an article ("I'm Black, You're White, Who's Innocent?") on racism by Shelby Steele, a professor at San Jose State University in California. In the same issue is an article entitled "Cyclone," about the giant roller coaster at Coney Island.
>
> The *Atlantic,* one of America's oldest continuously published magazines, contains much less whimsy than does *Harper's.* It tends to be more dignified and restrained than *Harper's.* Typical articles, from the July 1988 issue, are "An Insider's View of the Election," a twenty-five-page analysis of the race for the presidency, and "The Loneliest War," a study of the war conducted by Eritrean guerrillas in Ethiopia against the central government.
>
> In contrast to *Harper's* and the *Atlantic, The New Yorker* focuses mainly on the cultural scene: music, theater, dance, art, cinema, books. However, it does print frequent reports on politics and world events. For example, the issue of April 4, 1988, contains two short fictional works, a poem, an article about auctioning art, reviews of current cinema, theater, dance, and books, and, finally, "Letter from Washington," by political analyst Elizabeth Drew.

Some Other Forms

It can be useful to look at some other obvious paragraph forms.

The following paragraph is built on an interesting plan. The author states a topic, he gives an illustration supporting that generalization, and then he restates the topic.

a.   *Topic*   America is by far the most criminal nation in the world.

Illustration   On a per capita basis, Americans commit about twice as many assaults as Frenchmen, triple the number of rapes as Italians, and five times as many murders as Englishmen.

Restatement   From the price manipulations of Westinghouse-General Electric and the mass violence of Los Angeles down to the subway muggings and the petty thievery of juvenile gangs, it is apparent, in James Truslow Adams' words, that "lawlessness has been and is one of the most distinctive American traits."

—William M. McCord, "We Ask the Wrong Questions About Crime," *New York Times Magazine*

The following two paragraphs are interesting both in their structure and in their subject matter. Look closely at how they work.

b.   FIRST PARAGRAPH

Example 1   Once another woman and I were talking about male resistance to Woman's Liberation, and she said that she didn't understand why men never worry about women taking their jobs away but worry only about the possibility that women may stop making love to them and bearing their children.

Example 2   And once I was arguing with a man I know about Woman's Liberation, and he said he wished he had a motorcycle gang with which to invade a Woman's Liberation meeting and rape everybody in it.

Conclusion based on examples   There are times when I understand the reason for men's feelings.

Explanation of conclusion   I have noticed that beyond the feminists' talk about the myth of the vaginal orgasm lies a radical resentment of their position in the sexual act. And I have noticed that when I feel most militantly feminist I am hardly at all interested in sex.

SECOND PARAGRAPH

Topic sentence for both paragraphs   Almost one could generalize from that: the feminist impulse is anti-sexual.

Restriction of the topic   The very notion of women gathering in groups is somehow anti-sexual, anti-male, just as the purposely all-male group is anti-female.

Extended illustration   There is often a sense of genuine cultural rebellion in the atmosphere of a Woman's Liberation meeting. Women sit with their legs apart, carelessly dressed, barely made-up, exhibiting their feelings or the holes at the knees of their jeans with an unprovocative candor which is hardly seen at all in the outside world. Of course, they are demonstrating by their postures that they are in effect off duty, absolved from the compulsion to make themselves attractive, and yet, as the world measures these things, such demonstrations could in themselves be seen as evidence of neurosis: we have all been brought up to believe that a woman who was "whole" would appear feminine even on the barricades.

—Sally Kempton, "Cutting Loose," *Esquire*

The second of these paragraphs is an example of a common and useful pattern: topic, one or more restrictions, and one or more illustrations.

Another common pattern is question-answer.

c. Psychotic experience goes beyond the horizons of our common, that is, our communal, sense.

Question What region of experience does this lead to?

Answers It entails a loss of the usual foundations of the "sense" of the world that we share with one another. Old purposes no longer seem viable; old meanings are senseless; the distinctions between imagination, dream, external perceptions often seem no longer to apply in the same old way. External events may seem magically conjured up. Dreams may seem to be direct communications from others; imagination may seem to be objective reality.

—R. D. Laing, *The Politics of Experience*

Here is another example of the question-answer pattern:

d. Did Babe Ruth think up and execute that wonderful, simple visit to a sick child? Or was it cooked up by his wise, hard-boiled syndicate manager or some smart newspaperman scenting a heart story that would thrill the country? I don't know. I never really wanted to know, but I remember that at the time I had my suspicions. There were too many reporters and photographers present.

—Paul Gallico, *Farewell to Sport*

Paragraph Practice

Choosing your own subjects, use the preceding example paragraphs a, b, c, and d as models for writing four paragraphs of your own. (In the case of example b, you will be writing two closely related paragraphs.)

FUNCTIONS OF PARAGRAPHS

Any piece of writing that contains more than two paragraphs has a beginning paragraph, a concluding paragraph, and body paragraphs. The paragraphs that we have dealt with so far have been "body" paragraphs, the kinds of paragraphs that develop ideas within essays. And there is yet another kind: *transitional* paragraphs, which help us get from one paragraph to another, to see the connection between the two.

The following brief essay illustrates the function of the four kinds of paragraphs.

Beginning   In this age of electronic marvels—of computers and calculators, tape recorders, television—we often forget that the book is an extremely efficient piece of technology. The glamour of the new hardware, the speed with which the machines function, the hint of futurism about them—these make books seem like quaint relics for some people.

Transition   And yet, the book has enormous advantages over all other information systems.

Body   Have you ever tried to glance quickly through the information on a computer screen, getting an almost instantaneous sense of the contents? As a matter of fact, the book allows just such sampling and riffling, for the main difference between a book and electronic devices is that the content of a book exists in space and is stationary, whereas the contents of electronic devices exist in time and are ephemeral. You can even turn the corner of a page down to help find your place, and you can make marginal notes and underline.

Body   The book is completely portable. It needs no hookups, power sources, or phone lines. You can carry it with you wherever you go, as is the case with other print media such as newspapers and magazines. If you want to make computer data portable in this way, you get a printout, which is nothing more than a kind of "book."

Transition   The book probably has less whimsical importance than has so far been indicated in this discussion.

     Body   It is just possible that the book enables humans to think in ways and with power that would be inconceivable in nonliterate electronic societies. We know, for instance, that literacy develops the logical, sequential powers of the brain's left hemisphere. The transfer of information from the printed page must be neurologically different from the transfer of information from a television screen; hence, we can safely speculate that total reliance on television for information would have a significant influence on the thought process. Furthermore, the book allows readers to get at information in "chunks" of varying sizes, and this is an important fact. For example, in reading a book on a subject that I am interested in and familiar with, I might race through one chapter, spend considerable time on a short section that contains information new to me, ponder an ambiguous sentence, and so on. In other words, I can choose my own reading speed and strategies.

Conclusion   It is unlikely that present or future electronic marvels will do away with the book. This means that the old literacy is here to stay—the old literacy and the joy that it brings to readers.

Notice in particular how the transitional paragraphs work. The first gets the reader into the subject; the second signals a change in tone and purpose.

What kinds of beginnings do professional authors use? And how do they conclude their writings?

The First Paragraph

Here are some typical kinds of opening paragraphs that you can adapt for your own writing.

A Summary Paragraph

American colleges and universities are wondering whether they are entering an era of basic changes in the relations between students and their professors. The rules of student life are probably going to be liberalized; militant undergraduates, viewing themselves not without reason as an "exploited class," will ask for more than an advisory role in the formation of courses and curriculums. A new mode of student self-government, which extends both the duties and the rights of self-discipline, is long overdue. At the same time there is a growing concern that the demands for students' "rights" may take on the character of ideological pressures on the university and pose a threat to its fundamental work as the bearer and transmitter of the heritage of science and learning. An "ideological university" has ceased to be a community of free-minded scholars.

—Lewis S. Feuer, "The Risk Is Juvenocracy," *New York Times Magazine*

This opening paragraph is a summary of the essay that follows. In fact, one could make a pretty good outline of the entire essay just by looking at the ideas in the opening paragraph. If you can write such a paragraph *before* you produce the rest of a first draft, then you will have made a great leap forward in your writing task, for it is clear that you have the body of your essay firmly in mind, and the remainder of your job is to deal with each of the ideas fully enough to satisfy the reader. Of course, we can't say whether this author wrote his opening paragraph before or after he had completed the rest of his essay.

An Unexpected Twist

The wife of a new neighbor from up on the corner came down and walked up to my wife and started acting nice, which must have exhausted her.

—Jimmy Breslin, *The World of Jimmy Breslin*

This short first paragraph does not indicate what is to come in the essay, but it is vivid and arresting; it catches the reader's interest with its unexpected twist.

A Question

Why were so few voices raised in the ancient world in protest against the ruthlessness of man? Why are human beings so obsequious, ready to kill and ready to die at the call of kings and chieftains?

—Abraham J. Heschel, *The Prophets*

An essay can begin with a general question that the body of the essay answers.

"Once Upon a Time"

There was once a town in the heart of America where all life seemed in harmony with its surroundings. The town lay in the midst of a checkerboard of prosperous farms, with fields of grain and hillsides of orchards where, in spring, white clouds of bloom drifted above the green fields. In autumn, oak and maple and birch set up a blaze of color that flamed and flickered across a backdrop of pines. Then foxes barked in the hills and deer silently crossed the fields, half hidden in the mists of the fall mornings.

—Rachel Carson, *Silent Spring*

This descriptive-narrative paragraph is a variation of the "once-upon-a-time" beginning.

A Statement of Purpose

You know you have to read "between the lines" to get the most out of anything. I want to persuade you to do something equally important in the course of your reading. I want to persuade you to "write between the lines." Unless you do, you are not likely to do the most efficient kind of reading.

—Mortimer J. Adler, "How to Mark a Book,"
Saturday Review

This is a clear, blunt statement of purpose, and it was a very effective way to start this particular essay.

An Analogy

Drawing a daily comic strip is not unlike having an English theme hanging over your head every day for the rest of your life. I was never very good at writing those English themes in high school, and I usually put them off until the last minute. The only thing that saves me in trying to keep up with a comic strip schedule is the fact that it is quite a bit more enjoyable.

—Charles M. Schulz, "But a Comic Strip Has
to Grow," *Saturday Review*

The analogy points up the main problem that a comic strip artist faces and thus indicates the direction that the essay will take.

An Anecdote

Recently I have had occasion to live again near my old college campus. I went into a hole-in-the-wall bakery where the proprietor recognized me after ten years. "You haven't changed a bit, son," he said, "but can you still digest my pumpernickel? The stomach gets older, no? Maybe you want something softer now—a nice little loaf I got here."

—Herbert Gold, *The Age of Happy Problems*

You can start an essay with an anecdote from personal experience—one that is relevant to the topic of the essay.

Using Ingenuity

The point about opening paragraphs is simple: there is no reason for every essay to begin with a simple announcement of the subject ("In the following paragraphs I intended to discuss . . ."), even though that bare, direct kind of beginning is just right for some pieces. The first paragraph you use in your final draft may be the last one that you write, but whenever you compose it, you should think of your purpose and your audience. Do you want to amuse, inform, or convince? Do you want your *tone* to be serious? Ironic? Informal? Chatty?

Exercise

If you are using a collection of essays in your class, go through them to discover the kinds of openings the authors use. If any of the beginnings interest you particularly, be prepared to explain why. (If your class does not use a "reader," you can probably borrow one from a friend or find one in the library.)

Transitional Paragraphs

Transitional paragraphs are bridges that get readers from one idea to the next; they show connections and establish relationships. In the following example, notice how the short middle paragraph allows us to go easily from the ideas of the first to the ideas of the third.

> But nothing in that end of town was as good as the dumpground that scattered along a little runoff coulee dipping down toward the river from the south bench. Through a historical process that went back, probably, to the roots of community sanitation and distaste for eyesores, but that in law dated from the Unincorporated Towns Ordinance of the territorial government, passed in 1888, the dump was one of the very first community enterprises, almost our town's first institution.
>
> More than that, it contained relics of every individual who had ever lived there, and of every phase of the town's history.
>
> The bedsprings on which the town's first child was begotten might be there; the skeleton of a boy's pet colt; two or three volumes of Shakespeare bought in haste and error from a peddler, later loaned

in carelessness, soaked with water and chemicals in a house fire, and finally thrown out to flap their stained eloquence in the prairie wind.

—Wallace Stegner, *Wolf Willow*

Transitional paragraphs can be very simple:

In Wonderland, Alice can shrink magically in an instant. Magic, though, can't shrivel prices.

Except perhaps the magic of technology.

A set of computations that cost $1.26 on an IBM computer in 1952 costs only 7/10ths of a cent today. That's because IBM scientists and engineers have put their imagination and intelligence to work to create and improve information technology.

—IBM advertisement, *Newsweek*

As a matter of fact, however, most transitions between paragraphs are words or phrases in the first sentence of the paragraph to be related to the one before it.

The best way to learn about transitions, though, is to see them in action, so read the following essay, and pay attention to all the words and phrases in italics, for they are *transitions*.

The Eureka Phenomenon
Isaac Asimov

In the old days, when I was writing a great deal of fiction, there would come, once in a while, moments when I was stymied. Suddenly, I would find I had written myself into a hole and could see no way out. To take care of that, I developed a technique which invariably worked.

It was simply this—I went to the movies. Not just any movie. I had to pick a movie which was loaded with action but which made no demands on the intellect. As I watched, I did my best to avoid any conscious thinking concerning my problem, and when I came out of the movie I knew exactly what I would have to do to put the story back on the track.

It never failed.

In fact, when I was working on my doctoral dissertation, too many years ago, I suddenly came across a flaw in my logic that I had not noticed before and that knocked out everything I had done. In utter panic, I made my way to a Bob Hope movie—and came out with the necessary change in point of view.

It is my belief, *you see,* that thinking is a double phenomenon like breathing.

You can control breathing by deliberate voluntary action: you can breathe deeply and quickly, or you can hold your breath altogether, regardless of the body's needs at the time. This, however, doesn't work well for very long. Your chest muscles grow tired, your body clamors for more oxygen, or less, and you relax. The automatic involuntary control of breathing takes over, adjusts it to the body's needs and unless you have some respiratory disorder, you can forget about the whole thing.

Well, you can think by deliberate voluntary action, too, and I don't think it is much more efficient on the whole than voluntary breath control is. You can deliberately force your mind through channels of deductions and associations in search of a solution to some problem and before long you have dug mental furrows for yourself and find yourself circling round and round the same limited pathways. If those pathways yield no solution, no amount of further conscious thought will help.

On the other hand, if you let go, then the thinking process comes under automatic involuntary control and is more apt to take new pathways and make erratic associations you would not think of consciously. The solution will then come while you think you are not thinking.

The trouble is, *though,* that conscious thought involves no muscular action and so there is no sensation of physical weariness that would force you to quit. What's more, the panic of necessity tends to force you to go on uselessly, with each added bit of useless effort adding to the panic in a vicious cycle.

It is my feeling that it helps to relax, deliberately, by subjecting your mind to material complicated enough to occupy the voluntary faculty of thought, but superficial enough not to engage the deeper involuntary one. In my case, it is an action movie; in your case, it might be something else.

I suspect it is the involuntary faculty of thought that gives rise to what we call "a flash of intuition," something that I imagine must be merely the result of unnoticed thinking.

Perhaps the most famous flash of intuition in the history of science took place in the city of Syracuse in third-century B.C. Sicily. Bear with me and I will tell you the story—

About 250 B.C., the city of Syracuse was experiencing a kind of Golden Age. It was under the protection of the rising power of Rome, but it retained a king of its own and considerable self-government; it was prosperous; and it had a flourishing intellectual life.

The king was Hieron II, and he had commissioned a new golden crown from a goldsmith, to whom he had given an ingot of gold as raw material. Hieron, being a practical man, had carefully weighed the ingot and then weighed the crown he received back. The two weights were precisely equal. Good deal!

But then he sat and thought for a while. Suppose the gold-smith had subtracted a little bit of the gold, not too much, and had substituted an equal weight of the considerably less valuable copper. The resulting alloy would still have the appearance of pure gold, but the goldsmith would be plus a quantity of gold over and above his fee. He would be buying gold with copper, so to speak, and Hieron would be neatly cheated.

Hieron didn't like the thought of being cheated any more than you or I would, but he didn't know how to find out for sure if he had been. He could scarcely punish the goldsmith on mere suspicion. What to do?

Fortunately, Hieron had an advantage few rulers in the history of the world could boast. He had a relative of considerable talent. The relative was named Archimedes and he probably had the greatest intellect the world was to see prior to the birth of Newton.

Archimedes was called in and was posed the problem. He had to determine whether the crown Hieron showed him was pure gold, or was gold to which a small but significant quantity of copper had been added.

If we were to reconstruct Archimedes' reasoning, it might go as follows. Gold was the densest known substance (at that time). Its density in modern terms is 19.3 grams per cubic centimeter. This means that a given weight of gold takes up less volume than the same weight of anything else! In fact, a given weight of pure gold takes up less volume than the same weight of any kind of impure gold.

The density of copper is 8.92 grams per cubic centimeter, just about half that of gold. If we consider 100 grams of pure gold, for instance, it is easy to calculate it to have a volume of 5.18 cubic centimeters. But suppose that 100 grams of what looked like pure gold was really only 90 grams of gold and 10 grams of copper. The 90 grams of gold would have a volume of 4.66 cubic centimeters, while the 10 grams of copper would have a volume of 1.12 cubic centimeters; for a total value of 5.78 cubic centimeters.

The difference between 5.18 cubic centimeters and 5.78 cubic centimeters is quite a noticeable one, and would instantly tell if the crown were of pure gold, or if it contained 10 per cent copper (with the missing 10 per cent of gold tucked neatly in the goldsmith's strongbox).

All one had to do, *then,* was measure the volume of the crown and compare it with the volume of the same weight of pure gold.

The mathematics of the time made it easy to measure the volume of many simple shapes: a cube, a sphere, a cone, a cylinder, any flattened object of simple regular shape and known thickness, and so on.

We can imagine Archimedes saying, "All that is necessary, sire, is to pound that crown flat, shape it into a square of uniform thickness, and then I can have the answer for you in a moment."

Whereupon Hieron must certainly have snatched the crown away and said, "No such thing. I can do that much without you; I've studied the principles of mathematics, too. This crown is a highly satisfactory work of art and I won't have it damaged. Just calculate its volume without in any way altering it."

But Greek mathematics had no way of determining the volume of anything with a shape as irregular as the crown, since integral calculus had not yet been invented (and wouldn't be for two thousand years, almost). Archimedes would have had to say, "There is no known way, sire, to carry through a non-destructive determination of volume."

"Then think of one," said Hieron testily.

And Archimedes must have set about thinking of one, and gotten nowhere. Nobody knows how long he thought, or how hard, or what hypotheses he considered and discarded, or any of the details.

What we know is that, worn out with thinking, Archimedes decided to visit the public baths and relax. I think we are quite safe in saying that Archimedes had no intention of taking his problem to the baths with him. It would be ridiculous to imagine he would, for the public baths of a Greek metropolis weren't intended for that sort of thing.

The Greek baths were a place for relaxation. Half the social aristocracy of the town would be there and there was a great deal more to do than wash. One steamed one's self, got a massage, exercised, and engaged in general socializing. We can be sure that Archimedes intended to forget the stupid crown for a while.

One can envisage him engaging in light talk, discussing the latest news from Alexandria and Carthage, the latest scandals in town, the latest funny jokes at the expense of the country-squire Romans—and then he lowered himself into a nice hot bath which some bumbling attendant had filled too full.

The water in the bath slopped over as Archimedes got in. Did Archimedes notice that at once, or did he sigh, sink back, and paddle his feet awhile before noting the water-slop. I guess the latter. But, whether soon or late, he noticed, and that one fact, added to all the chains of reasoning his brain had been working on during the period of relaxation when it was unhampered by the comparative stupidities (even in Archimedes) of voluntary thought, gave Archimedes his answer in one blinding flash of insight.

Jumping out of the bath, he proceeded to run home at top speed through the streets of Syracuse. He did not bother to put on his clothes. The thought of Archimedes running naked through Syracuse has titillated dozens of generations of youngsters who have heard this story, but I must explain that the ancient Greeks were quite light-hearted in their attitude toward nudity. They thought no more of seeing a naked man on the streets of Syracuse, than we would on the Broadway stage.

And as he ran, Archimedes shouted over and over, "I've got it! I've got it!" Of course, knowing no English, he was compelled to shout it in Greek, so it came out, "Eureka! Eureka!"

Archimedes' solution was so simple that anyone could understand it—once Archimedes explained it.

If an object that is not affected by water in any way, is immersed in water, it is bound to displace an amount of water equal to its own volume, since two objects cannot occupy the same space at the same time.

Suppose, *then,* you had a vessel large enough to hold the crown and suppose it had a small overflow spout set into the middle of its side. And suppose further that the vessel was filled with water exactly to the spout, so that if the water level were raised a bit higher, however slightly, some would overflow.

Next, suppose that you carefully lower the crown into the water. The water level would rise by an amount equal to the volume of the crown, and that volume of water would pour out the overflow and be caught in a small vessel. Next, a lump of gold, known to be pure and exactly equal in weight to the crown, is also immersed in the water and again the level rises and the overflow is caught in a second vessel.

If the crown were pure gold, the overflow would be exactly the same in each case, and the volume of water caught in the two small vessels would be equal. If, however, the crown were of alloy, it would produce a larger overflow than the pure gold would and this would be easily noticeable.

What's more, the crown would in no way be harmed, defaced, or even as much as scratched. More important, Archimedes had discovered the "principle of buoyancy."

And was the crown pure gold? I've heard that it turned out to be alloy and that the goldsmith was executed, but I wouldn't swear to it.

How often does this "Eureka phenomenon" happen? How often is there this flash of deep insight during a moment of relaxation, this triumphant cry of "I've got it! I've got it!" which must surely be a moment of the purest ecstasy this sorry world can afford?

I wish there were some way we could tell. I suspect that in the history of science it happens often; I suspect that very few significant discoveries are made by the pure technique of voluntary thought; I suspect that voluntary thought may possibly prepare the ground (if even that), but that the final touch, the real inspiration, comes when thinking is under involuntary control.

But the world is in a conspiracy to hide the fact. Scientists are wedded to reason, to the meticulous working out of consequences from assumptions to the careful organization of experiments designed to check those consequences. If a certain line of experiments ends nowhere, it is omitted from the final report. If an inspired guess turns out to be correct, it is not reported as an inspired guess. Instead, a solid line of voluntary thought is invented after the fact to lead up to the thought, and that is what is inserted in the final report.

The result is that anyone reading scientific papers would swear that nothing took place but voluntary thought maintaining a steady clumping stride from origin to destination, and that just can't be true.

It's such a shame. Not only does it deprive science of much of its glamour (how much of the dramatic story in Watson's *Double Helix* do you suppose got into the final reports announcing the great discovery of the structure of DNA?[1]), but it hands over the important process of "insight," "inspiration," "revelation" to the mystic.

The scientist actually becomes ashamed of having what we might call a revelation, as though to have one is to betray reason—when actually what we call revelation in a man who has devoted his life to reasoned thought, is after all merely reasoned thought that is not under voluntary control.

Only once in a while in modern times do we ever get a glimpse into the workings of involuntary reasoning, and when we do, it is always fascinating. Consider, for instance, the case of Friedrich August Kekule von Stradonitz.

In Kekule's time, a century and a quarter ago, a subject of great interest to chemists was the structure of organic molecules (those associated with living tissue). Inorganic molecules were generally simple in the sense that they were made up of few atoms. Water molecules, for instance, are made up of two atoms of hydrogen and one of oxygen (H_2O). Molecules of ordinary salt are made up of one atom of sodium and one of chlorine ($NaCl$), and so on.

Organic molecules, *on the other hand,* often contained a large number of atoms. Ethyl alcohol molecules have two carbon atoms,

---

[1] I'll tell you, in case you're curious. None! [Asimov's note]

six hydrogen atoms, and an oxygen atom (C_2H_6O); the molecule of ordinary cane sugar is $C_{12}H_{22}O_{11}$, and other molecules are even more complex.

Then, too, it is sufficient, in the case of inorganic molecules generally, merely to know the kinds and numbers of atoms in the molecule; in organic molecules, more is necessary. Thus, dimethyl ether has the formula C_2H_6O, just as ethyl alcohol does, and yet the two are quite different in properties. Apparently, the atoms are arranged differently within the molecules—but how to determine the arrangements?

In 1852, an English chemist, Edward Frankland, had noticed that the atoms of a particular element tended to combine with a fixed number of other atoms. This combining number was called "valence." Kekule in 1858 reduced this notion to a system. The carbon atom, he decided (on the basis of plenty of chemical evidence) had a valence of four; the hydrogen atom, a valence of one; and the oxygen atom, a valence of two (and so on).

Why not represent the atoms as their symbols plus a number of attached dashes, that number being equal to the valence. Such atoms could then be put together as though they were so many Tinker Toy units and "structural formulas" could be built up.

It was possible to reason that the structural formula of ethyl

$$\text{alcohol was} \quad \begin{array}{c} \quad H \quad\; H \\ \quad | \quad\; | \\ H-C-C-O-H \\ \quad | \quad\; | \\ \quad H \quad\; H \end{array} \quad \text{while that of dimethyl ether was}$$

$$\begin{array}{c} \;\; H \qquad\quad H \\ \;\; | \qquad\quad | \\ H-C-O-C-H \\ \;\; | \qquad\quad | \\ \;\; H \qquad\quad H \end{array}$$

In each case, there were two carbon atoms, each with four dashes attached; six hydrogen atoms, each with one dash attached; and an oxygen atom with two dashes attached. The molecules were built up of the same components, but in different arrangements.

Kekule's theory worked beautifully. It has been immensely deepened and elaborated since his day, but you can still find structures very much like Kekule's Tinker Toy formulas in any modern chemical textbook. They represent oversimplifications of the true situation, but they remain extremely useful in practice even so.

The Kekule structures were applied to many organic molecules in the years after 1858 and the similarities and contrasts in the structures neatly matched similarities and contrasts in properties. The key to the rationalization of organic chemistry had, it seemed, been found.

Yet there was one disturbing fact. The well-known chemical benzene wouldn't fit. It was known to have a molecule made up of equal numbers of carbon and hydrogen atoms. Its molecular weight was known to be 78 and a single carbon-hydrogen combination had a weight of 13. Therefore, the benzene molecule had to contain six carbon-hydrogen combinations and its formula had to be C_6H_6.

But that meant trouble. By the Kekule formulas, the hydrocarbons (molecules made up of carbon and hydrogen atoms only) could easily be envisioned as chains of carbon atoms with hydrogen atoms attached. If all the valences of the carbon atoms were filled with hydrogen atoms, as an "hexane," whose molecule looks

like this—
$$H-\overset{\overset{\displaystyle H}{|}}{\underset{\underset{\displaystyle H}{|}}{C}}-\overset{\overset{\displaystyle H}{|}}{\underset{\underset{\displaystyle H}{|}}{C}}-\overset{\overset{\displaystyle H}{|}}{\underset{\underset{\displaystyle H}{|}}{C}}-\overset{\overset{\displaystyle H}{|}}{\underset{\underset{\displaystyle H}{|}}{C}}-\overset{\overset{\displaystyle H}{|}}{\underset{\underset{\displaystyle H}{|}}{C}}-\overset{\overset{\displaystyle H}{|}}{\underset{\underset{\displaystyle H}{|}}{C}}-H$$
the compound is said

to be saturated. Such saturated hydrocarbons were found to have very little tendency to react with other substances.

If some of the valences were not filled, unused bonds were added to those connecting the carbon atoms. Double bonds were formed as in "hexene"—

$$H-\overset{\overset{\displaystyle H}{|}}{\underset{\underset{\displaystyle H}{|}}{C}}-\overset{\overset{\displaystyle H}{|}}{\underset{\underset{\displaystyle H}{|}}{C}}-\overset{\overset{\displaystyle H}{|}}{C}=\overset{\overset{\displaystyle H}{|}}{C}-\overset{\overset{\displaystyle H}{|}}{\underset{\underset{\displaystyle H}{|}}{C}}-\overset{\overset{\displaystyle H}{|}}{\underset{\underset{\displaystyle H}{|}}{C}}-H$$

Hexene is unsaturated, for that double bond has a tendency to open up and add other atoms. Hexene is chemically active.

When six carbons are present in a molecule, it takes fourteen hydrogen atoms to occupy all the valence bonds and make it inert—as in hexane. In hexene, on the other hand, there are only twelve hydrogens. If there were still fewer hydrogen atoms, there would be more than one double bond; there might even be triple bonds, and the compound would be still more active than hexene.

Yet benzene, which is C_6H_6 and has eight fewer hydrogen atoms than hexane, is less active than hexene, which has only two fewer hydrogen atoms than hexane. In fact, benzene is even less active than hexane itself. The six hydrogen atoms in the benzene molecule seem to satisfy the six carbon atoms to a greater extent than do the fourteen hydrogen atoms in hexane.

For heaven's sake, why?

This might seem unimportant. The Kekule formulas were so beautifully suitable in the case of so many compounds that one might simply dismiss benzene as an exception to the general rule.

Science, *however,* is not English grammar. You can't just categorize something as an exception. If the exception doesn't fit into the general system, then the general system must be wrong.

Or, take the more positive approach. An exception can often be made to fit into a general system, provided the general system is broadened. Such broadening generally represents a great advance and for this reason, exceptions ought to be paid great attention.

For some seven years, Kekule faced the problem of benzene and tried to puzzle out how a chain of six carbon atoms could be completely satisfied with as few as six hydrogen atoms in benzene and yet be left unsatisfied with twelve hydrogen atoms in hexene.

Nothing came to him!

And then one day in 1865 (he tells the story himself) he was in Ghent, Belgium, and in order to get to some destination, he boarded a public bus. He was tired and, undoubtedly, the droning beat of the horses' hooves on the cobblestones, lulled him. He fell into a comatose half-sleep.

In that sleep, he seemed to see a vision of atoms attaching themselves to each other in chains that moved about. (Why not? It was the sort of thing that constantly occupied his waking thoughts.) But then one chain twisted in such a way that head and tail joined, forming a ring—and Kekule woke with a start.

To himself, he must surely have shouted "Eureka," for indeed he had it. The six carbon atoms of benzene formed a ring and not a chain, so that the structural formula looked like this:

To be sure, there were still three double bonds, so you might think the molecule had to be very active—but now there was a difference. Atoms in a ring might be expected to have different properties from those in a chain and double bonds in one case might not have the properties of those in the other. At least, chemists could work on that assumption and see if it involved them in contradiction.

It didn't. The assumption worked excellently well. It turned out that organic molecules could be divided into two groups: aromatic and aliphatic. The former had the benzene ring (or certain other similar rings) as part of the structure and the latter did not. Allowing for different properties within each group, the Kekule structures worked very well.

For nearly seventy years, Kekule's vision held good in the hard field of actual chemical techniques, guiding the chemist through the jungle of reactions that led to the synthesis of more and more molecules. Then, in 1932, Linus Pauling applied quantum mechanics to chemical structure with sufficient subtlety to explain just why the benzene ring was so special and what had proven correct in practice proved correct in theory as well.

Other cases? Certainly.

In 1764, the Scottish engineer James Watt was working as an instrument maker for the University of Glasgow. The university gave him a model of a Newcomen steam engine, which didn't work well, and asked him to fix it. Watt fixed it without trouble, but even when it worked perfectly, it didn't work well. It was far too inefficient and consumed incredible quantities of fuel. Was there a way to improve that?

Thought didn't help; but a peaceful, relaxed walk on a Sunday afternoon did. Watt returned with the key notion in mind of using two separate chambers, one for steam only and one for cold water only, so that the same chamber did not have to be constantly cooled and reheated to the infinite waste of fuel.

The Irish mathematician William Rowan Hamilton worked up a theory of "quaternions" in 1843 but couldn't complete that theory until he grasped the fact that there were conditions under which $p \times q$ was not equal to $q \times p$. The necessary thought came to him in a flash one time when he was walking to town with his wife.

The German physiologist Otto Loewi was working on the mechanism of nerve action, in particular, on the chemicals produced by nerve endings. He awoke at 3 A.M. one night in 1921 with a perfectly clear notion of the type of experiment he would have to run to settle a key point that was puzzling him. He wrote it down and went back to sleep. When he woke in the morning, he found he couldn't remember what his inspiration had been. He remembered he had written it down, but he couldn't read his writing.

The next night, he woke again at 3 A.M. with the clear thought once more in mind. This time, he didn't fool around. He got up, dressed himself, went straight to the laboratory and began work. By 5 A.M. he had proved his point and the consequences of his findings became important enough in later years so that in 1936 he received a share in the Nobel prize in medicine and physiology.

How very often this sort of thing must happen, and what a shame that scientists are so devoted to their belief in conscious thought that they so consistently obscure the actual methods by which they obtain their results.

Conclusions

Conclusions bring a piece of writing to an end. They should not introduce new topics that leave the reader hanging. The following is the last paragraph of an essay on how off-road vehicles are ruining the desert, but notice that it does not really conclude, for it introduces a whole new line of thought about which the reader will be curious.

> The California desert is part of one of the largest relatively unbroken stretches of wild land left in the United States. Now it is threatened by off-road vehicles and could be ruined. More interesting than the desert, however, is the damage that small motorized vehicles are doing to mountain forests and even the arctic tundra.

The writer has introduced a subject "more interesting" than the one covered in the essay, namely, damage to forests and the arctic tundra. The reader has every right to expect that these subjects should be developed.

The actual ending of the essay does not introduce new subject matter, and thus it really concludes:

> The California desert is part of one of the largest relatively unbroken stretches of wild land left in the United States outside Alaska. Now it is threatened and could become the genuine wasteland we once thought deserts to be. The smoke tree and the desert tortoise, the ironwood and Gambel's quail, the intaglios and the petroglyphs are

disappearing. It is not yet too late, but the desert is a fragile place and cannot survive forever strip-mining by our adult playthings.

—David Sheridan, "Dirty Motorbikes and Dune Buggies Threaten Deserts," *Smithsonian*

Conclusions now and then provide a summary of the piece that they end, but if an essay is relatively brief, the reader does not really need a summary.

It is very difficult to talk about conclusions out of context. A good piece of advice is this: watch the conclusions of the essays and other materials that you read. By doing this, you can learn a great deal about how to end your own writings.

DEVELOPMENT

Here is a simple and important point about paragraphs: if they are not used just to show transitions or to isolate ideas for emphasis, *they need to be developed.* So far, you have seen that paragraphs can be developed with restrictions and illustrations, and you have read a discussion of the functions of paragraphs. On pages 105–15 of chapter 5, "Exposition," you had a useful and thorough discussion of methods of development, illustrating how writers use comparison and contrast, classification, definition, data, and other techniques to make the main ideas of their paragraphs specific.

Often you need only sense detail, or imagery, to develop your paragraphs. For example, James Thurber *might* have written this:

The room was big, and from its windows I could see the yard.

In fact, the room and the yard were important for his story "Remembrance of Things Past," and here is what he wrote about them:

The room was long and high and musty, with a big, soft bed, and windows that looked out on the courtyard of the place. It was like a courtyard, anyway, in form and in feeling. It should have held old wagon wheels and busy men in leather aprons, but the activity I remember was that of several black-and-white kittens stalking each other in a circular bed of red geraniums, which, of course, is not like a courtyard, but nevertheless I remember the place in front of the house as being like a courtyard. A courtyard, let us say, with black-and-white kittens stalking each other in a circular bed of red geraniums.

This paragraph is packed with sense details: the room *smells* musty; the bed *feels* soft; we *see* the black-and-white kittens and the red geraniums.

And notice how specific and detailed is the following paragraph from "Holiday Memory," by Dylan Thomas. (The bank holiday is celebrated in Great Britain in mid-August.)

August Bank Holiday—a tune on an ice-cream cornet. A slap of sea and a tickle of sand. A fanfare of sunshades opening. A wince and whinny of bathers dancing into deceptive water. A tuck of dresses. A rolling of trousers. A compromise of paddlers. A sunburn of girls and a lark of boys. A silent hullabaloo of balloons.

This paragraph does not even contain sentences, just a series of images expressed in phrases.

Exercise

By supplying one vivid *image*, develop a paragraph on one of the following topics:

a. Registration at my college is chaos.
b. Scenes of nature can be awesome.
c. The game was a battle to the death.
d. Christmas morning was a blur of sounds, tastes, and colors.
e. It sometimes takes courage to try new foods.

If none of these topics appeal to you, invent your own. Here is an example:

Doing exercises for composition is excruciating. The student sits at his desk, his brow wrinkled, his muscles tense, his mind as blank as the page before him. His pen hovers above the sheet, trembling, but does not make contact. Minutes elapse, dripping away one by one, like intravenous fluid from a bottle suspended above a patient. The glare of the lamp makes a circle of brightness in the icy darkness of the room as the hopeful learner waits for inspiration to strike.

FINALLY

In conclusion, I would like to say that . . .

No! That sort of trite statement will never serve to end this chapter—or anything else. A conclusion such as the one that I just started is enough to make any reader yawn, and who wants the last response of the readers to be a yawn (or a groan)? Instead, I'll end this chapter by purposely making it seem incomplete, by injecting, right here at the end, a note of inconclusiveness, thus:

This chapter has covered much territory, but has left some territory uncovered, for the subject of paragraphs is a very big one. Do you have any questions concerning paragraphs that the chapter has aroused but not answered?

12
Rewriting Sentences

Common sense might tell you that short sentences are easier to read than long ones, but in this case common sense turns out to be nonsense, as the structure of a sentence is more important for its readability than its length is.[1] We can demonstrate this point with the following two sentences, each of which contains eleven words:

1. A good teacher explains all concepts very clearly to his students.
2. In explanation of concepts to students a good teacher is clear.

Sentence 1 is easier to read, even though both sentences convey the same idea.

Here are further examples of how sentence structure affects readability:

3a. Mary turned off the lights that Jim turned on.
3b. Mary turned the lights that Jim turned on off.

4a. I can write difficult sentences without even trying.
4b. Difficult sentences can be written by me without even trying.

5a. It is unbelievable that Herb thinks that Bert told Mary that Helen is rude.

5b. That Herb thinks that Bert told Mary that Helen is rude is unbelievable.

The "Reference Guide" contains further discussion on sentences. See especially pages 456–68.

REWRITING SENTENCES FOR CLARITY

There are a few learnable and simple principles for writing readable prose, and it is to these that we will now turn.

Closure

Both of the following sentences are difficult to read:

1. A handsome, efficiently typing, bilingual secretary can always get a good job.
2. That to talk to the people of a foreign country we must learn their language sufficiently well to convey our meanings seems perfectly obvious.

They are difficult because we must overload our short-term memories in order to gain the meaning. In sentence 1, for instance, the words *handsome, efficiently typing,* and *bilingual* must be held in short-term memory until *secretary,* the noun that they modify, is reached. And in 2, twenty-three words must be held in mind until the final word, *obvious.*

What has been said so far should conform to your own experience, particularly when you compare examples 1 and 2 with rewritten versions that are easier to read:

1a. A handsome, bilingual secretary who types efficiently can always get a good job.
2a. It seems perfectly obvious that to talk to the people of a foreign country we must learn their language sufficiently well to convey our meanings.

Because of the nature of the human mind, 1a and 2a are easier to read for *all* readers, not just for some.

A bit of detail about sentence 1 will clarify this point. The adjectives *handsome, efficiently typing,* and *bilingual* must relate to a noun, since adjectives modify nouns. This means that the reader must, in fact, keep three questions in mind, questions that cannot be answered until the noun is reached:

Who is *handsome?*
Who is *efficiently typing?*
Who is *bilingual?*

The adjectives cannot be totally processed for meaning until they are related to *secretary*—another way of saying that *closure is delayed.* In 1a, however, closure is not delayed as long as it is in 1, for the reader can "process" *handsome* and *bilingual* as soon as the noun *secretary* is reached and can then process the modifying clause *who types efficiently.*

The principle is this: the more a reader must keep in mind before achieving semantic closure, the more difficult the reading will be. (For this reason, periodic sentences are often more difficult to read than their loose versions. See pages 375–79.)

Explaining sentence 2 is more difficult, and a completely accurate account of its difficulty would take several pages, but in general the difficulty is this: the reader must keep everything in short-term memory until the last word of the sentence, *obvious,* which is the true predicate. What the reader must keep in mind is three complete propositions, which might be represented like this:

[we] to talk to the people of a foreign country
we must learn their language sufficiently well
[we] to convey our meanings

The following examples give a hard-to-read sentence, an explanation of the problem, and a more readable version:

3. A snow-capped, sublime, jaggedly rising mountain peak was silhouetted against the horizon.

   EXPLANATION: We cannot "process" the modifiers *snow-capped, sublime,* and *jaggedly rising* until we reach the noun phrase that they modify: *mountain peak.*

   REVISION: A jagged mountain peak, snow-capped and sublime, was silhouetted against the horizon.

4. Whatever the family couldn't buy at the country store located at the crossroads five miles from town they did without.

   EXPLANATION: Until the reader comes to the main clause, *they did without,* he or she cannot determine how the subordinate (noun) clause will relate. The subordinate clause consists of seventeen words, putting a great strain on short-term memory: *Whatever the family couldn't buy at the country store located at the crossroads five miles from town.*

REVISION: The family did without whatever they couldn't buy at the country store located at the crossroads five miles from town.

5. The program was a concert of relatively pleasant newly discovered Appalachian dulcimer music.

   EXPLANATION: The noun phrase *dulcimer music* is preceded by too many modifiers that must be held in suspension.

   REVISION: The program was a concert of relatively pleasant dulcimer music that had been newly discovered in Appalachia.

6. Fixing a broken dishwasher, without the proper tools, can be difficult.

   EXPLANATION: The phrase *without the proper tools* interrupts the sentence and delays the process of reaching the pivot word, *difficult.*

   REVISION: Fixing a broken dishwasher can be difficult without the proper tools.

7. To bake potatoes on an open bonfire, as we did when we were kids, was always a great adventure.

   EXPLANATION: The interrupting clause *as we did when we were kids* delays closure.

   REVISION: It was always a great adventure to bake potatoes on an open bonfire, as we did when we were kids.

All this technical detail aside, most of us can recognize and improve difficult sentences, if we pay attention. And, of course, such attention to readability and the effort to achieve it are extremely worthwhile, for *the best style is that which expresses the writer's meaning and intention with the least effort for the reader.* If part of your intention is to write a difficult sentence, then the less readable version is better than the more readable one. But, of course, most of the time we want to express our ideas so that they can be understood with a minimum of effort. As a rule, we want our prose to be relatively straightforward rather than relatively complicated.

This is not to say that all reading can be made easy for any or all readers. Difficult ideas are hard to grasp, regardless of how well the writer constructs the sentences in which they appear. It is perverse, however, to *want* to make difficult ideas even more difficult by expressing them in unreadable sentences.

Exercise

1. All the following sentences can be made more readable. Play around with them until you feel that you have created more readable versions *without changing their basic meaning.* You might want to test your revisions by asking the opinions of some of your classmates.

   a. That Herman thought that Hermione believed that Herbert was a thief was tragic.
   b. The child threw the mush that it had forced down up.
   c. The rapidly rising, disastrous, unnecessary rate of inflation must be controlled.
   d. To learn history, a fascinating subject that most people know little about, takes time and intelligence.
   e. What we once thought was necessary for the good life we have found we can do away with without any trouble.
   f. The conclusively predicted spring flood was upon us.
   g. Asking questions that are likely to bring productive answers in regard to any problem is a skill that can be developed.
   h. Students complaining about grading standards that instructors adopt are usually those who are doing poorly in classes.
   i. To write sentences that are hard to read, I am discovering, is sometimes more difficult than writing readable sentences.
   j. George is eager to help when the opportunity arises anyone who is in trouble.
   k. Often exemplary poorly constructed exercise sentences such as this one or the one above, which have been cooked up out of context, sound artificial.
   l. Whenever the surf is up is the time when I load my surfboard in the car and head for the beach.
   m. It is a custom in our family on Saturday afternoon to wash and polish our cars.
   n. What, since I am the world's greatest expert on the subject, you say about fishing, people's most glorious recreation, I completely deny.
   o. Over the fence to the cow some hay the farmers threw.

2. In your own writing, find ten sentences that can be made more readable. On a sheet of paper, write each one, and below it write an improved version.

Subjects and Doers

Typically, a sentence has a subject and a predicate, a concept that is more easily illustrated than explained:

SUBJECT	PREDICATE
The girl	ran ten kilometers.
She	won the race.
The Constitution of the United States of America	guarantees the principle of trial by a jury of one's peers.
Whatever you say	must be the truth.

In sentences that express an action, the doer of the action is called the *agent,* but the agent and the subject are not always the same. Compare the following sentences, all of which mean roughly the same thing:

1. Bill hit the nail with a hammer.
2. The nail was hit with a hammer by Bill.
3. A hammer was what Bill hit the nail with.

In all three sentences, Bill is the *agent,* the person who performs the action of hitting, but only in sentence 1 is Bill the *subject.*

In general, *those sentences in which the subject and the agent are identical are the most readable.* In each of the following examples, the *a* version is easier to read than the *b* version, since in the *a* versions subject and agent are identical.

4a. *Bertrand* teased Mary about her bad habit.
4b. Mary's bad habit was the reason for *Bertrand's* teasing her.

5a. *Alyosha* enjoyed caviar, a taste that was very expensive.
5b. The enjoyment of caviar by *Alyosha* was a very expensive taste.

6a. *Marvin* gave Moira a sloppy kiss.
6b. A sloppy kiss was given to Moira by *Marvin.*

7a. *Myrtle* grew petunias as a hobby.
7b. Growing petunias was *Myrtle's* hobby.

As you can see, in the *b* versions of the sentences, the agent—the doer of the action—has been displaced from the subject position, thus decreasing readability.

All this is simple enough, but there are some complications. Finite verbs like *teased, enjoyed, gave,* and *grew* obviously have subjects: "Bertrand teased . . . Alyosha enjoyed . . . Marvin gave . . . Myrtle grew . . . ." Although less obviously, nonfinite verbs also have subjects in sentences. The nonfinite verb forms that we will be concerned with are infinitives (*to tease, to enjoy, to give, to grow*) and present participles (*teasing, enjoying, giving, growing*).

8. FINITE VERB: My friend Kyoko *makes* sushi.
8a. INFINITIVE: My friend Kyoko likes *to make* sushi.
8b. PRESENT PARTICIPLE: My friend Kyoko enjoys *making* sushi.

Why do we say that *to make* in 8a and *making* in 8b have subjects? Simply because we must know who is performing the action or we cannot understand the sentence. In a way, when we read the sentences we supply the subjects:

8aa. My friend Kyoko likes [Kyoko (implied subject)] *to make* sushi.
8bb. My friend Kyoko enjoys [Kyoko (implied subject)] *making* sushi.

Another example. In sentence 9, we know that it is Ted who is doing the pleasing, but in 10 it is Ted who is being pleased. The implied subjects and objects are in brackets.

9. Ted is eager to please.
   Ted is eager [Ted] to please [someone].

10. Ted is easy to please.
    Ted is easy [someone] to please [Ted].

In 11, we know that the subject of *To become* must be *you.*

11. To become a millionaire, you must be lucky.

In 12, we know that the subject of *Fighting* must be *Naomi.*

12. Fighting the violent wind, Naomi struggled onward.

And in 13, we know that the subject of *Having graduated* must be *Irma.*

13. Having graduated from college, Irma began to look for a job.

The problem with the following sentences is that there is momentary confusion about the subjects of the nonfinite verbs.

14. *Darting* under a mossy rock, the trout was seen by us.
    (We saw the trout *darting* under a mossy rock.)

15. *To save* time, the shortcut must be taken.
    (*To save* time, you should take the shortcut.)

16. The child was found by us *hiding* in the closet.
    (We found the child *hiding* in the closet.)

17. Not *to proceed* without chains was told us by the policeman.
(The policeman told us not *to proceed* without chains.)

The principles, then, are very easy: (1) In the most readable sentences, the doers of the actions (the agents) are also the subjects. (2) If the reader cannot immediately supply the agent for a nonfinite verb in a sentence, the sentence will be confusing and hence difficult to read.

Exercise

You can improve the readability of *some* of the following sentences by revising them so that the doer of the action (the agent) and the subject coincide. If you feel that the sentence is easily readable as it stands, do not revise.

1. The cake was baked by Mary in the oven.
2. A screwdriver is what Bill opened the can with.
3. The captain of the ship hosted a reception for the passengers.
4. Playing marbles is enjoyed by the children.
5. All my friends like to attend ball games.
6. To clean chicken coops is detested by everyone I know.
7. With great enthusiasm Alvin set out on the hike.
8. To become an investment banker is the reason Lola wanted to attend college.
9. Lack of time was why the job wasn't completed by the crew.
10. A cup of strong tea is what I drink every morning.
11. Don't forget to take your pills before you go to bed.
12. To leave the key with the desk clerk should not be forgotten by guests who are checking out.
13. Taking the bus is the best way for residents to get to the park.
14. To take a taxi to the Music Center is the quickest way for concertgoers to get there.
15. Growing up in the city is found to be difficult by many youngsters.
16. Living in the country has advantages for many youngsters.
17. The members of the club, once a wild party was held by them in the Student Union Building, and to punish them they were put on academic probation by the dean.
18. Fame and fortune—that's the reason I'm studying to be an English teacher.
19. What Elvira explained to us was that we needed baking powder to make biscuits.
20. Hesitating because he was not sure which button to push, Jurgen stood before the soft drink dispenser.

Nouns Versus Verbs

Many verbs have noun equivalents, for example:

VERB	NOUN
act	action
complete	completion
decide	decision
grow	growth
hate	hatred
illuminate	illumination
resolve	resolution

It is a general rule that ideas expressed with verbs are more readable than ideas expressed with nouns.

Which sentences in the following pairs do you think are most readable?

1a. I *acted* foolishly.
1b. My *action* was foolish.

2a. When we *completed* the course, we took the final test.
2b. Upon *completion* of the course, we took the final test.

3a. I hope that you *decide* to take the course.
3b. I hope that your *decision* is to take the course.

4a. Everyone knows that corn *grows* tall in Iowa.
4b. Everyone knows about the tall *growth* of corn in Iowa.

5a. Gregory tried to conceal the fact that he *hated* Mary.
5b. Gregory tried to conceal the fact of his *hatred* for Mary.

Undoubtedly, the *a* versions are easier to read, a claim that you can test by submitting them to one group of good readers and the *b* versions to another group and clocking the reading speed.

The following two passages dramatically illustrate this principle. Though both convey nearly the same information, the first passage, which uses verbs, is more readable than the second version, which is loaded with nouns.

> To write readable prose, you must follow certain principles. For example, express your ideas with verbs rather than nouns whenever possible; try to make subject and agent coincide; and avoid uncommon words. At times, however, the less readable version of a sentence will fulfill your purpose better than the more readable one. You must use judgment.

To write readable prose, *the following* of certain principles is necessary, for example, *the expression* of ideas with verbs rather than nouns, *the coincidence* of subject and agent, and *the avoidance* of uncommon words. At times, however, *the fulfillment* of your purpose is better achieved with the less readable version of a sentence than with the more readable one. *The use* of judgment is necessary.

We have seen that finite verbs can be turned into nouns, as when we write *my failure* rather than *I failed:*

6a. I knew about *my failure* on the test.
6b. I knew that *I failed* the test.

Exactly the same principle applies with nonfinite verbs.

NONFINITE VERBS	NOUNS
Some farmers raise turkeys *to supplement* their incomes.	Some farmers raise turkeys for *the supplementation* of their incomes.
Fernando denied *having associated* himself with the dissenters.	Fernando denied *the association* of himself with the dissenters.
To avoid sickness, you must eat the proper food.	For *the avoidance* of sickness, you must eat the proper food.
Criticizing a play is easy, but writing one is difficult.	*The criticism* of a play is easy, but writing one is difficult.

Strangely enough, there is evidence that some readers prefer the nominal style even though it is less readable. They seem to feel that the ideas expressed with nouns are more profound than those expressed with verbs, fancier and more philosophical. This observation, of course, brings us right back to one of our main principles: when we write, we must consider our purpose and the audience for whom we are writing. Out of context, nothing in language is good or bad.

Exercise

Some of the following sentences use nouns where verbs could express the same meanings. Rewrite those sentences, changing them from the nominal to the verbal style. You will probably feel that some of the sentences do not need revision.

1. The appearance of the comet was low over the horizon.
2. Many scholars use their knowledge for the intimidation of others.

3. Marylou's success was in convincing the judge that she was innocent.
4. Because of its excitement of great interest, the new opera was a financial success.
5. Sometimes one asks whether or not all of the work to get a college degree is worthwhile.
6. Most students think that the failure of a course is tragic.
7. The construction of a good alibi is difficult.
8. Building a solid reputation for reliability is not easy.
9. Farley enjoyed the refusal of any request received.
10. Acceptance of responsibility for your actions is a must.
11. Publication of the stories of E. M. Forster was by Knopf.
12. For the achievement of success, you must work hard unless the inheritance of your rich uncle's money happens to you.
13. Unquestionably the greatest health hazard today is cigarette smoking.
14. The Hatfields were eager in their connivance against the McCoys, for neither family wanted settlement of the feud.
15. Because Marlene planned the commission of a murder, she was saving for the purchase of a shotgun.
16. When I first made the collection of them, the stamps had only face value.
17. Because the rivers were flooding, schools were closed in Rock Island and Davenport.
18. In his attempt at proof that the language was decaying, Harvey did not fail to quote his beloved Dr. Johnson.
19. The suggestion of the committee was for the erection of a monument to honor Vronsky by the city.
20. With its abstraction and frequent angularity, modern art leaves many viewers cold.
21. It is unwise to drink the water when contamination by raw sewage has taken place.
22. Finally, the coast glimmered into view, the sandstone cliffs of Laguna rising from the blue of the calm sea.
23. The attempt at argument against a dogmatic person is a frustration to most of us.
24. The orchestration of the concerto for Berman was by Bernstein.
25. The milking of a wild cow by anyone takes patience and strong hands.

Sentence Sequences

So far, we have dealt with the readability of individual sentences, but readers also must easily be able to see how one sentence relates to the next. A string of clear but unrelated sentences amounts to an unreadable passage. One of the main principles in creating readable passages involves the content of sentences.

Every sentence consists of a topic and a comment on that topic (or information about it). For example, in

1. Norma brought the lunch.

Norma is the topic, and *brought the lunch* is the comment. The topic is frequently the subject of the sentence, but it need not be. In

2. As to the sentence, it is the basic unit of language.

the sentence is the topic, *is the basic unit of language* is the comment, and *it* is the subject.

In the following examples, the topic is printed in *italics* and the comment is in capital letters.

3. Nowadays *farming* IS BIG BUSINESS.
4. In the *agribusiness*, THERE ARE MANY RISKS.
5. CARE by *the farmer* SHOULD BE EXERCISED IN CHOOSING WHAT CROPS HE WILL PLANT DURING THE SEASON.

As a general rule, a passage of writing is more readable if the topics of the sentences in it do not shift unnecessarily. In the following example, each sentence has a different topic, with the result that the passage is somewhat difficult to read:

6. As their name implies, *structural linguists* analyze the structure of language. *Transformational generative grammar* attempts to explain how the human brain creates language. *The control of language* is not the purpose of the science of linguistics.

Without loss of essential meaning, this passage can be rewritten so that it is more readable:

7. As their name implies, *structural linguists* analyze the structure of language. *Transformational generative linguists* attempt to explain how the human brain creates language. Neither *structural* nor *transformational generative linguists* presume to control language.

In passage 6, the topics are *structural linguists, transformational generative grammar,* and *the control of language.* But in passage 7, all of the topics have *linguists* as their main element.

Example 8 is easier to read than 9, for the topics in 8 are all related in meaning:

8. *The writer* does not need a theoretical knowledge of grammar, but often must have a sure command of language to avoid offending readers. *He* must be able to produce well-edited texts that contain no serious errors in such matters as verb agreement and pronoun reference. However, if he pays too much attention to these matters during the writing process, *the beginner* may find that the well of ideas dries up.

9. *The writer* does not need a theoretical knowledge of grammar, but often must have a sure command of language to avoid offending readers. *The well-edited text* contains no serious errors in such matters as verb agreement and pronoun reference. However, *too much attention* to these matters during the writing process may dry up the well of ideas.

In example 8, all the topics relate to "the writer," but in 9, the topics do not have this close relationship: *the writer, the well-edited text, too much attention.* This diversity makes 9 more difficult to read than 8.

The topic-comment principle is not an absolute, but it is a concept worth paying attention to. Especially in paragraphs, if topics shift unnecessarily from sentence to sentence, coherence disappears, and "incoherence" and "unreadability" are synonymous. (Pages 320–22 in this book also deal with the concept of paragraph unity.)

REWRITING SENTENCES FOR FLUENCY

When you read the following passage, you will probably have the sense that the expression of ideas is out of kilter:

The core of the good ole boy's world is with his buddies. It is the comfortable, all-male camaraderie. It is hyperhearty. It is joshing. It is drinking. It is regaling one another with tales of assorted, exaggerated prowess. Women are outsiders. Some social events are unavoidably mixed. Then the good ole boys cluster together at one end of the room. They leave wives at the other. The GOB's magic doesn't work with women. He feels insecure. He feels threatened by them. In fact, he doesn't really like women. He likes them only in bed.

You might say that the passage is choppy or even a bit incoherent. As a reader, you probably had some trouble determining how the ideas related to one another. The passage is simply not fluent.

It is a mangled version of a passage written by Bonnie Angelo, London bureau chief for *Time* magazine. Here is the original version:

> The core of the good ole boy's world is with his buddies, the comfortable, all-male camaraderie, joshing and drinking and regaling one another with tales of assorted, exaggerated prowess. Women are outsiders; when social events are unavoidably mixed, the good ole boys cluster together at one end of the room, leaving wives at the other. The GOB's magic doesn't work with women; he feels insecure, threatened by them. In fact, he doesn't really like women, except in bed.
>
> —"Those Good Ole Boys"

You will probably agree that this fluent version just sounds better—seems to have been produced by a more skilled writer and, perhaps, even a more intelligent person. Furthermore, the fluent version is much easier to read, for the relationships among the ideas are shown by the sentence structure, the writer having done the grouping that the reader must do for himself or herself in the choppy first version.

Here is an interesting experiment that you can easily perform. Show the following passages 1 and 2 to ten of your fellow students (who are not in your English class and thus have not been tipped off). Tell them that two writers answered the question "What does the gesture of tapping the temple mean?" After your subjects have read the passages, ask them the following questions: (1) Which passage "sounds" better? (2) Which passage is easier to read? (3) Which writer is more intelligent?

1. *Tapping the Temple*
   Many people understand this as a sign of stupidity. You might instead twist your forefinger against your temple. This makes the meaning more precise. It indicates "a screw loose." You might rotate your forefinger close to your temple. This signals that the brain is going round and round. But even these actions would be confusing to some people. In Saudi Arabia stupidity can be signaled by touching the lower eyelid with the tip of the forefinger. Other local stupidity gestures include tapping the elbow of the raised forearm. They also include flapping the hand up and down in front of half-closed eyes. Also, they include rotating a raised hand or laying one finger flat across the forehead.

2. *Tapping the Temple*

Many people understand this as a sign of stupidity. To make the meaning more precise, you might instead twist your forefinger against your temple, indicating "a screw loose," or rotate your forefinger close to your temple, signaling that the brain is going round and round. But even these actions would be confusing to some people. In Saudi Arabia, for example, stupidity can be signaled by touching the lower eyelid with the tip of the forefinger. Other local stupidity gestures include tapping the elbow of the raised forearm, flapping the hand up and down in front of half-closed eyes, rotating a raised hand, or laying one forefinger flat across the forehead.

The second passage is by the zoologist and author Desmond Morris, from *Manwatching*. As some of the subjects in your experiment might realize, the first passage is a mangled rewrite of the second.

If the experiment works as it is intended, most subjects will say that the second passage sounds better, is easier to read, and is written by the more intelligent author. However, both convey exactly the same information about gestures. The essential difference—as you will see if you compare the two passages—is in the style.

In general, then, fluent prose is more effective than prose that stops, starts, and stutters—though sometimes, for specific reasons, you may want your prose to lack fluency. You should, however, have the ability to write the kind of prose that best fits your purpose in communicating with a given audience.

Exercise

Most people have a great deal of skill in writing fluent prose, an ability that perhaps they are unaware of. You can make a rough test of your own ability to create fluent prose. Here are examples of how short sentences can be combined into single well-formed sentences. Following the examples are groups of sentences that you can combine into single sentences.

These are the examples:

a. The typewriter spills words onto the page. It clatters on. Its operator is in a trance. He does not care what comes out.
(Spilling words onto the page, the typewriter clatters on, its operator in a trance, not caring what comes out.)

b. The clouds massed below us. They were in great billows. They looked almost solid. We could jump from the plane. We could land safely in them. It would be like jumping from the barn into a huge featherbed. (Massing below us in great billows, the clouds looked almost solid, as if we could jump from the plane and land safely in them, like jumping from the barn into a huge featherbed.)

c. Of one thing we are certain. We are certain that writing is hard work. It is hard. It is rewarding. A well-written essay says something. It says just what we want it to. It conveys our exact meaning to our readers. (Of one thing we are certain: that writing is hard work, hard but rewarding, for a well-written essay says just what we want it to and conveys our exact meaning to our readers.)

d. The wind normally dies down. It dies down during the afternoon. That creates a peaceful interlude. During the interlude students stroll along the river. They sit under the elms on campus. They read. They chat. They just daydream.
(During the afternoon, the wind normally dies down, creating a peaceful interlude during which students stroll along the river or sit under the elms on campus, reading, chatting, or just daydreaming.)

e. The professor was a fascinating lecturer. He was an expert on the early lyrics of Christopher Smart. He was a fascinating lecturer for anyone interested in his subject. Few people are interested in his subject, as a matter of fact.
(The professor, an expert on the early lyrics of Christopher Smart, was a fascinating lecturer for anyone interested in his subject, which, as a matter of fact, few people are.)

Now you combine the following sentences:

1. The book has been in print for fifty years. It is utterly boring to most readers.
2. The assignment was given. The class asked the professor something. They asked when the paper was due. The professor was a kindly old duffer.
3. You do not know how to punctuate. You must go to the writing lab. It is located in the basement of Phillips Hall. You must learn that important skill. You must work with exercises until you have mastered it.
4. Students often discover something. They discover that they haven't left themselves enough time to do the essay question. They discover this toward the middle of the test.
5. The furniture was lovely to look at. Nevertheless, it was not awfully sturdy. The legs of the chairs often snapped under the weight of hefty occupants.

6. The wind was blowing at twenty miles per hour. It created a chill factor of −20°. This was enough to keep most of us indoors. Some hardy adventurers explored the fields and streams. The fields and streams were around the lodge.
7. Ethan Hatch claims something. It is easier to learn Chinese than English. I find this idea totally ridiculous. I know that young children learn all languages with equal speed and ease.
8. The second edition of the book was a great improvement over the first. The second edition appeared in 1975. It gave a more complete explanation of the history of typography. It included a full index. This feature is essential if the book is to be used as a reference source.
9. The computer is fast but dumb. It makes astronomical numbers of decisions in fractions of a second. Its speed allows it to complete infinitely complex problems in the wink of an eye. The programmer must know how to ask the right questions.
10. The day is ending. The sun is sinking in the west. It gives the sky and ocean a bronze sheen.

Purposes, Audiences, Situations

Here are two passages conveying essentially the same ideas:

Opera is a great art form, combining music and drama, providing a visual as well as aural spectacle, which is one reason fans prefer opera to any other art form.

Opera is a great art form. It combines music and drama. It provides a visual as well as aural spectacle. This is one reason fans prefer opera to any other art form.

The first is, of course, more fluent, but is it for this reason better? The only answer is this: better for what? *No language form is good or bad out of context.* A skilled writer will be able to produce either version, but to determine which is best, we would need to know

- the writer's purpose,
- the audience,
- and the situation.

Depending on these considerations, one or the other version might be preferable. In other words, neither example can be judged until it is in context.

This much seems obvious, but what might not be so clear is the value of being able to write fluent sentences when the occasion demands. If the writer is capable of producing only the kinds of sentences in the second example, then he or she is severely limited—like the mechanic who has only a monkey wrench and a hammer, when, in fact, auto repairs demand a well-stocked toolbox. As an old saying goes, if the only tool you have is a hammer, then you treat everything like a nail.

A Theory of Sentence Combining

Perhaps a bit of theory will be helpful at this point. The grammar of a language is nothing other than an instrument of mind. In this instance, we do not mean the grammar that you studied in high school when you learned to find the subjects and predicates of sentences or defined *noun* as "the name of a person, place, or thing." Grammar, as we are using it here, refers to the structures that carry ideas or meaning. One can say that the brain invented grammar, and, this being the case, obviously grammar must be important to thought and certainly to the expression of that thought. The writer who has not mastered grammar—in the sense of the structure of sentences—will have some difficulty getting his or her ideas down on paper, will fumble about, use more words than necessary, and find writing to be enormously frustrating. To convey your ideas, you must be a fluent writer—that is, you must be able to call on the grammatical resources or the language when you need them. Lack of this ability is a severe handicap to writing.

We can push this subject just a bit further. Every sentence contains one proposition or more than one, and we can define *proposition*, roughly, as a minimal sentence, carrying a single idea. The following is an example of a one-proposition sentence:

The man bites the dog.

This next example, however, is a two-proposition sentence:

Being vicious, the man bites the dog.

Why do we say that this sentence contains two propositions? Well, *the man bites the dog* is obviously a proposition in our sense, but what about *being vicious?* In the first place, note the following:

The man is vicious. The man bites the dog.

Doesn't that convey essentially the same information as the second example? Furthermore, in "Being vicious, the man bites the dog," we must know who it is that is vicious, or we won't understand the sentence; so when we read the sentence, it is as if we were reading "[*The man*] Being vicious, the man bites the dog."

Or take the following:

> The dog, a German shepherd, yelped with pain.

We can express these ideas in two sentences:

> The dog yelped with pain. The dog was a German shepherd.

So in the first of these, we actually have two propositions that could be expressed as two sentences.

Here are some further examples:

1. Strong tea, which is easy to make, revives the spirits.
   (Strong tea revives the spirits. Strong tea is easy to make.)
2. We smelled the aroma of coffee, pungent in the cold of the mountain cabin.
   (We smelled the aroma of coffee. The aroma was pungent in the cold of the mountain cabin.)
3. It is strange that a ham sandwich always tastes good.
   (It is strange. A ham sandwich always tastes good.)

   That a ham sandwich always tastes good is strange.
   (*Something* is strange. A ham sandwich always tastes good.)
4. Watching the embers glow in the fireplace, I felt completely at peace with the world.
   (I was watching the embers glow in the fireplace. I felt completely at peace with the world.)
5. The fire having nearly died out, we decided it was time to crawl into our bunks.
   (The fire had nearly died out. We decided *something*. It was time to do *something*. We crawled into our bunks.)

Example 5 has four propositions, yet the meaning of the sentence remains clear.

Exercise

If you gain the meaning of a sentence that contains more than one proposition, then you have gained the meanings of all the propositions in that sentence. In other words, when you read, you isolate propositions, even though you are not consciously aware that you do this. Each of the following sentences contains more than one proposition. What are they?

Here are some examples:

a. People who live in glass houses shouldn't throw stones.
(People shouldn't throw stones. People live in glass houses.)

b. Being careful not to break the yolk, I let the egg slide from the shell into the pan.
(I was careful not to break the yolk. I let the egg slide from the shell into the pan.)

c. The omelet, a tasty dish, pleased my son, his appetite having been whetted by the smell of cooking.
(The omelet pleased my son. The omelet was a tasty dish. His appetite had been whetted by the smell of cooking.)

d. Too hot for tennis, the weather kept us from taking any exercise and drained us of energy.
(The weather was too hot for tennis. It kept us from taking any exercise. It drained us of energy.)

Now separate the propositions in the following sentences:

1. Thus he fought his last fight, thirsting savagely for blood.

—H. L. Mencken

2. Walking through the fields, we learn quite a number of things about snails.

—Danilo Dolci

3. I am injected into this enormous silver monster, floating gently on a sea of Muzak, the sweet Karo Syrup of existence.

—Jean Shepherd

4. My own house faced the Cambridge world as a finely and solidly constructed mansion, preceded by a large oval lawn and ringed with an imposing white-pine hedge.

—e. e. cummings

5. To snare a sensibility in words, especially one that is alive and powerful, one must be tentative and nimble.

—Susan Sontag

6. Heads up, swinging with the music, their right arms swinging free, they stepped out, crossing the sanded arena under the arclights, the cuadrillas opening out behind, the picadors riding after.

—Ernest Hemingway

7. When the notion of man as machine was first advanced, the machine was a very simple collection of pulleys and billiard balls and levers.

—Wayne C. Booth

8. The babies were all under one year old, very funny and lovable.

—Grace Paley

9. Under the changes of weather, it may look like marble or like sea water, black as slate in the fog, white as tufa in the sunlight.

—Saul Bellow

10. One afternoon the previous May, a month when the fields blaze with the green-gold fire of half-grown wheat, Dewey spent several hours at Valley View, weeding his father's grave, an obligation he had too long neglected.

—Truman Capote

REWRITING SENTENCES FOR EMPHASIS

The grammar of English gives the writer many techniques for producing different effects with sentences. For example, the following all convey essentially the same information, but are quite different in effect:

> Most people enjoy peace and quiet.
> Peace and quiet are enjoyed by most people.
> What most people enjoy are peace and quiet.
> Peace and quiet—that's what most people enjoy.
> Most people enjoy this: peace and quiet.

If you understand and can use some of the important sentence strategies, you will be able to make your point in just the way you want to, with the right emphasis at the right time.

The following pages will give you practice in using various sentence strategies.

Periodic and Loose Sentences

A sentence "base" is the main clause of a sentence. In the following, the bases are printed in italics:

> *We decided not to take our vacation* because the price of gasoline had skyrocketed.
>
> Although our car gets excellent mileage, *we feel that we should conserve energy by not driving.*
>
> *A large park is near our house,* giving us the chance to get outdoors without using gasoline.
>
> The weather having been sunny and warm, *the park was crowded all weekend.*

As you can see, modifiers sometimes follow the base and sometimes precede it. When the modifiers follow the base, the sentence is called *loose;* when they precede it, the sentence is called *periodic.*

Here are two examples of loose sentences, printed to show how the modification works.

1. *Life disappears or modifies its appearances so fast that everything takes on an aspect of illusion—*
     a momentary fizzing and boiling with smoke rings,
        like pouring dissident chemicals into a retort.

—Loren Eiseley

2. *We caught two bass,*
     hauling them in briskly
        as though they were mackerel,
     pulling them over the side of the boat
     in a businesslike manner
        without any landing net
     and stunning them with a blow on the back of the head.

—E. B. White

The indentations in examples 1 and 2 indicate what modifies what. For example, "hauling them in briskly," "pulling them over the side of the boat," "and stunning them with a blow on the back of the head" all modify the base, but "as though they were mackerel" relates to "hauling them in briskly," and "without any landing net" refers to "in a businesslike manner."

Here are two periodic sentences, the modifiers preceding the bases:

3.   As the least drop of wine tinges the whole goblet,
     so the least particle of truth colors our wonderful life.

—Henry David Thoreau

4.   Instead of a squad of Nazi supermen in shiny boots, and packing
        Lugers,
     *we were confronted by five of the most unkempt, stunted, scrubby specimens
     I have ever had the pleasure of capturing.*

—Donald Pearce

Compare the effect of the following periodic sentence, example 5, with its loose version, example 6:

5. Having entered the House of Commons in the customary manner
   for peers' sons, from a family-controlled borough in an uncon-

tested election at the age of twenty-three, and, during his fifteen years in the House of Commons, having returned unopposed five times from the same borough, and having for the last twenty-seven years sat in the House of Lords, *he had little personal experience in vote getting.*

—Barbara Tuchman

6. *He had little personal experience in vote getting,* having entered the House of Commons in the customary manner for peers' sons, from a family-controlled borough in an uncontested election at the age of twenty-three, and, during his fifteen years in the House of Commons, having returned unopposed five times from the same borough, and having for the last twenty-seven years sat in the House of Lords.

In 5, readers are held in suspense, waiting for the main clause and thus for the sentence to resolve itself. The main predicate, *had,* is the sixty-third word in the sentence, and, of course, readers cannot organize the sentence until they reach the predicate or pivot word. In 6, *had* is the second word, and the phrases that follow its clause fall into place immediately, not needing to be held in suspension.

In 5, there is a certain force and finality that one does not sense in 6, which seems to run on and on. But this is not to say that one version is better than the other; each of the two achieves a different effect, and the value of that effect can be judged only in context, in the light of purpose, audience, and subject. Being able to perceive the different effects—and to achieve them when appropriate—is, however, important.

Here is another example of a sentence in periodic and loose forms:

7. In the autumn following Custer's expedition, the Sioux who had been hunting in the north began returning to the Red Cloud agency.

—Dee Brown

8. The Sioux who had been hunting in the north began returning to the Red Cloud agency in the autumn following Custer's expedition.

The principles governing the use of periodic and loose sentences are fairly simple.

First, the end-of-sentence position is the most important "slot."

Most Bostonians are prim and proper.

The first part of the sentence, "Most Bostonians," simply announces the topic; the last part, "prim and proper," gives information about the topic. The writer of that sentence has assumed that the readers would already know what "Bostonians" refers to, but that the information concerning them would be "news." In other words, sentence ends tend to carry more information than their beginnings and are thus, in general, more important.

Second, the periodic arrangement creates suspense; the reader must wait for the main clause, which will allow the meaning to be derived.

> Even in simple sentences like the following, *the end-of-sentence position is the most important "slot."*

Third, readability often determines one's choice between periodic and loose. For example, the following passage is slightly difficult to read because one does not find the subject of the second sentence immediately (and probably assumes that it is the same as that of the first):

> Since they end emphatically, periodic sentences can be more forceful than loose. Since their main clauses come first, loose sentences are usually easier to read than periodic ones.

The following version is easier to read:

> Since they end emphatically, periodic sentences can be more forceful than loose. Loose sentences are usually easier to read than periodic ones, since their main clauses come first.

Through practice, you can develop the ability to use the periodic and loose arrangements effectively.

Exercise

Some of the following sentences are loose, and some are periodic. Rearrange the periodic ones so that they become loose and the loose so that they become periodic.

1. In certain kinds of writing, particularly in art criticism and literary criticism, it is normal to come across long passages which are almost completely lacking in meaning.

—George Orwell

2. The human species, according to the best theory I can form of it, is composed of two distinct races, *the men who borrow* and *the men who lend.*

—Charles Lamb

3. The dog has long been bemused by the singular activities and the curious practices of men, cocking his head inquiringly to one side, intently watching and listening to the strangest goings-on in the world.

—James Thurber

4. The rolling period, the stately epithet, the noun rich in poetic associations, the subordinate clauses that give the sentence weight and magnificence, the grandeur like that of wave following wave in the open sea; there is no doubt that in all this there is something inspiring.

—W. Somerset Maugham

5. From the very beginning of school we make books and reading a constant source of possible failure and public humiliation.

—John Holt

6. I plodded on with the lesson, trying to get the class to locate Broad and Market Streets, the site of Philadelphia's City Hall, on maps that had been passed out.

—Peter Binzen

Parallelism and Balance

Two traditional principles involving sentences are parallelism and balance. Parallelism is a grammatical principle, and balance has to do with sentence effect. (See also pages 449–51 in the "Reference Guide.")

Two or more items that are in the same sentence "slot" are usually grammatical equivalents. Thus, the sentence

    1. Barbara likes *ice cream, candy,* and *soda pop.*

is parallel, for the coordinate objects of the verb *likes* are all nouns:

    2. Barbara likes *ice cream*
                  candy
                  soda pop

But this sentence

    3. Barbara likes *ice cream, candy,* and *to dance.*

is not parallel, for *ice cream* and *candy* are nouns, but *to dance* is a verbal.

Here is another sentence that is faulty in parallelism:

> 4. Robert wants to learn algebra, play tennis, and he goes to college.

The best way to explain the faulty parallelism in sentence 4 is to analyze the sentence:

> 5. Robert wants *to learn algebra* [verbal phrase]
> *(to) play tennis* [verbal phrase]
> *he goes to college* [clause]

The faulty parallelism is easily corrected:

> 6. Robert wants to learn algebra and play tennis, and he goes to college.

We can analyze this as

> 7. Robert wants *to learn algebra*
> *(to) play tennis*
> and [conjunction]
> he goes to college

As Virginia Tufte points out in her excellent book *Grammar as Style*, some professional writers deliberately create sentences in which parallelism is faulty, to achieve specific effects.[2] She cites these examples:

> 8. Here was himself, *young* [adjective]
> *good-looking* [adjective]
> *snappy dresser* [noun phrase]
> *and making dough* [verbal phrase]
>
> —John Steinbeck

> 9. Is there any one period of English literature to which we can point as being *fully mature* [adjective phrase]
> *comprehensive* [adjective]
> *and in equilibrium* [prepositional phrase]
>
> —T. S. Eliot

> 10. *Religiously* [adverb]
> *politically* [adverb]
> *and simply in terms of the*

> *characters' efforts to get* [prepositional phrase]
> *along with one another*
> this incongruity is pervasive.

—Frederick C. Crews

Closely related to parallelism, *balance* is a matter of the rhetoric of the sentence, not the grammar. As the word implies, it is a device in which structures are balanced, for emphasis or effect.

In the following sentence, coordinated noun phrases are balanced:

> 11. There was a time also when in the first fine flush of
>   *laundries and bakeries,*
>   *milk deliveries and canned goods,*
>   *ready-made clothes and dry cleaning,*
>   it did look as if the American life was being enormously simplified.

—Margaret Mead

Here are three more examples of balanced sentences:

> 12. There is no sense in hoping
>   for that which already exists
>   or
>   for that which cannot be.

—Erich Fromm

> 13. We go
>   wherever the wind blows,
>   we take
>   whatever we find.

—Danilo Dolci

> 14. The difference
>   between tragedy and comedy
>   is
>   the difference
>   between experience and intuition.

—Christopher Fry

Most balance is not quite that perfect, however. In the following, we find phrases that *nearly* balance:

> 15. The view that neurosis is a severe reaction to human trouble
>   is as
>   revolutionary in its implications for social practice
>   as it is
>   daring in formation.

—Jerome S. Bruner

Exercise

Using the example sentences in the preceding section as models, write ten sentences in which balance is an obvious principle. Then rewrite those sentences so that balance is eliminated.

Active and Passive Voice

The most common definition of *passive voice* is "the form of the sentence in which the subject receives the action." Thus, the first example is passive and second is active:

> Mary was punched by George. [passive]
> George punched Mary. [active]

In the *active voice,* the subject (George) performs the action (punching) and the object (Mary) receives the action.

However, using the definition of the *passive* above, we could argue that

> Mary received the blow.

is in the passive, for *Mary,* the subject, receives the action. But, as we shall see, this example is actually in the active voice.

To give an adequate definition of passive voice versus active voice would involve us in unnecessary complications. Perhaps the following is enough explanation for our purposes: some sentences allow you to flip-flop the subject and the object and insert a form of the verb "to be." When you do this, you change an active-voice sentence into a passive one. (See also pages 457–58 in the "Reference Guide.")

ACTIVE	PASSIVE
Mary received the blow.	The blow was received by Mary.
The man had bitten the dog.	The dog had been bitten by the man.
Lyle is mowing the lawn.	The lawn is being mowed by Lyle.
The reporter will write the story.	The story will be written by the reporter.

We also know that we can delete the *by* phrases from passive sentences.

ACTIVE	PASSIVE
The technician drew five cubic centimeters of blood from the patient.	Five cubic centimeters of blood were drawn from the patient.
Someone tipped over the pickle barrel.	The pickle barrel was tipped over.
You must complete the work before you are paid.	The work must be completed before you are paid.
The mechanic replaced the sparkplugs in the auto.	The sparkplugs in the auto were replaced.

Students have often been told that the active voice is more direct, vigorous, and effective than the passive; therefore, the passive should be avoided. But once again: it all depends! In the following paragraph, the passive sentences are italicized:

> I had a couple of close ones during this show. *On the way in, my platoon was evidently silhouetted against the night sky, and was fired on four times at a range of maybe 300 yards by an eighty-eight.* (This is a notorious and vicious gun. The velocity of the shell is so high that you hear it pass or explode near you almost at the same instant that you hear the sound of its being fired. You really can't duck. Also, it's an open-sights affair—*you are aimed at particularly: not, as with mortars, aimed at only by approximation.*) Anyway, they went past me about an arm's length above or in front of me. I don't know which. We hit the ditches. *After pointing a few more, the gun was forced off by our return tank fire.*
>
> —Donald Pearce, *Journal of a War*

Surely this passage would not be improved if all its sentences were in the active voice.

Exercise

Some of the following sentences are in the active voice, some in the passive. Change them to their opposites and discuss the changes in emphasis that result.

1. Rats and dogs are conditioned and are usually incapable of breaking that conditioning.

   —Henry F. Ottinger

384

2. Classroom dynamics can be described in terms of student and teacher roles.

3. The reader knows best how a productive wedding is arranged in his own field.

—William G. Perry, Jr.

4. I am using the word *image* in a wide meaning, which does not restrict it to the mind's eye as a visual organ.

—Jacob Bronowski

5. The presence of pleasure areas in the brain was discovered accidentally in 1954 by James Olds and Peter Milner in Canada.

—H. J. Campbell

6. The subject is told to administer a shock to the learner each time he gives a wrong response.

—Stanley Milgram

Repetition

Another interesting and useful device in sentence strategies is *repetition:*

1. He had drunk a lot of *rezina* in his time: he said it was good for one, good for the kidneys, good for the liver, good for the lungs, good for the bowels and for the mind, good for everything.

—Henry Miller

This daring extensive repetition certainly underscores the opinion about the goodness of *rezina,* a Greek wine.

In the following passage, the author uses repetition with great effect:

2. To be human, to be human, to be fully human. What does it mean? What is required?

—Wayne C. Booth

Not only does Booth repeat the infinitive phrase (with a variation on the last one), but he also repeats the question form twice. To illustrate the force of repetition, I will rewrite this example, removing the repetition:

3. What is meant by and required to be fully human?

Further examples of repetition for emphasis:

4. Just as the prophets of the eighth century B.C. left their villages and carried their "thus saith the Lord" far beyond the boundaries of their home towns, and just as the Apostle Paul left his village of Tarsus and carried the Gospel of Jesus Christ to the far corners of the Greco-Roman world, so am I compelled to carry the gospel of freedom beyond my own home town.

—Martin Luther King, Jr.

5. Now what does this Let Him Be Poor mean? It means let him be weak. Let him be ignorant. Let him become a nucleus of disease. Let him be a standing exhibition and example of ugliness and dirt. Let him have rickety children.

—George Bernard Shaw

Exercise

Using the preceding example sentences as models, write ten sentences (or passages) in which you employ obvious repetition to achieve emphasis.

Framing and Emphasis

The *frame* of a sentence is its first element. Since sentences usually begin with their subjects, the frame is also most often the subject, as in the following:

1. *Laurel and Hardy* provided laughter for millions of people in my generation.

However, sentences can be arranged so that the frame is not the subject:

2. *In my generation,* Laurel and Hardy provided laughter for millions of people.
3. *Laughter*—that's what Laurel and Hardy provided for millions of people in my generation.

Each of these three sentences achieves a different emphasis, the frame giving the sentence its direction. Indeed, any of the major elements can serve as a frame, as the following passive-voice sentence demonstrates:

4. *Millions of people* were provided laughter by Laurel and Hardy in my generation.

The point is that sentences can be manipulated so that the desired emphasis is achieved—or so that they achieve the desired emphasis. Not every sentence must begin with the logical subject. However, a word of caution: you should use restraint in departing from the normal word order. Excessive use of emphasis will defeat your purpose. If every sentence is emphatic, then none will have the force of emphasis, and your prose will seem unclear.

Look closely at how the following sentence arrangements create specific emphases:

5. *It was a heavenly place for a boy,* that farm of my Uncle John's.

—Mark Twain

(My Uncle John's farm was a heavenly place for a boy.)

6. *Patience, horses or a fine carriage, a widow to wive, a sloping lawn with a river at the bottom, a thriving field, an adopted daughter—* that was as far as his desire wandered.

—William Carlos Williams

(His desire wandered only as far as patience, horses or a fine carriage, a widow to wive, a sloping lawn with a river at the bottom, a thriving field, an adopted daughter.)

7. *To sing "Yankee Doodle"* is easy.
(It is easy to sing "Yankee Doodle.")

8. *That Mary missed the show* was a pity.
(It was a pity that Mary missed the show.)

9. *Of all virtues,* magnanimity is the rarest.

—William Hazlitt

(Magnanimity is the rarest of all virtues.)

10. *Stress* he could endure but peace and regularity pleased him better.

—William Carlos Williams

(He could endure stress but peace and regularity pleased him better.)

The point is that you don't have to begin every sentence with the subject. As the examples make clear, the frame that you choose for your sentence determines what is stressed.

Exercise

To change emphasis, rearrange each of the following sentences at least once:

1. The mail having arrived, we left for the city.
2. The students cheered, their team being seven points ahead.
3. The day, drizzlingly damp, depressed Deborah.
4. The waitress smiled toothily, artificial in her unctuous friendliness.
5. If winter comes, can spring be far behind?
6. Computer programming, though it fascinates many students, takes a long time to learn.
7. *Heart of Darkness,* a masterpiece of fiction, baffled La Wanda.
8. A spry octogenarian, my grandfather still plays golf.
9. In the morning, our whole family drinks tea.
10. Germans drink beer during the Oktoberfest.

Review

In the following sentences, various strategies are used to achieve various effects. Point out these strategies, and rearrange the sentences to achieve different effects.

1. The good fortune of the physicist—and these matters are always relative, for the material monism of physics may have impeded nineteenth-century thinking and delayed insights into the nature of complementarity in modern physical theory—this early good fortune or happy insight has no counterpart in the sciences of man.

   —Jerome S. Bruner

2. Since RKO-Radio Pictures first released *King Kong,* a quarter-century has gone by; yet year after year, from prints that grow more rain-beaten, from sound tracks that grow more tinny, ticket-buyers by thousands still pursue Kong's luckless fight against the forces of technology, tabloid journalism, and the DAR. They see him chloroformed to sleep, see him whisked from his jungle to New York, and placed on show, see him burst his chains to roam the city (lugging a frightened blonde), at last to plunge from the spire of the Empire State Building, machine-gunned by model airplanes.

   —X. J. Kennedy

3. I went as far as the sixth grade in school. I'm 57 now. I was 16 and didn't want to be 16 in the seventh grade so I quit.

   —Linda Lane

4. What is the function of sound in music? What is the function of sound in poetry? What is the function of sound in prose composition? What is the function of sound in drama?

5. Just praise is only a debt, but flattery is a present.

   —Samuel Johnson

6. And he took the pain of it, if not happily, like a martyr, at least willingly, like an heir.

—Edward Lewis Wallant

7. *Mansions* there are—two or three of them—but the majority of the homes are large and inelegant.

—John Barth

8. I am sure of this, that by going much alone a man will get more of a noble courage in thought and word than from all the wisdom that is in books.

—Ralph Waldo Emerson

9. These times—they try men's souls.

10. A sudden idea of the relationship between "lovers." We are neither male nor female. We are a compound of both. I choose the male who will develop and expand the male in me; he chooses me to expand the female in him. Being made "whole."

—Katherine Mansfield

11. Now I think—I happen to think—that those three beliefs that I speak of, the self-belief, the love-belief, and the art-belief, are all closely related to the God-belief, that the belief in God is a relationship you enter into with Him to bring about the future.

—Robert Frost

12. are you ready for the demystification of diamondback terrapins???????? they ain't nothing but salt water turtles.

—Verta Mae Smart-Grosvenor

13. I was a caged panther. It was a jungle. Survival was the law of the land. I watched so many partners fall along the way. I decided the modus operandi was bad. Unavailing, non-productive.

—Studs Terkel

14. Finally, one night they had Junior trapped on the road up toward the bridge around Millersville, there's no way out of there, they had the barricades up and they could hear this souped-up car roaring around the bend, and here it comes—but suddenly they can hear a siren and see a red light flashing in the grille, so they think it's another agent, and boy, they run out like ants and pull those barrels and boards and sawhorses out of the way, and then—Ggghhzzzzzzzzhhhhhh gggggggzzzzzzzeeeeeong!—gawdam! there he goes again, it was him, Junior Johnson! with a gawdam agent's sireen and a red light in his grille.

—Tom Wolfe

15. There are still islands where you can laze on the beach for hours and hear no sound louder than the trade winds in the palm fronds; or

breakfast on a flower-decked patio and sniff the frangipani and oleander; or wander through tumble-down towns without being jostled by cars or crowds.

—Ian Keown

Notes

[1]Many of the ideas in this section derive from Joseph M. Williams, *Style: Ten Lessons in Clarity and Grace* (Glenview, Ill.: Scott, Foresman, 1981), and E. D. Hirsch, Jr., *The Philosophy of Composition* (Chicago: University of Chicago Press, 1978).
[2]Virginia Tufte, *Grammar as Style* (New York: Holt, 1971), pp. 207–08.

13
Words

This chapter has two purposes. First, it will help you write more accurately and effectively for your audience, but it will also give you some interesting—and ultimately useful—concepts about language in a society as diverse as our own. (See also pages 469–85 in the "Reference Guide.")

DICTION AND USAGE

Words are symbols that convey concepts and, therefore, are basic to the thought process. In fact, words and their functions in sentences are topics that ought to interest the intellectually curious, and some knowledge of words is necessary to the writer.

This much said, let us turn to Jonathan Swift, whose best-known work tells of the marvelous adventures of Gulliver during his travels. Everyone knows about Gulliver's voyage to Lilliput, where he met the little people, but not everyone knows about his voyage to Balnibarbi, where he visited the great Academy of Lagado. In the academy, all sorts of learned and scientific projects were under way. One scientist, for instance, was attempting to distill sunbeams from cucumbers so that they could be used on gloomy days, and another was working at turning ice into gunpowder. Gulliver's tour of the academy progresses:

> We next went to the School of Languages, where three Professors sat in Consultation upon improving that of their Country.
>
> The first Project was to shorten Discourse by cutting Polysyllables into one, and leaving out Verbs and Participles; because in Reality all things imaginable are but Nouns.
>
> The other, was a Scheme for entirely abolishing all Words whatsoever: And this was urged as a great Advantage in Point of Health as well as Brevity. For, it is plain, that every Word we speak is in some Degree a Diminution of our Lungs by Corrosion; and consequently contributes to the shortening of our Lives. An Expedient was therefore offered, that since Words are only Names for *Things*, it would be more convenient for all Men to carry about them, such *Things* as were necessary to express the particular Business they are to discourse on. And this invention would certainly have taken place, to the great Ease as well as Health of the Subject, if the Women in Conjunction with the Vulgar and Illiterate had not threatened to raise a Rebellion, unless they might be allowed the Liberty to speak their Tongues, after the Manner of their Forefathers: Such constant and irreconcilable Enemies to Science are the common People. However, many of the most Learned and Wise adhere to the new Scheme of expressing themselves by *Things;* which hath only this Inconvenience attending it; that if a Man's Business be very great, and of various Kinds, he must be obliged in Proportion to carry a greater Bundle of *Things* upon his Back, unless he can afford one or two strong Servants to attend him. I have often beheld two of those Sages almost sinking under the Weight of their packs, like Pedlars among us, who when they meet in the Streets, would lay down their Loads, open their Sacks, and hold Conversation for an Hour together; then put up their Implements, help each other to resume their Burthens, and take their Leave.
>
> But, for short Conversations a Man can carry Implements in his Pockets and under his Arms, Enough to supply him, and in his House he cannot be at a Loss; therefore the Room where Company meet who practice this Art, is full of all *Things* ready at hand, requisite to furnish Matter for this kind of artificial Converse.
>
> Another great Advantage proposed by this Invention, was, that it would serve as a universal Language to be understood in all civilized Nations, whose Goods and Utensils are generally of the same Kind, or nearly resembling, to that their uses might easily be comprehended. And thus, Embassadors would be qualified to treat with foreign Princes or Ministers of State, to whose Tongues they were utter Strangers.

In this piece, Swift is poking fun at those who hold oversimplified views of how language works. Words, of course, denote *things,* as *table, book, mountain; concepts,* as *democracy, honesty, guilt; states of mind,* as *happiness, sadness, glee.* But words, obviously, do not gain their total meaning from what they refer to—even concrete words such as *book* or *table.* On the contrary, words gain much of their meaning from other words, through definition. Our understanding of the term *God,* for instance, depends on the other words that make up the "definition."

In any case, all words have shades of meaning.

Denotation and Connotation

Consider the word *man* in the following two sentences:

A man is a male human.
Keith is a real man.

The first means something cut and dried, almost like this: male + adult + human = man. But the meaning of the second sentence is harder to make clear: Keith is strong and virile; he is courageous and trustworthy; there is nothing soft or effeminate about him.

In these two kinds of meaning can be seen the difference between *denotation* and *connotation.* The core of meaning—the sort of thing that we can define with features such as "male," "adult," "human," or with the kind of statement found in a dictionary—is *denotation.* The associations that words carry with them, either in context or out of it, are called *connotation.*

The denotation of all these phrases is the same: *to die, to kick the bucket, to pass away.* But to illustrate the power of connotation, let's make up a little story.

A teenage girl is deeply attached to her grandmother, who becomes ill and is hospitalized. One afternoon, the girl goes to the hospital and meets her grandmother's physician in the hall. "How's Grandma today?" she asks. The physician replies with *one* of the following:

Your grandmother died this morning.
Your grandmother kicked the bucket this morning.
Your grandmother passed away this morning.

If the physician made the first reply, we might assume he was a callous sort of person, for *to die* is a bit harsh in its connotative value. The second reply is utterly tactless, for *to kick the bucket* has humorous connotations. Undoubtedly the physician gave the third reply, for the connotation of *to pass away* is not as harsh as that of *to die*.

Many terms with unfavorable connotations can be replaced: *garbage man–sanitary engineer, toilet–water closet, mortician–funeral director, shit–feces, dirty underwear–soiled linen, to lie–to fib, to vomit– to upchuck.*

The word *toilet* is interesting. Here is the *American Heritage Dictionary* definition of the word:

> **1.** A disposal apparatus consisting of a hopper, fitted with a flushing device, used for urination and defecation. **2.** A room or booth containing such an apparatus and often a washbowl. **3.** The act or process of grooming and dressing oneself. **4.** A dressing table. **5a.** Dress: attire. **b.** A costume or gown. —make one's toilet.

Thus, in *The Rape of the Lock*, Alexander Pope wrote,

> And now, unveiled, the Toilet stands displayed,
> Each silver Vase in mystic order laid.
> First, robed in white, the Nymph intent adores,
> With head uncovered, the Cosmetic powers.

But, of course, in modern English it is highly unlikely that one would hear, "Gloria is at her toilet, making herself beautiful." The word *toilet* simply has picked up too many unfavorable connotations. In the attempt to avoid these, *ladies' room* was substituted, and when that term picked up too many unfavorable connotations, *powder room* was substituted—a powder room being, presumably, where one goes to take a powder.

Here are some interesting sets of terms, each set having roughly the same denotations, but varying broadly in connotations:

UNFAVORABLE	NEUTRAL	FAVORABLE
legal murder	euthanasia	mercy killing
birth control	contraception	family planning
spying	surveillance	intelligence
peddling	selling	marketing
farting	flatulation	breaking wind
crazy	psychotic	mentally unbalanced
cancer	carcinoma	lingering illness
soggy (day)	rainy (day)	misty (day)

And, of course, to the residents of Los Angeles, *smog* is often *haze*.

The practice of substituting a word with favorable connotations for one with unfavorable connotations is known as *euphemism,* and the word so substituted is also known as a euphemism. Thus one might substitute *fibber* for *liar (Mike is a liar/Mike is a fibber)* because *fibber* has much less harsh connotations than *liar.* In the preceding list all the words in the "favorable" column might be viewed as euphemisms for the equivalents in the "unfavorable" column.

Levels of Usage

To the delight of most people who think about language, speakers and writers are gaining freedom from the strictures that society imposed so rigidly in the past. There was a time, for instance, when contractions (*isn't, haven't, don't,* and so on) were found only in extremely informal writing, and much fuss was made about the usage of *shall* and *will* (*shall* with the first person, as in *I shall return,* but *will* with the other persons, as in *you/he/they will return*). No sensible person nowadays would raise an eyebrow at finding an *isn't,* let alone an *I will,* even in such publications as scholarly journals, which typically demand a great deal of formality.

On the other hand, society does impose boundaries on usage, reacting against or proscribing certain features of so-called nonstandard English (see pages 396–97 and 408–14).

Unwritten, tacitly accepted dress codes provide a good analogy with language usage. Not many years ago, the better restaurants in, say, Atlanta demanded that male patrons wear ties and jackets, and not many years before that suits were demanded. Now only the most exclusive restaurants expect men to wear ties and jackets, and one would have to search for a restaurant that demanded suits. In short, dress codes have become much more flexible.

But there are regional variations in this permissiveness. For instance, in San Francisco, dress tends to be a good deal more formal than in Los Angeles, while in Las Vegas anything goes.

From my point of view, in the best of all possible worlds, we would dress just as we pleased, but we do not live in the best of all possible worlds. For this reason, I sometimes break down and put on a tie and a suit, either because I could not gain admittance to a certain place without such dress or because I would feel conspicuous and uncomfortable if I did not conform to the expectations that the situation imposed.

Dress codes and language codes are alike in that they result from custom, and they are socially imposed. The individual is quite free (*most* of the time) to conform to them or to ignore them, but ignoring them has its consequences.

To divide language into levels of usage is, to a certain extent, artificial. Nonetheless, such a division is instructive in that it allows one to grasp very real differences in language use.

Formal and Informal Usage

At one end of the usage scale is what might be called *formal*, both written and spoken. Formal written English might well contain fewer contractions than informal, and it avoids slang.

Here is an example of formal writing from a respected publication:

> It is easy to grasp why stringed instruments make the sounds they do. When the strings are struck or plucked, they vibrate at different natural frequencies in accordance with their tension and diameter. The energy of the vibration is then transferred to the air by way of a vibrating plate of wood and a resonating air chamber, with the sound eventually dying away. The musician can vary the pitch, or frequency, of individual strings by changing their vibrating length with the pressure of his fingers on the frets or the fingerboard.
>
> —Arthur H. Benade, "The Physics of Brasses," *Scientific American*

And here is an example of informal usage. A woman writes to Abigail Van Buren, "Dear Abby." The letter explains that the writer must pick up her boyfriend and drive him home because he doesn't have a car, and, to add insult to injury, the woman must also pay a toll to cross a bridge to get to her boyfriend's house. Abby answers:

> Thirty minutes in an automobile beats two and a half hours in a subway, no matter who does the driving. If he hasn't offered to pay for the toll, suggest it. If he can't or won't pay for it, you will have to decide whether dating him is worth the portal to portal service you're providing.

The characteristics of this informal usage, as opposed to the formal, are obvious. First are the contractions: *hasn't, can't, won't, you're.* In fact, Abby's failure to contract *you will* is almost jarring.

The slang is also a feature of informality: "Thirty minutes in an automobile *beats* two and a half hours in a subway."

Here is an example of formal spoken English:

> I don't look at aggression in such traditional terms as Reich or Lowen. I don't make the assumption that there is any one right way to reach out to the world, nor any single correct pattern for sexual expression. In a primitive culture if a man couldn't be aggressive, kill and rape a little, he wouldn't survive. But that has all changed. Civilization has allowed some of us to become artists and poets, to assert our existence in soft ways.
>
> —Stanley Keleman, interview in *Psychology Today*

The contractions, the double negative ("I don't make the assumption . . . *nor* any single correct pattern"), the relative brevity of the sentences—all these features mark the passage as spoken. Indeed, this example demonstrates that the line between formal written and formal spoken is thin.

Informal written and spoken English differ from formal largely on the basis of the words that they allow. For instance, in formal English, one might speak of being very *fond* of sherry; in informal English, one might be *crazy about* sherry. In informal English, one might *get a job,* but in extremely formal English, one would probably *obtain a position.*

Nonstandard Usage

Nonstandard usage has nothing to do with good or bad, and nonstandard usage is *not sub*standard. In fact, every society contains a power elite—the group of people who control the economy, who set educational policy, who determine the program content of the media, who edit the newspapers—and the concept of standard is derived from the usage that this power group finds acceptable.

It would be wrong to assume that there is a monolithic, well-defined entity called standard English. But standard can be defined by the usages that it does not allow, if not by a complete description of what it permits. For instance, standard allows midwesterners to sit on the *stoop* while westerners sit on the *front porch.* It doesn't matter whether you carry a *bucket* or a *pail* in standard, but you can't *tote* either one. In standard, you are perfectly free to say either *I know* WHO *you gave it to* or *I know* WHOM *you gave it to,* but you can't say HIM *and* ME *went.*

The concept of levels of usage is no great mystery. The importance of usage is a social condition that we might deplore but that we nonetheless must recognize. Both *Sandy ain't been here for an hour* and *Sandy hasn't been here for an hour* convey the same meaning, so from one point of view it's silly to prefer one form over the other. On the other hand, the second of those sentences is more acceptable than the first to the power elite in society.

A Word About Slang

Slang terms can be characterized as follows. They are used to produce an effect, such as humor, hipness, or cynicism. They are markedly excluded from formal usage. And they frequently are *nonce words,* or terms that appear in the language briefly and then fade away, even though some slang persists for decades or even centuries. As an illustration of how short-lived most slang is, think about the following terms: *twenty-three skiddoo, bundling, petting, necking, hubbahubbahubba, skirt* (for "woman"), *frail.* On the other hand, some slang terms last forever, it seems: *bones* (for "dice"); *shake a leg, nuts, screwy; rod* (for "pistol").

Sometimes, interestingly, a slang term appears to have no nonslang equivalent. When a child runs with a sled and then slams it down and jumps on it face down to ride downhill, he is doing a *belly-flop.* In his *Linguistic Atlas of the Upper Midwest,* Harold B. Allen lists these synonyms for belly-flop, all of them slang: *belly-bump, belly-gut, belly-buster, belly-bust, belly-booster, belly-bunt, belly-wopper, bellity-bumper, belly-butting, belly-coaster, belly-down, belly-slam, belly-slide.*[1] Allen also lists *slamming,* which is unfamiliar to me.

The big problem with slang in writing, of course, is that it is so rapidly dated, and nothing sounds so trite as yesteryear's or yesterday's slang. Another problem with slang is its vividness. Writing that uses slang is likely to sound as if the author is straining for effect.

Jargon

Jargon refers to those words and expressions that are used by members of an occupation, profession, or social set. Thus, physicians speak of a *sphygmomanometer,* not of a *blood pressure machine.* A patient has *phlebitis,* never inflammation of a vein. Every physician would much prefer to mention *iatrogenic* disease than to talk about diseases that are caused by the treatments that physicians administer.

Modern linguistics has its own, virtually impenetrable jargon: *suprasegmental phonemes* for intonation patterns in speech; *deep structure* for meaning; and a whole array of such exotics as *phoneme, morpheme, complementation,* and *deletion transformation.*

Subcultures also develop their own jargons. One example is the vernacular of jazz, as described by Robert S. Gold in an extremely interesting article.[2] Gold calls the language of the jazz world *jive.* Like jazz, it was developed by black Americans as a unique form of expression, creating a social identity. It has been said that the word *jive* itself was derived from the standard English word *jibe,* "to scoff at, to sneer at, to ridicule." A brief jazz glossary lists these items: *apple:* the earth, the universe, New York City; *balling:* having a good time (but in current slang this term means something quite different); *beat:* tired (this bit of jive has been adopted as slang in general usage); *benny:* overcoat; *capped:* excelled; *cat:* a musician, a man; *chick:* a girl; *conk:* the head; *dicty:* snobbish; *dig:* understand; *dims and brights:* days and nights; *drape:* a suit; *groovy:* great; *hep, hip:* aware of; *juice:* liquor; *kick:* a pocket; *kill:* thrill, fascinate; *mad:* fine, capable, able, talented; *nod:* sleep; *ofay:* white person; *pad:* house, apartment, room; *scoff:* food; *sky:* hat; *troll:* street, avenue; *trey:* three; *twister:* key.

There is nothing inherently wrong with jargon. One physician talking to another would be deemed naive if he spoke of the blood pressure machine rather than the *sphygmomanometer;* one plumber speaking to another is quite justified in talking about *P-traps, U-joints,* and *nipples;* literary critic to literary critic, there's nothing at all wrong with the terms *affective fallacy* and *objective correlative.*

It's all a matter of audience. When one specialist is addressing another, the jargon of the group is useful and informative, but when a specialist (a jazz musician or a plumber or a linguist) is addressing a layman, jargon is simply confusing.

Gobbledygook

Stuart Chase, in *Power of Words,* had this to say about gobbledygook:

> Said Franklin Roosevelt, in one of his early presidential speeches: "I see one-third of a nation ill-housed, ill-clad, ill-nourished." Translated into standard bureaucratic prose this statement would read:

It is evident that a substantial number of persons within the Continental boundaries of the United States have inadequate financial resources with which to purchase the products of agricultural communities and industrial establishments. It would appear that for a considerable segment of the population, possibly as much as 33.3333 percent of the total, there are inadequate housing facilities, and an equally significant proportion is deprived of the proper types of clothing and nutriment.

This rousing satire on gobbledygook—or talk among the bureaucrats—is adapted from a report prepared by the Federal Security Agency in an attempt to break out of the verbal squirrel cage. "Gobbledygook" was coined by an exasperated Congressman, Maury Maverick of Texas, and means using two, or three, or ten words in the place of one, or using a five-syllable word where a single syllable would suffice. Maverick was censuring the forbidding prose of executive departments in Washington, but the term has now spread to windy and pretentious language in general.

Here is another example of gobbledygook:

Due to the fact that hydroelectric generation of electrical current now involves costly materials and operations, it is respectfully requested that personnel be assiduous in ascertaining that all electrical appliances, particularly those used for illumination, are turned off if not in use.

That sloggy sentence means nothing more than this: Since electricity is expensive, please turn off the lights.

Abstractness

Closely related to the disease called gobbledygook is another, just as frustrating: abstractness. Here is an example:

Objective consideration of contemporary phenomena compels the conclusion that success or failure in competitive activities exhibits no tendency to be commensurate with innate capacity, but that a considerable element of the unpredictable must invariably be taken into account.

The preceding example is George Orwell's rewrite of a glorious passage from the Bible:

I returned and saw under the sun, that the race is not to the swift, nor the battle to the strong, neither yet bread to the wise, nor yet riches to men of understanding, nor yet favour to men of skill; but time and chance happeneth to them all.

400

Orwell wrote his parody in order to illustrate what happens to prose when it becomes totally abstract. In the Bible passage, concrete images not only convey but also reinforce the idea; the reader is given specific examples of what the passage means. In the Orwell parody, the reader has nothing specific to grasp, nothing to peg ideas on.

The best prose is concrete and imagistic, even when it is dealing with abstruse subject matter. Here is a brilliant example. The American thinker William James is discussing habit, certainly an abstract subject, but notice how he handles it concretely:

> Habit is thus the enormous fly-wheel of society, its most precious conservative agent. It alone is what keeps us all within the bounds of ordinance, and saves the children of fortune from the envious uprisings of the poor. It alone prevents the hardest and most repulsive walks of life from being deserted by those brought up to tread therein. It keeps the fisherman and the deck-hand at sea through the winter; it holds the miner in his darkness, and nails the countryman to his log-cabin and his lonely farm through all the months of snow; it protects us from invasion by the natives of the desert and the frozen zone. It dooms us all to fight out the battle of life upon the lines of our nurture or our early choice, and to make the best of a pursuit that disagrees, because there is no other for which we are fitted, and it is too late to begin again. It keeps different social strata from mixing. Already at the age of twenty-five you see the professional mannerism settling down on the young commercial traveler, on the young doctor, and the young minister, on the young counselor-at-law. You see the little lines of cleavage running through the character, the tricks of thought, the prejudices, the ways of the "shop," in a word, from which the man can by-and-by no more escape than his coat-sleeve can suddenly fall into a new set of folds. On the whole, it is best he should not escape. It is well for the world that in most of us, by the age of thirty, the character has set like plaster, and will never soften again.
>
> —*The Principles of Psychology*, I

James starts off with a metaphor: habit is the flywheel of society, the force that keeps all the other parts moving. He then gives a number of examples of how habit keeps people in their appointed places. Next, he points out that members of given professions adopt the habits of those professions. Finally, he ends with two wonderful figures of speech: it is as unlikely that people will change their habits as that a coat will suddenly change its folds, and the character sets like plaster.

Review

1. Characterize the following passages as nonstandard, informal, or formal. Indicate the features that led you to make your characterization.

   a. *What about the young dissenters?*

   If you gave 'em a push, they'd turn into homosexual. When the German hordes fifty years ago surrounded Paris, Marshall Petain brought out the pimps, whores, thieves, underground operators, he says: Our playground is jeopardized by the German Hun. Well, all Paris, every thief, burglar, pimp, he come out and picked up a musket. Stopped the German hordes.

   —Quoted in Studs Turkel, *Hard Times*

   b. My recall is nearly perfect, time has faded nothing. I recall the very first kidnap. I've lived through the passage, died on the passage, lain in the unmarked, shallow graves of the millions who fertilized the Amerikan soil with their corpses; cotton and corn growing out of my chest, "unto the third and fourth generation," the tenth, the hundredth. My mind ranges back and forth through the uncounted generations, and I feel all that they ever felt, but double. I can't help it; there are too many things to remind me of the 23½ hours that I'm in this cell. Not ten minutes pass without a reminder. In between, I'm left to speculate on what form the reminder will take.

   —George Jackson

   c. Now about Yolanda is a good friend to me all my friend is very nice to me, but Yolanda is the most good friend to me. In my class Yolanda and me we are always talking about people especially about boy and a teacher the teacher is a nice teacher he teach me and Yolanda in a school called ———— Junior High School it is located in Los Angeles, California. Yolanda has a brother name Orlando she has two more brother but I do not know their name but if Yolanda is a good friend to me well I guess her brothers are nice but one of them had got kick out of school.

   —A junior high school student

   d. An abundant and increasing supply of highly educated people has become the absolute prerequisite of social and economic development in our world. It is rapidly becoming a condition of national survival. What matters is not that there are so many more individuals around who have been exposed to long years of formal schooling—though this is quite recent. The essential new fact is that a developed society and economy are less than fully effective if anyone is educated to less than the limit of his potential. The uneducated man is fast becoming an economic liability and unproductive. Society must be an "educated society" today—to progress, to grow, even to survive.

   —Peter F. Drucker

2. Make an inventory of the slang that is current on your campus right now. Define the words and terms now in use. Do any of them seem to

have been around for some time? (For example, *flunk* is a slang term that has had great staying power.)
3. Are you familiar with the jargon of any particular field or group? If so, list and explain the words and terms that appear.
4. Revise the following sentences to eliminate the gobbledygook:

   a. Return with the utmost haste.
   b. Before he retires for the night, Paul scrupulously observes a regimen of oral hygiene.
   c. Do not enumerate your domestic fowls before they emerge from the ovarian state.
   d. Feathered vertebrates of the same genus show a decided tendency to congregate.
   e. George always set aside a portion of his earnings so that he would be prepared in the event that inclement weather should precipitate unforeseen circumstances that would necessitate his having extra coin of the realm.
   f. The domestic canine is frequently *Homo sapiens'* most devoted ally.

THE BASIC WORD STOCK OF ENGLISH

To put the English language in perspective, we will draw a thumbnail sketch of the development of the vocabulary.

In about the middle of the fifth century, three Germanic tribes—the Angles, the Saxons, and the Jutes—invaded the island of Britain, driving out the native Celts. The invaders isolated themselves from their native lands (now Germany), and one of the results of isolation (either geographical or social) is the development of new linguistic forms. The first English language, often called Old English, was Anglo-Saxon, a dialect of German.

In 597, Saint Augustine of Canterbury and some forty monks arrived in England, their mission to bring Christianity to the island. They soon converted King Ethelbert, and the church was established in the British Isles. Since Latin was the language of the church, the Latin vocabulary soon began to appear in Old English.

Toward the end of the eighth century, Danes (the Vikings) began to attack England, conquering all of the northern and most of the eastern parts of the island. Because King Alfred expelled the Danes a century later, Scandinavian did not become the language of the ruling classes, but many Scandinavian words came into English.

The most famous date in English history is, perhaps, 1066—when the Norman French conquered England. Because the language of Normandy was that of the power elite, English changed drastically, adjusting itself to the language of the conquerors. So it is fair to say that modern English is basically a Germanic language with a heavy overlay of French.

The point is this: our basic word stock is Anglo-Saxon and French, with an admixture of Latin, Scandinavian, and other languages.

Before we go on, we ought to wring the moral from this brief historical sketch: all varieties of language aspire toward that of the power elite. If the president of the United States, his cabinet, and the members of Congress today spoke French, anyone who wanted to be successful in the system would attempt to master that language. If the urban black dialect were the language of the power elite, everyone who wanted to enter the power structure would attempt to master the phonetic and grammatical characteristics of Black English.

According to Edward L. Thorndike,[3] English is composed of these elements:

WORDS OF	PERCENT
Old English origin	61.7
French	30.9
Latin	2.9
Scandinavian	1.7
Mixed	1.3
Uncertain	1.3
Low German and Dutch	.3

French has had a double influence, because English speakers first got vocabulary items from the Normans and then picked up many French words when that language became an international means of communication among the elite.

Words Borrowed from French

By about 1154, Norman French words had begun to appear in English writing: *castel* ("castle"), *tur* ("tower"), *justice, pais* ("peace"). By the time Geoffrey Chaucer started writing, late in the fourteenth century, French had really taken hold, and it is estimated that about 13 percent of Chaucer's words are of French origin. Some of the words from French that ultimately established themselves in English: *contract, import, debt, felony, criminal, judge, ointment, medicine, surgeon, chamber, lodge, chapel, buttress, portal, vault.*

The following list will give you some idea of the influence that French has had on English since about 1500. The words are categorized by general subject to which they apply, and the first date of their appearance in print is indicated in parentheses.

Military and naval   colonel (1548), dragoon (a doublet of *dragon,* 1622), reveille (1644), corps (1711 in the military sense; *corpse,* "body," is from 1325), sortie (1795), barrage (1859 "dam"; 1917 in the sense of "bombardment").

People   viceroy (1524), bourgeois (1564), coquette (1611), chaperon (1720, used earlier to mean "hood"), habitué (1818), chauffeur (1899).

Buildings and furniture   scene (1540), parterre (1639), attic (1696), salon (1750), chiffonier (1806), hangar (1902).

Literature, art, music   rondeau (1525), hautboy (1575; later spelled oboe), burlesque (1656), tableau (1699), connoisseur (1714), brochure (1756), carillon (1803), renaissance (1840), matinée (1880).

Dress, fashion, and materials   grogram (1562; borrowed again as *grosgrain,* 1869), cravat (1656), denim (1695), chenille (1738), corduroy (1787), blouse (1840), cretonne (1870), suede (1884).

Food and cooking   fricassee (1568), table d'hôte (1617), soup (1653), croquette (1706), aspic (1789), restaurant (1827), chef (1842), mousse (1892).[4]

Etymology

Etymology is the history of a word's derivation. It is interesting to discover that English is truly an international language in that it has borrowed words from every part of the world. The following is a sample of English words and their etymologies. You might like to use this list for a game, the rules for which are simple: cover the right-hand column, and then guess the language from which the word came. Only the language from which the word came into English is the right answer. For instance, suppose that a word came from Latin into French and then into English from French; French would be the right answer. (The source here is *The American Heritage Dictionary of the English Language.*)

1. alcohol   New Latin. Latin got the word from the Arabic *al-kuhl* or *al-kohl.* In Medieval Latin, the word meant a fine powder of antimony used to tint the eyelids. By the way, we adopted the Arabic definite article along with the word, for *al* means "the."

2. assassin   French. The first source of the word was the Arabic *hashshashin,* meaning "hashish addicts." You might look up the fascinating story of this word in an encyclopedia.

3. basenji   Bantu, an African language.

4. Bible   Old French. The word was adopted during the Middle English period. The ultimate source was *Byblos,* the name of the Phoenician port from which papyrus, used for making paper, was shipped to Greece.

5. blitzkrieg   German. It means "lightning war."

6. booze   Dutch. It came into Middle English and originally meant "to carouse."

7. brougham   Scotch. From Henry Peter Brougham, Baron of Brougham and Vaux (1778–1868), a Scottish jurist. (Along the same lines, you might want to look up *sandwich.*)

8. burlesque   French. From the Italian *burlesco.* The *-que* ending should tip you off.

9. cigar   Spanish *cigarro,* possibly taken from the Mayan word meaning "tobacco."

10. didactic   From Greek *didaktikos,* "skillful in teaching."

11. egg   Old Norse. It came into Middle English.

12. flak   German *Fl(ieger)a(bwehr)k(anone),* "aircraft defense gun." Thus, the word is an acronym, like NASA, NATO, and countless others that are derived from the initial letters of their words.

13. gin   From Dutch *jenever,* which came from the Latin word *juniperus,* "juniper."

14. goulash   Hungarian.

15. goy   Yiddish.

16. gumbo   Bantu. The Louisiana French adopted it.

17. hamburger   From the German city Hamburg; short for *hamburger steak.*

18. jazz   The origin is uncertain, so you can give yourself credit for this one.

19. junk (ship)   From Portuguese *junko* and Dutch *jonk.* The Portuguese and Dutch took the word from Malay *jong,* "seagoing ship." Give yourself credit if you said either Portuguese or Dutch.

20. khaki   From Urdu (a language of India), "dusty" or "dust-covered." Urdu borrowed it from Persian.

21. kimono   Japanese.

22. lariat   From Spanish *la reata*.

23. lemon   Old French. The French borrowed it from Arabic, and Arabic borrowed it from Persian.

24. marijuana   Mexican Spanish. If you said Spanish, give yourself credit.

25. moose   From Natick, an American Indian language.

26. mukluk   Eskimo.

27. obnoxious   Latin.

28. papoose   Algonquian. If you said American Indian, give yourself credit.

29. polka   French and German. Borrowed from Polish.

30. ranch   From the Mexican Spanish *rancho*.

31. robot   From Czech.

32. rodeo   Spanish.

33. safari   Arabic.

34. samovar   Russian.

35. sauerkraut   German, "sour cabbage."

36. sauna   Finnish.

37. schlemiel   Yiddish.

38. schmaltz   German.

39. smorgasbord   Swedish.

40. stucco   Italian, but the Italians got it from Old High German.

41. syphilis   Latin. Syphilis was the title character of a poem (1530) by Girolamo Fracastoro, a Veronese physician who supposedly had the disease.

42. tamale   Mexican Spanish.

43. tavern   Old French. The French took it from the Latin *taberna*, "hut." It is interesting to note that *tavern* and *tabernacle* come from the same source.

44. thug   From Hindi, a language of India.

45. tomato   Spanish. The Spanish borrowed it from Nahuatl, the language of the Aztecs and other related tribes.

46. totem   From Ojibwa, an American Indian language.

47. verandah   From Hindi.

48. vodka	Russian. It is the diminutive of *voda,* "water," so *vodka* literally means "little water."
49. whiskey	From the Irish *usquebaugh.*
50. xenophobia	Made up of *xeno* from the New Latin, meaning "stranger" and adopted from the Greek, plus the Greek *phobos,* "fearing."

Other Sources for the English Vocabulary

It should now be obvious that borrowed words make up a great portion of our word stock, but there are other interesting ways in which new words enter the language.

Many English words are derived from an existing word to which a prefix or suffix is added. That was the process used to make the word *passive* into a verb by the addition of the suffix *-fy: passify.* The corresponding adjectival form would be *passific,* the noun would be *passification.* Once the word *telegraph* came into the language by the process of combining the Greek root *tele,* meaning "far," with the Greek root *graph,* meaning "write," the words *telegraphy, telegrapher,* and *telegraphic* were easily derived.

Compounding is a common source of new words: *air-plane, free-loader, light-house-keeper.*

Words also undergo *functional shift:* that is, they move from one category to another. The noun *freak* is now used as a verb: "Gloria *freaked* Tony." Or perhaps it would be better to say that the categories of English words are to some extent fluid. The noun *head,* for instance, is also used as an adjective:

The *head* man is the president.

and a verb:

Thompson *headed* the investigation.

Here is another example of functional shift:

A secretary says, "I didn't back-file the letter; I waste-basketed it."[5]

In the process of *back-formation,* a new word is created by removing a suffix from an existing word: *editor/edit, burglar/burgle, lazy/laze,* and many more. *Clipping* is much like back-formation, but does not limit itself to the deletion of suffixes: *dormitory/ dorm, omnibus/bus, examination/exam, laboratory/lab.*

In the etymologies, we saw a word that entered the language from a proper name: *brougham*. There are many more such words: *sandwich, pasteurization, pander* (from the character Pandarus in Chaucer's *Troilus and Cressida*), *calico* (from Calcutta), and *bowdlerize* (from Thomas Bowdler, who produced a "cleaned-up" edition of Shakespeare).

Some words are simply *coined*. *Kodak* is one such word that was made up, and more recently Standard Oil coined *Exxon* as a trade name.

These are only some of the sources of words in English. If this discussion has aroused your interest in words and their nature, it has served its purpose. To be a good writer, you should be interested in—even fascinated by—words and their ways, and in your writing you must make careful choices of words.

WHAT ARE DIALECTS?

A *dialect* is a version of a language spoken by a group of people—for example, the Brooklyn and Southern dialects in American English and Cockney in Britain. Dialects are mutually intelligible; that is, the speaker of one dialect of a language can understand the speakers of other dialects. *And everyone in the language group speaks a dialect,* whether it be the dialect of the majority or a minority, of a limited geographical area or as widespread as what is sometimes called *standard,* the dialect of Tom Brokaw and other television newscasters.

Even an untrained observer can recognize dozens—if not hundreds—of dialects of English. From one point of view, at least, there is no such thing as the English language, but merely a number of mutually intelligible dialects.

No two people—even those in the same dialect group—speak exactly alike, which is to say that we all have our own *idiolects*. So we can look at language this way:

- A *language* is a collection of dialects (and dialects of a language are mutually intelligible).
- A *dialect* is a collection of idiolects with certain features in common.
- An *idiolect* is the language used by the individual speaker.

It is possible, therefore, to say that *idiolect* reflects the speaker's personal identity in speech. *Dialect* represents his or her social or geographical identification.

Development of Dialects

Dialects develop, it seems, because of either cultural or geographical isolation. For example, the West Indies have been relatively isolated, and they have developed and maintained their own dialects, such as that spoken in Jamaica. Similarly, the social isolation of blacks in the United States undoubtedly contributed to the development of the urban black dialect that one hears in large cities from coast to coast.

The following chart makes this point vividly:

	NORTHERN	SOUTHERN
EDUCATED	you (men, women)	you all
UNEDUCATED	youse	you all

The Northern *you* and *youse* mark a cultural distinction; the Southern *you all* is a regional usage. Therefore, when we consider dialect, we must think of the cultural and geographic variations of speech.

Prestige Dialects

As we have seen, every speaker of every language belongs to a dialect group—that is, all of us speak dialects. However, not all dialects in a language have equal prestige. The most common prestige dialect in America is standard, which is the kind of language spoken by most newscasters.

Since there is a standard dialect, we can say that any other dialect is *nonstandard,* but the word "nonstandard" does *not* imply "substandard." Nor should you assume that the only prestigious dialect in America is standard. For instance, there is considerable evidence that a certain kind of British accent confers an advantage in America—namely, the accent used by announcers of the British Broadcasting Corporation. To a great many Americans, this dialect sounds refined, cultured, while a dialect such as that spoken by some Brooklynites sounds uncultured, even crude.

A Look at a Nonstandard Dialect

The differences among dialects of a language are always fairly superficial. To give you some idea of how dialects differ from one another, I would like to present a brief description of Sanpete, spoken in central Utah, where Sanpete County is located. Like other dialects, Sanpete can be identified by certain of its *vocabulary items,* by *pronunciation,* and by some ways in which words are put together in sentences.

A vocabulary difference: the word *husband* is practically nonexistent in spoken Sanpete, so that one might speak of "Mary and her *man,*" whereas standard would use "Mary and her *husband.*" In Sanpete, the noun *drink* means almost exclusively a carbonated beverage other than cola. Therefore, if a Sanpeter asks you if you want a drink, he does not mean water, nor does he mean a martini, but rather root beer, orange soda, or something of the kind.

Sanpete has one noticeable *phonetic* variation from standard: the pronunciation of the sequence of letters *or* as in *horse.* The Sanpeter pronounces *horse* as a speaker of standard would pronounce *harse,* if there were such a word. Thus, "fork" is /fark/, and "corn" is /carn/.

The structural variations that differentiate Sanpete from standard are limited. The phrase *and them* means something like "and the others." Thus, "Let's go visit Ken and them" means something like "Let's go visit Ken and the other members of his family." Also, the phrase *to home* is used for *at home:* "I wonder if Evelyn and them are *to home.*"

Let's go on briefly to discuss the Sanpete dialect, for we can learn some important lessons from it. People who have lived in Sanpete all their lives and have become respected members of the community have pronounced nonstandard dialects, that is, they speak Sanpete. They have no cultural reason to change, and they have maintained their relative geographical isolation. However, when young people move from Sanpete into other societies, they tend to lose their native dialect, for they often enter communities in which Sanpete is not a prestige dialect. Therefore, they change their speech patterns in order to avoid the sneers and snickers that their nonstandard dialect would arouse in the standard-speaking community.

Dialect and Social Mobility

The next point to be made is fairly complex, but it is interesting and important. Take a look at the graph on page 411, from William Labov's *The Study of Nonstandard English.*[b] As is generally known, many New Yorkers tend to suppress the /r/ sound in such words as *guard, car,* and *beard,* pronouncing them something like this: /guahd/, /cah/, /behd/. From the point of view

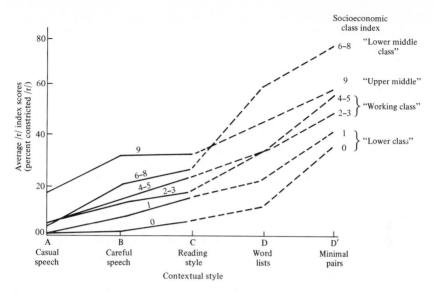

Class stratification of /r/ in *guard, car, beer, beard,* etc., for native New York City adults.

of standard English, this pronunciation is, of course, "improper." In casual speech, none of the groups of speakers pronounce the /r/ more than 20 percent of the time, but as the types of usage change from casual speech to careful speech to reading sentences to reading word lists and finally to reading minimal pairs (such as *car* and *far*), all groups increase the percentage of pronounced /r/s. But notice which group increases most dramatically: the lower middle class, even more than the upper middle class.

The explanation for this fact is most interesting. As Labov says, "This 'hypercorrect' behavior, or 'going one better,' is quite characteristic of second-ranking groups in many communities." The more motivated a group is toward upward social mobility, the harder that group will try to speak the power dialect. Therefore, it would seem, change in dialect is intimately connected both with one's place in the social-economic hierarchy and with one's aspirations to move upward. No group will change its dialect as long as the members of the group feel that they have no chance to improve their lot in the prevailing economic and social system.

In highly stratified situations, where society is divided into two major groups, the values associated with the dominant group are assigned to the dominant language by all. Lambert and his colleagues at

McGill University have shown how regular are such unconscious evaluations in the French-English situation in Quebec, in the Arabic-Hebrew confrontation in Israel, and in other areas as well. When English-Canadians heard the same person speaking Canadian French, on the one hand, and English, on the other, they unhesitatingly judged him to be more intelligent, more dependable, kinder, more ambitious, better looking and taller—when he spoke English. Common sense would tell us that French-Canadians would react in the opposite manner, but in fact they do not. Their judgments reflect almost the same set of unconscious values as the English-Canadians show. This overwhelmingly negative evaluation of Canadian French is a property of the society as a whole. It is an omnipresent stigma which has a strong effect on what happens in school as well as in other social contexts.[7]

In other words, the social stratification of dialects is tragic not only because the speakers of prestige dialects look down on the speakers of nonprestige dialects, but also because the speakers of nonprestige dialects *look down on themselves.* It is hard to estimate the damage that this linguistic arrogance causes, but any American can look around and sense the devastation that whole classes and races have undergone because of attitudes toward dialect.

Two points are worth repeating. By definition, the dialects of a language are mutually comprehensible. When a dialect becomes incomprehensible to other speakers of a language, that dialect has become another language, as is the case with Dutch, which drifted so far away from High German as to become a separate language.

The second point is equally important. All the evidence indicates that no language or dialect is inferior to any other language or dialect. Every language and dialect will do everything that its speakers want it to do. The idea that you can "think better" in one language or dialect than in another is simply a destructive myth.

Switching Dialects

Now a significant problem arises—one that you must solve for yourself: should the individual speaker make an effort to change his or her dialect? Though it is very difficult, if not impossible, for some people to change their pronunciation, every normal speaker of English can master the grammatical and structural niceties of standard spoken and written English. Let's take a representative structure from urban black dialect as an example of the insignificant differences between urban black and standard.

A typical urban black sentence is

Didn't nobody see it.

At first glance, it may seem to be far removed from standard

Nobody saw it.

Both sentences are in past tense. In the urban black sentence it is the auxiliary verb *didn't* that shows this tense, while in the standard version of the same idea tense is carried by *saw*. In this case, then, nonstandard can be changed to standard simply by changing the tense carrier. (No speaker of urban black would say *Didn't nobody saw it.*)

Another characteristic of urban black is the omission of the possessive *'s,* so that a typical sentence would be

Fido is John dog.

rather than

Fido is John's dog.

There are other differences between urban black and standard, but the point is this: surely a child or young person who can master the complications of surviving in a modern city can, *if he or she wants to,* also master the negatives, possessives, tense systems, and other features of standard English.

In my own opinion, the best solution to the problem of dialect change is this: don't do it. We should change society's attitudes toward dialects and leave the dialects alone. America avowedly honors its cultural diversity, and certainly one of the most important aspects of a culture is its dialects. Why should people give up so important a part of themselves as the way in which they and the other members of their culture speak?

But, sadly, until society's attitudes do change, I honestly believe that the ability to speak and write standard can well mean money in your pockets and power in your hands.

Exercise: Watch Your Language

1. Find someone who speaks a minority dialect, and do an informal study of it, recording its features in notes. How does it differ from standard in vocabulary, pronunciation, and structure? You may want to report on your "field work" in class discussion or in a brief essay.
2. What seem to be the outstanding features of your idiolect?
3. Listen to and think about the language of someone who speaks your dialect. What are the features of that person's idiolect?
4. Do some features of a person's idiolect or dialect annoy you? What are they? Why are they annoying?
5. In a standard encyclopedia, look up "Gullah." What did you learn about dialect? Discuss your findings.

FIGURATIVE LANGUAGE

Meanings can be expressed either literally or figuratively. For instance, here is an idea expressed literally:

> Nature is holy and mysterious, and can be understood only dimly by man.

The French poet Charles Baudelaire (as translated by R. G. Stern) expressed that idea figuratively in this way:

> Nature is a temple from whose living pillars
> Confusing words are now and then released.

Comparison of these examples raises a question: why express ideas figuratively at all? The answer is complicated and will take up the rest of this chapter, but to get our discussion under way, a couple of tentative answers might be advanced.

First, the figurative statement is more imagistic; it presents something for the reader's mind to "see." As has been pointed out again and again in this book, concrete, specific language has a special power that general, abstract language does not. For total comprehension of ideas, the mind often seems to need images.

Second, as if by magic, a great deal more meaning can usually be compressed into a figurative statement than into a literal one. Everyone would agree, I think, that the second example is a good deal more suggestive than the first—which is simply another way of saying that figurative language compresses meaning and is thus economical. The figure *Nature is a temple* is a good example. The word *temple* implies the whole history of humanity's veneration of something higher than itself: a magnificent structure (for a temple is not a mere church), a holy place, the concept of worship, the notion of the universality of worship (for all religions have temples), the smallness of the individual in relation to the structure (for a temple is not the Little Brown Church in the Vale), the concept of deity, a sense of quietness and wonder, mystery and awe—and on and on. So, everyone would grant, figurative language has considerable power. But not everyone—in fact, almost no one—wants to write poetry.

It turns out, however, that figurative language is not only vivid and useful, but absolutely essential in most kinds of writing.

For example, explaining how an airplane flies, the author of the following passage first states Bernoulli's theorem in literal terms and then explains it with an *analogy*, a form of comparison you are already familiar with (see pages 67–70).

> The ordinary airplane is held up by air pressure on its wings and this is explained by a very strange theorem first propounded by the Swiss mathematician Bernoulli. Bernoulli's theorem states that when a fluid flows past a fixed object the pressure exerted sideways on the object decreases as the velocity of flow increases.
>
> For example, start a water hose spurting a jet of water straight up in the air, then place a Ping-Pong ball on top of the jet. The ball bounces and twists but manages to stay on top of the stream of water—defying all apparent logic. What actually happens as the water flows around the ball? First it tends to slip to one side, say to the left. The water divides around the ball, much of it shooting straight up on the right side of the ball: some of it forced to take the long way around to the left. The detour makes the water slow down and as it slows its sidewise pressure builds up. Simultaneously the pressure of the high speed water shooting up the right side of the ball has lowered, and so the ball moves toward the low-pressure side, away from the high-pressure side and back into the center of the jet.
>
> The shape of an *airfoil* (wing section) is so designed as to increase the pressure of passing air on the underside and decrease it on the upper surface of the wing. This is accomplished in two ways—by tilting the wing slightly up at the front so that the incoming air hits the underside of the wing and slows down (increasing the pressure), and by forcing the air to travel a longer path over the upper surface than it travels along the lower surface of the wing.
>
> —Richard Korff, "How Does It Work?—The Airplane"

416

This passage draws an analogy between what happens when a Ping-Pong ball dances at the top of a stream of water and the function of an airplane's wing, the purpose being to clarify Bernoulli's principle. The analogy clearly has made understanding easier.

Much like analogy, in that they draw comparisons, are metaphor and simile.

Metaphor

The meaning of the term *metaphor* will become obvious as this section progresses. For the moment, let's take a look at metaphors that present different views of human beings:

> Humans are machines.
> Humans are biochemical systems.
> Humans are gods.

The first example implies that human beings do not have free will, but respond to the laws of mechanics as do such machines as pulleys or gears; in the next one, humans are only a collection of chemicals, such as might emerge from a laboratory; and in the last, humans assume the qualities of divinity. In a real sense, we can think of metaphors as instruments whereby we generate and organize our knowledge of the world. If we view humans as machines, our conclusions about them will be quite different from those that are based on a view of humanity as a divine image of God.

The following passage is metaphoric because we do not believe that people on New York sidewalks actually dance, and yet we sense that their movements can be viewed as if they were a ballet company in a theater:

> The stretch of Hudson Street where I live is each day the scene of an intricate sidewalk ballet. I make my own entrance into it a little after eight when I put out the garbage can, surely a prosaic occupation, but I enjoy my part, my little clang, as the droves of junior high school students walk by the center of the stage dropping candy wrappers.
>
> —Jane Jacobs, "Sidewalk Ballet"

Verbs frequently carry the metaphorical sense of a passage:

> Headstones *stagger* under great draughts of time. . . .
>
> —John Berryman

Literally, the line would read something like this:

> The headstones stand at odd angles. . . .

Drunks stagger, carriers stagger under heavy loads, and even dogs can stagger; only animate, humanlike beings can literally stagger.

Adjectives can also carry the metaphorical burden:

> After great pain a *formal* feeling comes—
> The nerves sit *ceremonious* like tombs;
> The *stiff* Heart questions—was it He that bore?
> And yesterday—or centuries before?
>
> —Emily Dickinson

In what sense is a feeling formal? We know of formal statements, dress, dinners. But feelings? The adjective *formal* seems to apply only to nouns that are in some way tangible; we can hear the formality of a speech and see the formality of a dinner, but there is no direct way for us to experience someone else's feelings. The adjective *ceremonious* seems to have the same quality; it will not apply literally to that which cannot be experienced directly in some way. And, of course, the adjective *stiff* applies only to substances like rubber that have varying degrees of flexibility.

Finally, adverbials can create metaphorical sense:

> When men were all asleep the snow came flying,
> In large white flakes falling on the city brown,
> *Stealthily* and perpetually settling and loosely lying. . . .
>
> —Robert Bridges

The point here is that only humans or animals can be stealthy: a cat or a burglar, for instance. Snow, rain, and soot can merely fall.

As these explanations have pointed out, metaphor arises when meanings don't quite add up. If I say that *Herman is a young Greek god,* you will undoubtedly take my statement to be metaphorical, for you will assume that I don't really believe that Herman is an immortal living on Mount Olympus, but that I intend something like this: Herman is extremely handsome and well proportioned.

However, not every break in meaning creates metaphor. For instance, if I encountered the following, I would be puzzled by it and interpret it as nonsense, not as a metaphor:

A carrot is a revolution.

The meaning of *carrot* is simply too far removed from the meaning of *revolution* for me to make any connection.

Metaphor, then, depends on some kind of interpretability, the exact nature of which is especially hard to explain. This is why the sentence

Colorless green ideas sleep furiously.

is taken to be not metaphorical but surrealistic.

The "poems" that computers write have this enigmatic, surreal quality:

Poem No. 078

THOUGH STARS DRAINED SICKLY UPON IDLE HOVELS
FOR LIFE BLAZED FAST UPON EMPTY FACES
WHILE BLOOD LOOMED BITTER ON IDLE FIELDS
NO MARTIAN SMILED

—RCA *Electronic Age*

Even the most sophisticated computers are unable to make the intricate decisions necessary to create metaphors. For, as should now be apparent, it takes knowledge of the world to create and interpret metaphors. If a reader believes that Greek gods exist and that Herman might well be one, then *Herman is a young Greek god* will not be a metaphorical statement for that reader; it will be literal.

Four Types of Metaphors

In an extremely interesting discussion, Laurence Perrine sheds further light on the nature of metaphor. Here is his definition:

A metaphor . . . consists of a comparison between essentially unlike things. There are two components in every metaphor: the concept actually discussed, and the thing to which it is compared. I shall refer to these, ordinarily, as the literal term and the figurative term. The two terms together compose the metaphor.[8]

Keeping in mind that a metaphor always consists of a literal term and a figurative term, we can identify four classes of metaphors: (1) those in which both terms are named; (2) those in which only the literal term is named, the figurative term being supplied by the reader; (3) those in which only the figurative term is named, the literal term being supplied by the reader; (4) those in which neither the literal nor the figurative term is named, both being supplied by the reader. Let's see how this works, using mostly Perrine's examples.

Type 1

Shakespeare provides an example of the first type, in which both literal and figurative terms are named:

> All the world's a stage,
> And all the men and women merely players.

This metaphor is "equational": *world* (literal term) = *stage* (figurative term). But the linking need not take place with the copula ("literal term *is* figurative term"). Prepositions can establish the link:

> Too long a sacrifice
> Can make a stone *of* the heart.
> > —William Butler Yeats

Here the literal term is *heart* and the figurative term is *stone*. The link can be established through a variety of other grammatical relationships:

> Come into the garden, Maud,
> > For the black bat, night, has flown.
> > —Alfred, Lord Tennyson

In this case, the metaphorical link between the literal term *night* and the figurative term *bat* is established through grammatical apposition. In the next example, the demonstrative *that* establishes the link between *beauty*, the literal term, and *lamp*, the figurative term:

> Be watchful of your beauty, Lady dear!
> How much hangs on that lamp, you cannot tell.
> > —George Meredith

Type 2

In metaphors that state only the literal term, the reader must supply the figurative term.

> Sheathe thy impatience; throw cold water on thy choler.
>
> —William Shakespeare

To understand these two metaphors the reader must supply the figurative terms *sword* and *fire,* for one *sheathes* a sword and *throws cold water on* a fire. Indeed, the metaphorical equation comes out something like this: *impatience = sword* and *choler = fire.*

> The tawny-hided desert crouches watching her.
>
> —William Butler Yeats

Here, the reader makes the equation *desert = lion,* because the adjective *tawny-hided* and the verb *crouches* suggest that animal.

Type 3

Here is an example of a metaphor in which the figurative term is given and the literal term must be supplied by the reader:

> Night's candles are burnt out.
>
> —William Shakespeare

The reader makes the inevitable equation *night's candles = stars.* Riddles often take this form:

> In spring I look gay
> Decked in comely array,
> In summer more clothing I wear;
> When colder it grows,
> I fling off my clothes,
> And in winter quite naked appear.

A child might ask, "What am *I?*" And the answer is the equation *I = tree.*

Type 4

The most difficult type of metaphor to interpret is that in which neither the literal term nor the figurative term is expressed.

> Let us eat and drink, for tomorrow we shall die.
>
> —Isaiah 22:13

The literal meaning of this is *Life is very short.* But the word *tomorrow* gives the clue to the proper figurative term: *day.* The quote from Isaiah means *Life is only a day*. *Life* is the literal term, and *day* is the figurative one.

Metaphor in Prose

Metaphor does not occur only in poetry; it can often be found in prose also, as the following example illustrates:

> The thesis which these lectures will illustrate is that this quiet growth of science has practically recoloured our mentality so that modes of thought which in former times were exceptional are now broadly spread through the educated world. This new colouring of ways of thought had been proceeding slowly for many ages in the European peoples. At last it issued in the rapid development of science; and has thereby strengthened itself by its most obvious application. The new mentality is more important even than the new science and the new technology. It has altered the metaphysical presuppositions and the imaginative contents of our minds; so that now the old stimuli provoke a new response. Perhaps my metaphor of a new colour is too strong. What I mean is just that slightest change of tone which yet makes all the difference. This is exactly illustrated by a sentence from a published letter of that adorable genius, William James. When he was finishing his great treatise on the *Principles of Psychology*, he wrote to his brother Henry James, "I have to forge every sentence in the teeth of irreducible and stubborn facts."
>
> —Alfred North Whitehead, *Science and the Modern World*

Simile

Simile is really a variety of metaphor, but one in which the equation between the literal and the figurative is expressed, usually by *like* or *as*. Examples:

> The inflated style is itself a kind of euphemism. A mass of Latin words falls upon the facts *like* soft snow, blurring the outlines and covering up all the details.
>
> —George Orwell, "Politics and the English Language"

> I ran, I shouted, I climbed, I vaulted over gates, I felt *like* a schoolboy let out on a holiday.
>
> —Vita Sackville-West

> So Elvis Presley came, strumming a weird guitar and wagging his tail across the continent, ripping off fame and fortune as he scrunched his way, and, *like* a latter-day Johnny Appleseed, sowing seeds of a new rhythm and style in the white souls of the white youth of America.
>
> —Eldridge Cleaver

And here is a simile from John Donne's "A Valediction: Forbidding Mourning":

> Our two souls therefore which are one,
>   Though I must go, endure not yet
> A breach, but an expansion,
>   *Like* gold to airy thinness beat.

Irony

The tapestry of language is richly woven with figurativeness, not only metaphor and simile, but a variety of other non-literal ways of conveying meaning.

Suppose I want to convey the notion that I disapprove of cheating on tests. I can state this idea literally:

> Cheating on tests is bad.

I can also convey my attitude through a metaphor or a simile:

> Cheating on tests is assassination of academic integrity.
> Cheating on tests is like playing cards with a marked deck.

I might also use irony:

> Cheating on tests is obviously an extremely noble thing for students to do.

For the last example to have an ironic effect, the reader must somehow see that I intend something quite different from what I say literally.

Metaphor comes about because of a mix of semantic features. Another way of saying this is that metaphor is a function of the denotations of words. Irony can result from a mix of *connotations*.

For example, the connotative value of *emperor* is one of glory, magnificence, and power. *Ice Cream* suggests the common and everyday. Therefore, when Wallace Stevens titled a poem "The Emperor of Ice-Cream," he created a verbal irony. The irony is reinforced by the opening of the poem:

> Call the roller of big cigars,
> The muscular one . . .

What does an emperor have to do with ice cream or rollers of big cigars?

Another example of this sort of irony:

> Rod McKuen is the poet laureate of the pimpled generation.

The phrase *poet laureate* is elevated in connotation, but *pimpled generation* is just the opposite The clash of connotations between these two terms conveys irony, which reveals a highly unfavorable attitude toward Rod McKuen.

An Example of Irony

The following is an ironic passage, and the irony stems largely from the word *momma* applied to America, for *momma* has a richly (perhaps overly) sentimental connotation, and the writer's attitude toward America is hardly sentimental:

> Now that I am a man, I have "given up childish ways." I realize that America is my momma and America was Momma's momma. And I am going to place the blame for injustice and wrong on the right momma. Even today, when I leave my country to appear on television and make other public appearances in foreign countries, I find it difficult to speak of the injustices I experience in this country. Because America is my momma. Even if Momma is a whore, she is still Momma. Many times I am asked if I would go to war if drafted. I always answer, "Yes, under one condition; that I be allowed to go to the front line without a gun. Momma is worth dying for, but there is nothing worth killing for. And if I ever change my opinion about killing, I will go to Mississippi and kill that Sheriff who spit in my wife's face."
>
> America is my momma. One fourth of July, I want to go to the New York harbor and talk to Momma—the Statue of Liberty. I want to snatch that torch out of her hand and take her with me to the ghetto and sit her down on the street corner. I want to show her the "tired, the poor, the huddled masses yearning to breathe free." I want to show Momma what she has been doing to her children. And Momma would weep. For the grief of the ghetto is the grief of the entire American family.
>
> —Dick Gregory, *The Shadow That Scared Me*

The passage is not, of course, unrelieved irony. It is a mixture of the ironic and the straightforward. In particular, the last sentence in each paragraph is completely straight.

A Second Example

In this passage, Lenny Bruce attacks Americans' homogenized version of themselves and their country:

> I credit the motion picture industry as the strongest environ-mental factor in molding the children of my day.
>
> Andy Hardy: whistling; a brown pompadour; a green lawn; a father whose severest punishment was taking your car away for the weekend.
>
> Warner Baxter was a doctor. All priests looked like Pat O'Brien.
>
> The superintendent of my school looked like Spencer Tracy, and the principal looked like Vincent Price. I went to Hollywood High, folks. Lana Turner sat at the next desk. Roland Young was the En-glish teacher and Joan Crawford taught general science. "She's got a fabulous body, but she never takes that shop apron off."
>
> Actually, I went to public school in North Bellmore, Long Is-land, for eight years, up until the fifth grade. I remember the routine of milk at 10:15 and napping on the desk—I hated the smell of that desk—I always used to dribble on the initials. And how enigmatic those well-preserved carvings were to me: BOOK YOU.
>
> —*How to Talk Dirty and Influence People*

The irony in this passage comes from the fact that the reader knows what Bruce's attitude is, even though he does not specify it. He is saying something like this: Americans' vision of them-selves is false and callow and unthinking. The last paragraph, in which Bruce begins to tell it like it really was, is the tip-off to the irony of what has gone before.

The effect of irony is powerful, for it makes the reader a conspirator with the writer. The reader says unconsciously, "I know what this guy is getting at; I'm in on the secret of his meaning—even though he doesn't give that meaning directly, in so many words."

Other Figures

Literally hundreds of kinds of figures of speech have been identified and given such tongue-twisting names as *aposiopesis, diacope, epitimesis, hypozeuxis, poiciologia,* and so on. We will let most of these rest in peace, but a few of them are useful enough to deserve brief mention.

Metonymy and Synecdoche

Metonymy is a kind of metaphor in which a term that is closely associated with the literal term is substituted for it. Thus

> He lived by the sword and died by the sword.

substitutes the word *sword* for *force or violence,* the sword being closely associated with force and violence.

Closely related to metonymy is *synecdoche,* the figure of speech in which a part stands for the whole.

> At least fifty sails set out for the race.

The sails are only parts of the racing yachts, but they stand for the whole.

Oxymoron

An *oxymoron* joins two contradictory terms to create a paradox. When this device is used unintentionally, it can produce confusion and seem foolish. But when it is used well, as for example by Shakespeare in *Romeo and Juliet* ("O heavy lightness! serious vanity!"), an oxymoron can convey additional insights through its startling combinations. "Holy devil" and "Hell's Angels" are two contemporary examples of oxymoron.

Overstatement and Understatement

Overstatement and *understatement* (*hyperbole* and *litotes* in the jargon) also are figurative devices. The figurative effect arises when the reader understands that the writer is overstressing or understressing a statement. In other words, there is a disjunction between the importance that the writer *seems* to put on a statement and its actual importance. Here is an example of overstatement:

> He [a lion] roared so loud, and looked so wonderous grim,
> His very shadow durst not follow him.
>
> —Alexander Pope

And here is an example of understatement:

> God loves his children not a little.

This means, of course, that God loves his children a very great deal.

Review

The following passages use a variety of kinds of figurative language. Underline the figurative elements, and name them if you can. Try to restate the ideas, eliminating the figures. What is lost? What is gained, if anything? Why?

1. Madison Avenue frequently exaggerates the importance of new features and encourages consumers to dispose of partially worn-out goods to make way for the new.

   —Alvin Toffler

2. Nobody knows how many people in America moonlight. . . .

   —Peter Schrag

3. In the magazines and newspapers, top management, formerly so autocratic (think of Henry Luce), now casts itself at the feet of the publicity intellectuals, seeking their intercession with the youth-worshipping public. One picks up *The New York Times* and reads on the front page that the posthumous homosexual novel of E. M. Forster is about to appear in England. Why not simply Forster's posthumous novel, on page 40? No, the word is HOMOSEXUAL and it is on the front page. The *Times* still keeps up its statesmanlike and grave appearance, but its journalism is yellower than ever. It has surrendered without a fight to the new class.

   —Saul Bellow

4. The bridge by which we cross from tragedy to comedy and back again is precarious and narrow.

   —Christopher Fry

5. Miss Nims, take a letter to Henry David Thoreau. Dear Henry: I thought of you the other afternoon as I was approaching Concord doing fifty on Route 62. That is a high speed at which to hold a philosopher in one's mind, but in this century, we are a nimble bunch.

   —E. B. White

6. Sex is dead. Nobody seems to have noticed its passing, what with the distraction caused by recent reports of the death of God, the death of Self, the death of the City, the death of Tragedy, and all the other cultural obituaries of the past few years. Yet it is a fact: sex is dead and we must begin to learn how to live in a world in which that is an incontrovertible fact.

   —Earl H. Brill

7. I have been told to "look down from a high place over the whole extensive landscape of modern art." We all know how tempting high places can be, and how dangerous. I usually avoid them myself. But if I must do as I am told, I shall try to find out why modern art has taken its peculiar form, and to guess how long that form will continue.

   —Kenneth Clark

8.   I am the daughter of earth and water,
            And the nursling of the sky:
       I pass thro' the pores of the ocean and shores;
         I change, but I cannot die.

For after the rain when with never a strain,
    The pavilion of heaven is bare,
And the winds and sunbeams with their convex gleams,
    Build up the blue dome of air,
I silently laugh at my own cenotaph,
    And out of the caverns of rain,
Like a child from the womb, like a ghost from the tomb.
    I arise and unbuild it again.

        —Percy Bysshe Shelley, "The Cloud"

Notes

[1] Harold B. Allen, *Linguistic Atlas of the Upper Midwest,* I (Minneapolis: Univ. of Minnesota Press, 1973), pp. 390–92.

[2] Robert S. Gold, "The Vernacular of the Jazz World," *American Speech,* 32 (Dec. 1957), 271–82.

[3] Edward L. Thorndike, "The Teacher's Word-Books," in Stuart G. Robertson, ed., *The Development of Modern English,* rev. Frederic G. Cassidy (Englewood Cliffs, N.J.: Prentice-Hall, 1954), p. 155.

[4] W. Nelson Francis, *The English Language: An Introduction* (New York: W. W. Norton, 1965), p. 144.

[5] Francis, p. 157.

[6] William Labov, *The Study of Nonstandard English* (Urbana, Ill.: National Council of Teachers of English, 1969).

[7] Labov, p. 31.

[8] Laurence Perrine, "Four Forms of Metaphor," *College English,* 33 (Nov. 1971), 125–38.

REFERENCE GUIDE

John S. Nixon, Rancho Santiago College

The Sentence
Style
Diction
Punctuation and Mechanics

This "Reference Guide" will be especially useful as you edit, or clean up, your writing. We recommend that you compose a first draft of any manuscript before you consult the Guide or try to do any editing. Although the composing process is different for each of us, and some of us edit as we compose, editing should not interfere with the more creative and challenging activities of discovering and organizing ideas. You can turn to the Guide later, as you revise your drafts, whenever you are uncertain about any of the conventions or whenever your instructor finds you are weak in a certain topic.

The Sentence

 **Words** alone are relatively useless without the contexts and connections provided by sentences. To make good sense, words must be connected in a manner that fits a particular context of communication and conforms to the rules of the language. A group of words that does not respect the rules of language is nonsense: "Sleep blue frozen pillow hurry Tom." Words connected to each other in a manner that conforms to the rules of language and that relates to a context familiar to the reader make perfect sense: "Grammar is not my favorite subject." The section that follows offers a review of basic sentence patterns and a number of useful variations and cautions.

REVIEW OF BASIC SENTENCE ELEMENTS

The ability to recognize the basic elements of sentences is an important first step toward effective editing.

Subjects and Predicates

All sentences have two basic elements, the subject and the predicate. The four simple sentences that follow illustrate the basic subject and predicate pattern:

Those students / registered late.
    SUBJECT   PREDICATE

The woman / ordered a rare steak.
    SUBJECT   PREDICATE

His brother / is a test pilot.
     SUBJECT   PREDICATE

George / laughed.
SUBJECT   PREDICATE

The complete subject identifies who or what the sentence is about and includes the simple subject and all the words associated with it. In the first sentence, *students* is the simple subject, and *those students* makes up the complete subject. What the sentence says about the subject is called the predicate. The complete predicate includes the verb and all the words associated with it. In the first example, *registered* is the verb, and *registered late* makes up the complete predicate.

The subject and the predicate often contain other elements that connect, complete, or modify the meaning of the sentence. The subject may be one word, as in the fourth example, but more often than not it includes one or more modifiers, like the word *those* in the first sentence. We can also substitute a pronoun for the complete subject *those students:*

They registered late.

When a pronoun is the subject of a sentence, the reader must never be in doubt as to what noun the pronoun is replacing (see Pronoun-Antecedent Agreement, pages 444–45).

A complete subject may be a group of words, or phrase:

Most of the students registered late.

A complete subject may also contain a verb:

What most students want is to register early.

This construction is called a clause, and it can function as the subject of a sentence. A clause always has a subject and a verb of its own.

The predicate always contains a verb, and it too may have modifiers, usually expressed as phrases or clauses. In the sentence *George laughed, laughed* is a single-word predicate; if we expand the sentence to *George laughed at her funny costume,* the predicate includes the modifying phrase *at her funny costume.*

When a verb requires an object to complete the predicate, it is called a transitive verb, as in *Laura kicked the ball.* Here, the transitive verb *kicked* is completed by the direct object *ball.* When the verb does not require an object to complete the predicate, it is called an intransitive verb, as in *George laughed*. With many verbs, the structure of the sentence determines whether the verb is transitive or intransitive: *Mary eats* [transitive] *pizza every Saturday,* or *Mary eats* [intransitive] *well.*

A verb may also be a linking verb; that is, it completes the predicate by linking the subject to another noun or to a modifier, which is its complement, as in these examples:

> David *looks* tired.
>
> She *became* a lawyer.
>
> The surf *seems* unusually rough.

Notice that the subjects of these sentences perform no action. If the second example were to read *She visited a lawyer, lawyer* would become the direct object, the receiver of the action performed by the subject, *she.* But in the sentence *She became a lawyer,* the verb *became* merely links the subject, *she,* to the complement, *lawyer.* Linking verbs connect subjects to their complements.

Subjects and verbs may be compound (as in the sentence you are now reading, in which *subjects and verbs* is the complete subject):

> *Democrats* and *Republicans registered* and *voted* in record numbers.

Connectors

The compound subject and the compound verb in the preceding example are both joined together by the connector *and.* Connectors, which join other elements in a sentence, can be coordinating connectors or subordinating connectors. A coordinating connector (*and, but, or, nor, yet* . . .) joins two equal or similar sentence elements:

> Susan laughed *and* cried during the movie.
>
> Jason put the money in the bank, *but* he really wanted to spend it.

A subordinating connector joins two clauses (groups of words each containing a subject and a verb), making one of the clauses a subordinate clause, or grammatically dependent on the other. A subordinating connector may come between the clauses it joins, or it may come at the beginning of the sentence:

> We haven't decided *when* we will return.
>
> *If* you don't like the shirt, take it back.
>
> Chris likes the song *because* it reminds him of his first girlfriend.

Modifiers

Modifiers are words, phrases, or clauses that describe subjects, objects, complements, or other modifiers or that tell where, when, why, how, or under what conditions the action of verbs takes place. These sentences illustrate the various functions of modifiers:

A *perfect* game is rare.   [modifies the subject]

The group played an *old* hit.   [modifies the object]

She is the *best* candidate.   [modifies the complement]

We drove through *very* thick fog.   [modifies the modifier]

They ate *late.*   [modifies the verb—when]

He hid the money *in an empty can.*   [modifies the verb—where]

Taylor stopped eating *because he was full.*   [modifies the verb—why]

She fixed the vacuum *by replacing the plug.*   [modifies the verb—how]

If you go first, I will follow.   [modifies the verb—under what condition]

Exercise

Draw a single line under the simple subject and a double line under the verb in each of the following sentences.

1. The parachutist landed in the middle of the stadium.
2. He swerved to avoid a cat in the road.
3. Kelsey thought the recital was boring.
4. That curry dish is extremely spicy.
5. This humid weather has got to end soon.

Draw a single line under all the connectors and a double line under all the modifiers (words, phrases, and clauses) in the following sentences.

6. Although the surgery was difficult, she is expected to recover quickly.
7. The offer is tempting, but I think I should remain in town.
8. The delicate pattern of the embroidery is yet another example of her superior imagination and skill.
9. Godzilla and Rodan are squaring off again in Tokyo harbor.
10. If you are so sure, why not ask him yourself?

Problem Elements: Prepositional Phrases and Verbals

A common mistake in trying to locate the subject of a sentence is to pick a noun contained in a prepositional phrase. The subject of a sentence never appears within a prepositional phrase—a modifier consisting of a group of words that begins with a preposition. Here is a list of common prepositions:

about	below	from	out
above	beneath	in	over
across	beside	inside	past
among	between	into	through
around	by	of	to
at	during	off	toward
before	except	on	under
behind	for	onto	with

Notice how easily you can locate the subjects of the following sentences by crossing out the prepositional phrases:

> ~~During the thunderstorm~~, we sat ~~in the car~~.
>
> ~~From my vantage point~~, I could not see ~~inside the cave~~.
>
> She leaned ~~to the right~~ and nudged her opponent out ~~of bounds~~.
>
> ~~Despite their increasing representation in the workforce~~, women have failed to approach the income ~~of men~~.

Another problem element in sentences is verbals. Verbals are derived from their verbs, but they do not function grammatically as verbs and must not be confused with them. Notice that in these sentences

> *Dancing* is good exercise.
>
> I hope *to hear* from you soon.
>
> That is an *encouraging* sign.

the italicized words look like verbs, but they do not function as verbs. *Dancing* is the subject of its sentence; *to hear* is the complement of its sentence; and *encouraging* is the modifier of *sign*.

There are three different kinds of verbals: infinitives, participles, and gerunds. The infinitive usually begins with the infinitive marker *to*, followed by some form of a verb: *to win, to eat, to be thinking, to have chosen*. It may serve as a subject, an object, a complement, or a modifier:

> *To relocate* now would be a mistake.   [subject]
>
> He demanded *to be heard*.   [object]
>
> Laura hopes *to become* an actor.   [complement]
>
> The kitten climbed the drapes *to annoy* its owner.   [modifier]

The participle, also a word or phrase that derives from its verb, functions as a modifier. The present participle ends in *-ing* (*loving, worrying, smiling*). The past participle either ends in *-ed* (*disgruntled, recognized, inspired*) or is an irregular form (*sworn, stolen, broken, driven*). These sentences illustrate the forms and functions of participles:

> The *leading* candidate refuses to debate the issue. [modifies the subject]
>
> Ramon is a *paying* member. [modifies the complement]
>
> While in college, we lived on *frozen* foods. [modifies the object of *on*]
>
> *Having been disgusted* by his remark, she left home. [passive form of past participle; modifies the subject *she*]

The gerund functions as a noun and has the same form as the present participle. It is used as the subject, the object, or the complement of a sentence.

> *Eating* is my favorite pastime. [subject]
>
> David stopped *thinking*. [object]
>
> His top priority is *studying*. [complement]

Exercise

Draw a line under all the prepositional phrases in the following sentences.

1. You will find the flashlight in the bottom drawer.
2. In spite of his valiant efforts, David lost the business.
3. With all of her money, you would think she could dress better.
4. During the night, Judy walked in her sleep.
5. The clerk taped the receipt to the bottom of the box.

Draw a line under all the verbals in the following sentences. Then tell whether each verbal functions as a subject, an object, a complement, or a modifier.

6. Easing the pain is all we can do.
7. Disturbed by the latest figures, he promised to try harder.
8. The drunken man stumbled across the dimly lit street.
9. That was a most captivating performance.
10. The searing heat quickly penetrated the parched surface.

Sentence Sense and Good Writing and Editing

Sentence sense—an instinctive knowledge of where a sentence begins and ends and how a sentence is developed—is something every speaker of English already possesses. You began to acquire it as soon as you learned to talk, and you have been practicing it all your life. Sentence sense is an inherent part of your ability to speak English.

Using this sentence sense when you write can help you avoid or correct sentence fragments, run-ons, and other errors of mechanics and usage. It can also help you choose the best sentence style for a particular writing situation. That sounds great, you might say, but if I have sentence sense why do I make mistakes when I write? For many students, one of the blocks to using their sentence sense effectively is a fear of writing. Writing experiences in school are often unsatisfying and unpleasant; English classes may be confined to uninteresting writing topics and unending grammar lessons, or they may ignore sentence skills completely. For these and probably many other reasons, your instinctive sentence sense may be shut down by a fear or loathing of writing.

One way to turn on your sentence sense skills is to read your writing aloud. That may be old advice, but it works. As you revise and edit, read aloud, and you will find those sentence sense instincts returning. You will be able to hear where a sentence should begin and end. You will catch faults in punctuation and usage. In addition, you may hear weak sentences that do not communicate your ideas clearly and concisely. Just as sentence sense guides your speaking, it can guide your writing. It may, of course, need some fine-tuning, and the tools necessary for that are provided in this part of the Guide.

Fragments

A sentence fragment is a part of a sentence that is punctuated as if it were a whole sentence. Professional writers sometimes use fragments for emphasis or convenience, as in this passage from Stephen King's *Children of the Corn* (the fragments are italicized):

> The pop station they had been listening to was almost obliterated in static, and Burt switched, running the red marker slowly down the dial. *Farm reports. Buck Owens. Tammy Wynette. All distant, nearly distorted into babble.*

Putting words between a capital letter and a period does not necessarily make a sentence. Creative and casual writing aside, however, the English sentences you write should have a subject and a verb and should express a complete idea. Avoid fragments in formal writing—term papers, business reports and correspondence, scholarly essays, and so forth.

Fragment   Toxic waste poses a serious threat. Which we had better address.
Complete   Toxic waste poses a serious threat, which we had better address.
Complete   Toxic waste poses a serious threat—which we had better address.

There are a few exceptions, when fragments are acceptable even in formal writing. You may use them when asking and answering questions:

When is the report due? Tomorrow.

What's for dinner? Tacos.

Use fragments for recording conversations, since people do not always speak in complete sentences:

"He Who Walks Behind the Rows," Burt said, turning off the ignition. *"One of the nine thousand names of God only used in Nebraska, I guess. Coming?"*

—*Children of the Corn*

Remember that two constructions connected with a semicolon should be complete sentences, not fragments:

Incorrect   The lead singer appeared to slip on stage; although I couldn't see him very well.
Correct   The lead singer appeared to slip on stage, although I couldn't see him very well.

Frequently, fragments result from beginning a sentence with a subordinating word. A subordinate clause or phrase cannot stand alone as a sentence. A simple sentence beginning with one of the following subordinating words will come out as a fragment:

after	even	unless	whichever
although	if	until	while
as	since	when	who
as if	so that	where	whoever
because	that	wherever	
before	though	which	

Fragment   Until he leaves for home.
Complete   Until he leaves for home, I want you to stay close by.

Exercise

Rewrite these sentences to correct all the fragments. Rearrange phrases and clauses into complete sentences as you think best.

1. Although it was a beautiful day. I stayed inside.
2. We successfully completed the course. Realizing the experience would benefit us later.
3. Never forgetting the love she felt for us. We mourned her passing with happy memories.
4. To be or not to be. That is the question.
5. So Susan would not notice. Jeff hid the necklace in the closet.
6. She has only one ambition. To become a professional wrestler.
7. During the holidays. I always visit my grandparents.
8. At five o'clock in the morning. The newspaper always arrives.
9. Thickening the sauce before you add it to the meat. Always improves the texture of the stew.
10. Because the neighbors went on vacation. They asked me to feed their tropical fish.

Comma Splices

Using a comma to separate two complete thoughts (independent clauses) is a comma splice. The comma alone is not enough to join two complete thoughts, as this example shows:

> They have only circumstantial evidence on the suspect, he will be released this afternoon.

The most obvious way to correct a comma splice is to use a period to separate the independent clauses:

> They have only circumstantial evidence on the suspect. He will be released this afternoon.

Another method is to use a comma and a coordinating conjunction to separate the independent clauses. This is acceptable when you wish to give equal emphasis to the two clauses:

> They have only circumstantial evidence on the suspect, and he will be released this afternoon.

A third method of correcting a comma splice is to subordinate one independent clause to the other, acceptable when you do not wish to give the two clauses equal emphasis:

> Because they have only circumstantial evidence on the suspect, he will be released this afternoon.

When you use words like *however, consequently, therefore,* or *moreover* to join two independent clauses, the most common punctuation between the clauses is a semicolon:

> They have only circumstantial evidence on the suspect; consequently, he will be released this afternoon.

Fused or Run-On Sentences

Sentences connected with no punctuation at all between them are called fused or run-on sentences:

> Correcting fused sentences is easy the most common method is separating the sentences with a period.

Fused sentences are confusing to readers and should always be corrected.

> Correcting fused sentences is easy. The most common method is separating the sentences with a period.

Exercise

Using whatever method seems best, rewrite the following sentences to correct the fused sentences and comma splices.

1. The crisp autumn evening feels so good after such a long hot summer, any change in the weather is welcome.
2. The sandwiches in the commons are good, they are also very expensive.
3. Lydia arrived late she missed the crucial vote.
4. Although the instructor warned the students against excessive unexcused absences, his bark was worse than his bite, calling his bluff, several students were able to succeed in the class with minimal attendance.
5. The soccer coach had the team practice until dark, he said they would not have to practice tomorrow.
6. You should never use soap on a baby's face, its skin is very sensitive.
7. I usually agree with his foreign policy statements, however, he lost my vote with that last remark about human rights.
8. Bill's doctor suggests that he reduce his protein intake, red meat is the first food he should eliminate.
9. Margaret never questioned his sincerity, odd as it seems now, she would have done anything for him.

10. The computer program was difficult to learn, it sure saved a lot of time once I began using it.

When you string together a series of clauses that could stand alone as sentences with connectors like *and, but, for, so, yet,* you are probably writing a run-on sentence, as in this example:

> The church carnival began Friday evening, and all the volunteers were at their work stations by six o'clock, but the gates didn't open until seven o'clock, so the volunteers had plenty of time for setup.

This sentence can be improved by breaking it up into two sentences and subordinating two of the clauses:

> Because the church carnival began Friday evening, all the volunteers were at their work stations by six o'clock. And since the gates didn't open until seven o'clock, the volunteers had plenty of time for setup.

Run-on or fused sentences are difficult to understand and monotonous to read and to write. Avoid them in your writing.

Exercise

Using whatever method seems best, rewrite these sentences to avoid the run-on style.

1. The cost of housing has been steadily rising at an average rate of 23 percent each year, and this has forced more and more people to turn to low-income housing, but unfortunately there isn't enough of this type of housing available to those interested, so the government must supplement the construction industry so that it will build the necessary housing.
2. The children built a lavish castle of sand, but a particularly strong wave swamped it, so they moved farther back to build another, but a frisky, friendly dog wrecked their efforts, and they had to try again, so once more they put shovel and pail to sand, and on their last attempt produced a worthy castle, and it was admired by all passersby.
3. He jumped on his board and paddled out to where the waves were breaking; he spotted a wave and turned his board toward the shore, anticipating a good ride, but the wave was not as good as he had

expected, so he drifted with the current and waited for the next opportunity; patience and discipline are necessary qualities for skilled surfers.

SUBJECT-VERB AGREEMENT

Verbs must agree with their subjects in number and person. The rule seems simple enough, but the many variables that fall under the rule are often confusing to writers and readers alike.

A singular subject takes a singular verb. A plural subject takes a plural verb:

> His *collection* of stamps *is* extensive.   [singular]
> Their *collections* of stamps *are* extensive.   [plural]

If the subject is a personal pronoun (*I, we, they* . . .), the verb agrees in person with the pronoun. If the subject is a noun, the subject always takes the third-person form of the verb:

> *I am* hungry.   [subject and verb in first-person singular]
> *We are* late.   [subject and verb in first-person plural]
> The *bus stops* here.   [verb in third-person singular to agree with *bus*]

Many errors in subject-verb agreement arise because the writer has overlooked exceptions to the rule or has not allowed for unusual or difficult sentence constructions. We now review the more common variables you should be aware of.

Other Words Between Subject and Verb

Other words or phrases that come between the subject and the verb generally do not change subject-verb agreement:

> The *list* of resources *is* quite comprehensive.
> Political *campaigning*, with its increasing reliance on constant media exposure, *has become* a full-time job for most office seekers.

The subject (*list*) of the first sentence is singular. The phrase *of resources* that comes between the subject and the verb does not affect subject-verb agreement.

Inverted Word Order

Placing the verb before its subject in a sentence does not change subject-verb agreement. Also, words like *there, here, who, where, what,* and *which* can begin a sentence and precede the verb, but they do not offset subject-verb agreement:

There *are* two Mexican *restaurants* in my town.

Most severely affected by the early rains *were* the cotton *farmers.*

Where *are* the *Harvey's* now?

Compound Subjects

Subjects joined by the connector *and* usually take a plural verb:

The *choir* and the *organist work* well together.

Daily *watering* and weekly *fertilizing maintain* the plants in hot weather.

Susan's *mother* and *father are* out of town.

But there are several exceptions to this pattern that you should remember. If the compound subject stands for a single unit, the verb is singular:

The *cardiologist* and *chief* of medical staff *is* Doctor Bowen.

Raisin bran and *cream is* my favorite breakfast food.

When *every* or *each* precedes a group of singular subjects joined by *and,* the verb is singular:

Every Tom, Dick, and Harry *has* his own computer.

Each tree and shrub *was* carefully selected.

When subjects are joined by *or, either . . . or, neither . . . nor,* or *not only . . . but also,* the verb agrees with the subject nearest to the verb:

Either the United States or the Soviet Union *is hosting* the event.

Neither the doctor nor the nurses *were* able to respond in time.

Neither the nurses nor the doctor *was* able to respond in time.

Note the difference in the two sentences: the verb agrees with the part of the subject closest to it.

Relative Pronouns

When one of the relative pronouns (*who, which, that . . .*) is the subject of a subordinate clause, the verb in the clause agrees with the antecedent of the relative pronoun (the words it refers to):

This is one of those *situations that erode* our relationship. [The verb erode is plural because *that* refers to *situations*, which is plural.]

It is the *judge who decides* what is a fair punishment. [The verb *decides* is singular because *who* refers to *judge*, which is singular.]

Indefinite Pronouns

The following indefinite pronouns take singular verbs:

one	anyone	everyone	someone	each
no one	anybody	everybody	somebody	either
nobody	anything	everything	something	neither
nothing				

Anybody who drives under the influence of alcohol or drugs *is* a criminal.

Each of them *has* her merits.

Somebody has been sleeping in my bed.

Collective Nouns

A collective noun takes a singular verb when the unit it refers to is a whole, but it takes a plural verb when it refers to the parts of the whole:

SINGULAR (WHOLE)

His *family is* very conservative.

Two-thirds of the money *was* wasted.

The *jury is* deadlocked.

PLURAL (PARTS)

My *family have* all gone their separate ways.

Two-thirds of the receipts *have* been counted.

The *jury are* debating among themselves.

Exercise

In the following sentences, underline the correct form of the verbs in parentheses.

1. Neither Laura nor her mother (know, knows) the correct answer.
2. Each of the presidential candidates (has, have) experienced hecklers.
3. Tastes in exotic foods, of course, (vary, varies) greatly.
4. There (is, are) skiers on the slopes at daybreak.
5. The sentence (was, were) ten years in prison.

6. David's beach house, with beds for six, (is, are) available next week.
7. Anybody willing to work long hours (is, are) eligible.
8. Either Mary or Heather (plans, plan) to attend the meeting.
9. Which one of the horses (runs, run) in tomorrow's race?
10. An amusement park, as well as several hotels and restaurants, (is, are) planned for the site.

PRONOUN-ANTECEDENT AGREEMENT

A pronoun must always agree in number with its antecedent. Pronouns take the place of, or refer to, nouns or other pronouns, and the words they stand for are their antecedents. A singular antecedent requires a singular pronoun, a plural antecedent a plural pronoun.

> The *quarterback* forgot *his* audible play.   [singular]
> The *dancers* moved quickly through *their* routine.   [plural]

As with subject-verb agreement, the general rule for pronoun-antecedent agreement is simple and clear. Several problem constructions, however, offer variations on the rule, and it is these exceptions that you need to remember.

Such antecedents as *each, either, neither, one, anybody, anyone, everybody, a person,* and *one* take a singular pronoun:

> *Each* of the kittens has *its* distinctive marks.
> *A person* may indeed defend *herself* in court.

Notice that an antecedent like *a person* may take either a masculine or a feminine pronoun when the meaning is uncertain or the pronoun could refer to either sex. Your sense of purpose and audience should dictate the choice. Often, rewriting the sentence to eliminate gender reference or rewriting it in a plural form will prove more acceptable. For example:

> Self-defense in court is legal.
> People may indeed defend themselves in court.

When two or more antecedents are joined by *and,* the pronoun is plural; when two or more singular antecedents are joined by *or* or *nor,* the pronoun is singular:

> *Andy and Sarah* lost *their* place in line.
> Did *Andy or Sarah* lose *his or her* place in line?

A collective noun takes either a singular or a plural pronoun, depending on whether the unit is considered as a whole or as a group of parts:

SINGULAR (WHOLE)

The committee has to write *its* own objectives.

The choir has won many of *its* awards abroad.

PLURAL (PARTS)

The committee may argue in private, but *they* always agree in public.

The choir arranged most of *their* own music.

Exercise

In the following sentences, underline the correct form of the pronouns and verbs in parentheses.

1. The club sponsored (its, their) first dance last night.
2. Agreeing that (its, their) mission is to recommend policy, the committee appointed (its, their) chairperson as liaison to the president.
3. Neither the professor nor the students remembered when (he, they) discussed the final exam topics.
4. Each contestant must take (her, their) chances.
5. If any one of the patients (requires, require) transportation, (he, they) should call outpatient services.
6. The board of trustees may vote (itself, themselves) a stipend for attending meetings.
7. The piano instructor asked the class to play the tune (it, they) had studied the previous week.
8. A number of people (has, have) offered (his, her, their) suggestions for revising the election process.
9. The game warden moved the herd to (its, their) winter feeding ground.
10. Neither the bride nor the groom arrived on time for (his, her, their) wedding ceremony.

SHIFTS IN SUBJECTS AND VERBS

From our discussion of agreement, we can see that one factor influencing all the rules is consistency: what begins in the singular remains singular; what begins in the third person remains third person.

This kind of consistency is important beyond the requirements for sentence agreement. Using consistent forms of subjects and verbs not only in sentences but in paragraphs and longer compositions is an important element in clear, effective writing. (See chapter 11, "Paragraphs," for a more complete discussion.)

Subjects

A paragraph usually develops a single topic that is identified by subjects within the sentences of the paragraph. Readers have a better chance of understanding the topic of a paragraph when the topic is expressed through a consistent set of related subjects. You should avoid unnecessary shifts in the subject within the paragraph. The unity of the paragraph is enhanced when the general topic is expressed by the same subject or set of subjects. Of course, this is not an absolute rule, and you will have to make choices with your writing purpose and audience in mind. Notice the shifting subjects in this example:

> When Rush began, we had no idea how hectic and time-consuming it would be. Every fraternity had different traditions, and there was no time for us to prepare for the routines. The parties were fun; but always smiling and being polite grew old fast. Choosing the right fraternity was important. Knowing how to play their games was even more important. The pace of Rush was intense, but the end result meant a lot to us.

The topic of the paragraph is "the rewards and frustrations of Rush." The unity of the paragraph suffers because the topic is expressed through too many different subjects (fraternity, parties, games). Avoiding the unnecessary subject shifts improves the paragraph:

> When Rush began, we had no idea how hectic and time-consuming it would be. We had no time to learn the different traditions and routines of the fraternities. The parties were fun; but we tired of always smiling and being polite. We knew that choosing the right fraternity was important, and that knowing how to play their games was even more important. The pace of Rush was intense, but we knew the end result would be worth it.

Verbs

Unnecessary shifts in verb tense and voice are also awkward and often confusing to readers. As with unnecessary subject shifts, consistency is the guiding principle for verb shifts. Unless your topic demands a change in time, do not shift suddenly from present tense to past or from past tense to present. This passage illustrates the problem:

The pitcher *read* the catcher's sign. As he *moves* into his stretch, he *glanced* toward first base, checking the runner.

The time relationships signaled by the verbs in these sentences make no sense. The verbs should be consistently in the present or the past tense:

The pitcher *reads* the catcher's sign. As he *moves* into his stretch, he *glances* toward first base, checking the runner.

Consistency in voice is also important within sentences and para-graphs. Active and passive voice is discussed in more detail on pages 457–58. Here, we are only concerned with the principle of consistency, which is the same as for tense: a sentence is either passive or active, not both. This sentence illustrates the problem:

The lottery *was won* by Pete, but the officials *could not locate* him.

Shifting from the passive voice in the first clause to the active voice in the second clause is awkward. The sentence reads much better if both verbs are in the active voice:

Pete *won* the lottery, but the officials *could not locate* him.

Exercise

Revise the following passages to remove all the awkward shifts in subjects and verbs.

1. The temptation to skip classes is commonly felt by college students, and they sometimes ignore their academic responsibilities to take advantage of good weather. Instructors usually take a hard line on attendance, but the possible penalties incurred by the students who skip may not deter them from the outside pleasures of a summer day. Responsibility versus pleasure was always a natural part of student life. A person should consider the consequences carefully before they are completely consumed by the temptation to skip classes.
2. My composing process is begun by me finding an idea to write about, and I think this is the most difficult part of writing. The blank page stared at me while my blank mind stares back. Once an idea comes to mind, the challenge becomes writing a good first sentence. Choosing the right words to fit an idea is almost as difficult as finding the idea. One should relax with the composing process, and they should not get hung up by correctness and perfection on the first draft.

3. Cathy's birthday had finally arrived. We shopped all day Saturday in search of the right gift, and the electric wok seems perfect. Cathy always needs clothes, but we could not find anything at the right price that would fit her. Anyway, she loves to cook, and she just finished a Chinese cooking class. The gift is wrapped in red-striped paper, and we gave them to her at the party.

DANGLING MODIFIERS

A modifier should relate directly and only to the sentence element it modifies. Readers will easily misinterpret any sentence in which a modifier dangles—is not properly related to what it modifies. For example:

> *Standing on one leg in the swamp,* Joe saw the blue heron.

The sentence is unintentionally humorous because as it is written the first phrase modifies *Joe* rather than *blue heron,* and the reader pictures Joe standing on one leg in the swamp.

Here is another example of a dangling modifier:

> *To start a business venture,* money must be raised.

The reader is left to wonder: "Who is going to start the business venture?" Revised to change voice, the sentence no longer suffers from a dangling modifier:

> To start a business venture, you must raise money.

If you edit carefully—including listening to what you write—you ought to be able to find the dangling modifiers in your writing and revise the sentences that contain them. Here are several additional examples, with explanations and revisions:

DANGLING	REVISED
Skating on the ice, a log tripped Jane. [Who was skating? Not a log. *Jane* must be the subject.]	Skating on the ice, Jane tripped on a log.
To prepare a good stew, fresh ingredients must be used. [Who is preparing? Who is using? A subject must be added.]	To prepare a good stew, you must use fresh ingredients.

The boy and the girl argued loudly, telling him that she was right. [Who told him? You must add the subject *she*.]

The boy and the girl argued loudly, and she told him that she was right.

Darting under the rock, I saw the trout. [*I* should be the subject, so it is best to begin the sentence with *I*.]

I saw the trout dart under the rock.

Exercise

Revise the following sentences to eliminate the dangling modifiers.

1. Being very hungry, the stew tasted delicious.
2. The policeman eyed a jaywalker with his right hand on his nightstick.
3. After adjusting the thermostat, the room soon seemed comfortable.
4. Realizing something terrible waited behind the bedroom door, the adrenalin raced through my body.
5. To qualify for the team, the senior cheerleaders must judge the candidates' performance on all standard routines.
6. After planting the fuchsias, the garden showed a lot of spring color.
7. Planning the vacation well in advance, the best airline fares were available to Mike.
8. Studying the effects of radiation exposure, the consequences of nuclear war become more meaningful to us.
9. Looking through the microscope, the tiny microbe came into view.
10. Encouraged by the results of the last test, hope filled the room.

FAULTY PARALLELISM

Sentence elements in a pair or a series should always be parallel in their grammatical form. (Parallelism is discussed on pages 379–82.) Consistency is again the guiding principle. When the clauses, phrases, or words in a pair or series within a sentence are balanced so that they all have the same grammatical form, the sentence is clearer and easier to read. Notice how awkward and unbalanced this sentence is to read:

The hero was a man who believed in an ideal, fought for it, and finally shooting all those who didn't agree with him.

The coordinated elements are not parallel. The past tense verbs *believed* and *fought* should be paralleled by the past tense *shot,* not *shooting.* The sentence is easily revised to read:

> The hero was a man who believed in an ideal, fought for it, and finally shot all those who didn't agree with him.

The following sentences illustrate several other common problems of faulty parallelism. Notice how the balanced structures in the revised sentences make them smoother to read.

Faulty parallelism The novel is about decadence in nineteenth century England and that the disregard of the working classes brought about the decline of the monarchy.

Revision The novel is about decadence in nineteenth century England and the disregard of the working class, which brought about the decline of the monarchy. [The compound object of *about* should have two phrases, not one phrase and one subordinate clause.]

Faulty parallelism Eloise enjoys looking for antiques, partying with friends, and to play the piano.

Revision Eloise enjoys looking for antiques, partying with friends, and playing the piano. [The object of *enjoys* requires a balanced series of gerund phrases.]

Faulty parallelism Foreign cars are usually rated less expensive, safer, and having better mechanical reliability than American cars.

Revision Foreign cars are usually rated less expensive, safer, and more reliable mechanically than American cars. [The complement requires a balanced series of modifiers.]

Exercise

Revise the following sentences to correct all instances of faulty parallelism.

1. Uncle Al told me that my choice of automobile was extremely foolish in this age of expensive gasoline and to buy a small economy car that will get excellent mileage.
2. The problem with learning how to write clear, concise sentences and how you should avoid confusing your readers demonstrates why composition courses are required at most colleges and universities.
3. Those waiting to get in were noisy, rude, and were beginning to get violent.
4. Jeff's greatest ambitions were to attend UCLA as a drama major and having a successful career as an actor.
5. The candidates avoid the important issues and by appealing to the voters' fears and prejudices capture their votes through emotion.

6. Bob and Monica shopped for groceries in the morning, cleaned the apartment in the afternoon, and were entertaining friends in the evening.
7. Professor Thompson liked knowing what was going on and to mind other people's business.
8. My father told me to clean out the garage and dispose of all my treasured comic books and that I need to find a new place for my old baseball card collection too.
9. Listening to the surf, my body basking in the sun, eyes fixed on the gorgeous hunks a few feet away, I knew what heaven must be like.
10. I had to edit my essay for fragments, dangling modifiers, and there was faulty parallelism, too.

CASE

We use the term "case" to describe the grammatical function or relationship of pronouns to other words in a sentence. (Case also applies to nouns, but only when they function as possessives: "the *professor's* office hours.") Most pronouns have three case forms: subjective, when the pronoun functions as the subject of its clause; objective, when the pronoun functions as the object of its clause; and possessive, when the pronoun functions as a modifier in its clause. The case of a pronoun is determined by its grammatical function in the clause or sentence in which it appears. We generally use the correct case without conscious choice; however, a few constructions can cause problems.

The Relatives *who* and *whom*

Who is a subject pronoun, and *whom* is an object pronoun. When in doubt about which is the correct case to use, substitute a personal pronoun for the relative pronoun. If *she* or *they* fits the context, use *who;* if *her* or *them* fits the context, use *whom:*

Sandy is the woman *who* wrote the letter.

Clearly, *who* is the subject of *wrote* (note that *she* can substitute for *who*). In the following sentence, the relative pronoun performs a different function:

Sandy is the woman *whom* I hired.

Whom is the object of *hired* (note that *her* can substitute for *whom:* "I hired her").

Do not be confused by any extra words that come between a relative pronoun and its verb:

Sandy is the woman who *they said* wrote the letter.

Such a construction does not change the case of the pronoun.

One final note on the *whoever/whomever* relative pronouns. The objective case pronoun is often used incorrectly because it appears to be the object of a preceding preposition:

Hotel reservations will be made for *whomever* sends the deposit by the deadline.

This is incorrect and should read

Hotel reservations will be made for *whoever* sends the deposit by the deadline.

because *whoever* is the subject of *sends,* not the object of *for.* The object of *for* is the whole clause, *whoever sends the deposit by the deadline.*

The Verb *to be*

The conventions of standard written English dictate that a pronoun complement of the verb *to be* takes the subjective case:

It was *she.*

The Connectors *as* and *than*

When *as* and *than* are used to make comparisons, they function as connectors, and a pronoun that follows them takes the subjective case:

She is at least as heavy as *he.*

The rule is easy to follow if you remember that *as he* is a shortened version of *as he is.*

Possessive Pronouns with Gerunds

A pronoun that modifies a gerund is usually in the possessive case, because gerunds function as nouns:

Karen objected to *his removing* the furniture.
We are all embarrassed by *her* nonstop *talking.*
Their accepting the rejection doesn't surprise me.

Nouns that modify gerunds also take the possessive form:

Mary's napping did not interfere with our practice.

Exercise

In the following sentences, underline the correct form of the pronouns in parentheses.

1. The new president isn't sure (who, whom) he will appoint to his cabinet.
2. (We, Us) dancers are sure to be part of the touring troupe.
3. Her parents object to (his, him) watching television all afternoon.
4. There were no complaints from the committee members (who, whom) I thought opposed the amendment.
5. If Gregg had not finished nursing school, his parents would never have allowed Sherry and (he, him) to get married.
6. They have not played Trivial Pursuit as long as (we, us).
7. Christine and Tara are the ones (who, whom) I believe should be the starting forwards.
8. Straining to see through the dense fog, I thought (she, her) to be Diane.
9. The pastor did not appreciate (us, our) leaving the service early.
10. I would be happy to go with (whoever, whomever) you select.

VAGUE PRONOUN REFERENCES

A very common source of confusion to readers is a pronoun that appears to refer to more than one word or a pronoun that has no antecedent at all. These sentences illustrate some of the problems:

Robert explained to Michael that *he* had to wait another hour.

Julia's sister is a paramedic, but Julia is not interested in *it.*

In the first sentence, who had to wait another hour? The pronoun reference is unclear. Using quotation marks is one way to correct this fault:

Robert explained to Michael, "You have to wait another hour."

In the second sentence, no clear reference for *it* exists. The pronoun cannot logically be linked to *paramedic,* the word it appears to refer to. The sentence is best rewritten another way:

Julia's sister is a paramedic, but Julia is not interested in becoming one.

As a last illustration, vague pronoun references are commonly created by the misuse of relative pronouns:

I couldn't find my driver's license, which embarrassed me.

Which refers to the entire main clause, and the reference is unclear because we as readers are accustomed to looking for a single word or phrase as the reference for *which*. Rewriting the sentence to remove the relative pronoun avoids the vague reference:

I was embarrassed because I couldn't find my driver's license.

In summary, every pronoun should refer clearly and directly to a specific antecedent.

Exercise

Revise the following sentences to clarify all the vague pronoun references.

1. I love pepperoni on pizza, but it doesn't always agree with me.
2. Laura's sister let her wear her new necklace to school.
3. Their dog was friends with their cat until he bit him.
4. The student was very anxious. At that moment they were in the next room deciding his fate.
5. The doctor ordered the nurse to draw the blood because he didn't want to do it.
6. John quit the team because he thought it took too much time away from his studies.
7. My decision to join the army was based on careful consideration of training opportunities, which pleased my parents.
8. At football games it is common for them to form the human wave.
9. The sharpshooters should be careful about where they point their rifles when they are loaded.
10. At car repair shops it is common for them to offer you services that you don't need.

ADJECTIVES AND ADVERBS

As we briefly discussed earlier in this Guide (see page 433), modifiers qualify, restrict, or add to the meaning of other words. Adjectives and adverbs both function as modifiers in sentences, but their grammatical functions are not the same. Adjectives modify nouns and pronouns; adverbs modify verbs, verbals, adjectives, and other adverbs. To illustrate the careless use of adjectives and adverbs, read the following sentences, in which adjectives incorrectly modify either a verb, an adverb, or another adjective:

> Listen as *careful* as you can.
>
> He certainly plays tennis *good*.
>
> It is *real* important that she attend.
>
> That horse runs *considerable* faster than the other.

The errors seem obvious, yet the mistakes are easy to make and are easily overlooked in editing. Remember, adjectives do not modify verbs, adverbs, or other adjectives. The sentences should be revised to read:

> Listen as *carefully* as you can.
>
> He certainly plays tennis *well*.
>
> It is *really* important that she attend.
>
> That horse runs *considerably* faster than the other.

Exercise

Revise the following sentences to eliminate all the incorrect uses of adjectives for adverbs and vice versa.

1. The Ford Thunderbird has been produced continuous since 1955, and it still sells good today.
2. Soccer is an extreme popular sport around the world.
3. You should think positive about the report.
4. When David saw the cake rising in the oven, he looked happily.
5. The pledges thought the extra housework was absolute unnecessary.
6. We are sure pleased that the confrontation did not result in a permanently split between you.
7. Chew your food more slower.
8. The slight green tap water tasted most horrible.
9. Respond as quick as you can.
10. The personally computer has completely changed my writing.

Style

So far, this "Reference Guide" has presented advice on sentence structure (grammar) based on the conventions, or rules, of standard English. Learning the rules of sentence structure is an important step toward effective writing and editing, but the rules by themselves are not enough. The English language is complex, and exceptions to the rules are too numerous for a knowledge of grammar alone to make one a good writer. The writer's purpose and audience are likely to change with each writing task, and the choices the writer must make in forming sentences are as much governed by what we call style as by the conventions of standard English.

Style, like the clothes we wear or the way we comb our hair, is situational, and because of this you will find that frequently there is no one right or wrong answer to a stylistic question. Unlike the conventions of standard English, which generally apply to all purposes and audiences in formal writing, the elements of style vary with the writing situation. You must learn to match those elements to your writing purpose and your audience.

The earlier parts of this book have told you how to write grammatically correct sentences, how to focus your ideas, and how to gather and organize the information you need to move a clearly defined audience to a specific purpose. But you still have to get those ideas down on paper in a form that is not just grammatically correct but is reasonably clear, concise, and persuasive. That is style, and understanding its principles as they are presented in this section will help you make the choices that lead to clear and effective writing for different situations.

ACTIVE AND PASSIVE VOICE

In sentences written in the passive voice, the subject is not the performer of the action indicated by the verb. Thus, passive voice sentences are generally weaker than sentences in the active voice, in which the subject is the performer of the action. They are often awkward, wordy, and unnecessarily complex. For example, in the passive voice sentence

> The record was broken last year by the leading sprinter on the track team.

the grammatical subject is *record*, but the performer of the action indicated by the verb, *was broken*, is buried in the prepositional phrase, *by the leading sprinter*. Indirect, wordy sentences like this can be revised by turning them around and making the performer of the action the subject of the sentence:

> The leading sprinter on the track team broke the record last year.

The sentence is now in the active voice, which carries the action of the sentence forward more fluently and directly.

Using the passive voice is not always weak, particularly when you want your sentence to emphasize the receiver of the action rather than the performer, as in this example:

> His stereo was stolen from his car.

The important information here is the *stereo,* not the "someone" who stole it, the performer of the action. An active voice version of this sentence lacks the appropriate emphasis:

> Someone stole his stereo from his car.

In most writing situations, however, the stylistic choice should be the active voice because it is clear, concise, and direct. (See pages 382–84 for additional discussion of active and passive voice.) Compare these examples:

Passive   Her writing could be improved by working through these exercises.
Active   She could improve her writing by working through these exercises.

Passive   The decision was made by the dean.
Active   The dean made the decision.

Exercise

Revise the following sentences by changing the passive voice to the active voice.

1. Wrapped in the red-striped paper, the gift was given by Chris.
2. The quarterback was hurt during practice by a sharp tackle thrown by the defensive end.
3. Our problem was solved by Ellen's clever work on the computer.
4. Bruce Springsteen was surrounded by a crowd of screaming admirers.
5. Some children were seen by the workmen.
6. The national vote was challenged by Teamsters Local 415.
7. The expenses of the trip were shared by all of us.
8. Weeding is detested by everyone I know.
9. The distant church bells can be heard every evening from the balcony of my hotel room.
10. Great flocks of seabirds could be seen at the water's edge as we drew nearer.

WORDINESS

Wordiness—using more words than are needed to express an idea—is a common affliction of writers. A clear, effective writing style requires the concise, direct expression of ideas; yet at one time or another, for one reason or another, we have all padded our sentences with too many words—often redundant, meaningless, or unnatural. Readers are put off by such verbosity. Knowing what the more common wordiness traps are will help you avoid them as you write and remove them as you revise and edit.

Redundant Pairs

The English language has a long tradition of doubled words, a custom that grew as the language borrowed more and more words from Latin, French, and other languages. The borrowed word sounded more sophisticated, English speakers and writers thought, and they began using such redundant expressions as *true and accurate, hopes and desires,* and *so on and so forth.*

Revising for redundant pairs is usually a matter of choosing the more appropriate one of the words or phrases over the other, as in this example:

Redundant Jennifer asked me to give her my honest and sincere opinion.
Revised Jennifer asked me to give her my honest opinion.

Exercise

Revise the following sentences to eliminate the redundant pairs.

1. A psychologist is trained to help us with our concerns and worries.
2. Did Ms. McCarthy question the goals and ambitions of the characters in her novels?
3. The Sierra Club's report was highly praised for its direct and forthright attack on the American public for its extravagant and wasteful use of natural resources.
4. While the blizzard raged and howled outside, we roasted popcorn over the open fire and enjoyed the pleasures and comforts of the warm, cozy cabin.
5. All in all, Hubert's reasons for missing the Senate hearing were both understandable and justifiable, so he was excused from penalty, fair and square.

Redundant Modifiers

All words have synonyms or other words with the same meaning. But to use together, in the same phrase or clause, words that have the same meaning is another form of redundancy. *Memories* implies *past*, so *past memories* is redundant. *Personal* is a part of the meaning of *belief*, so *personal belief* contains a repeated thought. To revise this kind of wordy phrasing, just delete the redundant modifier, as in this example:

Redundant Sheldon turned around just in time to see Mario completely finish the pizza.
Revised Sheldon turned around just in time to see Mario finish the pizza.

Exercise

Revise these sentences to eliminate the redundant modifiers.

1. Harold asked the golf pro to again repeat the directions for accomplishing a guaranteed hole-in-one.

2. Mary and John's recipe for *huevos rancheros* calls for several important essentials, including hot sauce and corn tortillas.
3. Our initial preparation for the camping trip to Glacier National Park could not have taken more than thirty minutes.
4. The guide told us to ask Roberto to respond to any unanswered questions that we might have about the Toltec culture.
5. Tearfully, the patient urged her doctor to tell her the honest truth about her condition.

Redundant Categories

Specific words imply the general categories to which they belong. Consequently, it is redundant to use both the noun for the general category and the modifier for something within that category in a construction like this:

> The *educational process* can only be changed by the local *governmental system.*

The sentence reads better as

> Education can only be changed by local government.

Education is a process, and government is a system. It is therefore redundant to say *educational process* or *governmental system.*

The most common redundant categories are these:

- size, color, weight, taste, shape, form, time, number
- appearance, quality, character, condition, state, nature, type, kind, degree, manner, way
- process, system, context, activity, factor, action, concept, question, problem, subject, field, area, matter

If you notice you have used one of these category words with a specific descriptive word, you can almost always delete one or the other.

Exercise

Revise the following sentences to eliminate the redundant categories.

1. The fat dill pickle was of a long, round shape and had a very sour taste.
2. Once the dolly was in place, the heavy weight of the refrigerator could be moved in a relatively easy manner.

3. Sadly, it was the factor of poor health that forced Aunt Louise to retire at an early age.
4. Scientists are presently studying the ecological systems of our planet in order to recommend effective conservation efforts and appropriate recycling actions.
5. According to the insurance broker, our hospitalization plan is one of the finest in the entire area of the state.

Meaningless Modifiers

Some modifiers fall into our speech and writing almost as frequently and as unconsciously as we clear our throats. Words and phrases like *kind of, really, practically,* and *for all intents and purposes* are empty of meaning. Your sentences will be sharper and clearer if you excise such verbal clutter and, instead, state exactly what you mean. These sentences illustrate the problem and the solution:

Wordy   For all intents and purposes, American industrial productivity generally depends on certain factors that are really more psychological in kind than on any given technological aspect.

Revised   American industrial productivity depends more on psychology than on technology.

Exercise

Revise the following sentences to eliminate the meaningless modifiers and other redundancies.

1. Actually David has two tickets to the rock concert, but now that Corrine is ill he won't go regardless.
2. It certainly was not long ago when virtually all gasoline stations were closed on Sundays.
3. No matter how much we would like to help slow down inflation, basically we end up assisting it because of our particular and individual needs for various commodities.
4. I virtually refused to answer the telephone because I definitely did not want to talk to the particular person who was supposed to call me that afternoon.
5. For all intents and purposes, your writing will naturally improve as you generally watch for various meaningless modifiers and basically delete them from your individual writing.

Obvious Implication

Some writers cloud what they have to say by including needless words, phrases, and even whole sentences that state the obvious—things all of us already know about the world around us. This kind of redundancy often extends through an entire paragraph, as this example illustrates:

> Today, the period in history known as the Holocaust is alive in the interest of many people. Dozens of films have been made, books written, and TV shows produced recording the events that took place during the Holocaust, describing the various aspects of Nazism and the systematic destruction of six million Jews by the Germans under their leader, Adolf Hitler. On the surface, this popular interest in what happened to the Jews under Hitler would appear to be a healthy phenomenon. What could be wrong with a new examination by the media of what is certainly the one single most significant event of twentieth century history? Unfortunately, this popular interest by so many in the events of the Holocaust has brought with it serious misunderstandings about it, and inevitably incorrect views by those who have been exposed to those misunderstandings.

The passage provides far too much information that most of us already know, making it dull and awkward. If we remove the obvious implications, we create a far more fluid and informative passage:

> Many people have become interested in the Holocaust through dozens of films, books, and TV programs that have dealt with Hitler, Nazism, and the systematic destruction of six million Jews. On the surface, this interest would appear to be healthy: what could be wrong with reexamining the most significant event of the twentieth century? Unfortunately, this interest has also resulted in some serious misunderstandings.

Exercise

Revise the following sentences to eliminate all instances of obvious implication and other redundancies.

1. Imagine a mental picture of someone engaged in the intellectual activity of trying to learn what the rules are for how to play soccer.
2. As you read on in the book further, you discover that the character does an about-face, changing completely into a good man with admirable characteristics.
3. Uncle Sedrick, who lives in Minneapolis, which is a large city next to St. Paul, Minnesota, came out to California in August to attend the wedding of his niece, who got married last August.

4. Imagine a mental picture of a skier engaged in his sport coming down the white slope of a mountain covered with freshly fallen snow that is cold and powdery.
5. *Great Expectations* is a novel by Charles Dickens. Many people believe this novel is the best one ever written by Dickens. If it is not the best, then it is second only to *David Copperfield,* another novel by Dickens.

Excessive Detail

This final stylistic principle on wordiness is more dependent than any of the others on your purpose and audience. Excessive detail is the fault of providing too many details in your writing, but in order to determine how much detail is enough you have to evaluate the needs of your audience and the purpose of your message. What is too much detail for one audience may not be enough for another. This obviously overwritten sentence is at the extreme of detail that is excessive for almost any audience:

> Baseball, one of our oldest and most popular outdoor summer sports in terms of total attendance at ballparks and viewing on television, has the kind of rhythm of play on the field that alternates between the players passively waiting with no action taking place between the pitches to the batter and exploding into action when the batter hits a pitched ball to one of the players who fields it.

Although the sentence harbors more weaknesses than excessive detail, we can revise it to remove the unwieldy detail—more than any literate audience should have to endure:

> Baseball has a rhythm that alternates between passive waiting and explosive action.

Exercise

Revise the following sentences to eliminate the excessive detail. Assume that your classmates are your audience.

1. Punk rock, a seemingly violent and angry music that has attracted many young people in America today, has not done well on the charts, which indicate popularity, perhaps because many punk devotees do not want to participate in surveys or they simply do not purchase tapes or records, upon which most chart data is based.
2. Bicycle riding both for pleasure along country lanes or at the beach

and for business transportation is a perfect way to keep the body fit, for it provides exercise to thighs, calves, and feet, while it forces the rider to sit up straight and tall.

3. Whenever the bedroom fan that sits in the corner by the window breaks down, Maria has trouble falling asleep because the room is so warm from the heat of the day and so quiet because the usual lulling noise of the fan is not there to rock her to sleep.

PLACEMENT OF MODIFIERS

Your readers should be able to connect modifiers quickly and easily to the sentence elements they modify. As we found with dangling modifiers, when a modifying word, phrase, or clause is placed in a sentence so that it could modify either of two elements, its reference will be uncertain or ambiguous, and the intended meaning of the sentence unclear. To illustrate the problem:

David has followed the advice *faithfully* given by the manual.

Was the advice given faithfully or followed faithfully? The adverb should be placed nearer the word it modifies:

David has *faithfully* followed the advice given by the manual.

Another example:

I gave Laura a book for her birthday *that I had recently read about.*

Have I read about the book or the birthday? The sentence should be revised to place the modifying clause closer to the object of the sentence, *book:*

For her birthday, I gave Laura a book *that I had recently read about.*

Exercise

Revise the following sentences to correct every use of an ambiguous or misplaced modifier.

1. My father wore the new shirt I gave him at the party.
2. The audience stared while the escape artist wrestled with his bonds in frantic anticipation.

3. Professor Hines only wanted us to write good essays.
4. The film about revolution in Central America that I saw at the mall was interesting.
5. An excellent swimmer, like her sister, she worked as a lifeguard last summer.
6. Harrison Ford plays the part of the quiet academic turned daredevil adventurer effortlessly.
7. We stayed at a small motel near the edge of town that had been vacant for days.
8. The stereo is in the shop that he wrecked.
9. There is a debate tomorrow on legalized abortion in the commons.
10. Sheila said on the way to the mountains she was hungry.

LONG SENTENCES AND SPRAWL

Cutting excess wordiness and redundancy will make your sentences shorter and crisper. But even if you have expressed your ideas simply and directly, you can lose your readers by packing too many ideas into a single sentence:

> Adding water to the cake mix, the young cook looked uncertainly at the recipe, checking to make sure that he had done everything correctly so that he would not have the same unpleasant results as the last time, when his earlier creation had ended up a hard, burnt ball in the middle of the pan.

This sprawling sentence is grammatically correct, not breaking any rules that would make it a run-on. Correct writing, however, is not always the same as good writing, and the sentence does not read well. It can easily be revised into a more readable passage:

> Adding water to the cake mix, the young cook looked uncertainly at the recipe. He checked to make sure that he had done everything correctly so that he would not have the same unpleasant results as the last time. His earlier creation had ended up a hard, burnt ball in the middle of the pan.

Sentence length depends in part on the complexity of the ideas being expressed. A simple, unqualified idea needs only a short sentence; the statement of an idea that is subtle and full of modification requires more words. Sentence length can also vary with fashion; in the past fifty years, the trend has been toward shorter, more readable sentences. In addition, sentence length depends on context, audience, and the intention of the writer. Short sentences, for instance, carry greater emphasis or excitement than long ones.

Knowing the most common symptoms of sprawling sentences will help you to revise them, and three of these symptoms are illustrated in the following examples:

Sprawling coordination   The rising cost of housing has been steadily increasing at an average rate of 23 percent each year, and this has forced more and more people to turn to low-income housing, but unfortunately there isn't enough of this type of housing available to those interested, so the government must supplement the construction industry so that it will build this necessary housing.

Sprawling subordination   Although the criminal served eight years of his fifteen-year sentence, as soon as he was paroled he was again consorting with his underworld associates, planning what he hoped would be his greatest job.

Sprawling relatives   This is the horse that kicked the dog that bit the cat that chased the mouse that lived in the house that Jack built.

The simplest way to revise a sprawling sentence is to break it up into shorter sentences. Revisions of these sprawling sentence examples show how easily this is done:

The rising cost of housing has been steadily increasing at an average rate of 23 percent each year. This has forced more and more people to turn to low-income housing. But unfortunately, there isn't enough of this type of housing available. The government must supplement the construction industry so that it will build this necessary housing.

After serving eight years of his fifteen-year sentence, the criminal was paroled. Immediately, he was again consorting with his underworld associates and planning what he hoped would be his greatest job.

This horse kicked the dog that bit the cat. The cat chased the mouse that lived in the house, which Jack built.

Exercise

Revise the following sentences to correct the unnecessary sprawl.

1. The gardener spent three hours at his task and worked steadily all the while: he mowed, edged, pruned, and clipped; he raked the flower beds and he hosed down the patio, but his most painstaking task was to trim the dwarf star pine, which he did needle by needle with a tiny pair of shears and with single-minded concentration.

2. Even though economists traditionally are cautious about expressing either excessive hope or despair on the basis of a single month's statistics, they generally agreed this week that the current slump will end late this year.

3. Because the smog hung heavily in the brown sky against the brown hills as we drove down the freeway, we did not consider cracking a window to admit the polluted outside air, but instead allowed the air conditioner to blow cool air into the sealed interior.

4. The lava flew through the air and rolled freely down the incline of the volcano from which it had come as it invaded the seemingly unsuspecting village that sat at the base of this dangerous mountain.

5. Women have gained a good deal of political clout that they once lacked in electing candidates that would support programs that would benefit children and minorities.

SHORT SENTENCES AND CHOPPINESS

A reader may get lost trying to sort out the meaning in a sprawling sentence, and the same reader can become distracted, bored, or annoyed trying to stay with the meaning of a string of short, choppy sentences. The problem with such sentences is obvious in this passage:

> Of one thing we are certain. We are certain that writing is hard work. It is hard. It is rewarding. A well-written essay says something. It says just what we want it to. It conveys our exact meaning to our readers.

The passage is not only choppy; it is rather incoherent. When you read it, you probably had difficulty determining how the ideas related to one another. This revised version is much more fluent:

> Of one thing we are certain: that writing is hard work, hard but rewarding, for a well-written essay says just what we want it to and conveys our exact meaning to our readers.

The fluent version sounds better and is easier to read because the sentence structure now shows the relationships among the ideas. The writer has done the grouping of ideas that the reader had to do for herself or himself in the choppy first version.

Revising short sentences to eliminate choppiness is usually accomplished by combining sentences. Here is another example that shows how short sentences can be combined into a single well-formed sentence:

Choppy   The typewriter spills words onto the page. It clatters on. Its operator is in a trance. He does not care what comes out.

Fluent   Spilling words onto the page, the typewriter clatters on, its operator in a trance, not caring what comes out.

    The difference between choppy and fluent sentences is not grammatical; both versions of the preceding examples are grammatically correct. We find the second version more fluent and readable because of the expectations of language structure and meaning that we as readers bring to them. We judge sentence fluency by its context. That is to say, in order to recognize and to produce fluent writing, we need to know the writing purpose, the audience, and the situation, all of which comprise context.

Exercise

Combine each of the following groups of sentences to create a single fluent sentence.

1. The clouds massed below us. They were in great billows. They looked almost solid. We could jump from the plane. We could land safely in them. It would be like jumping from the barn loft into a huge feather bed.
2. The wind normally dies down. It dies down during the afternoon. That creates a peaceful interlude. During the interlude students stroll along the river. They sit under the elms on campus. They read. They chat. They just daydream.
3. The assignment was given. The class asked the professor something. They asked when the paper was due. The professor was a kindly old duffer.
4. Students often discover something. They discover that they haven't left themselves enough time to do the essay question. They discover this toward the middle of the test.
5. The computer is fast but dumb. It makes astronomical numbers of decisions in fractions of a second. Its speed allows it to complete infinitely complex problems in the wink of an eye.

Diction

Diction means word choice. The goal of good diction in writing is to use the right word in the right place at the right time. In working toward this goal, you must consider the characteristics of individual words. What parts of speech are important? Should the words be general or specific? Abstract or concrete? Common or unusual? Denotative or connotative?

Errors in diction reflect inaccurate or inappropriate choice of words. Unless you know what a word means, you cannot use it effectively in speech or in writing. A dictionary is the first resource you should consult on matters of diction.

This section offers guidance on choosing the right words, an explanation and exercises on using a dictionary, and a glossary of commonly misused words. (See also pages 390–427.)

POMPOUS DICTION

Using words that are unnecessarily long or obscure often destroys the clarity and effectiveness of writing. We can usually substitute a common word for a fancy one without altering the meaning. In our utilitarian writing, especially, we need to omit language that tries to sound impressive or pompous. Of course, there are times when the obscure word is exactly the right one. What we want to avoid is the use of unusual words to give our writing a false sense of importance, as in this example:

> The alleged felon effectuated entrance into the domicile by means of an appliance forcibly applied to the external locking mechanism.

This pompous sentence is easily revised to the language of everyday discourse:

> The alleged felon entered the house using a tool.

Exercise

Revise the following sentences to eliminate the use of pompous diction.

1. It is my individual and personal belief that the canine member of the animal kingdom provides the most affectionate behavior as man's domestic companion.
2. The installment plan equalizes all men in their ability to obtain the material goods of our great industrial society and to achieve a higher standard of living.
3. In order to fortify the probability of a successful response to my request for her company on an excursion to the local cinema, I promptly dispatched to Fran a garland of floral buds.
4. While a tyro in international diplomacy, Dr. J. P. Morgan effected a surprising number of perspicacious and synergistic communication programs for member nations of the Third World.
5. Reverend Parson's laconic discourse committed his credulous adherents to lachrymose exhibitions.

CHOOSING THE RIGHT WORDS

Always choose words that express precisely what you mean, since a reader expects your meaning to be exactly what your words say it is. Before writing the final draft of a paper, read the paper carefully to see that every word expresses your meaning in a way that cannot be misunderstood. The next few pages give guidelines for avoiding some common errors in diction. A review of the guidelines will help you choose the right words as you compose.

Vague Diction

Choose specific words rather than vague ones, unless you have a good reason to use general or vague diction.

A general term like *food* stands for a whole group of specific things—from vegetable soup to T-bone steak to strawberry pie. If you want to make a statement about all foods, the general term is appropriate: *Food is becoming more and more expensive.* But do not use the general term when concrete details and specific words are more appropriate:

Vague and general	For dinner we had some really good food.
Specific	For dinner we had barbecued steaks and sweet corn.
Vague and general	He liked to argue about controversial subjects.
Specific	He liked to argue about politics and religion.

Note that specific and general are relative, not absolute, terms as they apply to the choice of words. In the following list, which runs from specific to general, any of the four terms could be used to refer to a famous tree growing on campus, depending on which is most appropriate to your purpose and audience:

Specific	Charter Oak (one particular tree)
Less specific	oak (includes thousands of trees)
More general	tree (includes oaks, pines, palms, and so on)
More general	plant (includes trees, flowers, bushes . . .)

Tree is more specific than *plant* but more general than *oak.*

Make your language as specific as possible. If your writing is criticized for vagueness—the most common fault in undergraduate writing—revise it by using, wherever you can, a specific and concrete word that will create a definite and vivid picture in the reader's mind. A search for concrete words often helps to clarify your thinking. Here are some more examples:

Too abstract	My father showed his disapproval.
Concrete	My father growled, "Stop that!"
Vague	There are several factors that make *Fatal Attraction* a good movie.
Concrete	A sexy plot, suspense, and energetic acting make *Fatal Attraction* a lively movie.
Vague	One member of the ASB Cabinet has been irresponsible about performing his duties.
Concrete	Although he is a member of the ASB Cabinet, Pete Meyers has missed the last five meetings.

Note that a specific statement might contain a smaller number of words than a vague, indefinite one, but communicates a great deal more information:

Vague	One member of my family has recently begun her professional career.
Concrete	Last week my sister Karen joined a law firm.

Abstract Verbs

Whenever possible, replace weak, abstract verbs and verb phrases with direct, concrete ones.

Make your verbs work. In the sentence *He made a hasty exit,* the verb is abstract, and the adjective and the noun have to carry what meaning the sentence has. Choose a more exact and forceful verb: *He rushed from the room* or *He ran down the corridor.*

Occur, take place, prevail, exist, happen, and other verbs that express a state of affairs have legitimate uses, but too often they are colorless and appear tossed in merely to complete a sentence:

Weak	In the afternoon a sharp drop in the temperature occurred.
Stronger	The temperature dropped sharply in the afternoon.
Weak	Throughout the meeting an atmosphere of increasing tension existed.
Stronger	As the meeting progressed, the tension increased.

Copulative verbs (*be, seem, appear,* and the like) completed by an adjective or a participle are usually weaker than concrete verbs:

Weak	He was occasionally inclined to talk too much.
Stronger	Occasionally he talked too much.
Weak	In some colleges there is a very definite lack of emphasis on the development of a program in remedial English.
Stronger	Some colleges have failed to develop programs in remedial English.

Unnecessary use of the passive voice also produces weak sentences (see pages 457–58). The passive voice is appropriate when the doer of an action is unknown or is irrelevant to the statement, but do not use the passive needlessly. Usually the doer of an action is important enough to name as the subject of the verb:

Weak passive	The dinner was enjoyed by everyone.
Stronger active	Everyone enjoyed the dinner.
Weak passive	Every night Mr. Richardson's lawn had to be watered by me.
Stronger active	Every night I had to water Mr. Richardson's lawn.

Appropriate	Chicken and green peas were served at the banquet.
passive	Lost parcels may be claimed at the office.

One final word of caution: in an effort to avoid flat and colorless verbs, do not go to the opposite extreme and use verbs that are too explosive for their context, as in these examples:

Her angry words leaped at him and pounced upon him.

The evening breeze ravished her senses and cooled her forehead.

Inappropriate Connotation

Choose words with the exact connotation required by your context. (See also pages 392–94.)

In addition to their denotation, or literal meaning, most words have a connotation, a fringe of associations and overtones that makes them appropriate in certain situations but not in others. *House, home,* and *domicile* all have the same denotation—a place of residence. But their connotations are quite different: *house* emphasizes the physical structure; *home* suggests family life, warmth, comfort, affection; *domicile* has legal overtones.

The connotation of every word you use should be appropriate to its context. You would not write a sentimental song entitled "House, Sweet House," nor would you comfortably speak of the official residence of the president of the United States as "the White Home." Similarly, you might ask a stranger, "Are you married?" but not "Are you mated?" We learn the connotations of words by seeing and hearing them in different contexts. If you observe that the word *snug* usually appears in connection with the idea of warmth, comfort, an open fire, cozy shelter, or safety, you know the connotation of the word, and you will not use it indiscriminately in its literal sense of "sheltered from the weather." Many of the discussions of near-synonyms in your dictionary are really about the connotations of the words, and special dictionaries of synonyms, like *Roget's Thesaurus* and *Webster's Dictionary of Synonyms,* will also help you to understand connotations.

Incorrect Use of Idiom

Use the idiom most appropriate to your subject and your reader.

An idiom is an expression peculiar to the language and not definable by the principles of logic or the literal meaning of the individual words. Why do we say that a person is *on duty, in trouble,* or *at play?* The answer is that these are idiomatic combinations that have become fixed in our language. How can a person who is learning English and knows the words *take, in, up, down,* and *over* deduce the meaning of *take in* ("comprehend"), *take down* ("humiliate"), *take over,* and *overtake?* She can't; she must learn each idiom separately.

Idiom requires that certain words be followed by arbitrarily fixed prepositions. Something may be *required of* all students, *compulsory for* all, *necessary to* all, or *obligatory on* all. Here is a list of some idiomatic uses of prepositions:

agree *to* a proposal, *on* a procedure, *with* a person
angry *at* or *about* something, *with* a person
argue *with* a person, *for* or *against* or *about* a measure
correspond *to* or *with* a thing, *with* a person
differ *from* one another in appearance, *with* a person in opinion
independent *of*
interest *in*
listen *to* a person, argument, or sound, *at* the door
regard: *with regard to* or *as regards*
stay *at* home
superior *to* (for "better than")
wait *on* a customer, *for* a person, *at* a place

Idiom also demands that certain words be followed by infinitives, others by gerunds. For instance:

INFINITIVE	GERUND
able to go	capable of going
like to go	enjoy going
eager to go	cannot help going
hesitate to go	privilege of going

When two idioms are used in a compound construction, each idiom must be complete:

Incomplete	He had no love or confidence in his employer.
Complete but awkward	He had no love for or confidence in his employer.
Improved	He had no love for his employer and no confidence in her.
Incomplete	I shall always remember the town because of the good times and the friends I made there.
Complete	I shall always remember the town because of the good times I had and the friends I made there.

Exercises

A. Give several specific or concrete words for every one of the general or abstract words listed in each category. (Example: cloth—velvet, satin, taffeta, linen, burlap.)

1. *Nouns:* examination, car, bird, goodness, clothing, surprise
2. *Verbs:* look, laugh, talk, entertain, walk
3. *Adjectives:* unpleasant (person), cold (day), interesting (evening), young, dark

B. Rewrite each of the following sentences from student papers to make the sentences more specific and concrete.

1. We couldn't get started on the float that night because of bad weather.
2. The family liked to show its financial standing by driving expensive sports cars and wearing designer clothing.
3. Many tract homes are made with cheap materials and decorated in bad taste.
4. One reason that I enjoy football and basketball is that I like sports with real action to them.
5. During high school I had real trouble with my foreign language courses, but in college so far I have found them much easier.
6. The expedition encountered a serious difficulty, which delayed its departure for some time.
7. By her own efforts she overcame her handicap of bad health and the emotional problems it caused.
8. One of my hobbies is music.
9. Something was wrong with the elevator, so they had a hard time getting up to the office.
10. The effect of a setting like the Grand Canyon on people is truly remarkable.

C. Revise each of the following sentences from student papers by giving the sentences more forceful verbs or verb forms.

1. Most of the desert resorts at the foot of the mountains have been confronted by disastrous winter floods.
2. It was soon discovered by the new settlers that life in the colonies was not utopian.
3. But the ironic tone of the poem is necessary so that the realization that the characters are slaves to conformity can be made.
4. Later that afternoon a violent argument between my roommate and me occurred.
5. Our teacher was in a hurry to leave because there had been a phone call for him from his wife, who was expecting a child.
6. Throughout the whole series of discussions on student values, a feeling of candor and self-examination existed.
7. The increasing competition for college admissions would seem to illustrate the fact that students who have only an average record are going to have trouble getting any kind of higher education.

8. Great flocks of sandpipers and gulls could be seen rising from the beach as we approached.
9. Only about half of the freshman class was present at the last rally, and they appeared to be pretty feeble in their cheering.

D. Explain the difference in connotation between the two words in each of the following pairs. Use a dictionary if you are in doubt.

1. violin/fiddle	8. gobble/gorge
2. sympathy/pity	9. biased/prejudiced
3. marsh/swamp	10. infant/baby
4. upset/agitated	11. stare/gape
5. break/shatter	12. old/elderly
6. waste/squander	13. mutt/mongrel
7. joy/ecstasy	14. tease/torment

E. For each of the following words, list under the headings a synonym with the appropriate connotations. The first row across is filled in as a guide. Consult your dictionary if you become stuck for an appropriate synonym.

COMMONPLACE OR NEUTRAL	CRUDE OR DEROGATORY	SLANG	ELEVATED OR LITERARY
girl	slut	bod	maiden
boy			
food			
money			
complain			
go away			
car			
liquor			

F. Some of the following sentences from student papers tell truths unintended by the writer; some of the sentences are merely inappropriate in their connotations. Whatever their faults, revise the sentences for exactness of diction.

1. His immaturity may improve with age.
2. The basic objective of the indoctrination program is to build strong class spirit and to weed out those who are leaders in the class.
3. Lee had a fine formal education and he ended up going to West Point.
4. Darwin's *Origin of Species* began an epic of materialism.
5. Margaret Mead's book had a great success because Americans are grossly interested in sex.
6. The words that bring pictures to your mind are lovely and lush.
7. I fitted away my first three year in college.

8. Jefferson and Madison were two of the most prolific characters our nation produced at that time in history.
9. Watching attentively, I saw the tall lean stature of a man hop briskly from the car.
10. Her shrewish temper leads her to disregard common social politeness and essential consideration until she not only has debauched herself but her husband.

G. Revise each of the following sentences from student papers to correct the violations of English idiom. Also, correct any other diction faults you may find.

1. Shelley was washed out on the shore.
2. Most often, however, a taxpayer will cheat with his own incentive.
3. One of the main issues that came out concerned the adoption of a compulsory health program of the nation.
4. Sixth grade teachers first introduce homework to the student in any large scale.
5. If anyone does poorly in the first few games, chances are the bench will be next.
6. About his eyes are the etched lines caused by years of hard work.
7. Get a dog with a keen nose because you can teach a dog to point but you can't make him smell good.
8. Jonson thought Shakespeare knew no Latin and less Greek.
9. He has thoroughly analyzed, computed, and consulted the problem with renowned men all over the world.
10. One aspect of Joyce's writing I didn't care for was the way he exaggerated on certain unimportant parts in a story.

USING A DICTIONARY

A good dictionary is the one book a writer probably depends on the most. A dictionary is not just a place to check spellings, but is a record of all the current uses and meanings of words. Rather than prescribing what a word should mean and how it should be used, a dictionary sets down the various meanings a word has acquired and the ways in which it is used today. A good portable dictionary—such as *Webster's Ninth New Collegiate Dictionary, The Random House College Dictionary,* or *The American Heritage Dictionary of the English Language*—is an essential tool for even the most casual writer.

The sample dictionary entry on page 478, from *Webster's Ninth New Collegiate Dictionary,* shows where in that particular dictionary you can find various kinds of information about a word. Dictionaries vary

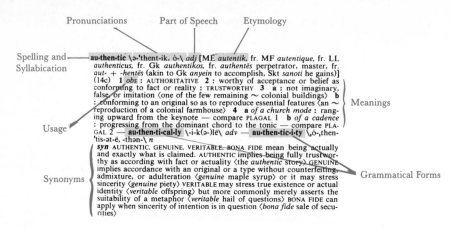

Sample Dictionary Entry

somewhat in their format, but for each separate entry, or word, all give the kinds of information explained in the following list. Compare this list and the sample entry with your own dictionary and make note of the variations.

spelling and syllabication   When more than one spelling is given, the spelling printed first is usually the preferred one. The division of the word into syllables (syllabication) is indicated by dots: **sub·tract.**

pronunciation   A key to the symbols used to indicate pronunciation is usually printed inside the front or back cover of a dictionary. Some dictionaries also run an abbreviated key to pronunciation at the bottom of each page or every other page. The syllable to be accented is shown either by the symbol ′ after the stressed syllable or by ' before it. As with spelling, when more than one pronunciation is given, the first one is usually preferred.

part of speech   Abbreviations (explained in the introductory section of the dictionary) indicate the word's part of speech, or grammatical function: **imply** *vt* means that *imply* is a transitive verb. Note that some words can be used as several different parts of speech. *Forfeit,* for example, is listed first as a noun *(n),* and its various meanings in this use are defined. Then its meaning when used as a transitive verb *(vt)* is given, and finally its meaning as an adjective *(adj).*

grammatical forms   Forms of the past tense and the past and present participles of verbs, alternative forms of the word, the comparative and superlative degrees of adjectives, and the plurals of nouns are given whenever the word is irregular or there might be doubt as to the correct form or spelling.

etymology   The word's etymology, or history, is shown through the form in which it was used in Middle or Old English *(ME, OE)* or in the language from which the word was borrowed. Earlier meanings are often given. See the introductory section of your dictionary for an explanation of the many abbreviations.

meanings   The different meanings of a word are arranged in numbered groups, sometimes with illustrative phrases or sentences. Some dictionaries give the oldest meanings first; others list the more common meanings first; still others—though this is rare—put the earlier meanings last.

usage labels   Descriptive labels, usually abbreviated, indicate the level of usage: archaic, obsolete, colloquial, slang, dialectal, substandard, nonstandard, and the like. Look up the meanings of these terms in your dictionary; the level of usage can be important to you in trying to choose the right word from several that mean the same thing. Sometimes a usage label indicates a special field rather than a level of usage: for example, poetic, Irish, chemistry. If a word has no usage label, you can assume that in the opinion of the dictionary editors the word is in common use on all levels; that is, it is standard English. Usage labels are defined and illustrated in the explanatory notes in the front of every dictionary; check yours and be sure you understand how the labels are used.

synonyms   Words that have nearly identical or closely related meanings often need careful discrimination to indicate the precise connotations of each. A full account of the distinctions in meaning between synonyms (for example, *suggest, imply, hint, intimate, insinuate*) may be given at the end of the entry for each of the words, or there may be a cross-reference to one entry under which the synonyms are explained.

abbreviations   Most dictionaries include entries for common abbreviations and their meanings.

Exercises

A. In looking up the meanings of words, get in the habit of trying to discover within what limits of meaning a word can be used. Read the definition as a whole; do not pick out a single synonym and suppose that it is interchangeable with the word you have looked up. For each of the following words, look up the definition in your dictionary, and then write a sentence that accurately illustrates one meaning of the word.

anachronism	increment	neologism	sabotage
duress	innocuous	nepotism	sinecure
eminent	irony	ostentatious	sophistication
fetish	matériel	philanthropy	taboo
hedonist	misanthropy	precocious	tempera
imminent	mundane	retroactive	travesty

B. Tell how the etymology given in your dictionary for each of the following words can help you to remember the meaning or the spelling of the word. (Note that for a series of words all stemming from the same base word, the etymology is usually given only for the base word.)

alibi	denouement	malapropism	sacrilegious
capitol	insidious	peer *(noun)*	sarcasm
cohort	isosceles	privilege	subterfuge
concave	magnanimous		

C. Some dictionaries list in a separate section all abbreviations in common use; others incorporate these abbreviations in the main alphabetical listing. Whichever arrangement your dictionary uses, look up the following abbreviations and be ready to explain what they mean:

at. wt.	e.g.	K.C.B.	OHG
CAA	ETA	lc	Pb
colloq.	ff.	LL.D.	q.v.

D. By studying your dictionary, explain what the distinctions in meaning are between the two words in each of the following pairs:

neglect/negligence	instinct/intuition
ingenuous/ingenious	contagious/infectious
fewer/less	eminent/famous
admit/confess	criticize/censure

E. In each of the following sentences, underline the more precise of the two words in parentheses. Be prepared to justify your choice.

1. The decadent Roman civilization was a(n) (feminine, effeminate) civilization.
2. Her charming innocence is (childlike, childish).
3. The problem is to assure the farm workers (continuous, continual) employment.
4. He is (continuously, continually) in trouble with the police.
5. I am quite (jealous, envious) of your opportunity to study in Europe.
6. She is so (decided, decisive) in her manner that people always give in to her.
7. If we give your class all these privileges, we may establish (precedents, precedence) that would be unwise.
8. She always makes her health her (alibi, excuse) for her failures.

GLOSSARY OF TROUBLESOME USAGES

This glossary discusses some of the more commonly misused words, but it is not meant to be comprehensive and should be supplemented by a good up-to-date dictionary for words not included here. Note that "colloquial" designates a word that is frequently used in everyday speech and in writing in a conversational style, as distinguished from carefully edited or formal writing.

a, an Indefinite articles; *a* is used before words beginning with a consonant sound, *an* before words beginning with a vowel sound. Before *h, an* precedes the few words in which the *h* is silent *(an herb);* usually when the *h* is pronounced, *a* is used *(a history book).*

accept Not to be confused with *except. Accept* means to receive *(He will accept the crops); except* indicates something left out *(The story is good except for some errors).*

A.D. An abbreviation for the Latin *anno domini,* "in the year of the Lord." In formal writing it precedes the year *(Arminius died in A.D. 21);* in informal writing it is used the same as B.C. *(in 312 A.D.; the third century A.D.).*

affect Not to be confused with *effect. Affect* means to influence or to change *(The wind may affect the crops); effect* means to bring to pass *(This method will effect great reforms).*

aggravate Means to intensify or to make worse *(The shock aggravated his misery).* Colloquially, it means to annoy, irritate, arouse the anger of.

ain't A nonstandard contraction of *am not, is not,* or *are not.*

all the Constructions like *all the farther* are colloquial when used to mean as far as.

a lot Spelled as two words; never write *alot.*

already An adverb meaning by this time *(The hotel was already full);* not to be confused with *all ready,* which means completely ready *(The cake was all ready to be picked up).*

alright A common misspelling for *all right.* When used before a noun *(He's an alright guy),* the phrase is slang no matter what the spelling.

among See **between.**

and etc. A redundancy. See **etc.**

anyplace, everyplace, no place, someplace Colloquialisms for *anywhere, everywhere, nowhere, somewhere.*

anyways, anywheres The first is dialectal for *anyway, in any case;* the second is dialectal for *anywhere.*

apt See **liable.**

at about *About* alone is preferred in writing; *at about* is overworked and redundant *(He came about three o'clock).*

awful, awfully Often colloquially used as an intensive for *very* or *extremely;* in writing use the latter words.

awhile An adverb, and hence incorrect when used as the object of *for (Stay awhile* or *Stay for a while).*

badly Colloquially used in place of *a great deal* or *very much* with verbs signifying want or need. (Colloquial: *I want badly to see you.* Preferred in writing: *I want very much to see you.*)

besides Means additionally or in addition to; not to be confused with *beside,* which is always a preposition meaning by the side of *(beside the house).*

between   Standard when referring to two objects or to more than two objects considered individually *(between Portland and Seattle; an agreement between all three states). Among* always refers to more than two and to things considered as a group *(He lived among the natives; The three heirs were fighting among themselves).*

bring   Not to be confused with *take. Bring* indicates motion toward the speaker *(Bring this order to me); take* indicates motion away from the speaker *(Take the forms to the office).*

can, may   In formal speech and writing, *can* indicates ability and *may* indicates permission *(If you can open that box, you may have what's in it).* In some kinds of questions, *can* is standard informal usage even though permission is meant *(Can I try it next? Why can't I?).*

compare to, compare with   *Compare to* represents similarity *(She compared him to a dog); compare with* represents an examination of both the similarities and the differences of two things *(We compared dolphins with sharks).*

continual, continuous   *Continual* is used to describe events that are intermittent but recurrent *(the continual dripping of the rain); continuous* is used of time and space and implies an absence of interruption *(the continuous expanse of the prairie).*

could of   Nonstandard for *could have.*

data, phenomena, strata   The *-a* ending is the Latin plural, not the singular, and the words are treated as plural in formal scholarly writing; however, the use of *data* with a singular verb is becoming widespread. The singular forms are *datum, phenomenon,* and *stratum.* (Informal: *This data has been taken from the last census report.* Formal: *These data have been taken from the last census report.)*

different   Usually followed by *from,* but *than* is gaining acceptance.

don't   A contraction of *do not;* illiterate when used with a subject in the third person singular, as in "He don't know."

due to   In formal writing, *due to* should not be used adverbially to mean *because of.* (Colloquial: *He made many mistakes due to carelessness.* Preferred in writing: *He made many mistakes because of carelessness.)*

effect   See **affect.**

either, neither   In writing, both words designate one of two persons or things; colloquially, one of three or more. In formal writing, *none* is preferred to *neither* for references to one of three or more items. (Colloquial: *I asked Leahy, Mahoney, and McGinty, but neither of them was willing.* Preferred in writing: *I asked Leahy, Mahoney, and McGinty, but none of them was willing.)*

emigrate   Means to leave a country; often confused with *immigrate,* to enter a country.

equally as good   A redundant combination of two phrases, *equally good* and *just as good;* use either of them in its place *(Their radio cost much more than ours, but ours is equally good; Our radio is just as good as theirs).*

etc.   The abbreviation of the Latin *et cetera,* "and others." Avoid its vague use; it is acceptable only to avoid needless repetition or, informally, to represent terms that are entirely obvious from the context. In formal writing, it is often spelled out rather than abbreviated. (Vague: *She was more* *beautiful, witty, virtuous, etc., than any other lady.* Preferred: *She was more beautiful, witty, and virtuous than any other lady.* Correct: *Use even numbers like four, eight, ten, et cetera.*)

everyplace   See **anyplace.**

except   See **accept.**

expect   Colloquial when used to mean suppose or presume. (Colloquial: *I expect it's time for us to go.* Preferred in writing: *I suppose it's time for us to go.*)

farther, further   In careful usage, *farther* indicates distance, while *further* indicates degree and can also mean additional; both words are used as either adjectives or adverbs (*a mile farther, further disintegration, further details*).

fewer, less   *Fewer* indicates a smaller number (*I have fewer students than she*); *less* refers to a smaller amount (*There is less noise here*). A helpful hint: use *fewer* in speaking of things that can be counted and *less* for something that cannot be counted.

further   See **farther.**

get, got, gotten   *Get to* (go), *get away with, get back at, get with* (something), and *got to* (for *must*) are widely used in speech but should be avoided in writing. Either *got* or *gotten* is acceptable as the past participle of *get*.

good   An adjective; not to be used in formal writing in place of the adverb *well*. (Substandard: *Do it good this time.* Standard: *Do it well this time; Do a good job.*)

had have, had of   Substandard for *had*. (Substandard: *If he had have* (or *had of*) *tried, he would have succeeded.* Standard: *If he had tried, he would have succeeded.*)

hardly   Since the word already conveys the idea of negation, it should not be used with another negative. (Substandard: *It was so misty that we couldn't hardly see.* Standard: *It was so misty that we could hardly see.*)

hopefully   Means in a hopeful manner (*We look hopefully to the future*); do not use it as a vague introductory phrase (*Hopefully, your son will make the team*). In using any form of *hope*, always indicate who is doing the hoping (*We hope your son makes the team*).

immigrate   See **emigrate.**

in regards to   A nonstandard combination of *in regard to* and *as regards*; either of the latter is acceptable in writing.

irregardless   A nonstandard combination of *irrespective* and *regardless*; the latter word is the more commonly used.

its, it's   Often confused; *its* is the possessive form of *it*, and *it's* is the contracted form of *it is*.

kind, sort   Colloquial when used with a plural modifier and a plural verb. (Colloquial: *These kind* (or *sort*) *of books are trash.* Preferred in writing: *This sort of book is trash; These kinds of books are trash.*) In questions, the number of the verb depends on the noun that follows *kind* or *sort* (*What kind of book is this?; What kind of books are these?*).

kind of, sort of   Colloquial when used for *rather*. (Colloquial: *I thought the lecture was kind of dull.* Preferred in writing: *I thought the lecture was rather dull.*) Also colloquial when followed by *a* or *an*. (Colloquial: *What kind of* *a house is it? It is a sort of a castle.* Preferred in writing: *What kind of house is it? It is a sort of castle.*)

lay, lie   The two are often confused. *Lay* is a transitive verb meaning to put or to place something; it always takes an object; its principal forms are *lay, laid, laid.* *Lie* is intransitive and means to recline or to remain; its principal forms are *lie, lay, lain.* When in doubt, try substituting the verb *place;* if it fits the context, you want some form of *lay.* (Present tense: *I lie down every afternoon; I lay the paper by his plate every morning.* Past tense: *I lay down yesterday after dinner; I laid the paper by his plate yesterday.* Present perfect tense: *I have lain here for two hours; I have laid the paper by his plate many times.*)

less   See **fewer.**

liable, likely, apt   In careful writing, these words are not interchangeable. *Likely* indicates a mere probability *(He is likely to be chosen); apt* implies a natural tendency or ability *(He is apt to win the scholarship); liable* is used when the possibility is unpleasant *(He is liable to get a parking ticket).*

lie   See **lay.**

like   Its use to introduce a subordinate clause is widespread in informal English, especially that used in advertising; in carefully edited writing, *as, as if,* and *as though* are preferred. (Colloquial: *He acted like the rest did.* Preferred in writing: *He acted as the rest did; He acted like the rest of us; I felt as if* (or *as though*) *I had done something generous.*)

likely   See **liable.**

lots, lots, a whole lot   Colloquial for *much, many, a great deal.*

may   See **can.**

most   As an adverb, means very; colloquial when used in the sense of *almost.* (Acceptable: *You are most kind.* Colloquial: *Most everyone was invited.* Preferred in writing: *Almost everyone was invited; Most of us were invited.*)

myself   Colloquial as a substitute for *I* or *me.* (Colloquial: *They received help from Mary and myself.* Preferred in writing: *They received help from Mary and me.*)

neither   See **either.**

no place   See **anyplace.**

nowhere near   A colloquialism for *not nearly.*

nowheres   Dialectal for *nowhere.*

off of   A colloquial usage in which *of* is superfluous *(Keep off* [not *off of*] *the grass).*

outside of   The *of* is usually superfluous; write simply *outside.* Also, *outside of* should not be used in writing for *aside from* or *except for.* (Colloquial: *Outside of this mistake, it is very good.* Preferred in writing: *Aside from this mistake, it is very good.*)

over with   The *with* is superfluous *(The regatta is over* [not *over with*]*).*

percent   Use the word *percent* (or *per cent*), not the % symbol, after the numeral in formal writing. *Percent* means literally "by the hundred" and therefore is more accurate to use in an exact numerical statement; *per-*

centage means, loosely, a part or proportion of a whole. (Colloquial: *A large percent were Chinese.* Standard: *Twenty percent were Chinese; A large percentage were Chinese.*) Note: in commercial writing, the % sign often is used, but only with a numeral.

phenomena   See **data.**

quite a few, quite a little   Colloquial for *a good many, a good deal (a good many people, a good deal of trouble).*

real, really   *Real* means true or genuine *(I have a real Australian boomerang); really* is an adverb meaning very much *(He is really interested in science).*

reason is because   *Reason is that* is the preferred phrase *(The reason I quit is that I did not get the promotion).*

set   A transitive verb often confused with *sit,* an intransitive verb. (Present tense: *I sit in the chair; I set the book on the table.* Past tense: *I sat in the chair; I set the book on the table.* Present perfect tense: *I have sat in the chair; I have set the book on the table.*)

sit   See **set.**

someplace   See **anyplace.**

sort   See **kind.**

strata   See **data.**

sure   Colloquially used for *certainly, surely.* (Colloquial: *He sure can play poker.* Preferred in writing: *He certainly can play poker; He plays poker very well.*)

take   See **bring.**

try and   Often used for *try to,* but should be avoided in writing *(I must try to* [not *try and*] *find a job).*

unique   Colloquial usage when such adverbs as *rather, more, most, very* modify *unique;* the word means the only one of its kind, and one thing cannot be *more* (or *less*) *unique* than another *(This copy of the book is unique; This copy of the book is very unusual).*

up   Do not attach a superfluous *up* to a verb unless you are sure that doing so will make your expression more accurate or effective. (Superfluous: *He opened up the box and divided the money up among the men.* Improved: *He opened the box and divided the money among the men.*)

wait on   Dialectal for *wait for.*

ways   Colloquial in such an expression as *a little ways;* in writing, the singular is preferred *(a little way).*

where to, where at   Colloquialisms in which the preposition is redundant or dialectal. (Colloquial: *Where are you going to?; Where is he at?* Preferred in writing: *Where are you going?; Where is he?*)

who, whom   *who* is nonstandard when used as an object, except in certain questions (see pages 451–52).

would have, would of   Nonstandard when the phrase is used instead of *had* in *if* clauses. (Nonstandard: *If he would have* [or *would of*] *stood by us, we might have won.* Standard: *If he had stood by us, we might have won.*)

Punctuation and Mechanics

Punctuation and the conventions of mechanics—capitalization, abbreviations, spelling, and so forth—help create order in the reader's mind. The rules and special marks that make up English punctuation and mechanics communicate sound patterns, special meanings, and significances about words as they appear on the page. Understanding and applying the conventions correctly will make you a better communicator.

PUNCTUATION

When you speak, your listeners hear and see you punctuate through your voice and your body language. They hear and see commas, periods, dashes, question marks, exclamation points, and quotation marks as you shout, whisper, pause, accentuate, wave your arms, roll your eyes, or shake your finger. In writing, punctuation marks play the role of the voice and body language. They help the reader hear you the way you want to be heard. You create sounds in the reader's mind with your words, and your punctuation gives order, sense, and emphasis to those sounds.

Although punctuation is essential in effective written communication, it cannot save a badly written sentence. If you find yourself struggling over commas, semicolons, and dashes, you probably have created a sentence that does not communicate well. It may be best just to toss it out and write a new one to a simpler design. The better the sentence, the easier it is to punctuate.

The Comma

Some dozen marks of punctuation are the most commonly used ones. With the exception of the comma, they all have specialized functions that are easy to understand. The comma, however, not only is the punctuation mark we use most often; it is also the most complex and uncertain.

The comma's primary uses are to separate coordinate elements in a sentence and to set off subordinate constructions in a sentence. In addition, the comma is occasionally used to prevent a misreading: to separate words that a reader might mistakenly group together. If you consistently apply the following comma rules and conventions in your writing, you can be assured that your readers will most likely comprehend the meaning as you intend them to.

1. Use a comma to separate two sentence elements that might be incorrectly connected by the reader and thus misunderstood:

    > Ever since she has devoted herself to the cause of the homeless.
    >
    > I do not care for raw fish simply appears gross.

    These sentences are confusing to read; adding commas clarifies their meaning:

    > Ever since, she has devoted herself to the cause of the homeless.
    >
    > I do not care, for raw fish simply appears gross.

    Preventing inaccurate reading is the most important use of the comma, and this rule supersedes all the other comma rules. Listen to your words as you write, and in general use a comma where you would pause briefly in speech.

2. Use commas to separate the words, phrases, or subordinate clauses in a series:

    > Smoothing back his hair, adjusting his tie, and staring in the mirror, Ronald thought about his date.

He remembered the seat cushions, the concert tickets, and his key to the house.

He was glad it was a warm, starry night.

The comma preceding the *and* in a series is optional, and many professional editors omit it today. Whichever style you choose, be consistent.

3. Use commas to separate the independent clauses in a compound sentence when the clauses are joined by a conjunction like *and, but, for, nor, because,* or *so,* unless the clauses are very short:

Ronald drove to Kathy's apartment, and he nervously pressed his finger to the doorbell.

The bell rang and Kathy answered.

4. Use a comma to separate an introductory adverb clause, participial phrase, or prepositional phrase from the rest of the sentence, unless the introductory phrase is very short:

Because she came to the door so quickly, he thought she must have been waiting.

Throughout the morning and afternoon, Kathy had been hoping that Ronald would come on time.

At that moment she was relieved.

5. Use commas to set off an appositive, a noun phrase that renames a noun or pronoun:

Kathy, an attractive, tall woman, invited Ronald into the apartment.

Note: do not use commas when the appositive and its noun form a unit, as in *my cousin Kathy* or *the novelist Conrad.*

6. In a direct quotation, use commas to set off a reference to the person being addressed and to set off a phrase or clause that interrupts the quotation:

"How are you, Ronald?"

"Kathy," called her roommate, "where are you going?"

7. Use commas to set off an introductory word or phrase or a parenthetical expression that does not modify any part of the sentence:

"Why, how gorgeous you look this evening, Kathy."

"Of course, I cannot forget my coat."

8. Use commas to set off a contrasting expression introduced by *not:*

Kathy said, "I was looking for the glasses, not the thermos."

9. Use commas to set off the individual elements in a date or an address:

February 23, 1988, was a date he would never forget.

Kathy lives at 29 Brookhollow Lane, Apartment 2, Irvine, California.

10. Use commas to set off a nonrestrictive phrase or clause. A nonrestrictive clause is a subordinate clause that is not essential to the meaning of the word or words it modifies:

The delivery boy handed the woman the package, which was wrapped in pink paper.

A restrictive clause is essential to the meaning of whatever it modifies and does not take a comma:

Ronald chose the seats that his brother had recommended.

Also use commas to set off a clause or phrase that is out of its normal order in a sentence:

Kathy was so excited that, although she tried to thank him, she could not speak.

11. Use commas as shown in the following miscellaneous constructions.
    (a) in numerals:

20,876   1,202,338

(b) in a name followed by a title:

Jerome S. Hunter, Ed.D.

(c) in the salutation of friendly letters and the complimentary closing of all letters:

Dear John,   Your friend,

(d) after an introductory "yes" or "no":

> Yes, I will cook dinner.

Comma Errors

Using a comma where it does not belong is a more flagrant error than omitting one where it ought to be. An omission could simply be carelessness, but erroneously putting in a comma shows ignorance. Contemporary practice favors a loose style of punctuation, so less punctuation is better than more. A good rule of thumb is to use no commas except those called for by the preceding rules and conventions.

To list all the situations in which a comma should not be used would be an endless task. But here are a few rules to save you from the more common kinds of comma errors.

1. Do not use a comma to connect two sentences. Using a comma here instead of a period is called a comma splice (see page 438), and it can result in serious misinterpretation:

   > She leaned over the pier railing to gain a better view, as I looked farther down the beach using my binoculars, I saw our son talking with a stranger.   [comma splice]

   > She leaned over the pier railing to gain a better view. As I looked farther down the beach using my binoculars, I saw our son talking with a stranger.   [correctly punctuated]

2. Do not use a comma to separate a verb from its complement:

   > My favorite authors are, Faulkner, Steinbeck, and Updike.   [wrong]

   > My favorite authors are Faulkner, Steinbeck, and Updike.   [correct]

3. Do not use a comma to separate a subject from its verb:

   > That our concept of public education must be revised, is now evident to all.   [wrong]

   > That our concept of public education must be revised is now evident to all.   [correct]

4. Do not use commas excessively:

   > Although, in my opinion, a loose system of punctuation makes for more readable prose, I do not like a prose style that does not reflect natural, speech patterns.   [wrong]

Although in my opinion a loose system of punctuation makes for more readable prose, I do not like a prose style that does not reflect natural speech patterns.   [acceptable]

Exercise

Insert commas in the following sentences wherever they are needed for ease of reading or are required by rule or convention.

1. Stephen is a dishwasher at the Hotel Paradise 350 First Street Eugene Oregon.
2. Jose was born in Havana Cuba but grew up in Miami Florida.
3. I have always wanted to visit Honolulu Hawaii.
4. Well said father we went to the beach but we couldn't find a parking place.
5. Weeding the lawn is hard work isn't it?
6. Be sure to tell Debbie John Henry and Linda where the party will be.
7. Mother wondered aloud who could that be at this hour?
8. I carefully filled in my name date of birth place of birth and social security number on the credit application.
9. Linus was on first base Pig Pen was catching Peppermint Patty was fielding Lucy was fielding also and Charlie Brown was pitching.
10. For breakfast we had ham and eggs orange juice and coffee.
11. Her large round brown eyes peeked from behind her mother's skirt.
12. New York New York is the largest city in the United States and Los Angeles California is the second largest city.
13. We go on Mondays and Wednesdays not Tuesdays and Thursdays.
14. Well some of my friends are in her class.
15. Mrs. Rice the lab teacher said that I needed to review one thing more before I took the test.
16. Paul are you taking the test tomorrow?
17. Dennis was excited and nervous when he thought of what lay ahead.
18. Because he was so excited he hardly ate any breakfast that morning.
19 As he looked back on the experience later he realized that he had nothing to be nervous about.
20. After he got out of the service Uncle Bob bought his own plane.

The Semicolon

The semicolon indicates a greater break in a sentence than the comma does. Its most common use is in compound sentences that work better without a conjunction between the clauses:

We searched the whole day and night; the results were nil.

Our plan was to fly from Rome to New York; however, a surprise summer storm forced us to fly to Philadelphia instead.

A semicolon is also used to separate the elements in a series when the elements contain internal commas:

One day of orientation was led by Dr. Joseph, a chaplain; Dr. Smith, a French professor; and the dean.

Similarly, a semicolon often is used to separate independent clauses where there are commas within the clauses:

A fine program, "Nightline," went on TV some time ago; but its late hour, 11:30, was too late for me.

The Apostrophe

The apostrophe is used to form the possessive case of nouns and indefinite pronouns, to mark the omitted letters in a contracted word or date, and sometimes to indicate the plural forms of letters, numbers, and abbreviations.

To form the possessive of all singular nouns and of all plural nouns not ending in *-s,* simply add an apostrophe and the letter *s (′s)* at the end of the word:

John's   mouse's   men's   oxen's   teeth's
anybody's   someone's

To form the possessive of plural nouns ending in *-s,* just add an apostrophe—nothing else:

babies'   coaches'   teachers'

Use the apostrophe to form contractions, inserting it in place of the omitted letters or numbers:

he's   we're   Mary's going   '50 (for *1950*)   hasn't

Use the apostrophe to form the plural of letters, numbers, and abbreviations when the meaning would not be clear without it:

the ABC's   8's, 9's, and 10's   I.D.'s

Quotation Marks

Quotation marks signify that you are quoting someone else's words and they are also used around certain kinds of titles. Follow theses rules when you quote someone or cite the title of a work of less than book length.

1. Use quotation marks to enclose a direct quotation:

    He said, "I shall not fail you this evening."

2. When the quotation is broken by explanatory words, use another set of quotation marks:

    "I shall not fail," he said, "to visit you this evening."

3. Do not use quotation marks to enclose an indirect quotation:

    He said that he would not fail us this evening.

4. When a direct quotation contains more than one paragraph, place an opening quotation mark at the beginning of each paragraph but the closing quotation mark at the end of only the last paragraph. (Remember to start a new paragraph when the speaker changes.)

5. Use single quotation marks to enclose a quotation within a quotation:

    "I heard you say, 'Let's not tell Donna!' " she pouted. "I want to know what you meant."

6. Use quotation marks to enclose the titles of short stories, short poems, essays, articles, and the chapters of a book:

    William Faulkner wrote the short story "The Bear."

7. When there is other punctuation at the end of a quotation, (a) place a comma or a period within the closing quotation mark:

    "I read the story called 'The Pit and the Pendulum,' " he said.

    (b) place a colon or a semicolon outside the closing quotation mark:

    She recited the theme of Frost's "Mending Wall": that men can never learn to be good neighbors with a wall between them.

(c) place a question mark or an exclamation point within the quotation marks when the punctuation mark belongs to the words quoted; when it relates to the whole sentence, place it outside:

> "Stop!" shouted the cop.
>
> What is the theme of Charles Lamb's essay "Dissertation upon a Roast Pig"?

8. When a word is defined or discussed within a sentence, place the word and its meaning in quotation marks:

> "Egregious," which originally meant "outstandingly good," today means "outstandingly bad."

The Period

The period is used to end declarative sentences and some imperative sentences:

> I will join you this afternoon.
>
> Please do as the doctor suggests.

In addition, the period is used in many abbreviations (but not usually in those for governmental agencies or for organizations, like *FBI, CIA, NAACP*):

> Thurs.   Feb.   e.g.   Ms.

Finally, the period is used in numbers to denote percentages and as a decimal point:

> .098 $10.50   4.657

The Question Mark and the Exclamation Point

Use a question mark at the end of a direct question:

> Did David really win the lottery?

But do not use a question mark with an indirect question or a polite request:

> He asked whether I would join him.
>
> Would you please turn down the stereo.

Use the exclamation point—but do not overuse it—in greetings and to express strong feelings:

> Hello!
>
> She really didn't do that!

The Colon

Use a colon to connect phrases or clauses that demonstrate a cause-and-effect relationship:

> The team's performance was miserable: the coach must make some changes.
>
> Here are the facts: we have neither the time nor the money to take such a trip.

A colon is also used to introduce a list, an illustration, or a statement:

> I had only three problems: my forehand, my backhand, and my serve.

Use a colon to introduce a long quotation.

The colon also appears in expressions of time: *8:30;* in the salutation of a formal letter: *Dear Ms. Parks:;* and in citing chapter and verse of the Bible: *John 4:7.*

Ellipses

Three spaced periods (. . .), called ellipsis marks, are used to indicate the omission of a word or words from a quoted passage. If the omitted words come at the end of a sentence, a fourth period is needed:

> We hold these Truths to be self-evident: that all Men . . . are endowed by their Creator with certain unalienable Rights. . . .

The Dash

The dash indicates a stronger degree of separation than a comma. It is used to set off, to highlight, or to emphasize:

> The application requested a transcript and had space to enter extracurricular activities, interests, hobbies—need I say more.

The dash is also used to summarize:

> Relaxation, repose, growth within—these are necessities of life, not privileges.

Although the dash can take the place of other punctuation marks, you should use it sparingly. Its overuse could suggest carelessness, an ignorance of other marks of punctuation, or an inability to shape sentences adequately. (Note that on a typewriter or a computer you make a dash by typing two hyphens, with no space on either side.)

Parentheses and Brackets

Parentheses enclose or set off nonessential explanatory or supplementary material. They may occur within a sentence, or they may enclose a whole sentence (as in the last sentence about the dash) or group of sentences. If the parenthetical statement occurs within a sentence, it never begins with a capital letter or ends with a period:

> He was a late sleeper (until noon every day).
>
> The professor wanted to give the class a surprise quiz (for which the class had not prepared).

Brackets are used to enclose an explanatory word or phrase inserted in a quotation by the person doing the quoting:

> "We know more about its state [the state of the language] in the later Middle Ages; and from the time of Shakespeare on, our information is quite complete.

The Latin word *sic* (meaning "thus") enclosed in brackets is sometimes inserted in a quotation following a misspelling or other error to indicate that the error occurs in the original:

> He sent that written confession: "She followed us into the kitchen, snatched a craving [*sic*] knife from the table, and came toward me with it."

Exercise

The following excerpt from an essay published in *Time* magazine is printed here with all punctuation deleted except that at the ends of the sentences. Add whatever internal punctuation you think is necessary and be prepared to explain your choices.

In Praise of the Humble Comma
Pico Iyer

Punctuation in short gives us the human voice and all the meanings that lie between the words. You aren't young are you loses its innocence when it loses the question mark. Every child knows the menace of a dropped apostrophe the parent's Don't do that shifting into the more slowly enunciated Do not do that and every believer the ignominy of having his faith reduced to faith. Add an exclamation point to To be or not to be and the gloomy Dane has all the resolve he needs add a comma and the noble sobriety of God save the Queen becomes a cry of desperation bordering on double sacrilege.

Sometimes of course our markings may be simply a matter of aesthetics. Popping in a comma can be like slipping on the necklace that gives an outfit quiet elegance or like catching the sound of running water that complements as it completes the silence of a Japanese landscape. When V. S. Naipaul in his latest novel writes He was a middle-aged man with glasses the first comma can seem a little precious. Yet it gives the description a spin as well as a subtlety that it otherwise lacks and it shows that the glasses are not part of the middle-agedness but something else.

Thus all these tiny scratches give us breadth and heft and depth. A world that has only periods is a world without inflections. It is a world without shade. It has a music without sharps and flats. It is a martial music. It has a jackboot rhythm. Words cannot bend and curve. A comma by comparison catches the gentle drift of the mind in thought turning in on itself and back on itself reversing redoubling and returning along the course of its own sweet river music while the semicolon brings clauses and thoughts together with all the silent discretion of a hostess arranging guests around her dinner table.

Punctuation then is a matter of care. Care for words yes but also and more important for what the words imply. Only a lover notices the small things the way the afternoon light catches the nape of a neck or how a strand of hair slips out from behind an ear or the way a finger curls around a cup. And no one scans a letter so closely as a lover searching for its small print straining to hear its nuances its gasps its sighs and hesitations poring over the secret messages that lie in every cadence. The difference between Jane whom I adore and Jane whom I adore and the difference between them both and Jane whom I adore marks all the distance between ecstasy and heartache. No iron can pierce the heart with such force as a period put at just the right place in Isaac Babel's lovely words a comma can let us hear a voice break or a heart. Punctuation in fact is a labor of love. Which brings us back in a way to gods.

MECHANICS

Capitalization

Capitals, also called uppercase letters, mark the first word of sentences and the first word of direct quotations (and of course there is the capital *I* as a pronoun). Beyond those rules, you need to become familiar with the conventions of capitalizing these proper nouns and their derivatives:

1. Days of the week and months of the year.
2. The names of organizations, such as political parties, governmental agencies and departments, societies, institutions, clubs, churches, and corporations.

3. Members of such organizations: *Democrats, Lions, Catholics.*
4. Historical events and periods: *the Battle of Hastings, the Medieval Age, the Baroque Era.*
5. Geographic areas: *the East, the Northwest, the Rocky Mountains.*
6. Names of races and languages: *Japanese, Mexican, English, Caucasian.*
7. Many words of religious significance: *the Lord, the Trinity, Allah.*
8. Words for family members when used in place of the person's proper name: *a call from Mother telling about my father's new position.*
9. In biological nomenclature, the names of genera but not of species: *Homo sapiens, Equus caballus.*
10. Stars, constellations, and planets, but not *the earth, the sun,* or *the moon* unless used as the astronomical name.
11. Titles of persons when used as part of the name: *Senator Byrd, Professor Marsh, Uncle Bob.*
12. Each word in the titles of books, plays, poems, articles, musical compositions, paintings, and many other artistic works: *Cats, Howl, David, The Godfather.* Note: do not capitalize articles, conjunctions, or prepositions in a title except when they are the first word or when the work's creator has capitalized them.

Italics and Underlining

In print, words are made to stand out through the use of a script-like type called *italic.* In handwriting or on the typewriter or computer, underlining serves the same purpose as italics.

Use italics for the titles of books, movies, plays, works of art, magazines or periodicals, ships, and aircraft:

> *The Last Emperor*
> *Consumer Reports*
> U.S.S. *Enterprise*

Use italics for foreign words or phrases that have not yet become accepted in English:

> The dancer unties a knot with her feet in the Mexican *reboza.*

Finally, use italics (sparingly) to show emphasis:

> When I say *stop,* I mean *stop.*

Hyphenation

Use a hyphen to break a word at the end of a line. The hyphen is always placed between syllables; never divide a word in mid-syllable. Incorrect word division suggests either ignorance or laziness, or both. Your dictionary will tell you what is correct.

Hyphens are also used to form compound words, such as *ready-made*, *sister-in-law*, and *half-truth*. The hyphenation of compound words tends to vary over time, and the best practice is to check a good dictionary whenever you are uncertain about a word.

Abbreviations and Numbers

In ordinary, nontechnical writing, avoid using abbreviations. Your dictionary gives all the standard abbreviations, and you should consult it whenever you think an abbreviation might be appropriate in your writing.

A few standard abbreviations are in general use for most kinds of writing: *i.e.* ("that is"); *e.g.* ("for example"); *etc.* ("and so forth"); *vs.* ("versus"); *A.D.* and *B.C.*; *A.M.* and *P.M.;* Washington, *D.C.* In addition, the initials of many organizations and government agencies are commonly used as their abbreviations: *CIA, FBI, GOP, NATO.*

The rules for using numbers in writing vary from handbook to handbook. Here are my references. For any number over twelve, use the numeral: *13, 14, 15,* and so on. For numbers *one* through *twelve*, spell out the word. For a series of numbers, however, use numerals: *she has 3 hats, 7 coats, 16 dresses, and 24 pairs of shoes.* If a number begins a sentence, always spell out the word. Always use numerals to express percentages.

Spelling

The misspelling of common words is almost universally regarded as a sign of ignorance. Most misspelling reflects bad habits, which can be corrected with little effort; no one—least of all a college graduate—needs to be a poor speller.

The first step is to make a list of the words that you consistently misspell. To find out what those words are, have someone give you a series of spelling tests based on the words listed in this section. These are all common words that are frequently misspelled. You have no need to learn difficult words, like *asphyxiate* or *symbiosis,* which occur infrequently in ordinary writing, since you can always consult a dictionary when you need to know how to spell them.

Add to your list other words that you know you tend to misspell (even the best writers have a few of these), and study the list. Look carefully at all the letters in each word, pronounce the word one syllable at a time, write the word repeatedly to fix its pattern in your mind. Invent mnemonic devices—pictures, jingles, associations—to help you remember particular spellings. For example, you might remember the distinction between *capital* and *capitol* by associating *capitAL* with *WAshington* and *capitOL* with *dOme*. Also learn the common prefixes and suffixes, and analyze words to see how their prefixes and suffixes are formed. For example:

disappoint = dis + appoint
dissatisfied = dis + satisfied
misspelling = mis + spell + ing
really = real + ly

unnecessary = un + necessary
government = govern + ment
carefully = care + ful + ly
incidentally = incident + al + ly

See how many of the words in your list of commonly misspelled words you can break down into a root word with prefixes or suffixes. If you find exceptions, look for an explanation in the Spelling Rules (pages 502–04).

Trouble Spots in Words

Learn to look for the trouble spots in words and concentrate on them.

Commonly misspelled words almost always fall into groups that are misspelled in the same way. That is, a particular letter or combination of letters is the trouble spot in a number of words, and if you can remember the correct spelling of the trouble spot, the rest of the word will take care of itself. *Receive,* like *deceive, perceive,* and *conceive,* is troublesome only because of the *-ei-* combination; if you can remember that it is *e* after *c,* you will have mastered all these words. To spell a word like *beginning* correctly, all you need to remember is to double the *n.*

Careful pronunciation can help you to avoid errors at trouble spots. In the following list, we often omit the letters in italics when we pronounce the words, and therefore we tend to misspell them. Say each of the words aloud, exaggerating the sound of the italicized letters:

acci*den*tally	*lab*oratory	*prob*ably	*strict*ly
*can*didate	*li*able	*li*brary	sur*prise*
*every*body	*li*brary	*recog*nize	*tem*perament
*Feb*ruary	*lit*erature	*soph*omore	*us*ually
*gen*erally	oc*cas*ionally		

Conversely, many people incorrectly add letters to words because of mispronouncing them. Pronounce each of the following words, making sure an extra syllable does not creep in at the spot indicated by the italics:

*ath*letics	*elm*	hin*drance*	remem*brance*
disas*trous*	en*trance*	*light*ning	simi*lar*
drown*ed*	*height*	mis*chievous*	um*brella*

The trouble spot in each of the following words is caused by a tendency to transpose the italicized letters when we say the word. Again, careful pronunciation will help you to remember the proper order of the letters:

children	perform	prefer	prescription
hundred	perspiration	prejudice	tragedy
irrelevant			

Similar Words Frequently Confused

Learn the meanings and spellings of similar words—pairs of words that look or sound almost the same.

Many errors that appear to be misspellings are caused by confusing such words as *effect* and *affect;* these are really errors in diction rather than spelling. It is useless to spell *principal* correctly if the word that belongs in your sentence is *principle.* Pairs of words that are frequently confused are given in the following list, along with brief definitions:

	DEFINITION		DEFINITION
accept	to receive	breath	*noun*
except	aside from	breathe	*verb*
access	admittance	capital	city
excess	greater amount	capitol	building
advice	*noun*	choose	*present tense*
advise	*verb*	chose	*past tense*
affect	to influence (*verb*)	clothes	garments
effect	result (*noun*) OR to bring about (*verb*)	cloths	pieces of fabric
aisle	e.g., in churches	coarse	not fine
isle	island	course	path, series
all ready	prepared	complement	to complete
already	previously	compliment	to praise
allusion	reference	conscience	sense of right and wrong
illusion	misconception	conscious	aware
altar	shrine	corps	group
alter	to change	corpse	dead body
alumna	a woman graduate	costume	dress
alumnae	*plural* (women)	custom	manner
alumnus	a man graduate	council	assembly
alumni	*plural* (men)	counsel	advice (*noun*) OR to advise (*verb*)
angel	celestial being		
angle	corner	dairy	milk supply
ascent	a climb	diary	daily record
assent	agreement (*noun*) OR to agree (*verb*)	decent	proper
		descent	downward slope
berth	bed	desert	wasteland
birth	being born	dessert	food
boarder	one who boards	device	*noun*
border	edge	devise	*verb*

	DEFINITION		DEFINITION
dual	twofold	quiet	still
duel	fight	quite	entirely
formally	in a formal manner	respectfully	with respect
formerly	previously	respectively	as relating to each
forth	forward	shone	*past tense* of shine
fourth	4th	shown	*past perfect* of show
ingenious	clever	stationary	*adjective*
ingenuous	innocent	stationery	*noun*
its	of it	their	*possessive*
it's	it is	there	in that place
later	subsequent to	they're	they are
latter	second of two	than	*comparison*
lead	a metal	then	at that time
led	*past tense* of lead	to	go *to* bed
loose	*adjective*	too	*too* bad, me *too*
lose	*verb*	two	2
peace	not war	weather	rain or shine
piece	portion	whether	which of two
personal	*adjective*	who's	who is
personnel	*noun*	whose	*possessive*
principal	most important	you're	you are
principle	basic doctrine	your	*possessive*

Spelling Rules

Learn the spelling rules we have for the English language.

Unfortunately, most English spelling rules apply to a relatively small number of words, and almost all the rules have exceptions. Nevertheless, knowing rules may help you to spell some of the common words that cause you trouble.

It is as important to learn when a rule should and should not be used as it is to understand the rule itself. Applied in the wrong places, the rules will make your spelling worse rather than better.

1. Final silent *-e*

Drop the final silent *-e* before suffixes beginning with a vowel (*-ing, -age, -able*). Keep the final silent *-e* before suffixes beginning with a consonant (*-ful, -ly, -ness*).

hope + ing = hoping		hope + ful = hopeful
love + able = lovable		nine + teen = nineteen
stone + y = stony		arrange + ment = arrangement
guide + ance = guidance		late + ly = lately

plume + age = plumage
white + ish = whitish
write + ing = writing
dote + age = dotage

pale + ness = paleness
white + wash = whitewash
sincere + ly = sincerely
bale + ful = baleful

Learn the following exceptions:

dyeing	ninth	awful
hoeing	truly	wholly
gluey	duly	

The final -*e* is also retained in such words as the following in order to keep the soft *c* or *g* sound:

noticeable   courageous
peaceable   outrageous

2. Doubling the final consonant

When adding a suffix that begins with a vowel to a word that ends in one consonant preceded by one vowel (*red/redder*), notice where the root word is accented. If it is accented on the last syllable or if it is a monosyllable, double the final consonant.

prefer + ed = preferred
omit + ing = omitting
occur + ence = occurrence
red + er = redder

benefit + ed = benefited
profit + ing = profiting
differ + ence = difference
travel + er = traveler

Note that in some words the accent shifts when the suffix is added:

referred   reference
preferring   preference

There are a few exceptions to this rule, like *transferable* and *excellent,* and many words that should follow the rule have alternative spellings: *worshiped* or *worshipped; traveling* and *traveler* or *travelling* and *traveller.*

3. Words ending in -*y*

If the -*y* is preceded by a consonant, change the *y* to *i* before any suffix except -*ing.*

lady + s = ladies   lonely + ness = loneliness
try + ed = tried   accompany + s = accompanies
            study + ing = studying

The *y* is usually retained if it is preceded by a vowel:

valleys   monkeys   displayed

Some exceptions: *laid, paid, said.*

4. *-ie-* or *-ei-*

When *-ie-* or *-ei-* is used to spell the sound *ee,*

> Put *i* before *e*
> Except after *c.*

achieve	grieve	retrieve	ceiling
belief	niece	shield	conceit
believe	piece	shriek	conceive
brief	pierce	siege	deceit
chief	relief	thief	deceive
field	relieve	wield	perceive
grief	reprieve	yield	receive

Some exceptions: *either, leisure, neither, seize, weird.*

Review Exercise

Following is a list of commonly misspelled words. Underline those words that you recognize as troublesome to you and review them from time to time. The list can also serve as a reference when you are editing your writing.

abbreviate	acquitted	ammunition	arising
absence	across	among	arithmetic
absorption	address	amount	arouse
absurd	aggravate	analogous	arranging
abundant	aggression	analysis	article
accelerate	airplane	analyze	artillery
accidentally	alleviate	annual	ascend
accommodate	alley	antecedent	association
accomplish	allotted	anxiety	athlete
according	allowed	apartment	athletics
accumulate	ally	apparatus	attempt
accustom	already	apparent	attractive
achievement	although	appearance	audible
acoustics	always	appropriate	audience
acquaintance	amateur	arctic	authorities
acquire	ambiguous	argument	automobile

auxiliary
awkward
bachelor
balance
balloon
barbarous
barring
battalion
bearing
becoming
beggar
beginning
believe
beneficial
benefited
biscuit
boundaries
breathe
brilliant
Britain
Britannica
bulletin
buoyant
bureau
buried
burying
business
busy
cafeteria
calendar
candidate
carburetor
carrying
casualties
causal
ceiling
celebrity
cemetery
certain
changeable
changing
characteristic
chauffeur
chief
choosing
chosen
clause
climbed
clothes

colloquial
colonel
column
coming
commission
commitment
committed
committee
companies
comparatively
compel
compelled
competent
competition
complaint
completely
compulsory
concede
conceit
conceivable
conceive
condemn
condescend
connoisseur
conqueror
conscience
conscientious
considered
consistent
contemptible
control
controlled
convenient
copies
corner
coroner
corps
corpse
costume
countries
courteous
courtesy
cries
criticism
criticize
cruelty
cruise
curiosity
curriculum

custom
cylinder
dealt
debater
deceitful
deceive
decide
decision
defendant
deferred
deficient
definite
definition
democracy
dependent
descendant
description
desirable
despair
desperate
destruction
developed
development
diaphragm
diary
dictionary
dietitian
difference
digging
diphtheria
disappearance
disappoint
disastrous
discipline
discussion
disease
dissatisfied
dissipate
distribute
doesn't
dominant
don't
dormitories
dropped
drunkenness
echoes
ecstasy
efficiency
eighth

eligible
eliminate
embarrass
emphasize
employee
encouraging
encyclopedia
enthusiastic
environment
equipment
equipped
equivalent
erroneous
especially
eventually
exaggerate
exceed
excel
excellent
exceptional
excitement
exercise
exhaust
exhilaration
existence
experience
explanation
extensive
extracurricular
extremely
exuberance
fallacious
fallacy
familiar
fascinate
February
fiery
financial
financier
forehead
foreign
foremost
forfeit
forty
frantically
fraternities
friend
fulfill, fulfil
gaiety

gauge
generally
genius
genuine
glorious
government
grammar
grandeur
grievous
guarantee
guardian
guidance
handicapped
handkerchief
harass
hearse
height
heinous
heroes
hesitancy
hindrance
hoarse
hoping
horde
humorous
hurriedly
hurries
hygiene
hypocrisy
hysterical
illiterate
illogical
imaginary
imagination
imitative
immediately
implement
impromptu
inadequate
incidentally
incredible
indefinitely
independent
indicted
indispensable
inevitable
influential
innocent
inoculate

intellectual
intelligence
intentionally
intercede
interested
interpret
interrupt
irreligious
irresistible
irresponsible
itself
judicial
khaki
knowledge
laboratory
legitimate
leisure
library
lightning
literature
loneliness
losing
magazine
magnificent
maintain
maintenance
maneuver
manual
manufacture
mathematics
mattress
meant
medicine
medieval
messenger
millionaire
miniature
minute
mischievous
misspelled
modifies
modifying
momentous
mosquitoes
mottoes
mountainous
murmur
muscle
mysterious

necessary
necessity
neither
nervous
nevertheless
nickel
niece
ninety
ninth
noticeable
notorious
nowadays
obedience
obliged
obstacle
occasionally
occur
occurred
occurrence
official
omission
omit
omitted
opinion
opportunity
optimistic
organization
original
orthodox
outrageous
overrun
pamphlet
parallel
parliament
participle
particularly
pastime
peaceable
perceive
perform
permissible
perseverance
persistent
persuade
phrase
physical
physician
picnicked
piece

playwright
pleasant
possess
possessive
possible
potatoes
practice
prairie
preceding
predominant
preference
preferred
prejudice
preparation
prevalent
primitive
privilege
probably
professor
prominent
pronounce
pronunciation
propeller
protein
psychology
pursue
pursuing
putting
quantity
quarantine
questionnaire
quizzes
realize
recede
receipt
receive
receiving
recognize
recommend
reference
referred
relevant
religion
religious
remembrance
reminiscence
rendezvous
repetition
replies

representative
reservoir
resistance
restaurant
rhetoric
rheumatism
rhythmical
ridiculous
sacrifice
sacrilegious
safety
salary
sanctuary
sandwich
scarcely
scene
scenic
schedule
secretarial
secretary
seized
sensible
sentence
sentinel
separate
sergeant
severely
shining
shriek
siege

similar
sincerely
sincerity
skeptical
slight
soliloquy
sophomore
source
specifically
specimen
spontaneous
statement
statue
stomach
stopped
strength
strenuously
stretched
struggle
studying
subordinate
subtle
succeed
success
successful
suffrage
superintendent
supersede
suppress
surprise

swimming
syllable
synonym
synonymous
tangible
tariff
tasting
technical
technique
temperament
tenant
tendency
thorough
thought
tournament
traffic
tragedy
transferred
tremendous
tries
truly
twelfth
typical
tyranny
unanimous
undoubtedly
unnecessary
until
usage
useful

using
usually
vacancy
vacuum
valuable
vengeance
victorious
view
vigilant
vigorous
village
villain
warrant
warring
weird
welfare
whole
wholly
wiry
woman
women
won't
worried
worrying
writing
written
yacht
your
you're (you are)
zoology

Copyrights and Acknowledgments

Index

A 9
B 0
C 1
D 2
E 3
F 4
G 5
H 6
I 7
J 8

Reference Guide: Proofreading

Adjectives and Adverbs

Adjectives and adverbs both function as modifiers in sentences, but their grammatical function is not the same.   /   454–55

Case

The case (form) of a pronoun is determined by its grammatical function in the clause or sentence in which it appears.   /   451–53

Comma Splices

Using a comma to separate two complete thoughts (independent clauses) is a comma splice.   /   438–41

Dangling Modifiers

A modifier should relate directly and only to the sentence element it modifies.   /   448–49

Fragments

A sentence fragment is a part of a sentence that is punctuated as if it were a whole sentence.   /   436–38

Mechanics

Capitalization   /   497–98
Italics and Underlining   /   498
Hyphenation   /   498–99
Abbreviations and Numbers   /   499
Spelling   /   499–507

Parallelism

Sentence elements in a pair or a series should always be parallel in their grammatical form.   /   449–51

Pronoun-Antecedent Agreement

A pronoun must always agree in number with its antecedent.   /   444–45

Pronoun Reference

A very common source of confusion to readers is a pronoun that appears to refer to more than one word or a pronoun that has no antecedent at all.   /   453–54

Punctuation

The Comma   /   487–91
The Semicolon   /   491–92